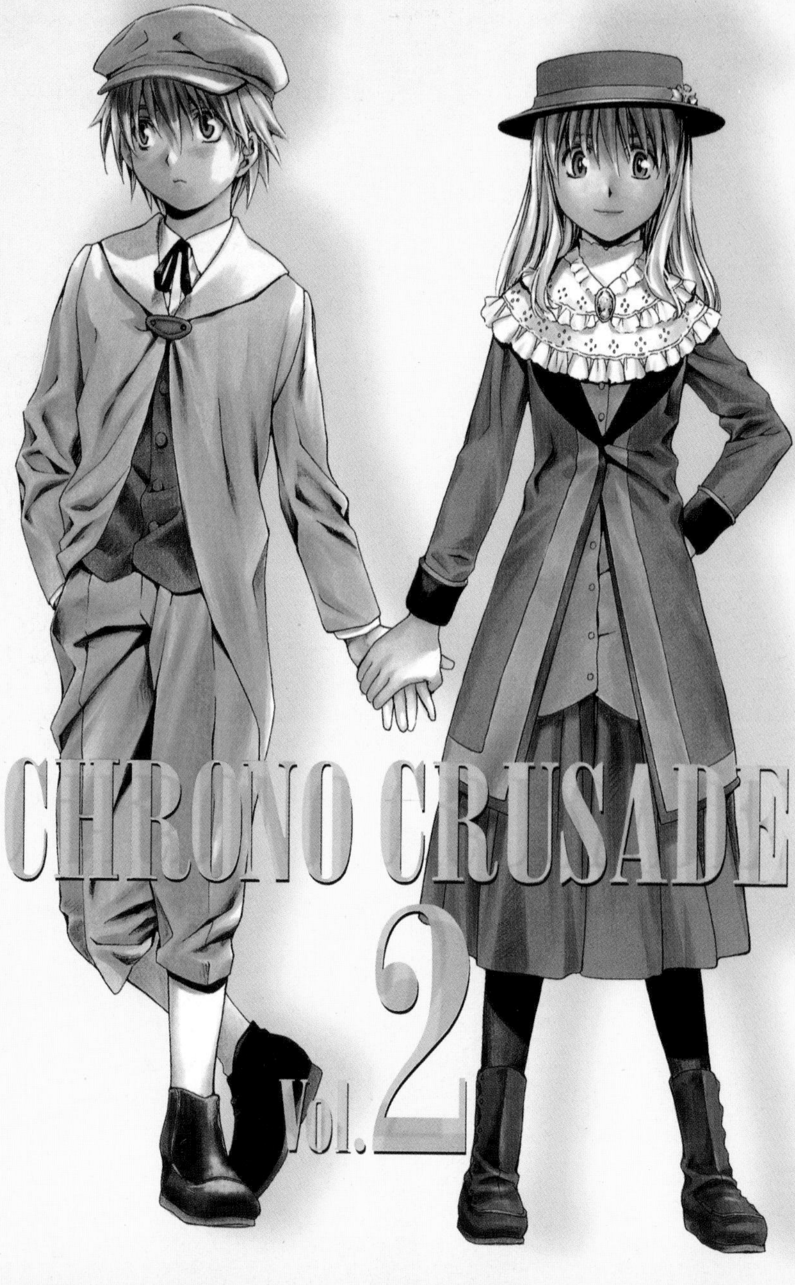
CHRONO CRUSADE
Vol. 2

CONTENTS

ACT 7
GHOST IN THE WATCH ———————— 3

ACT 8
FALLING RAIN ———————————— 25

ACT 9
THE BEGINNING ————————————— 43

ACT 10
TWO DECISIONS ————————————— 69

ACT 11
TO MOVE FORWARD AGAIN ———————— 93

ACT 12
GIRL'S STEP ————————————————— 119

ACT 13
RAGING TORNADO ——————————— 143

ACT 14
I AM HERE ————————————————— 169

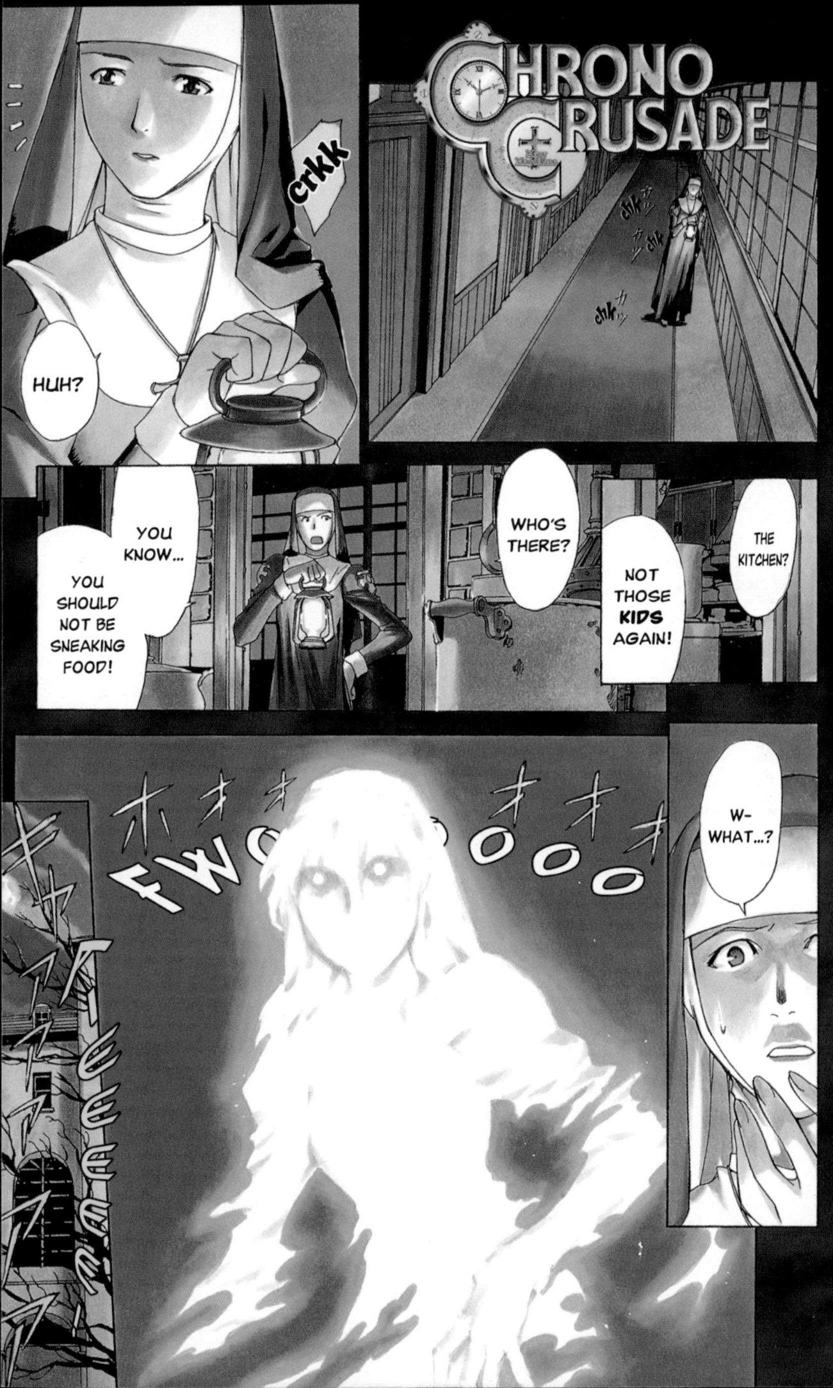
CHRONO CRUSADE
chk
chk
chk
crkk
HUH?
THE KITCHEN?
NOT THOSE KIDS AGAIN!
WHO'S THERE?
YOU KNOW...
YOU SHOULD NOT BE SNEAKING FOOD!
W-WHAT...?
FWOOOOO

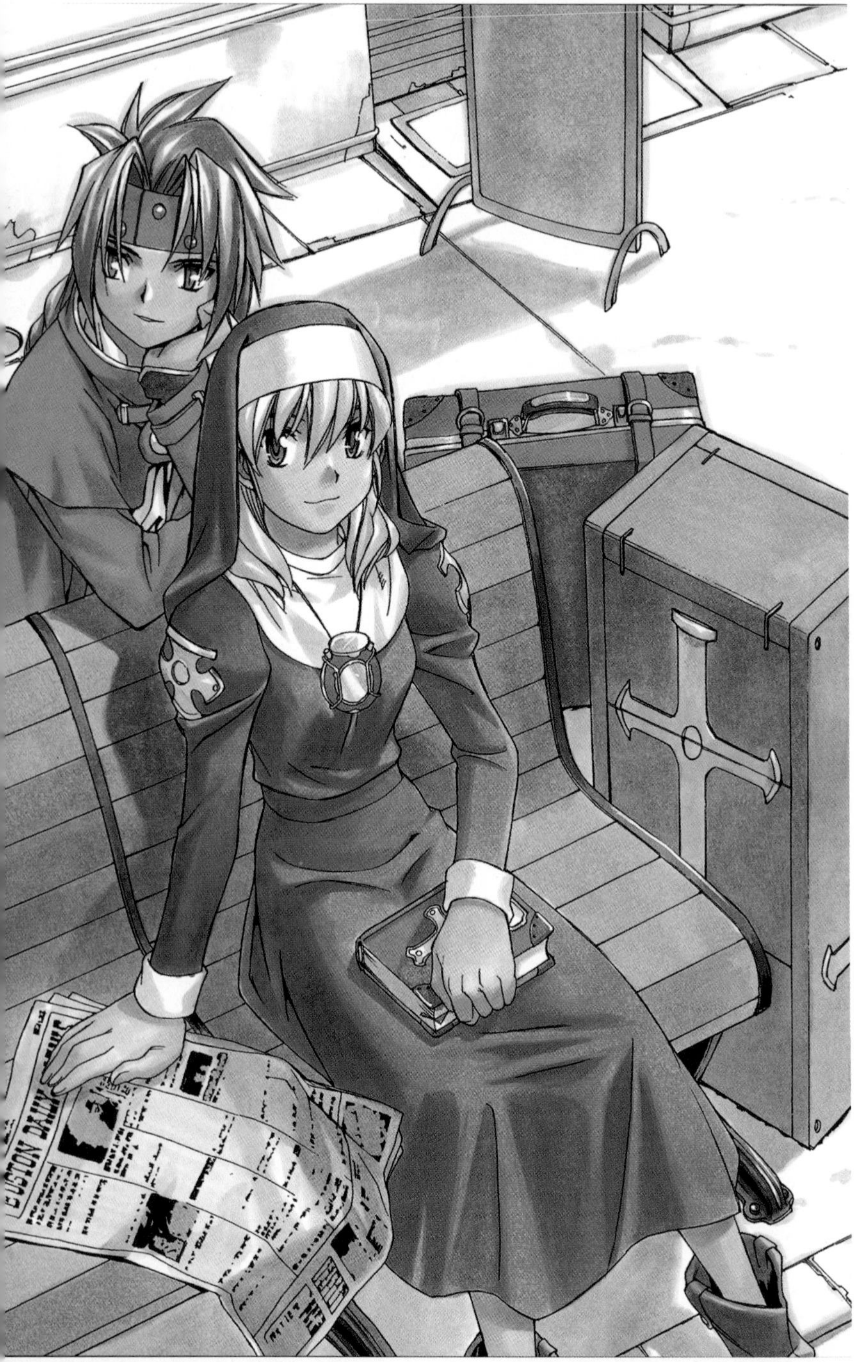
DAILY

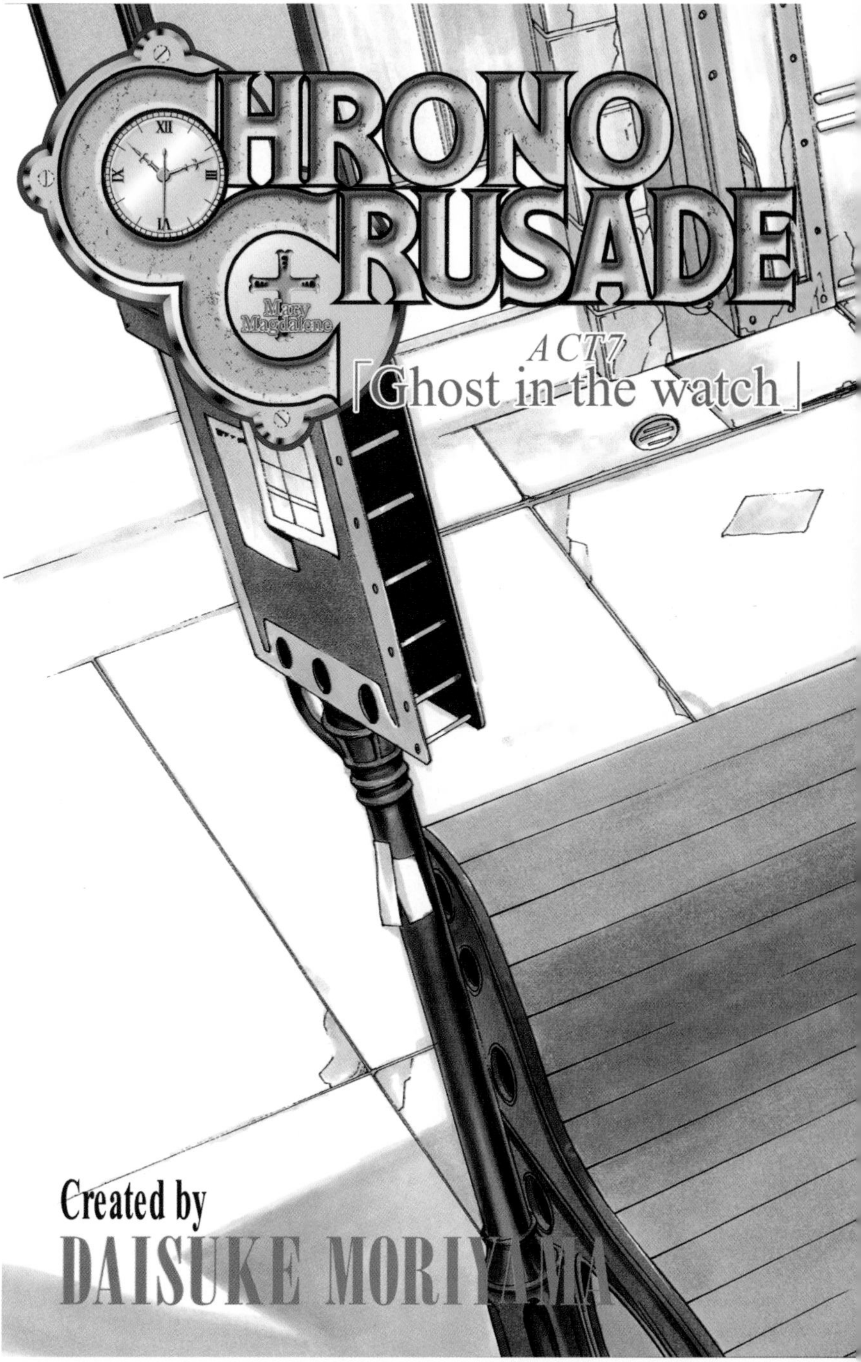
CHRONO CRUSADE
Mary Magdalene
ACT7
「Ghost in the watch」
Created by
DAISUKE MORIYAMA

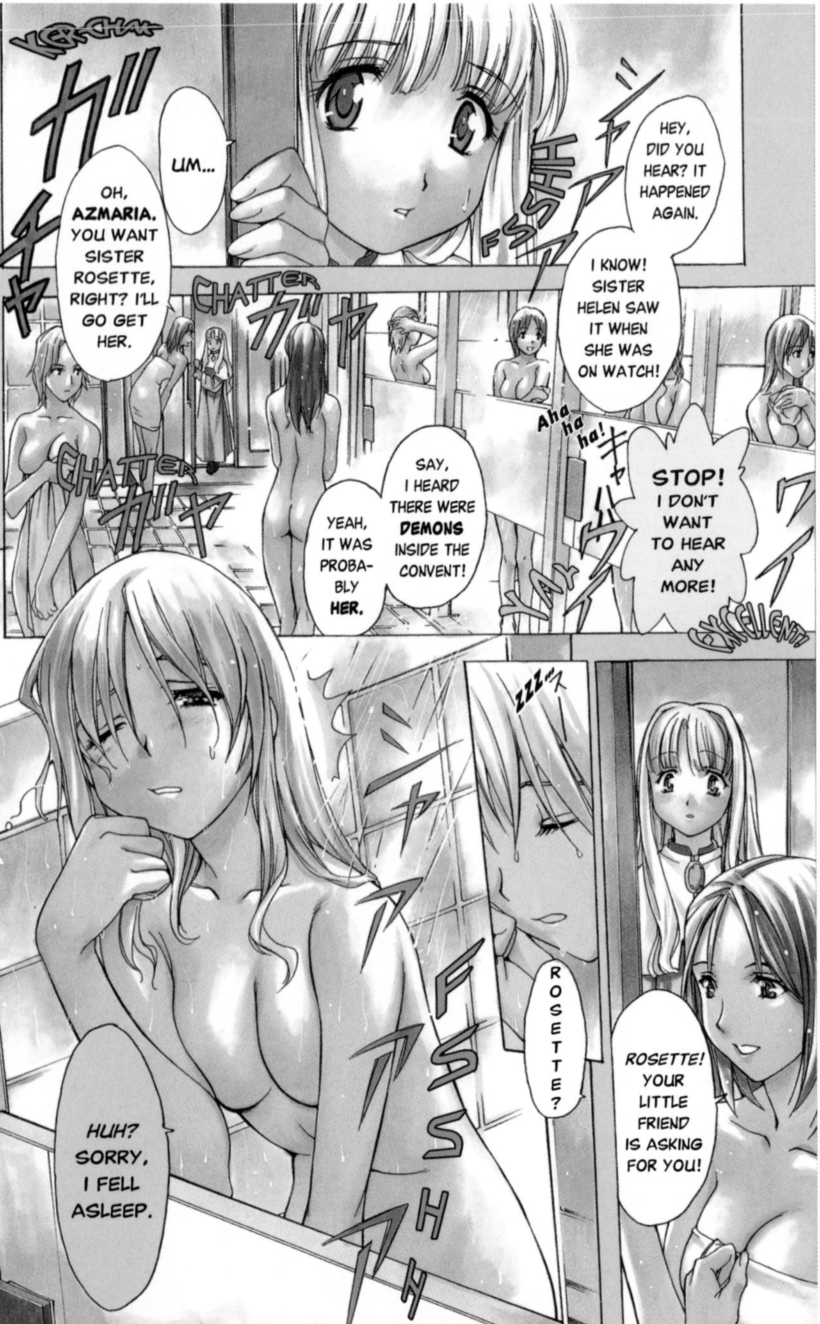
KER-CHAK
HEY, DID YOU HEAR? IT HAPPENED AGAIN.
FSSH
UM...
OH, AZMARIA. YOU WANT SISTER ROSETTE, RIGHT? I'LL GO GET HER.
I KNOW! SISTER HELEN SAW IT WHEN SHE WAS ON WATCH!
CHATTER
STOP! I DON'T WANT TO HEAR ANY MORE!
Aha ha ha!
SAY, I HEARD THERE WERE DEMONS INSIDE THE CONVENT!
YEAH, IT WAS PROBA-BLY HER.
CHATTER
ROSETTE! YOUR LITTLE FRIEND IS ASKING FOR YOU!
ROSETTE?
ZZZ...
FSSH
HUH? SORRY, I FELL ASLEEP.

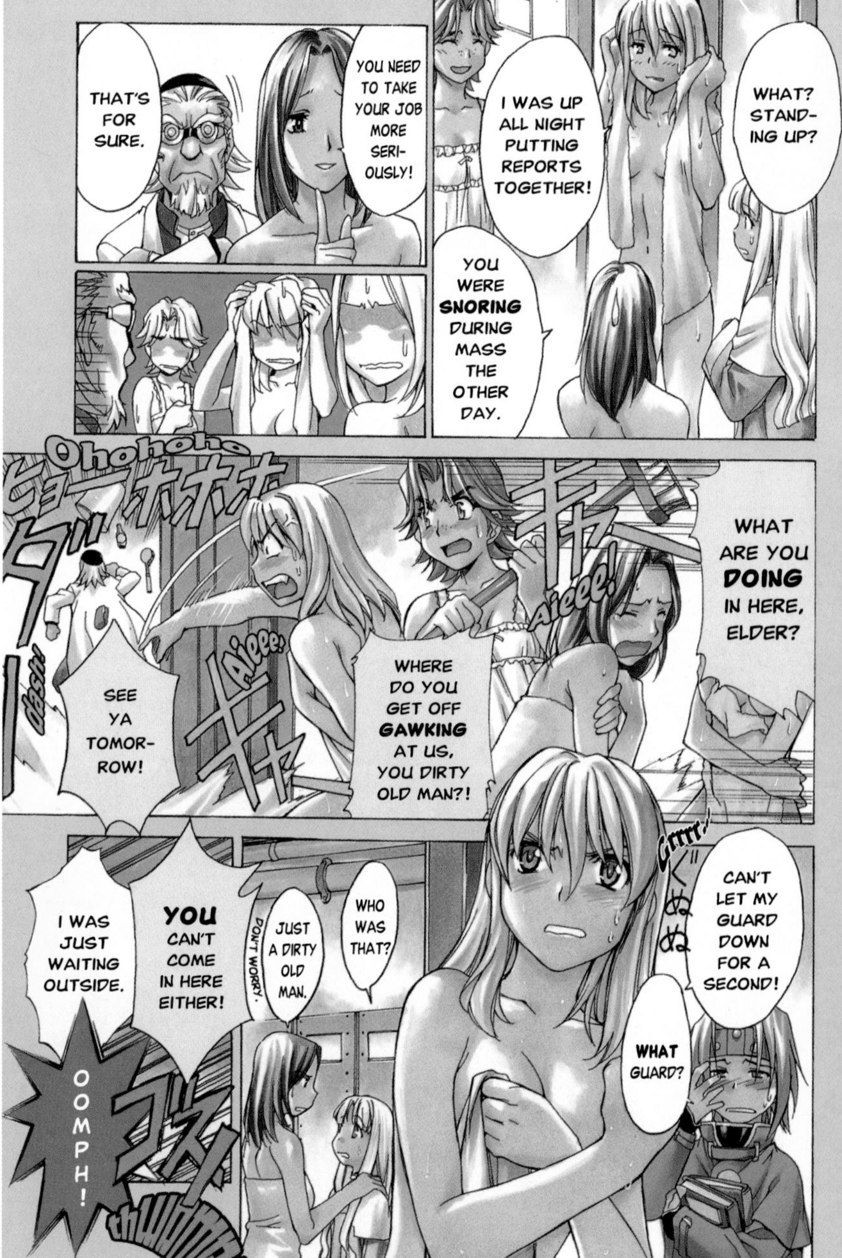
WHAT? STANDING UP?
I WAS UP ALL NIGHT PUTTING REPORTS TOGETHER!
YOU WERE SNORING DURING MASS THE OTHER DAY.
YOU NEED TO TAKE YOUR JOB MORE SERIOUSLY!
THAT'S FOR SURE.
WHAT ARE YOU DOING IN HERE, ELDER?
Aieee!
WHERE DO YOU GET OFF GAWKING AT US, YOU DIRTY OLD MAN?!
Aieee!
Ohohoho
SEE YA TOMORROW!
dash!
Grrrr...
CAN'T LET MY GUARD DOWN FOR A SECOND!
WHAT GUARD?
WHO WAS THAT?
JUST A DIRTY OLD MAN.
DON'T WORRY.
YOU CAN'T COME IN HERE EITHER!
I WAS JUST WAITING OUTSIDE.
OOMPH!
thwump!

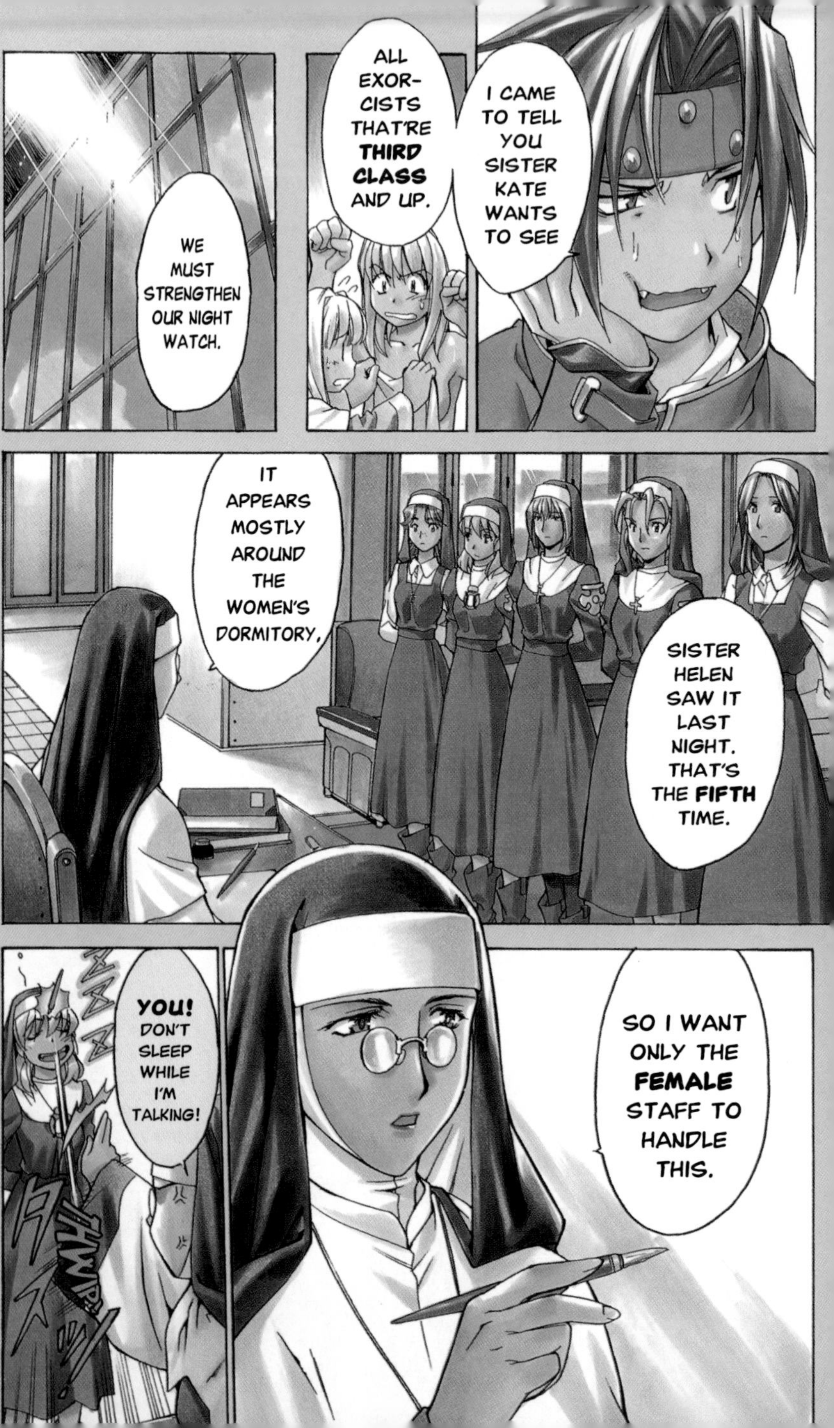
I CAME TO TELL YOU SISTER KATE WANTS TO SEE
ALL EXOR-CISTS THAT'RE **THIRD CLASS** AND UP.
WE MUST STRENGTHEN OUR NIGHT WATCH.
IT APPEARS MOSTLY AROUND THE WOMEN'S DORMITORY,
SISTER HELEN SAW IT LAST NIGHT. THAT'S THE **FIFTH** TIME.
SO I WANT ONLY THE **FEMALE** STAFF TO HANDLE THIS.
YOU! DON'T SLEEP WHILE I'M TALKING!
THWAP!

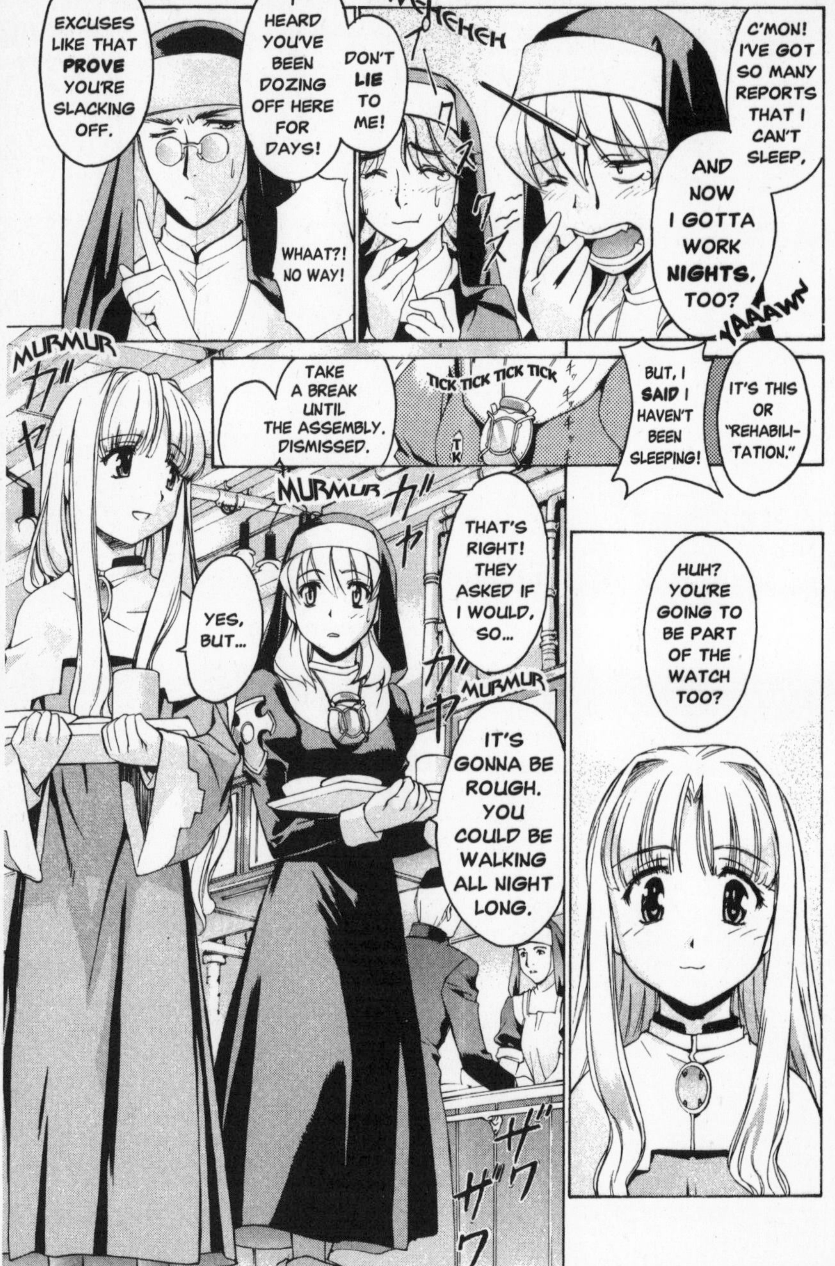

PWEHEHEH
C'MON! I'VE GOT SO MANY REPORTS THAT I CAN'T SLEEP,
AND NOW I GOTTA WORK NIGHTS, TOO?
YAAAWN
I HEARD YOU'VE BEEN DOZING OFF HERE FOR DAYS!
DON'T LIE TO ME!
WHAAT?! NO WAY!
EXCUSES LIKE THAT PROVE YOU'RE SLACKING OFF.
IT'S THIS OR "REHABILITATION."
BUT, I SAID I HAVEN'T BEEN SLEEPING!
TICK TICK TICK TICK
TK
TAKE A BREAK UNTIL THE ASSEMBLY. DISMISSED.
HUH? YOU'RE GOING TO BE PART OF THE WATCH TOO?
MURMUR
MURMUR
THAT'S RIGHT! THEY ASKED IF I WOULD, SO...
YES, BUT...
MURMUR
IT'S GONNA BE ROUGH. YOU COULD BE WALKING ALL NIGHT LONG.
MUMBLE MUMBLE

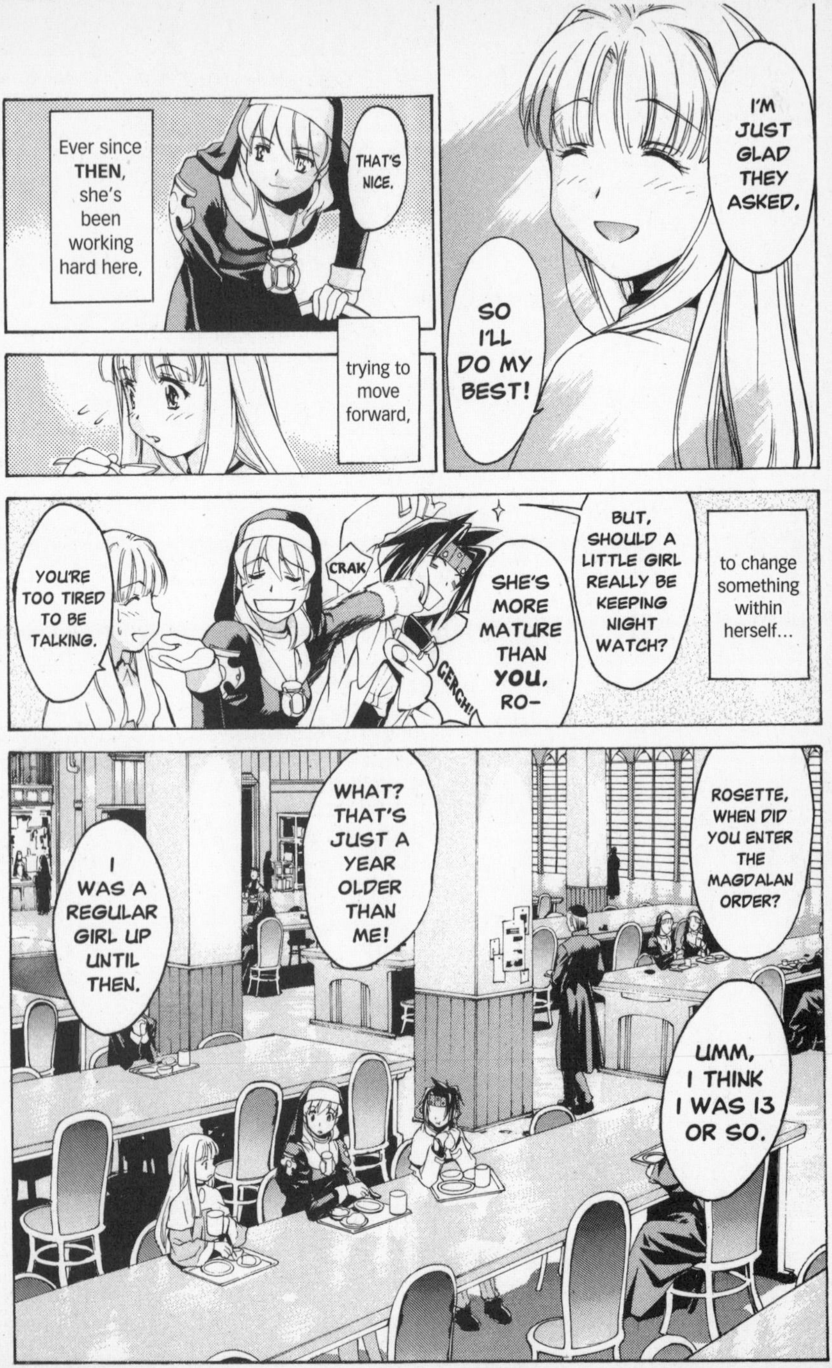

I'M JUST GLAD THEY ASKED.
SO I'LL DO MY BEST!
THAT'S NICE.
Ever since THEN, she's been working hard here,
trying to move forward,
to change something within herself...
BUT, SHOULD A LITTLE GIRL REALLY BE KEEPING NIGHT WATCH?
SHE'S MORE MATURE THAN YOU, RO-
CRAK
GERCH!
YOU'RE TOO TIRED TO BE TALKING.
ROSETTE, WHEN DID YOU ENTER THE MAGDALAN ORDER?
UMM, I THINK I WAS 13 OR SO.
WHAT? THAT'S JUST A YEAR OLDER THAN ME!
I WAS A REGULAR GIRL UP UNTIL THEN.

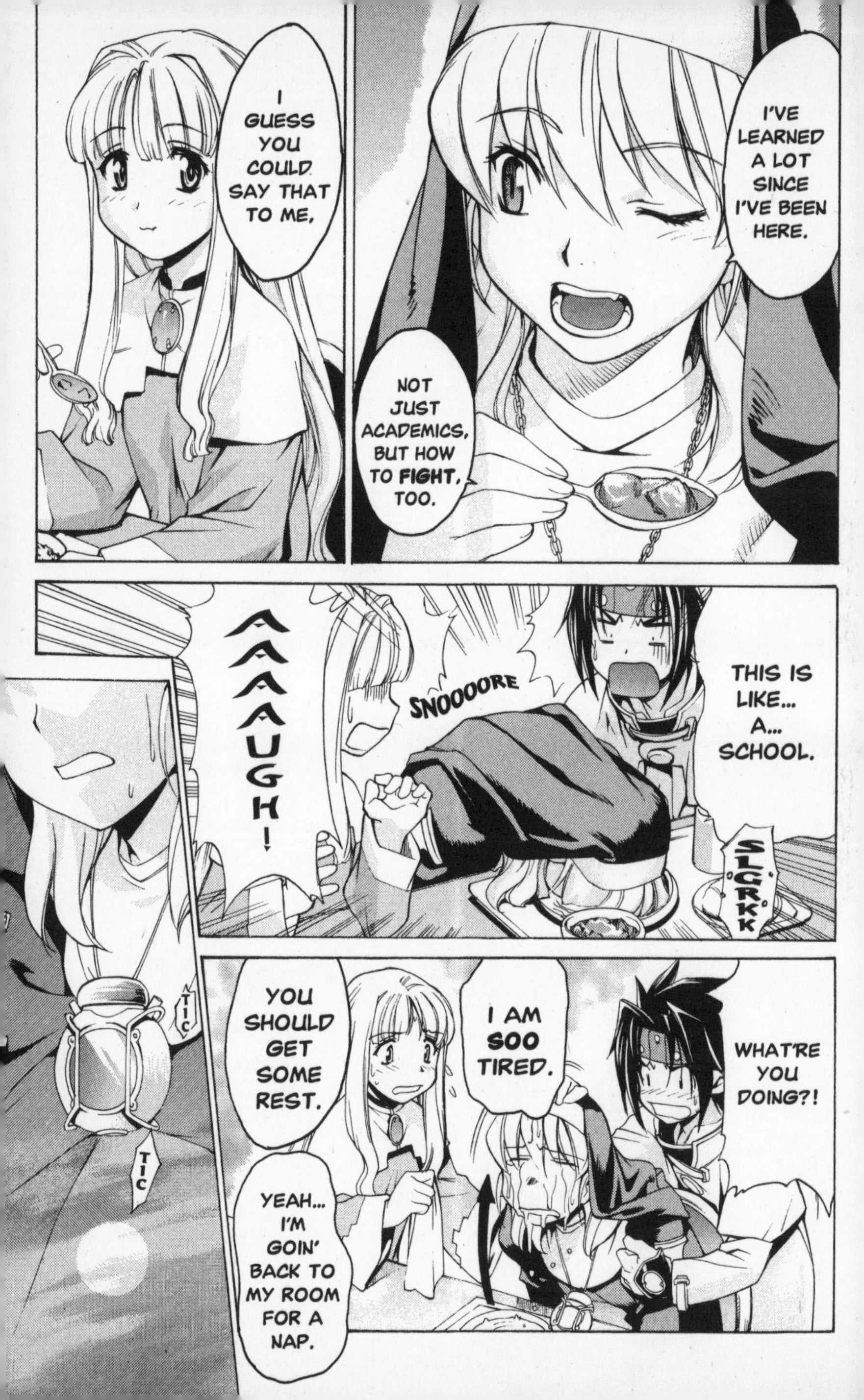

I'VE LEARNED A LOT SINCE I'VE BEEN HERE.
NOT JUST ACADEMICS, BUT HOW TO FIGHT, TOO.
I GUESS YOU COULD SAY THAT TO ME,
THIS IS LIKE... A... SCHOOL.
SNOOOORE
AAAAAUGH!
SLGRKK
WHAT'RE YOU DOING?!
I AM SOO TIRED.
YOU SHOULD GET SOME REST.
YEAH... I'M GOIN' BACK TO MY ROOM FOR A NAP.
TIC
TIC

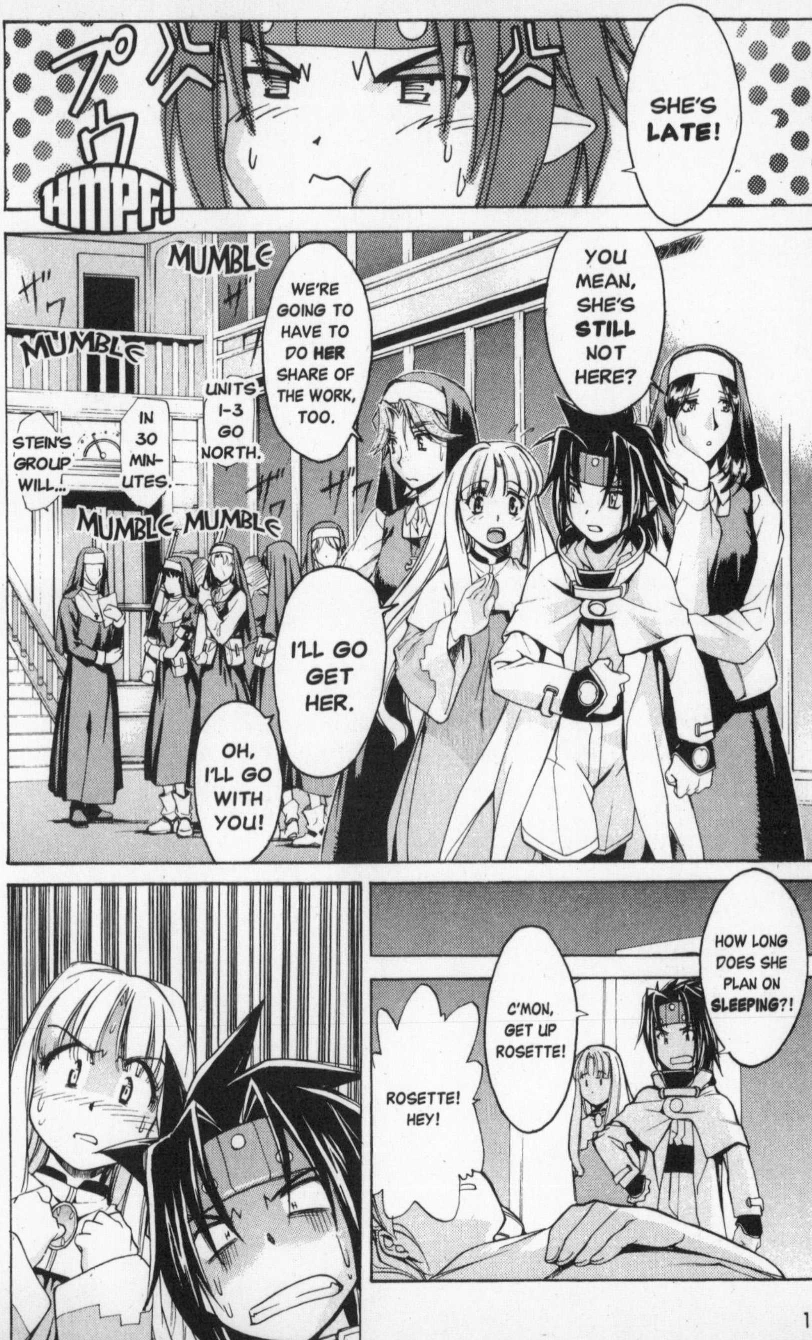
SHE'S LATE!
HMPF!
YOU MEAN, SHE'S STILL NOT HERE?
WE'RE GOING TO HAVE TO DO HER SHARE OF THE WORK, TOO.
MUMBLE
MUMBLE
UNITS 1-3 GO NORTH.
IN 30 MIN-UTES.
STEIN'S GROUP WILL...
MUMBLE MUMBLE
I'LL GO GET HER.
OH, I'LL GO WITH YOU!
HOW LONG DOES SHE PLAN ON SLEEPING?!
C'MON, GET UP ROSETTE!
ROSETTE! HEY!

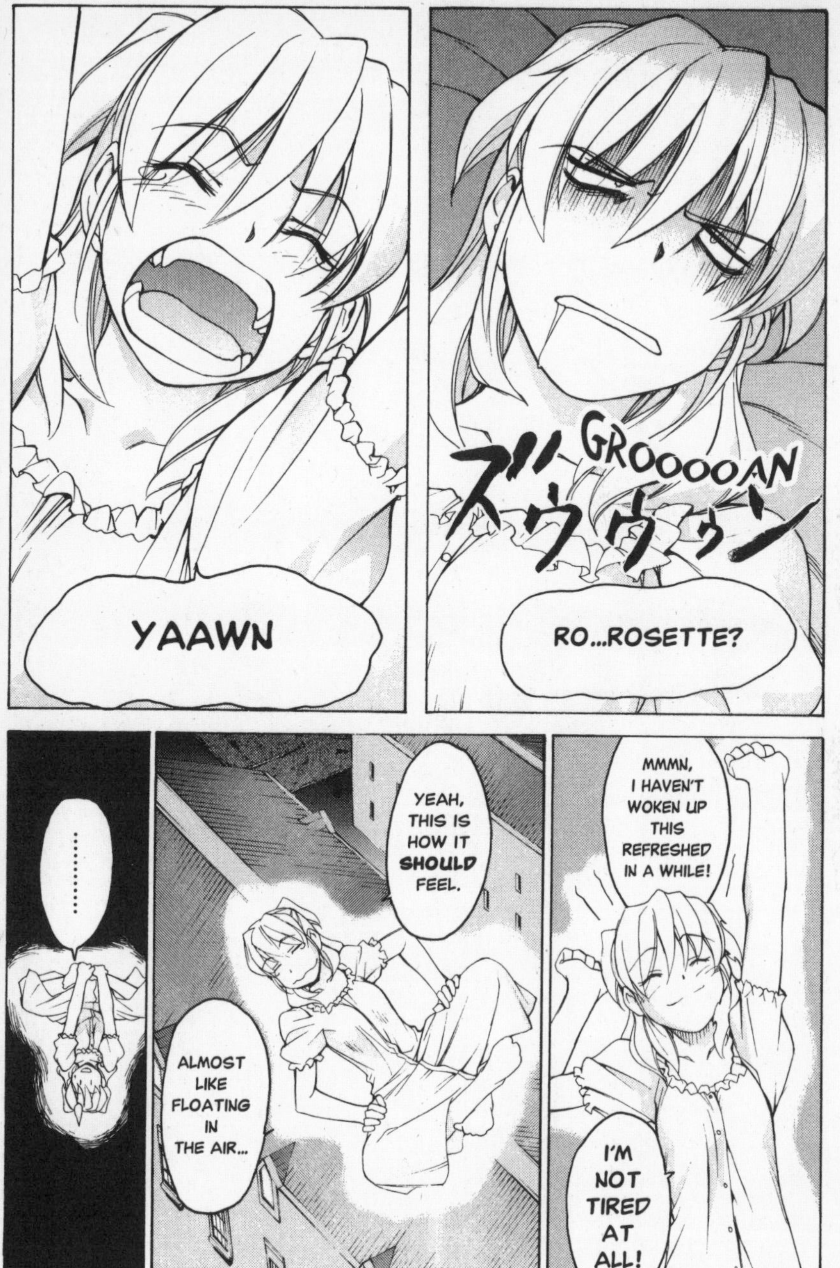
YAAWN
ズウウゥン
GROOOOAN
RO...ROSETTE?
MMMN, I HAVEN'T WOKEN UP THIS REFRESHED IN A WHILE!
I'M NOT TIRED AT ALL!
YEAH, THIS IS HOW IT SHOULD FEEL.
ALMOST LIKE FLOATING IN THE AIR...
....

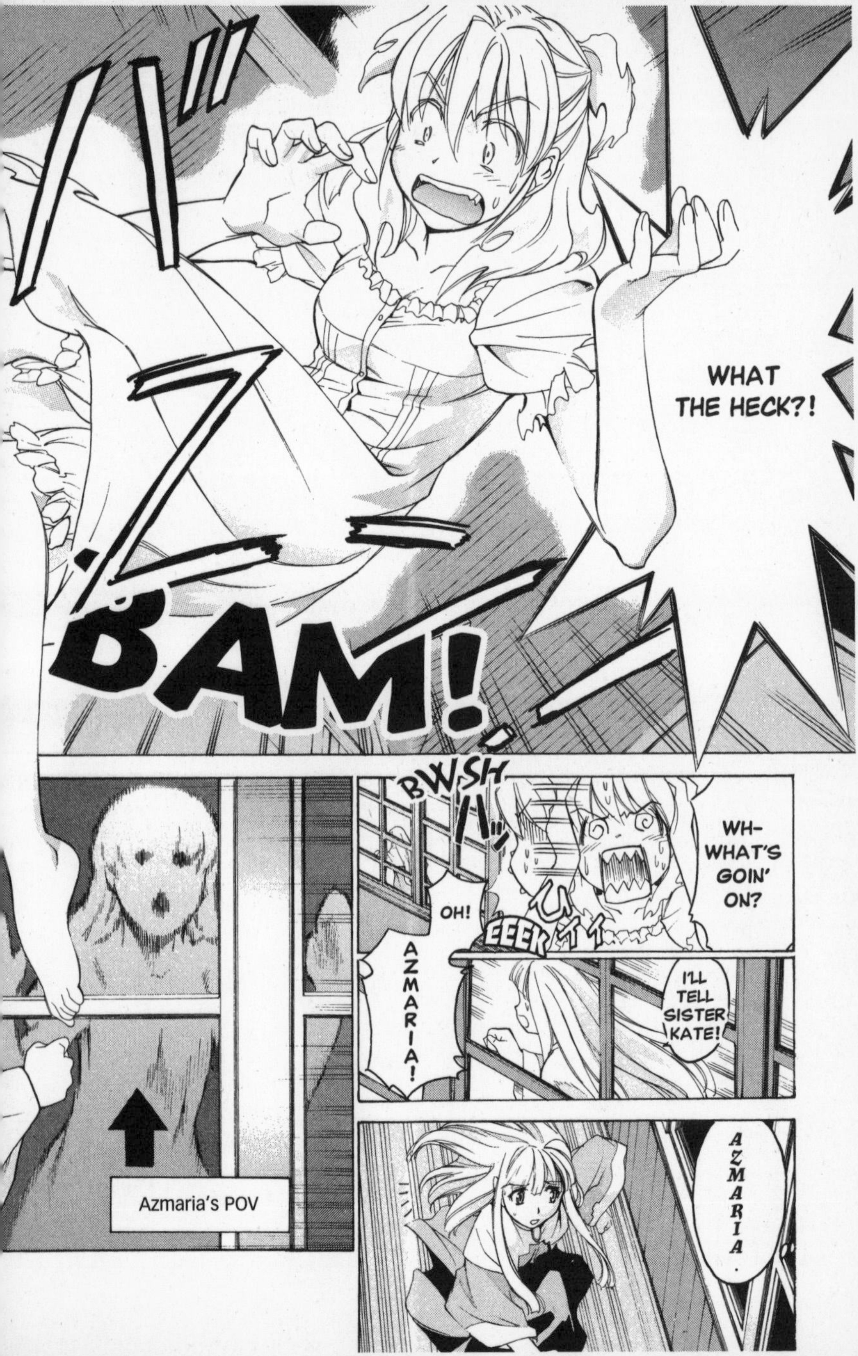
WHAT THE HECK?!
BAM!
WH- WHAT'S GOIN' ON?
BWSH
EEEK
OH!
AZMARIA!
I'LL TELL SISTER KATE!
AZMARIA.
Azmaria's POV

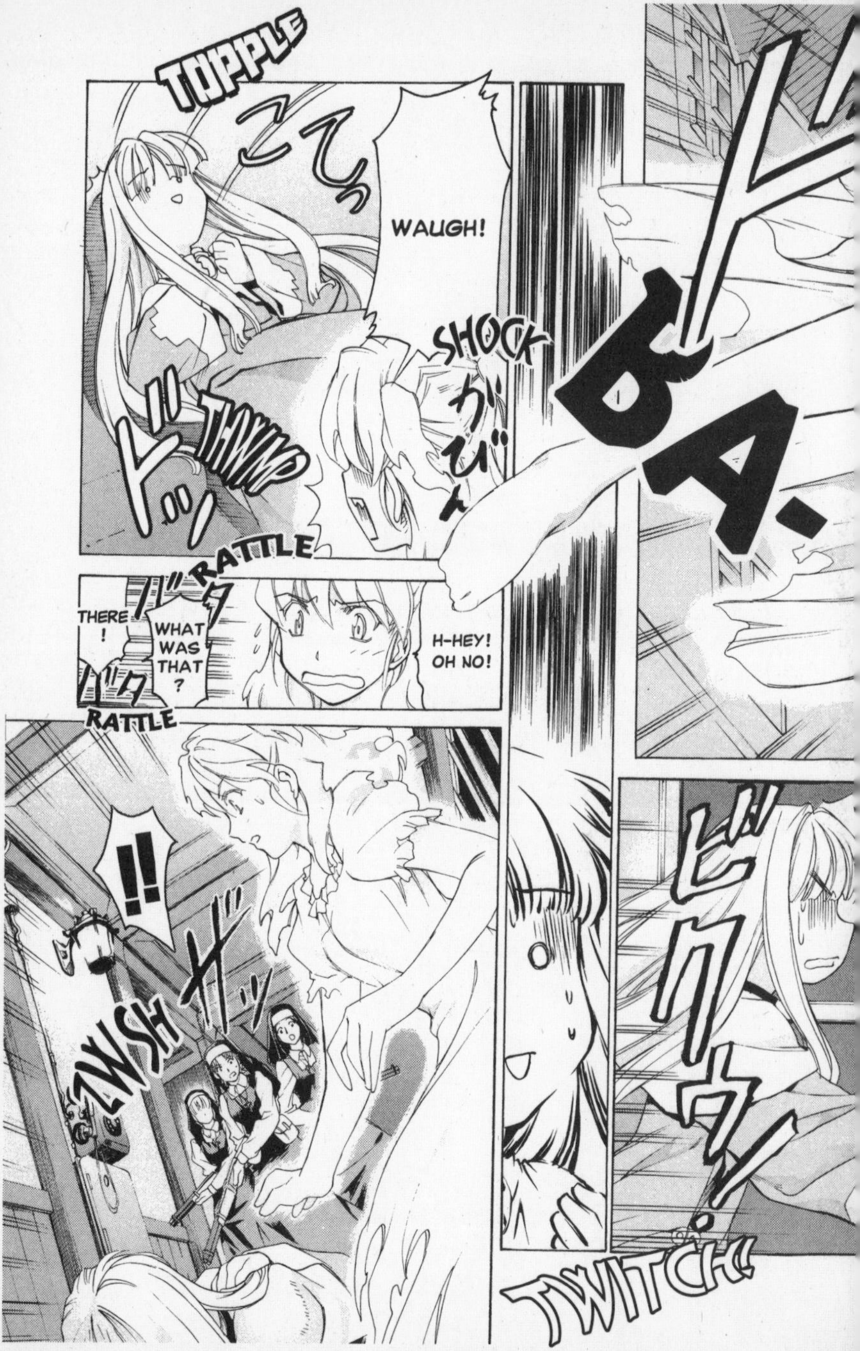

TOPPLE
WAUGH!
SHOCK
THWMP
BA.
RATTLE
THERE!
WHAT WAS THAT?
H-HEY! OH NO!
RATTLE
!!
ZWSH
TWITCH!

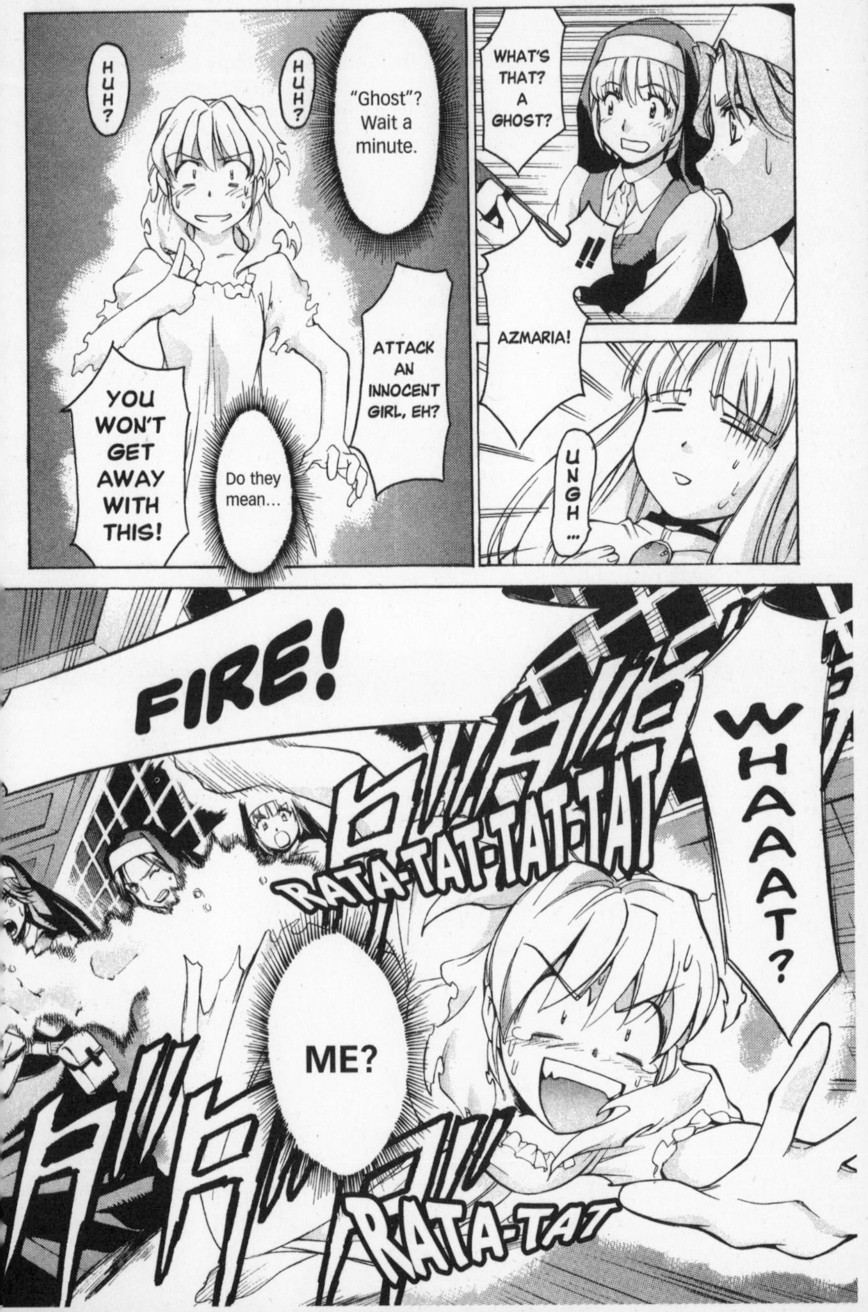
WHAT'S THAT? A GHOST?
!!
AZMARIA!
UNGH...
"Ghost"? Wait a minute.
HUH?
HUH?
ATTACK AN INNOCENT GIRL, EH?
YOU WON'T GET AWAY WITH THIS!
Do they mean…
FIRE!
WHAAAT?
RATA-TAT-TAT-TAT
ME?
RATA-TAT

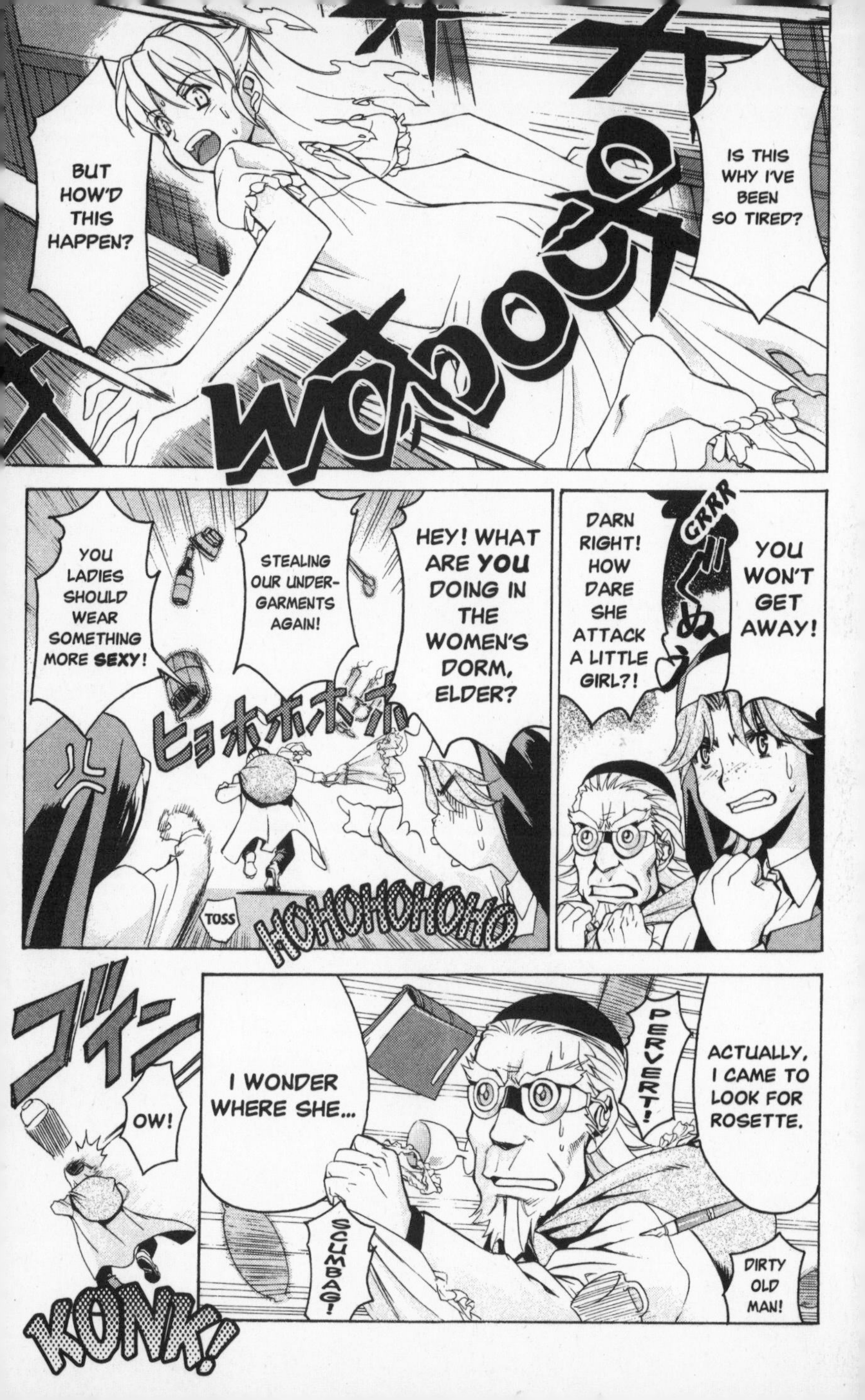
IS THIS WHY I'VE BEEN SO TIRED?
BUT HOW'D THIS HAPPEN?
GRRR
YOU WON'T GET AWAY!
DARN RIGHT! HOW DARE SHE ATTACK A LITTLE GIRL?!
HEY! WHAT ARE **YOU** DOING IN THE WOMEN'S DORM, ELDER?
STEALING OUR UNDER-GARMENTS AGAIN!
YOU LADIES SHOULD WEAR SOMETHING MORE **SEXY**!
HOHOHOHOHOHO
TOSS
ACTUALLY, I CAME TO LOOK FOR ROSETTE.
PERVERT!
I WONDER WHERE SHE...
DIRTY OLD MAN!
SCUMBAG!
OW!
KONK!

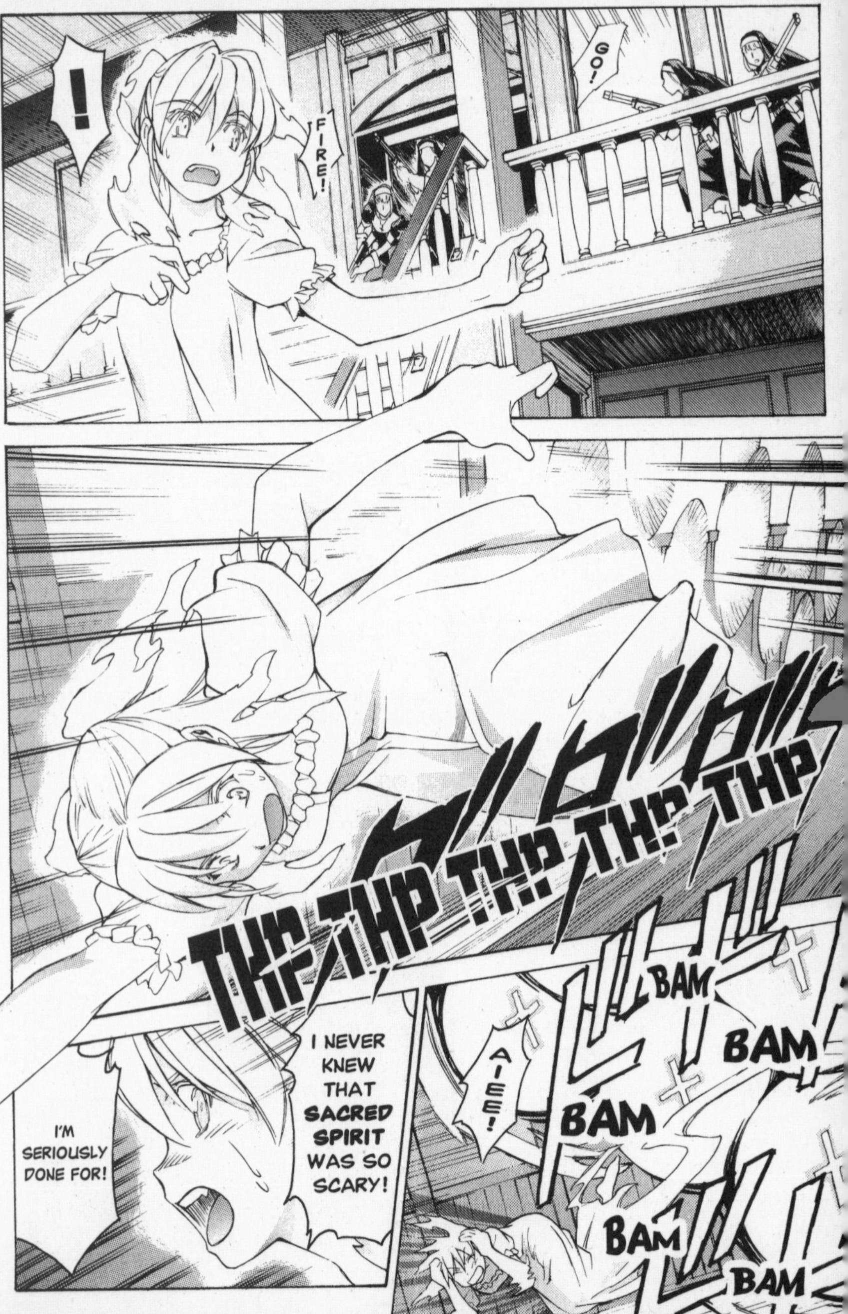
GO!
FIRE!
!
THP THP THP!! THP! THP
BAM
BAM
BAM
BAM
BAM
AIEE!
I NEVER KNEW THAT SACRED SPIRIT WAS SO SCARY!
I'M SERIOUSLY DONE FOR!

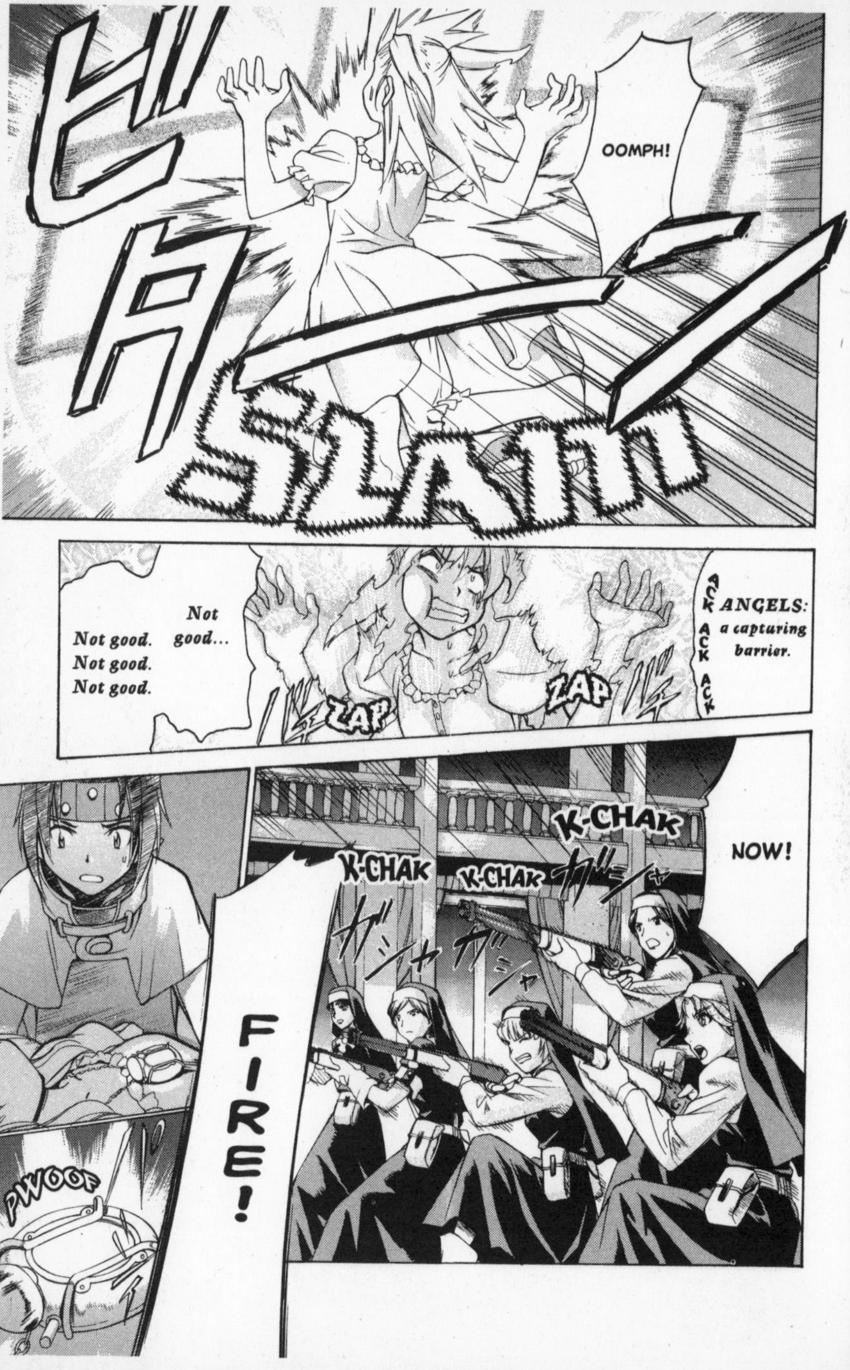
OOMPH!
SLAM
ANGELS: a capturing barrier.
ACK ACK ACK ACK
ZAP
ZAP
Not good...
Not good.
Not good.
Not good.
NOW!
K-CHAK
K-CHAK
K-CHAK
FIRE!
PWOOF

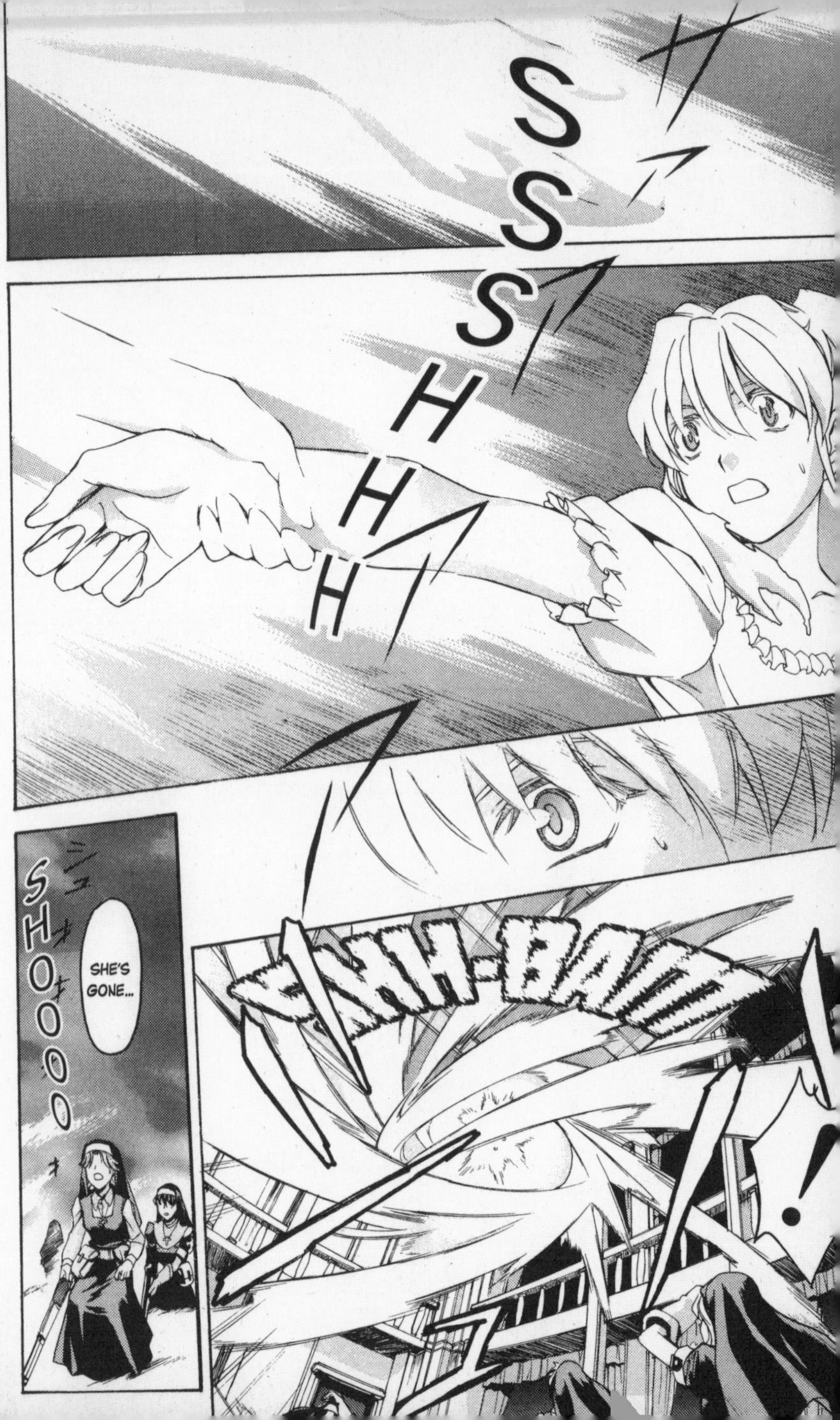
SSSHHH
SHOOOOO
SHE'S GONE...

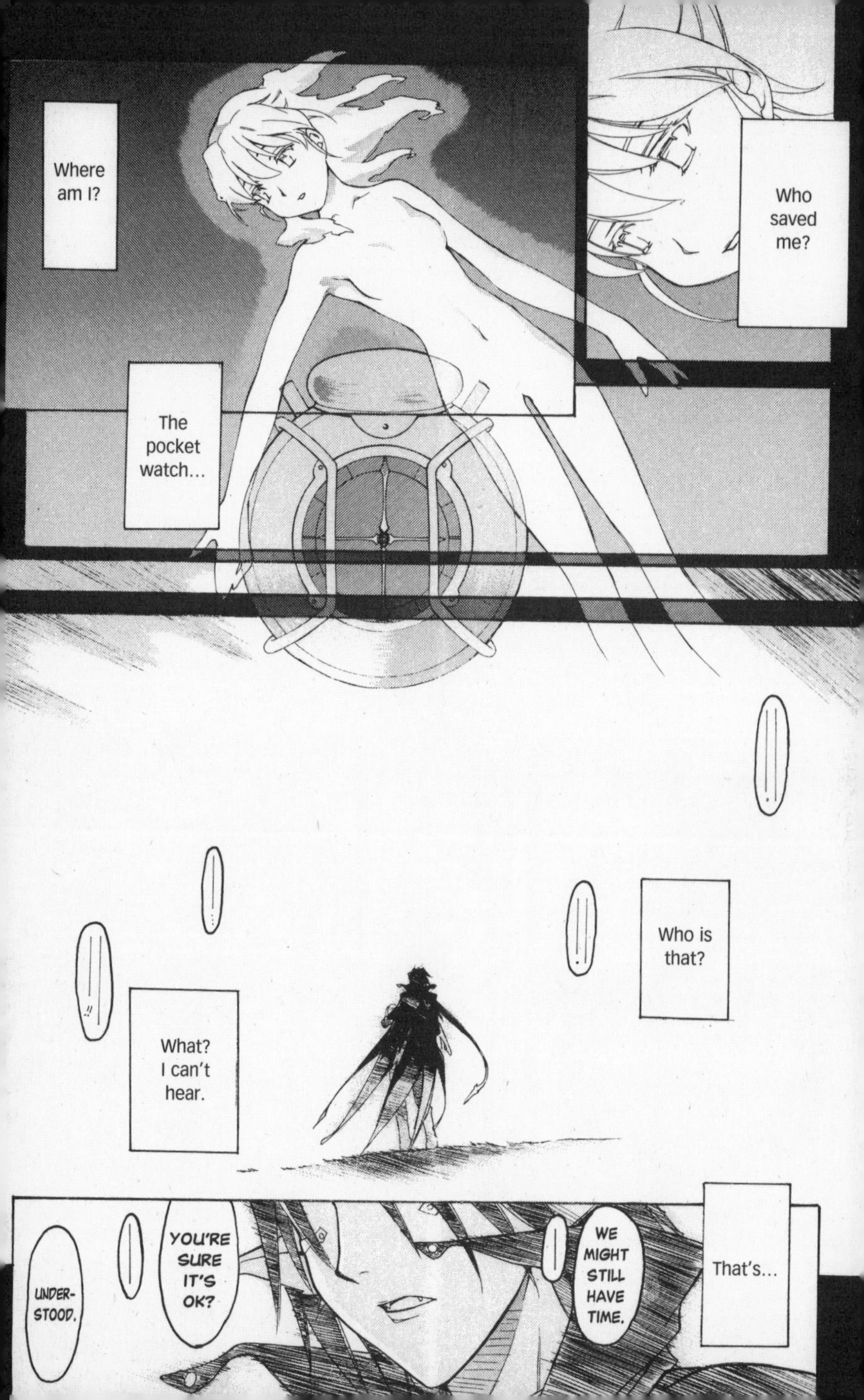
Who saved me?
Where am I?
The pocket watch...
Who is that?
What? I can't hear.
That's...
WE MIGHT STILL HAVE TIME.
YOU'RE SURE IT'S OK?
UNDER-STOOD.

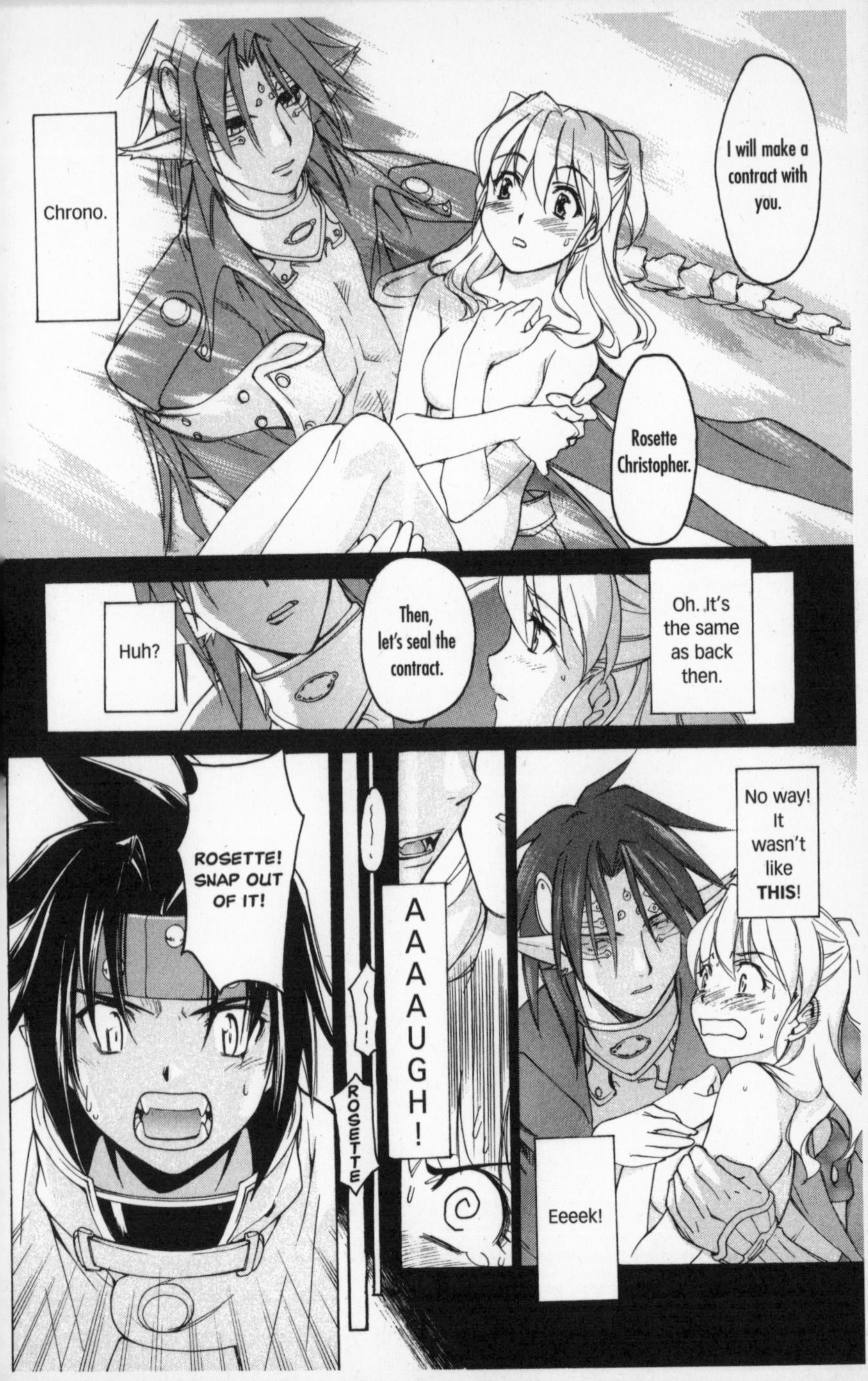
I will make a contract with you.
Chrono.
Rosette Christopher.
Oh. It's the same as back then.
Then, let's seal the contract.
Huh?
No way! It wasn't like **THIS**!
Eeeek!
AAAAUGH!
ROSETTE
ROSETTE! SNAP OUT OF IT!

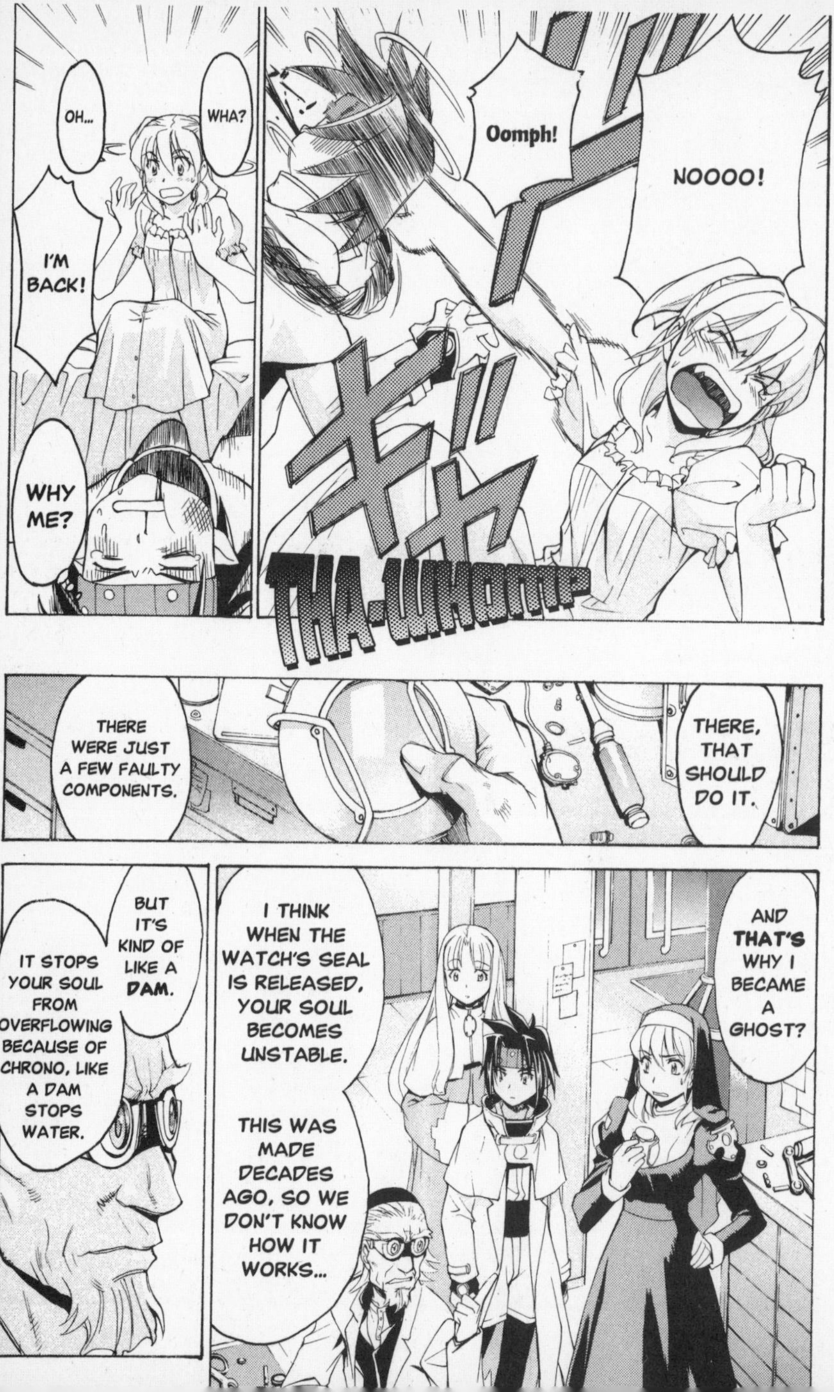
NOOOO!
Oomph!
THA-WHOMP
WHA?
OH...
I'M BACK!
WHY ME?
THERE, THAT SHOULD DO IT.
THERE WERE JUST A FEW FAULTY COMPONENTS.
AND THAT'S WHY I BECAME A GHOST?
I THINK WHEN THE WATCH'S SEAL IS RELEASED, YOUR SOUL BECOMES UNSTABLE.
THIS WAS MADE DECADES AGO, SO WE DON'T KNOW HOW IT WORKS...
BUT IT'S KIND OF LIKE A DAM.
IT STOPS YOUR SOUL FROM OVERFLOWING BECAUSE OF CHRONO, LIKE A DAM STOPS WATER.

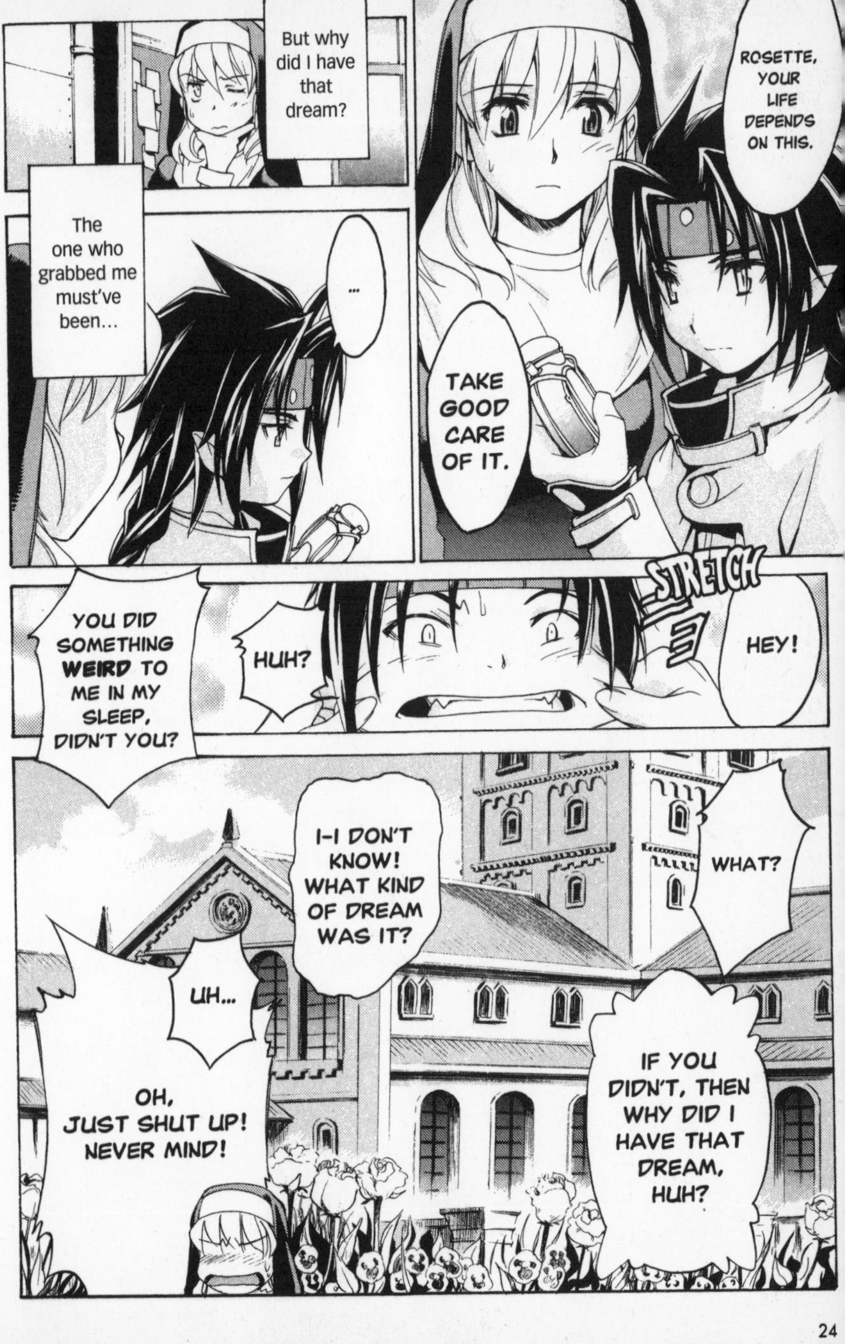
ROSETTE, YOUR LIFE DEPENDS ON THIS.
TAKE GOOD CARE OF IT.
But why did I have that dream?
The one who grabbed me must've been...
...
STRETCH
HEY!
HUH?
YOU DID SOMETHING WEIRD TO ME IN MY SLEEP, DIDN'T YOU?
WHAT?
I-I DON'T KNOW! WHAT KIND OF DREAM WAS IT?
UH...
IF YOU DIDN'T, THEN WHY DID I HAVE THAT DREAM, HUH?
OH, JUST SHUT UP! NEVER MIND!

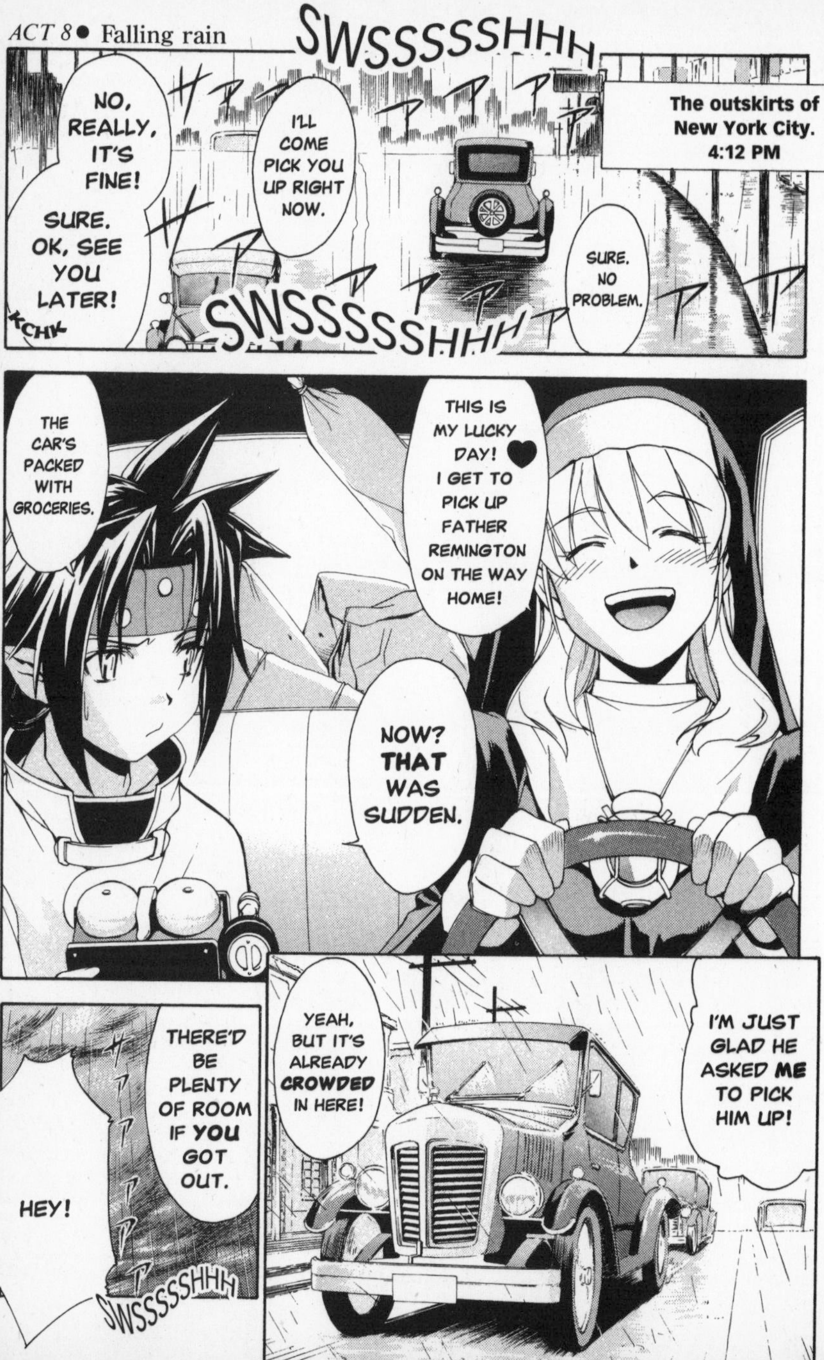
SWSSSSSHHH
The outskirts of New York City. 4:12 PM
SURE. NO PROBLEM.
I'LL COME PICK YOU UP RIGHT NOW.
NO, REALLY, IT'S FINE!
SURE. OK, SEE YOU LATER!
KCHK
SWSSSSSHHH
THIS IS MY LUCKY DAY! ♥ I GET TO PICK UP FATHER REMINGTON ON THE WAY HOME!
THE CAR'S PACKED WITH GROCERIES.
NOW? THAT WAS SUDDEN.
I'M JUST GLAD HE ASKED ME TO PICK HIM UP!
YEAH, BUT IT'S ALREADY CROWDED IN HERE!
THERE'D BE PLENTY OF ROOM IF YOU GOT OUT.
HEY!
SWSSSSSHHH

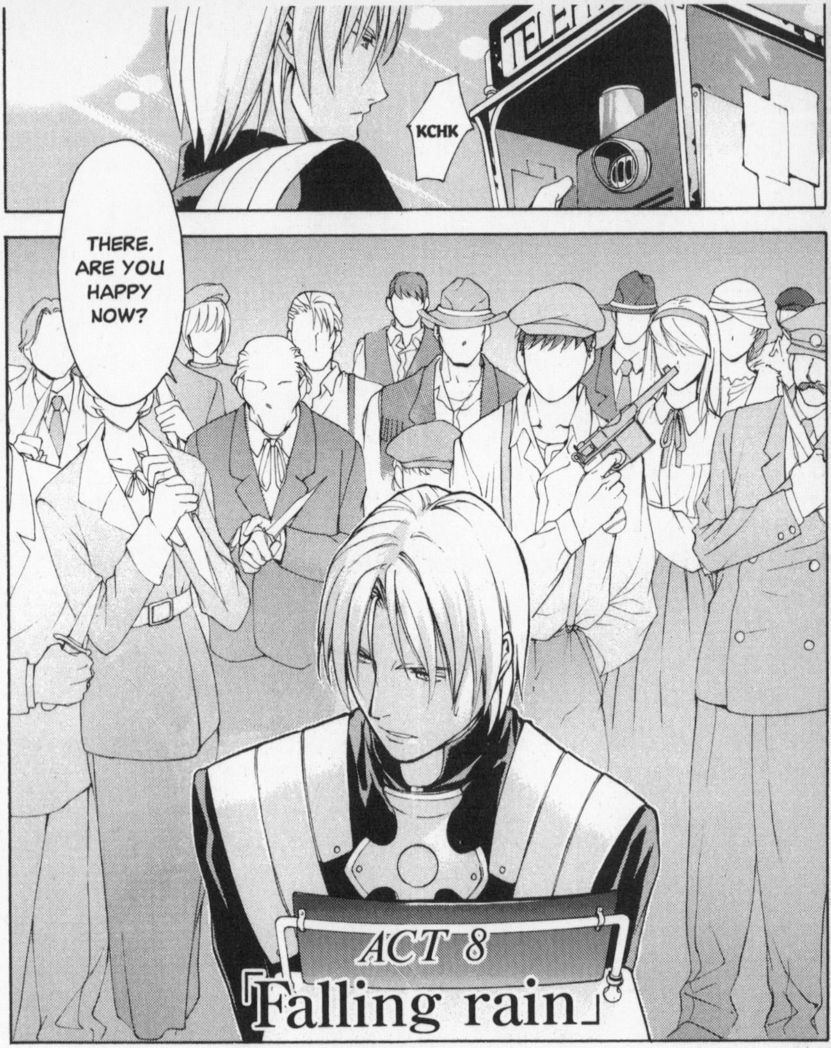
KCHK
THERE. ARE YOU HAPPY NOW?
ACT 8
「Falling rain」

This has turned into a very dangerous situation.

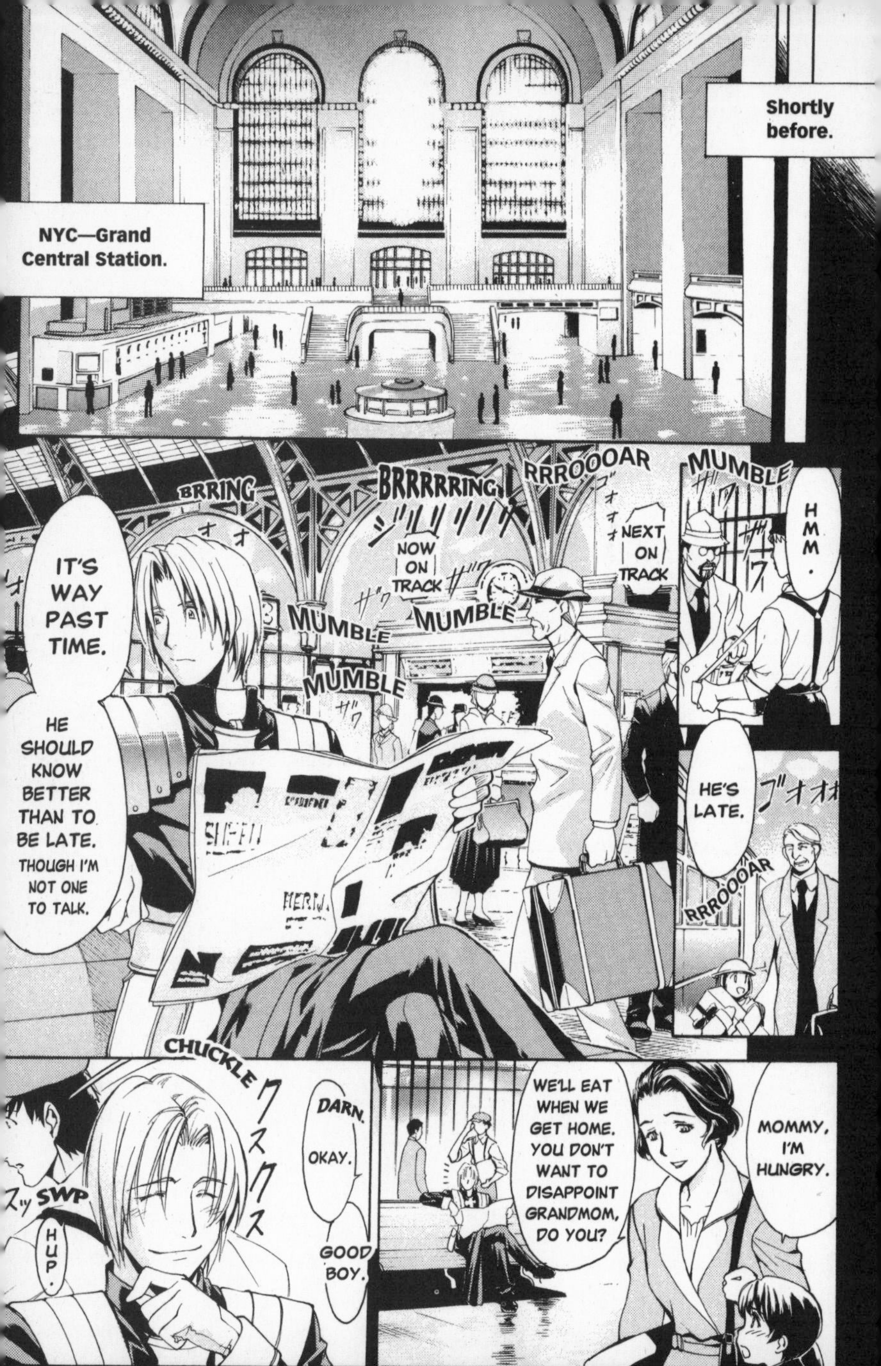
Shortly before.
NYC—Grand Central Station.
MUMBLE
HMM.
HE'S LATE.
RRROOOAR
RRROOOAR
BRRRRRING
BRRING
NOW ON TRACK
NEXT ON TRACK
MUMBLE
MUMBLE
MUMBLE
IT'S WAY PAST TIME.
HE SHOULD KNOW BETTER THAN TO BE LATE.
THOUGH I'M NOT ONE TO TALK.
MOMMY, I'M HUNGRY.
WE'LL EAT WHEN WE GET HOME. YOU DON'T WANT TO DISAPPOINT GRANDMOM, DO YOU?
DARN.
OKAY.
GOOD BOY.
CHUCKLE
SWP
HUP.

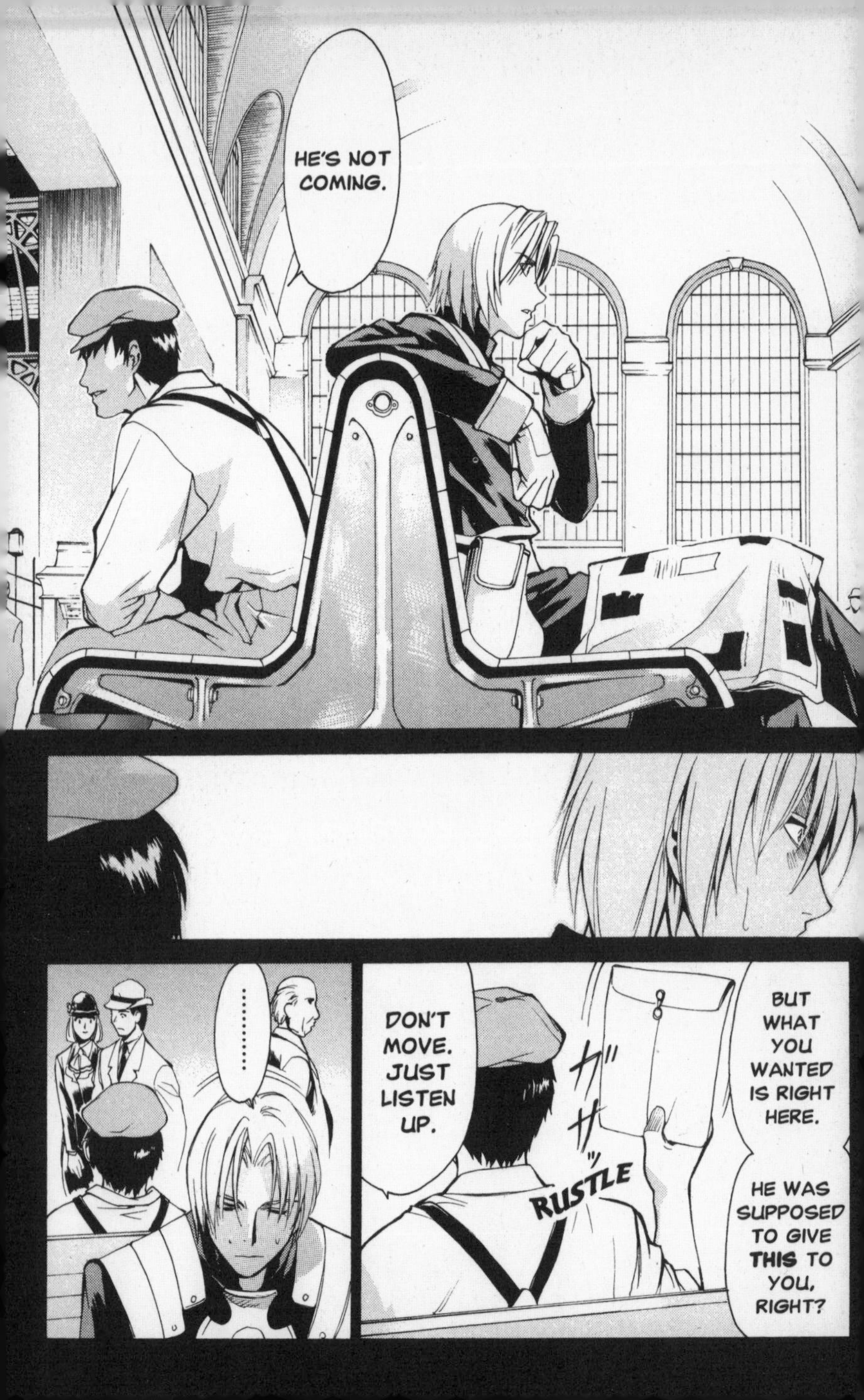
HE'S NOT COMING.
......
DON'T MOVE. JUST LISTEN UP.
RUSTLE
BUT WHAT YOU WANTED IS RIGHT HERE.
HE WAS SUPPOSED TO GIVE THIS TO YOU, RIGHT?

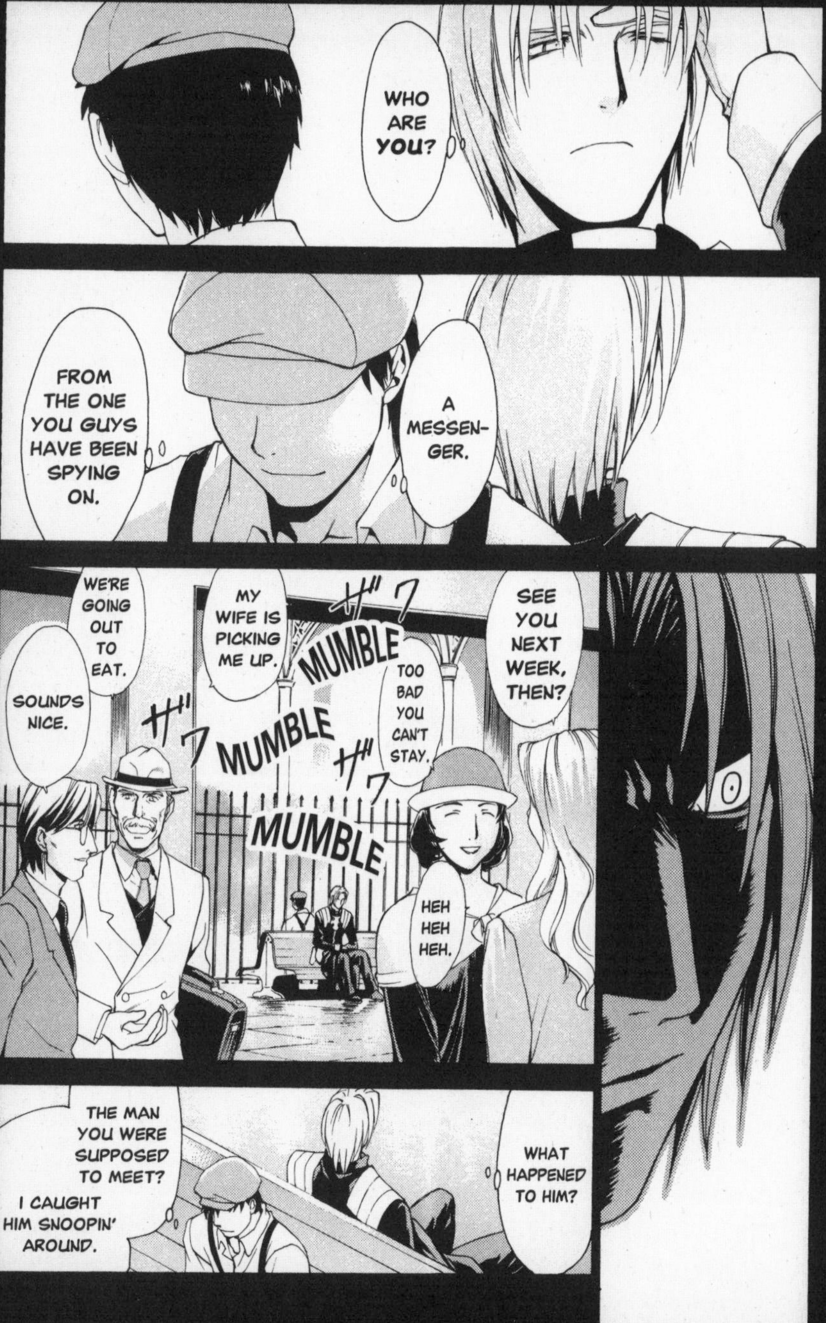
WHO ARE YOU?
A MESSENGER.
FROM THE ONE YOU GUYS HAVE BEEN SPYING ON.
SEE YOU NEXT WEEK, THEN?
TOO BAD YOU CAN'T STAY.
MY WIFE IS PICKING ME UP.
WE'RE GOING OUT TO EAT.
SOUNDS NICE.
ザワ MUMBLE
ザワ MUMBLE
ザワ MUMBLE
HEH HEH HEH.
WHAT HAPPENED TO HIM?
THE MAN YOU WERE SUPPOSED TO MEET?
I CAUGHT HIM SNOOPIN' AROUND.

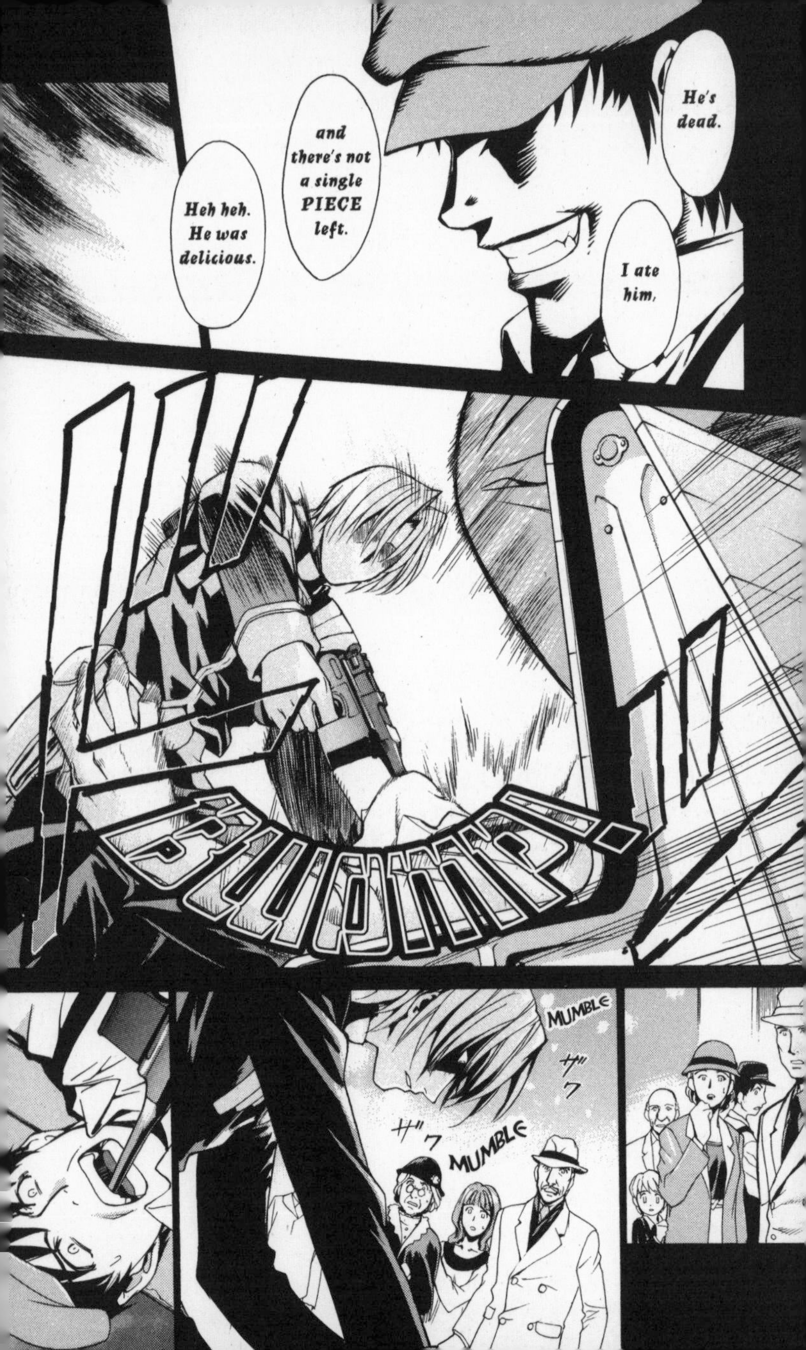
He's dead.
I ate him,
and there's not a single PIECE left.
Heh heh. He was delicious.
MUMBLE
ザワ
ザワ
MUMBLE

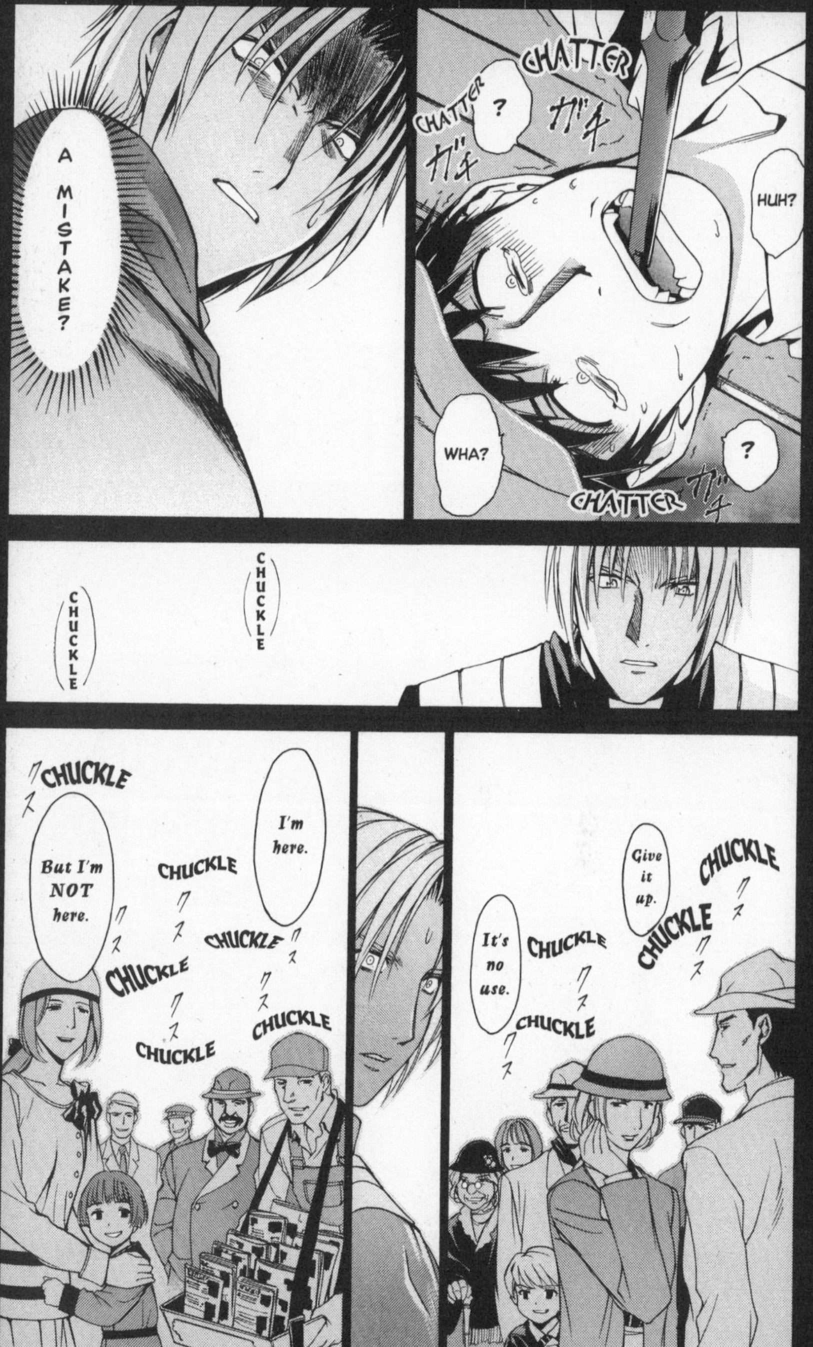
CHATTER
ガチ
CHATTER
ガチ
?
HUH?
WHA?
?
CHATTER
ガチ
A MISTAKE?
CHUCKLE
CHUCKLE
CHUCKLE
クス
Give it up.
CHUCKLE
クス
It's no use.
CHUCKLE
クス
CHUCKLE
クス
I'm here.
CHUCKLE
クス
But I'm NOT here.
CHUCKLE
クス
CHUCKLE
クス
CHUCKLE
クス
CHUCKLE
CHUCKLE
CHUCKLE

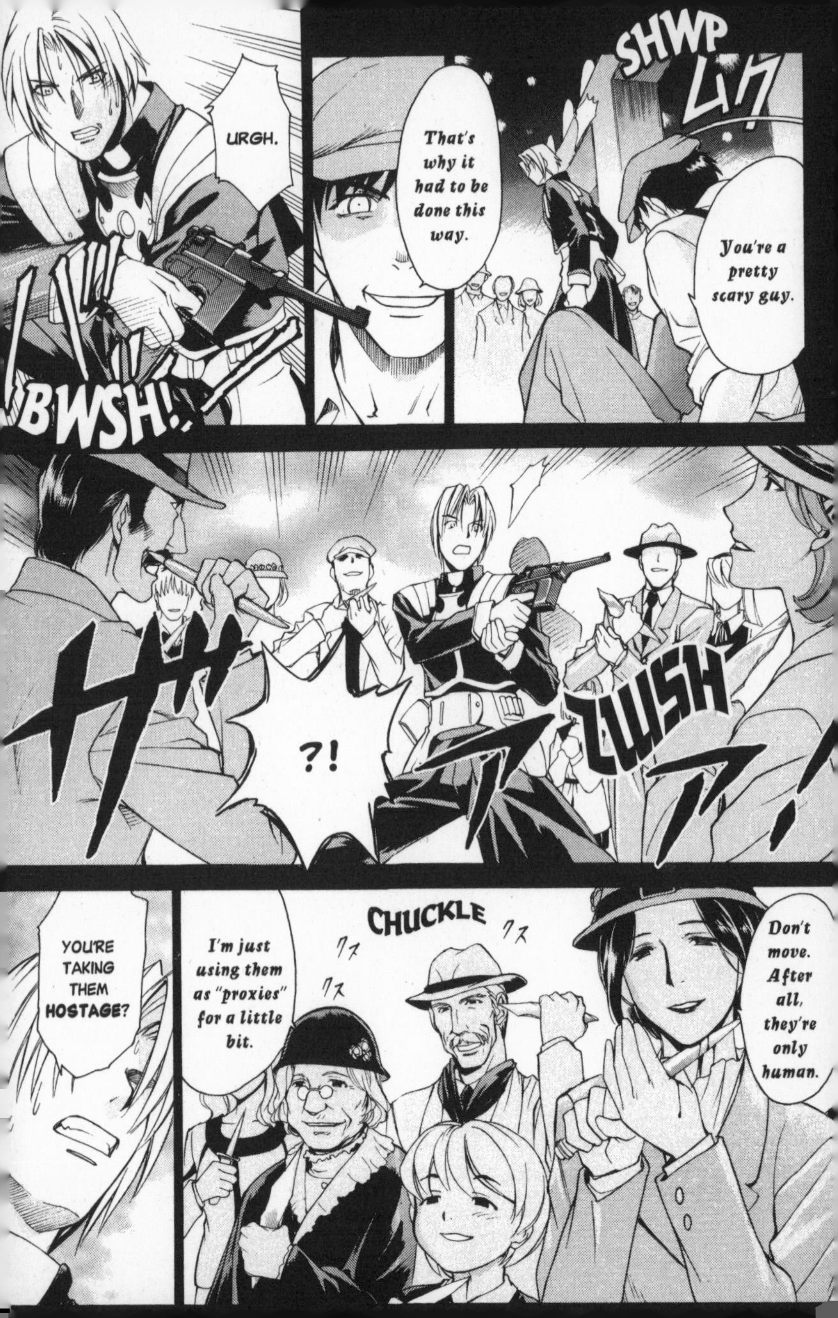
SHWP
You're a pretty scary guy.
That's why it had to be done this way.
URGH.
BWSH!!
ZWSH
?!
Don't move. After all, they're only human.
CHUCKLE
I'm just using them as "proxies" for a little bit.
YOU'RE TAKING THEM HOSTAGE?

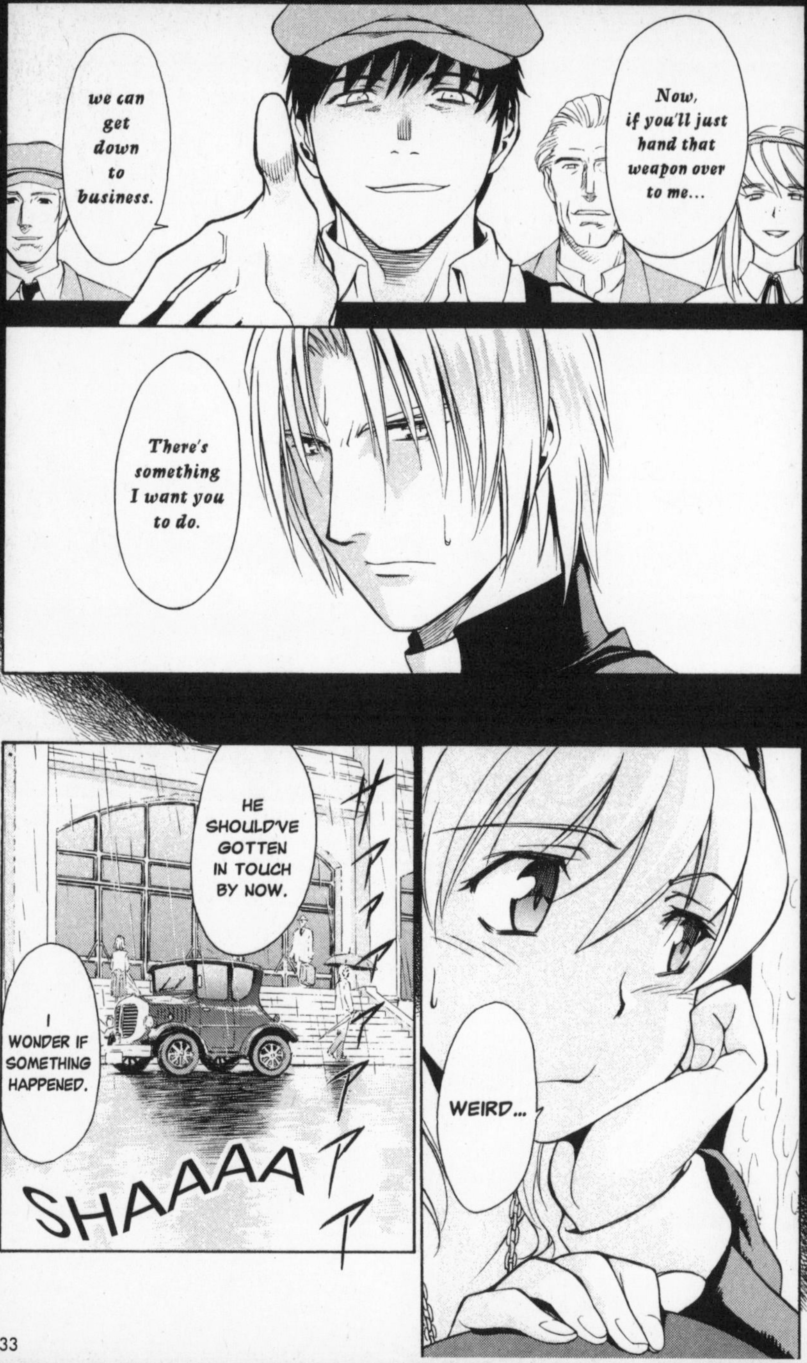
Now, if you'll just hand that weapon over to me...
we can get down to business.
There's something I want you to do.
WEIRD...
HE SHOULD'VE GOTTEN IN TOUCH BY NOW.
I WONDER IF SOMETHING HAPPENED.
SHAAAA

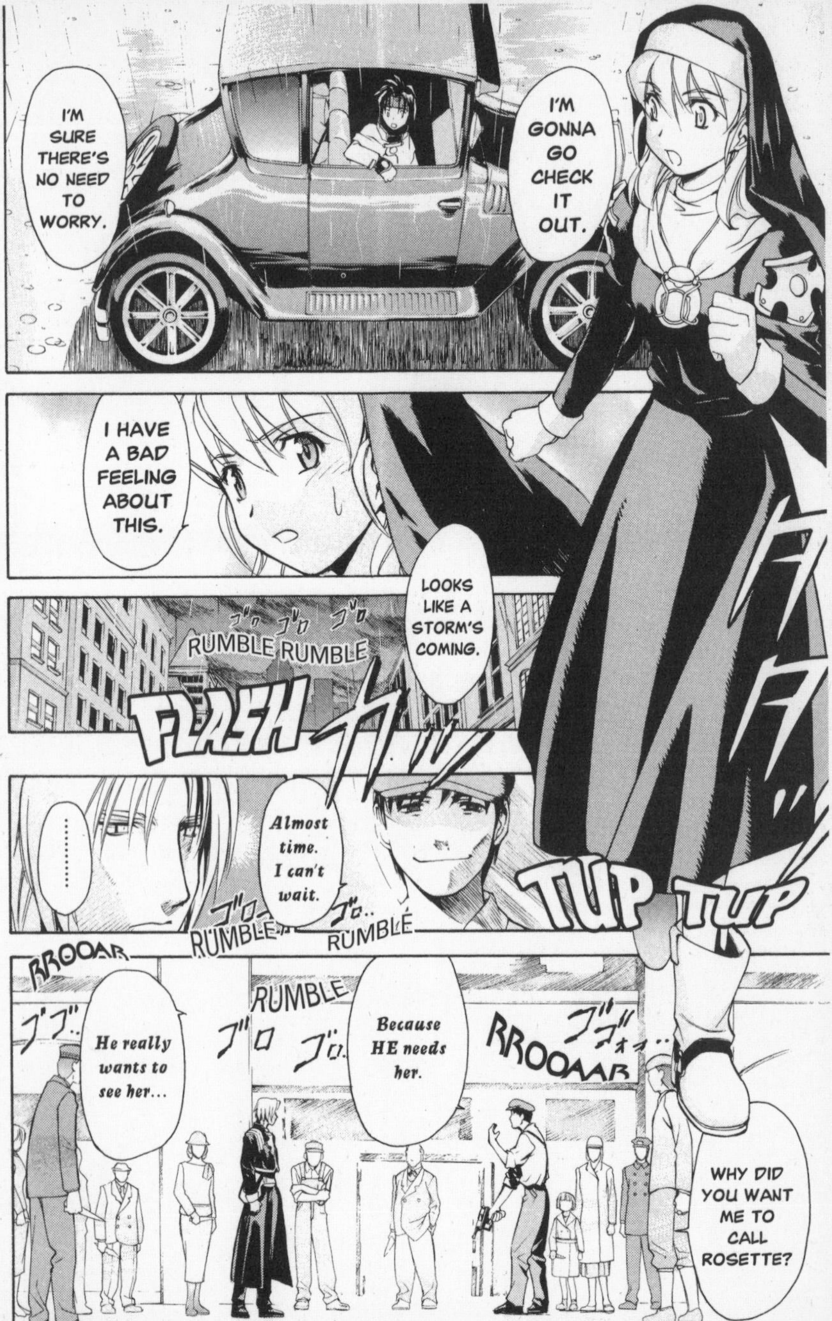
I'M GONNA GO CHECK IT OUT.
I'M SURE THERE'S NO NEED TO WORRY.
I HAVE A BAD FEELING ABOUT THIS.
LOOKS LIKE A STORM'S COMING.
RUMBLE RUMBLE
FLASH
Almost time. I can't wait.
......
RUMBLE
RUMBLE
TUP TUP
WHY DID YOU WANT ME TO CALL ROSETTE?
BROOAAR
Because HE needs her.
RUMBLE
He really wants to see her...
BROOAR

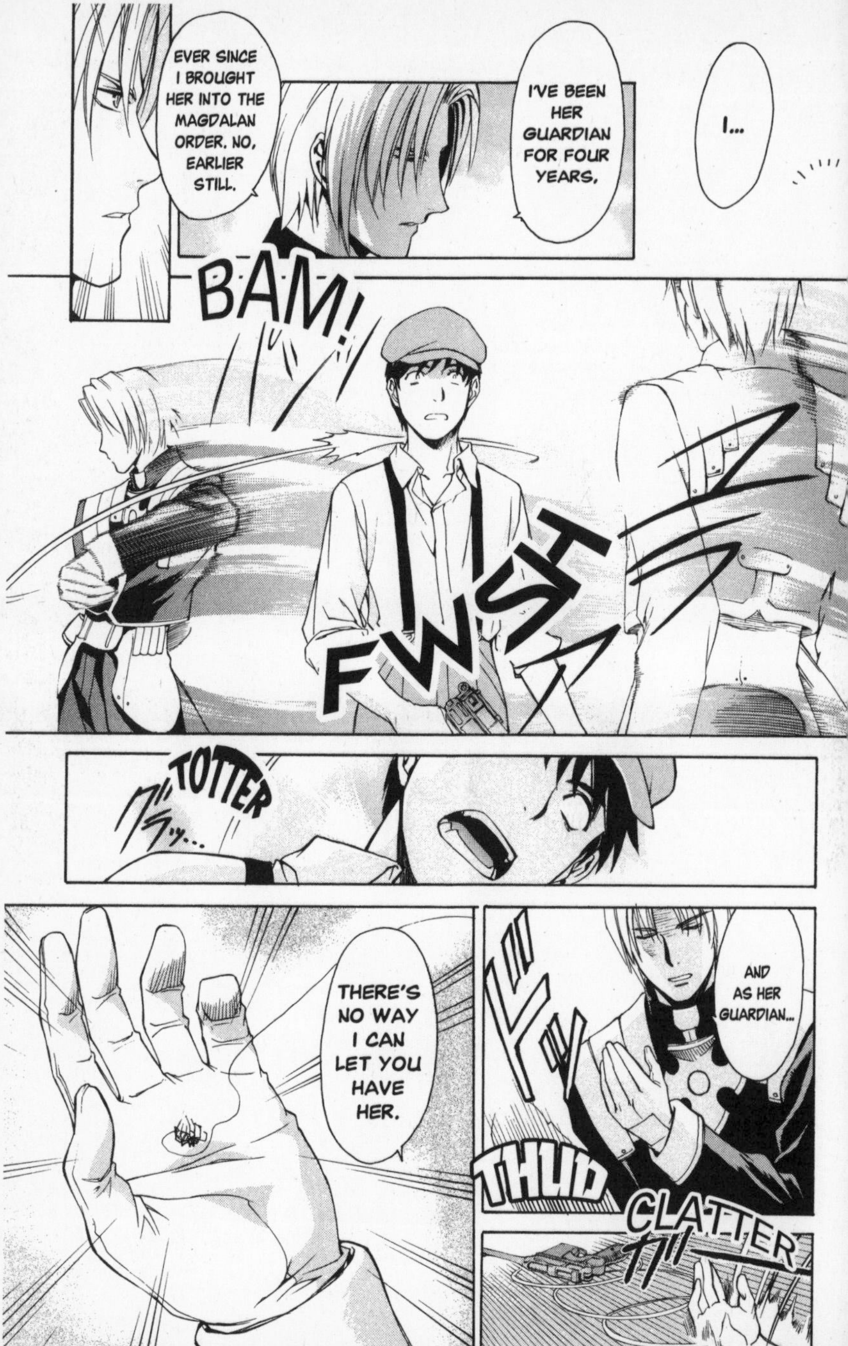
I...
I'VE BEEN HER GUARDIAN FOR FOUR YEARS.
EVER SINCE I BROUGHT HER INTO THE MAGDALAN ORDER. NO, EARLIER STILL.
BAM!
FWSH
TOTTER
AND AS HER GUARDIAN...
THUD
CLATTER
THERE'S NO WAY I CAN LET YOU HAVE HER.

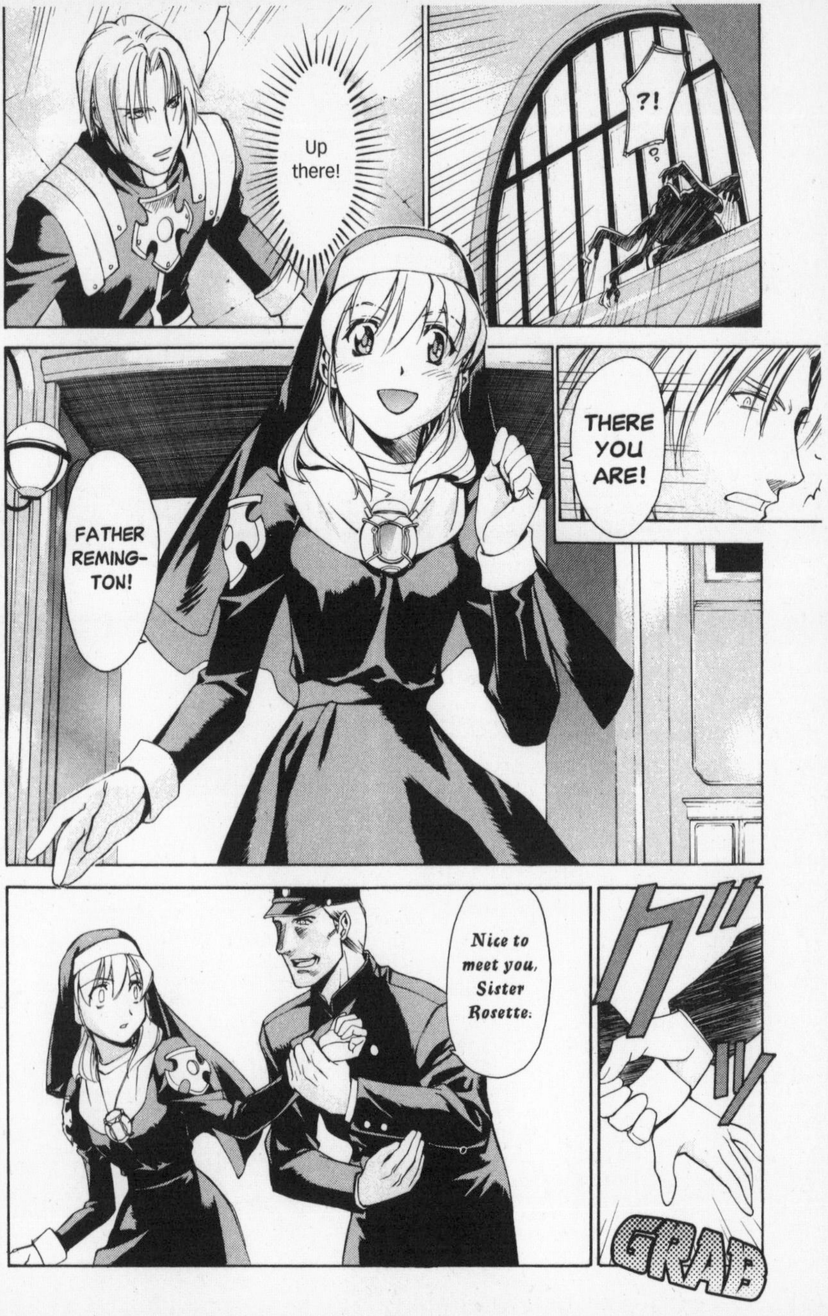
?!
Up there!
THERE YOU ARE!
FATHER REMINGTON!
GRAB
Nice to meet you, Sister Rosette.

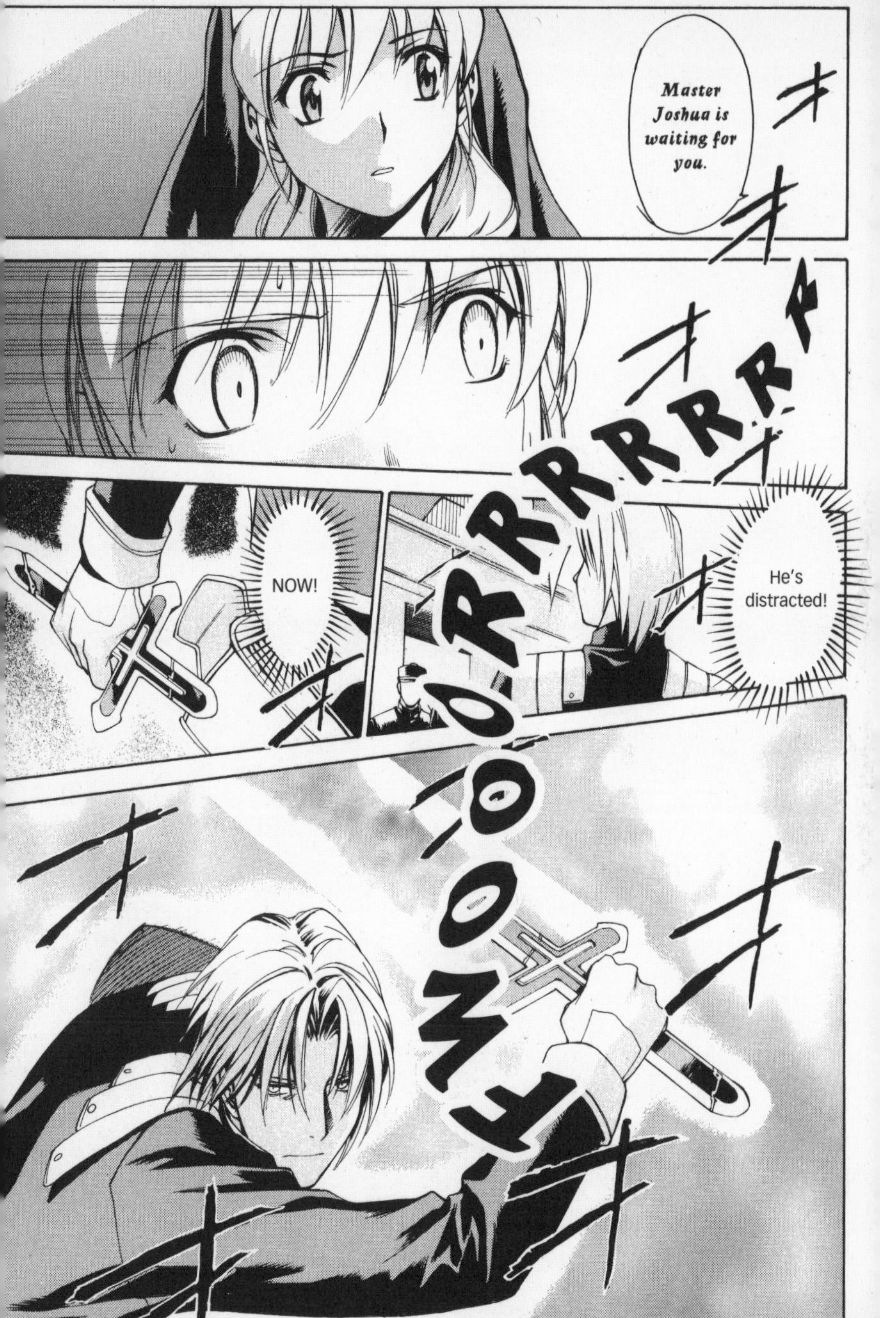
Master Joshua is waiting for you.
He's distracted!
NOW!

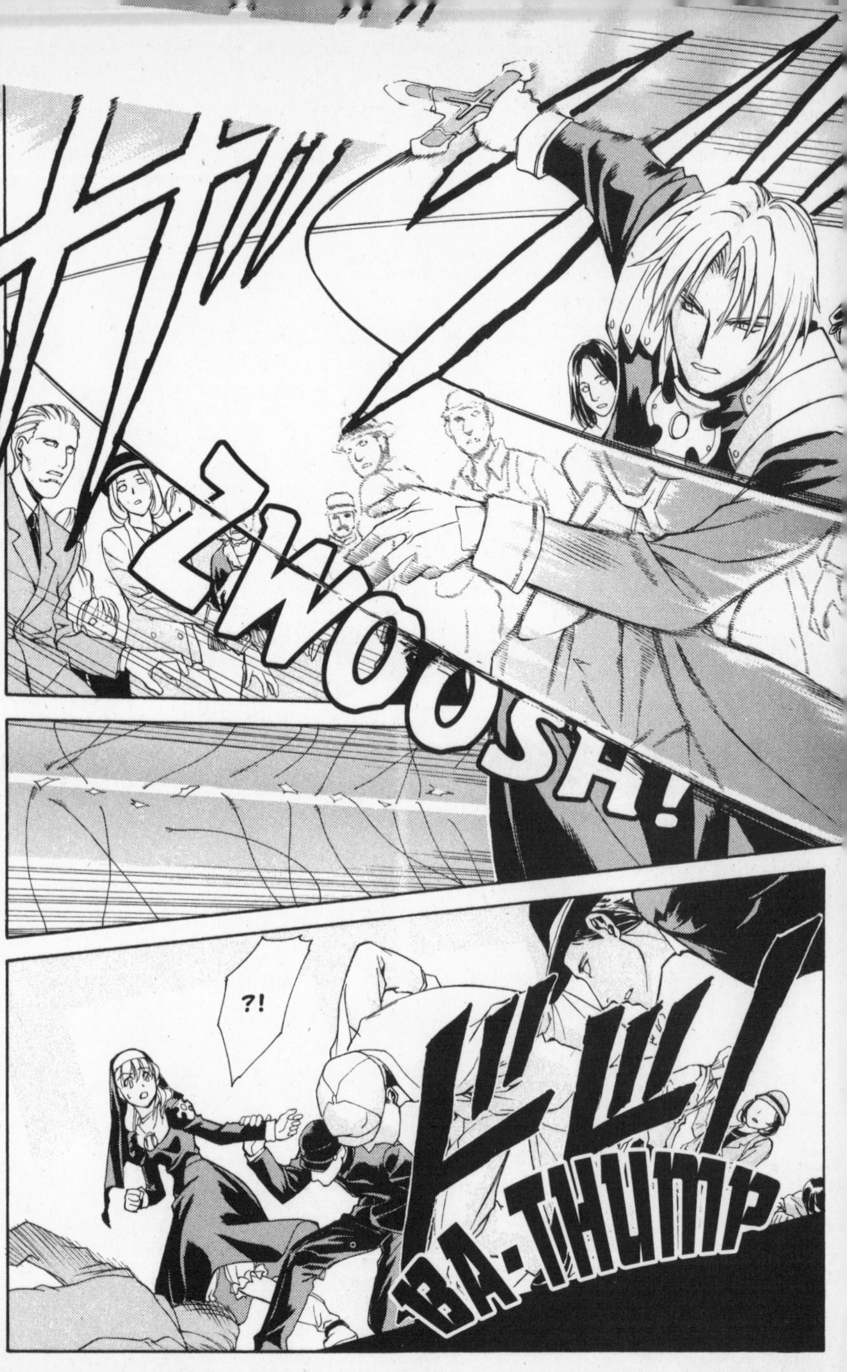

ZWOOSH!
?!
BA-THUMP

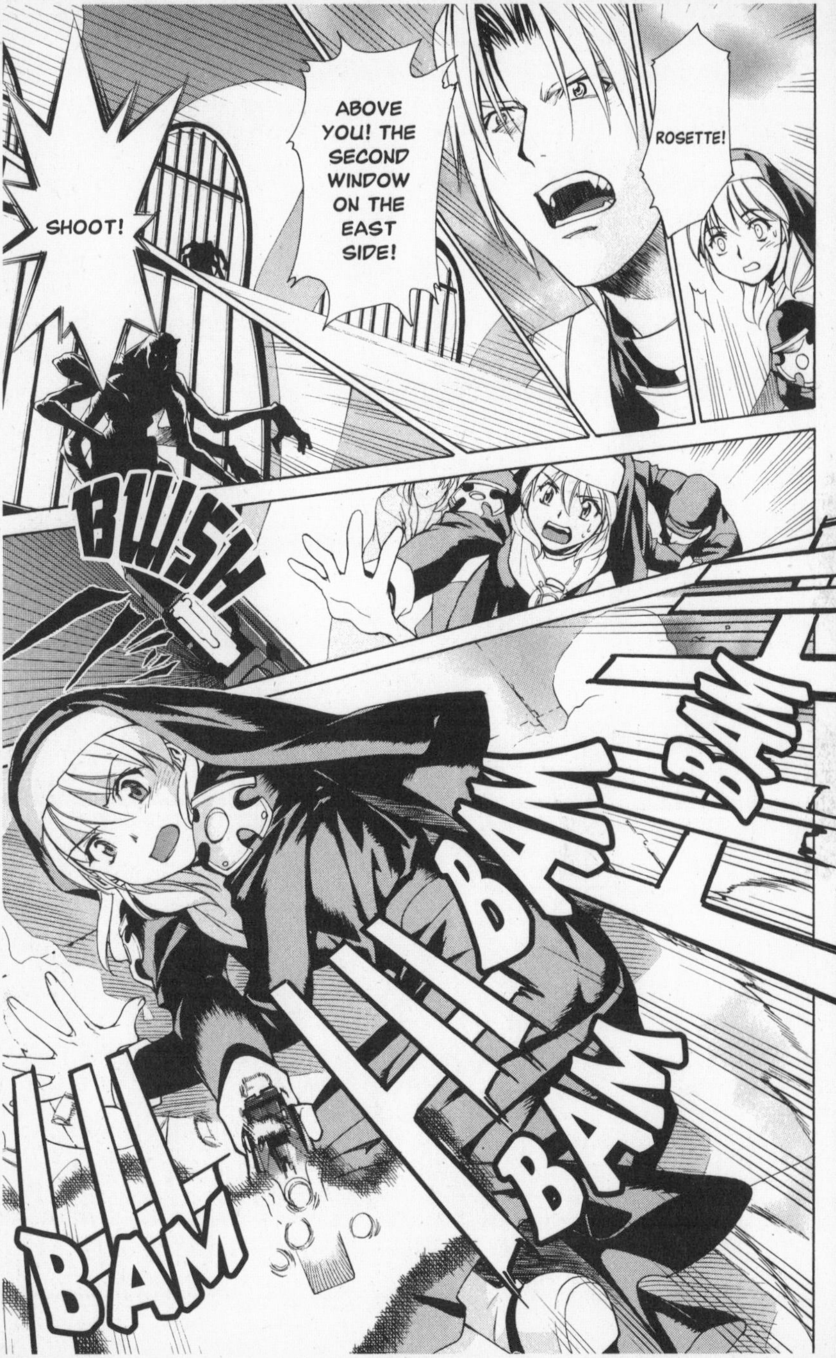
ROSETTE!
ABOVE YOU! THE SECOND WINDOW ON THE EAST SIDE!
SHOOT!
BWSH
BAM
BAM
BAM
BAM

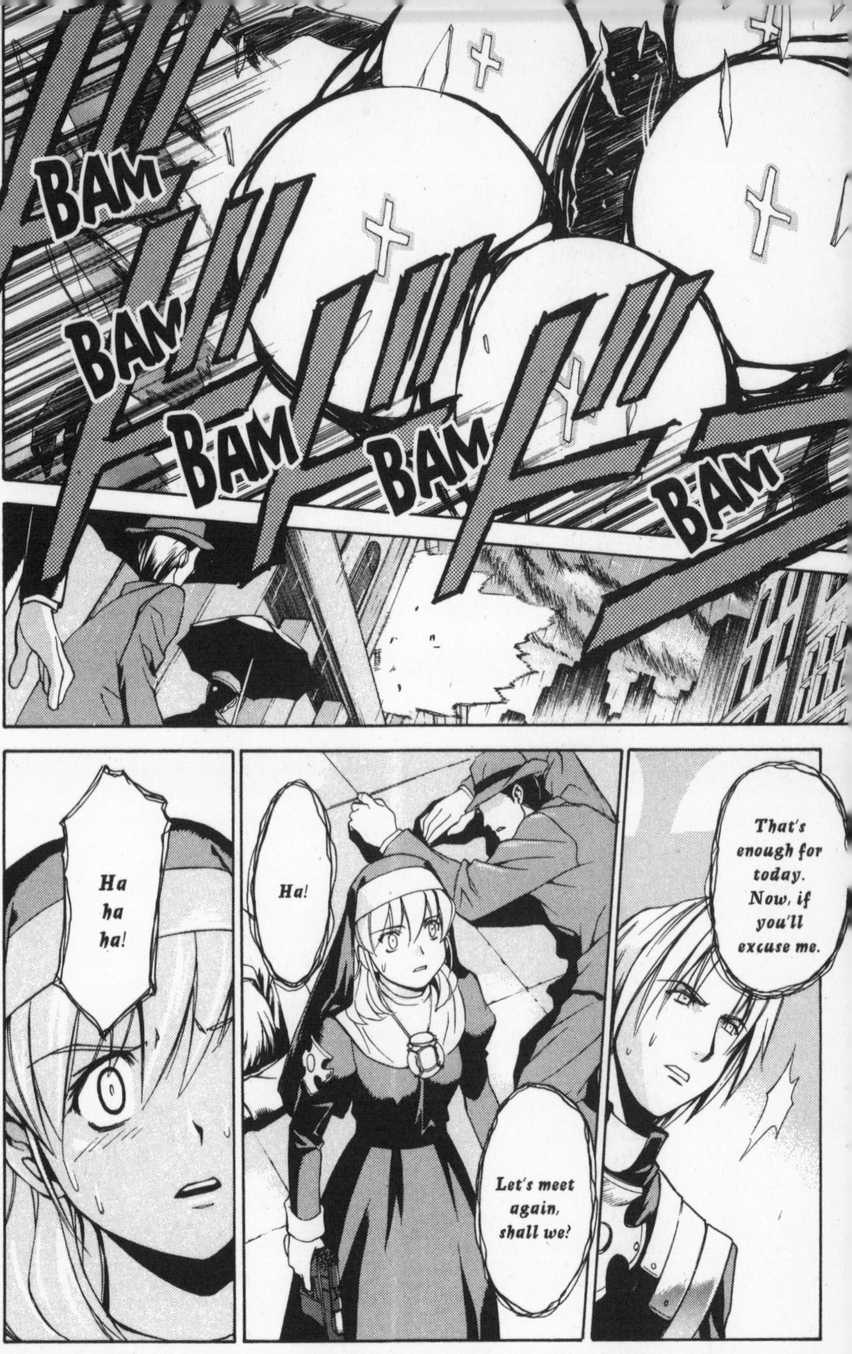
BAM
BAM
BAM
BAM
BAM
That's enough for today. Now, if you'll excuse me.
Let's meet again, shall we?
Ha!
Ha ha ha!

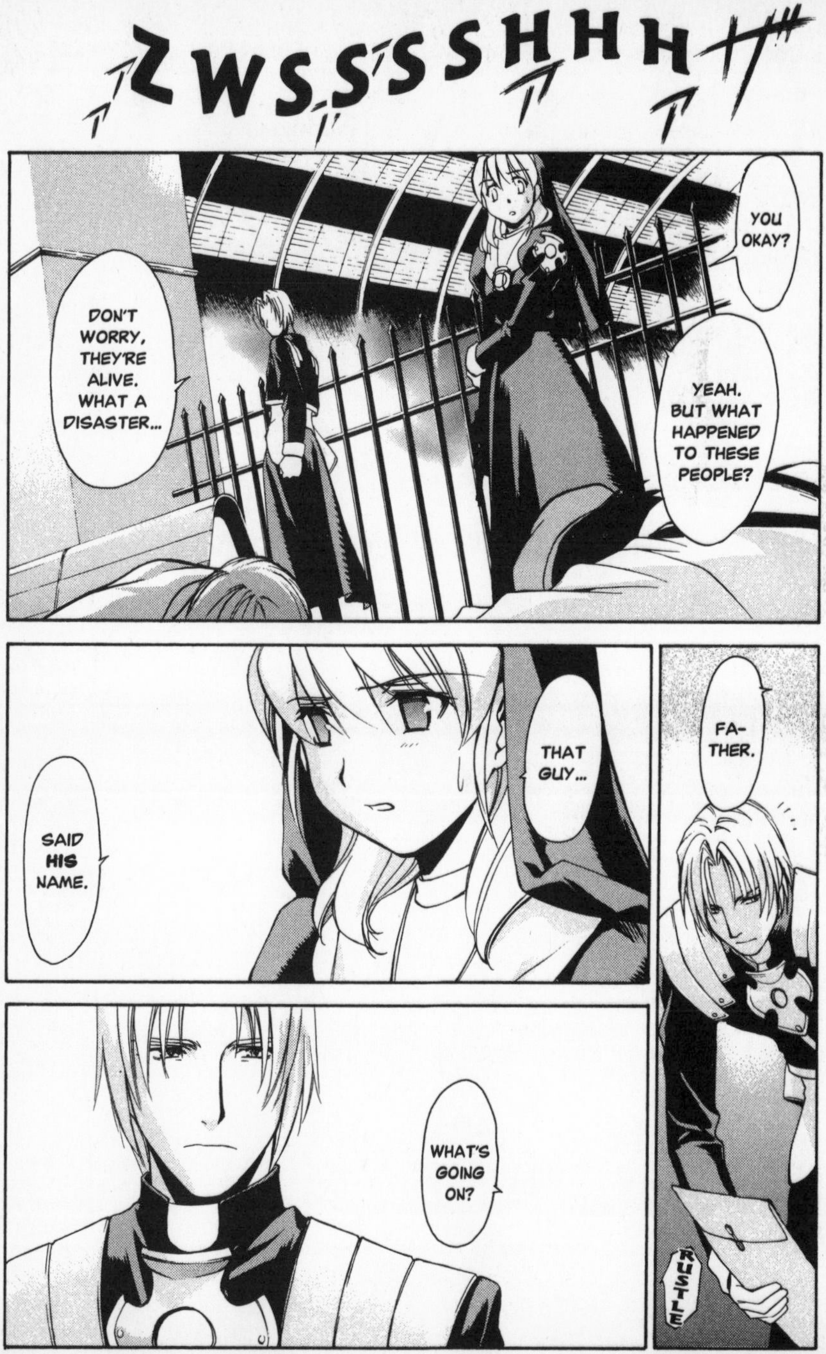
ZWSSSSHHHH
YOU OKAY?
YEAH. BUT WHAT HAPPENED TO THESE PEOPLE?
DON'T WORRY, THEY'RE ALIVE. WHAT A DISASTER...
FA-THER.
THAT GUY...
SAID HIS NAME.
RUSTLE
WHAT'S GOING ON?

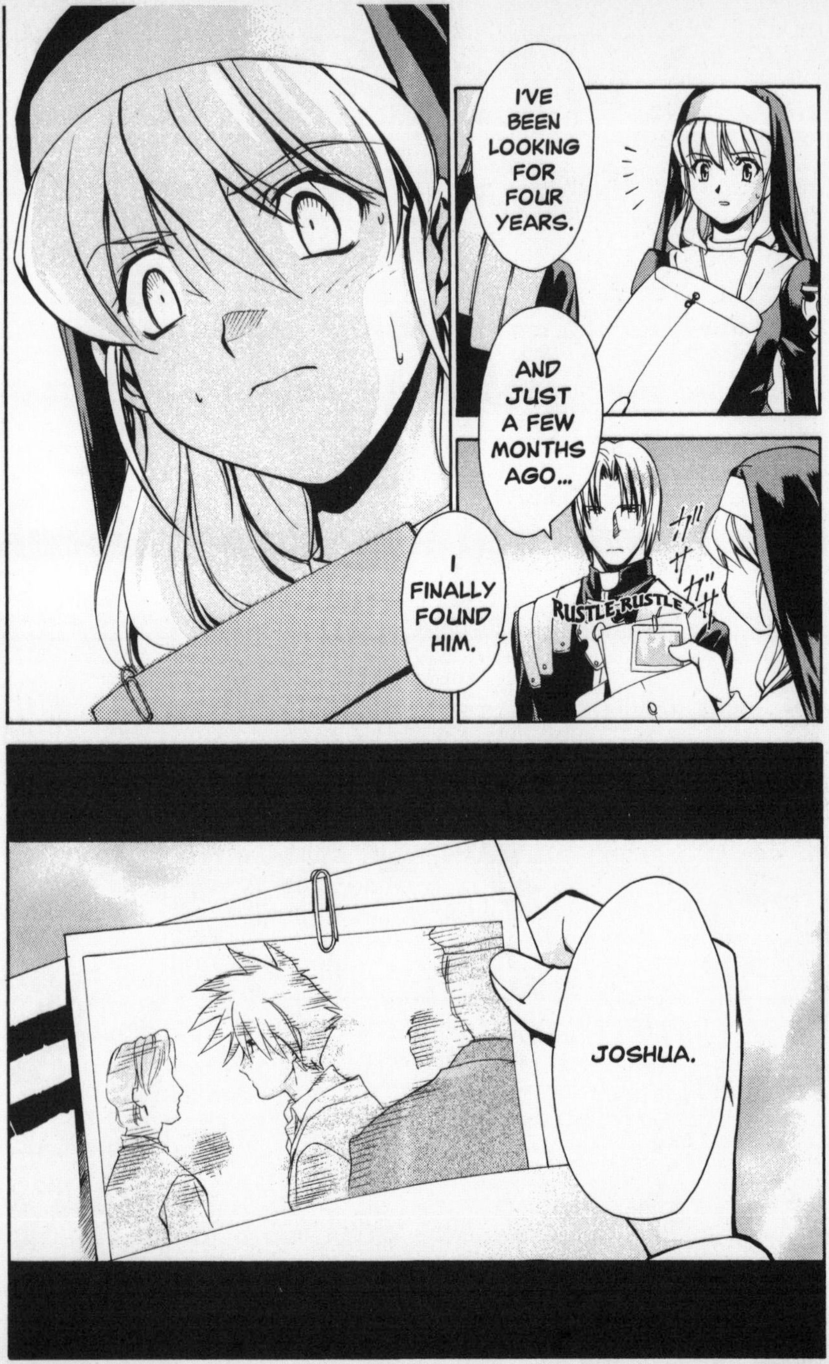
I'VE BEEN LOOKING FOR FOUR YEARS.
AND JUST A FEW MONTHS AGO...
I FINALLY FOUND HIM.
RUSTLE RUSTLE
ガサガサ
JOSHUA.

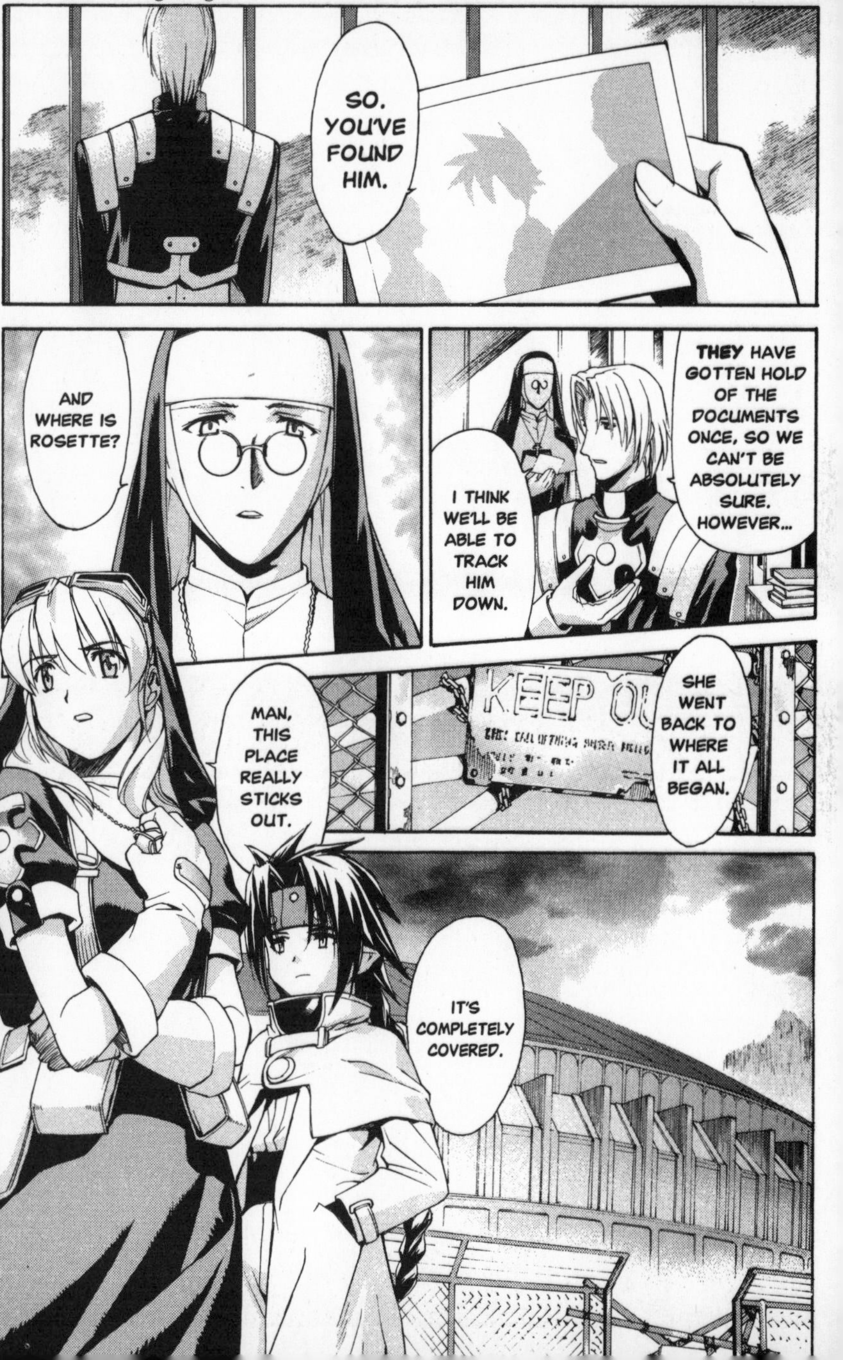
SO. YOU'VE FOUND HIM.
AND WHERE IS ROSETTE?
THEY HAVE GOTTEN HOLD OF THE DOCUMENTS ONCE, SO WE CAN'T BE ABSOLUTELY SURE. HOWEVER...
I THINK WE'LL BE ABLE TO TRACK HIM DOWN.
SHE WENT BACK TO WHERE IT ALL BEGAN.
KEEP OU
MAN, THIS PLACE REALLY STICKS OUT.
IT'S COMPLETELY COVERED.

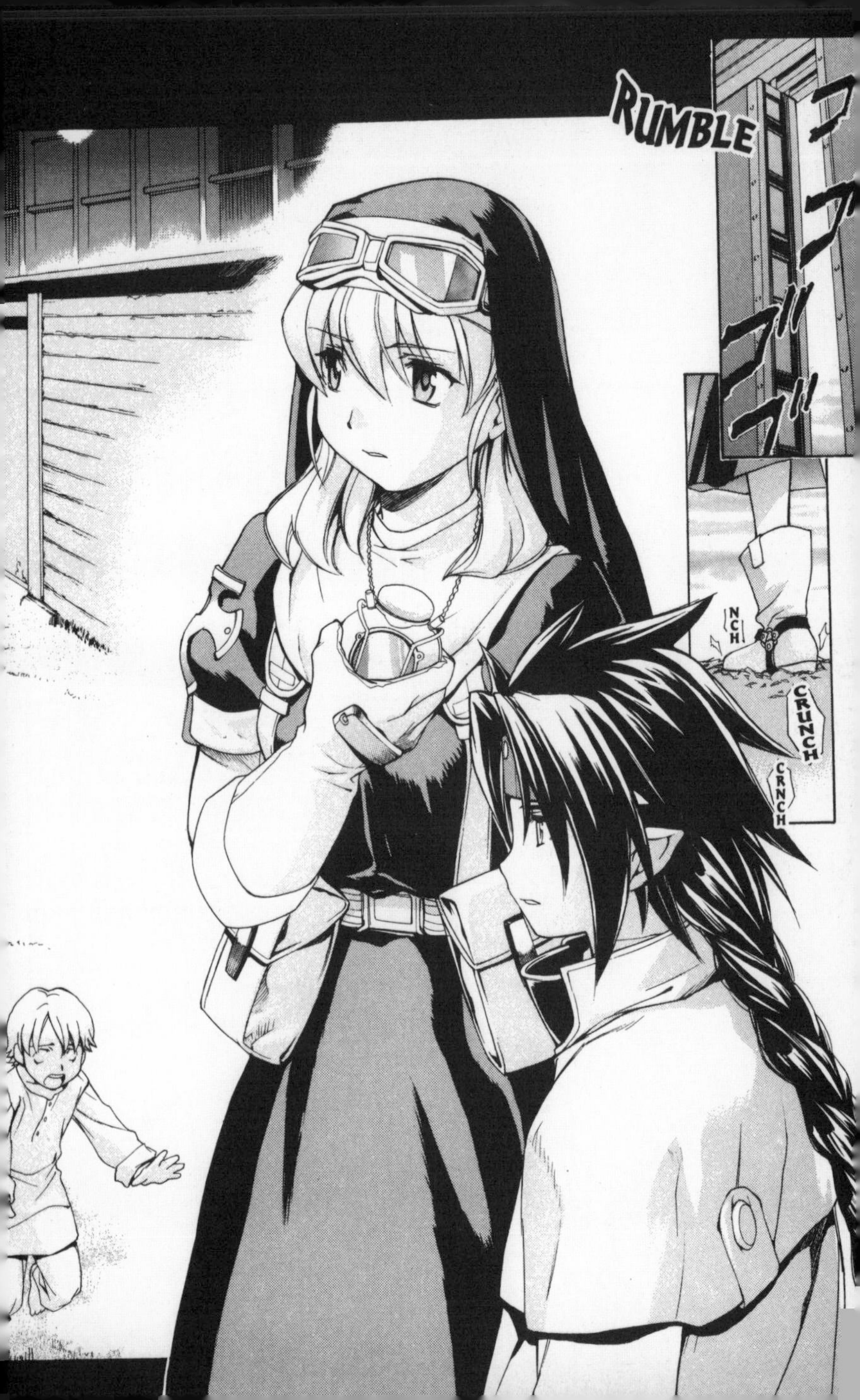
RUMBLE
NCH
CRUNCH
CRNCH

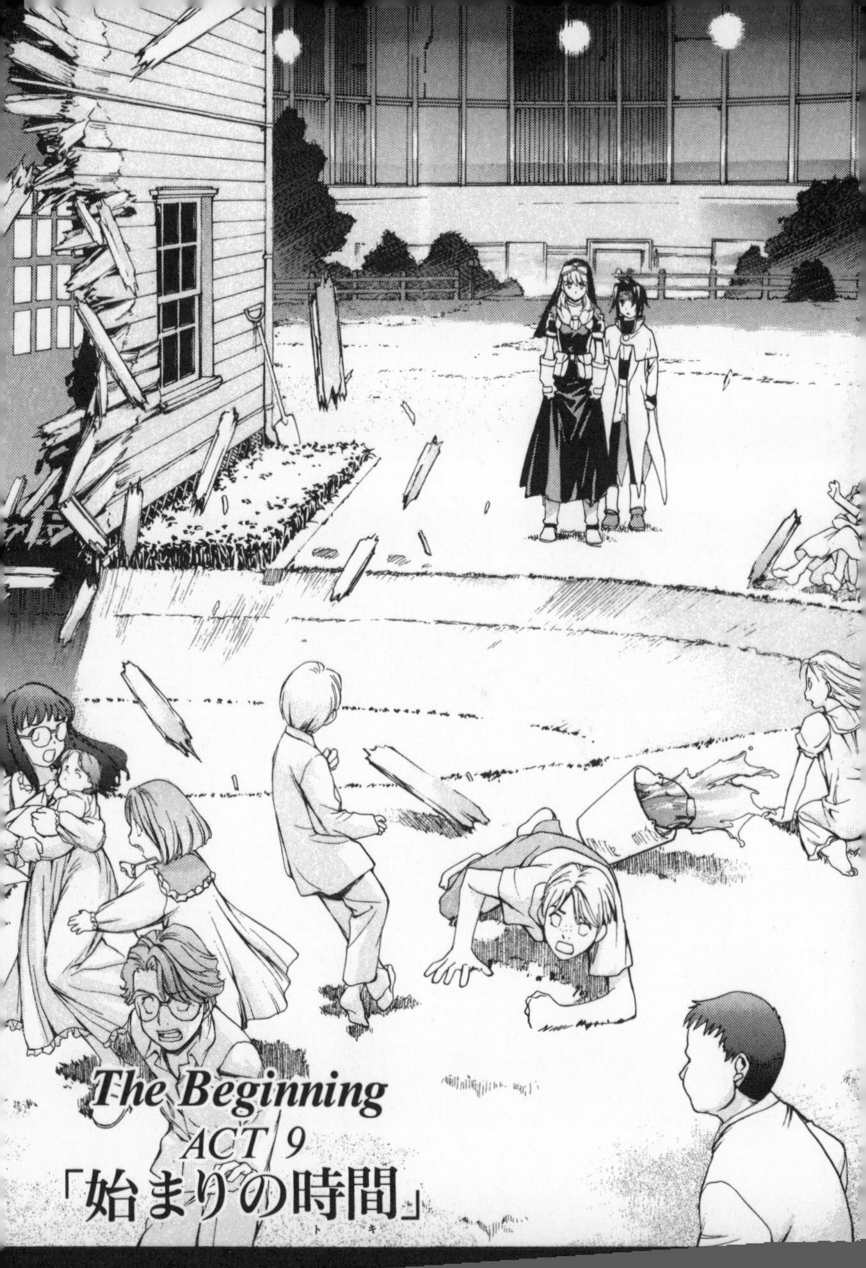
The Beginning
ACT 9
「始まりの時間」
トキ

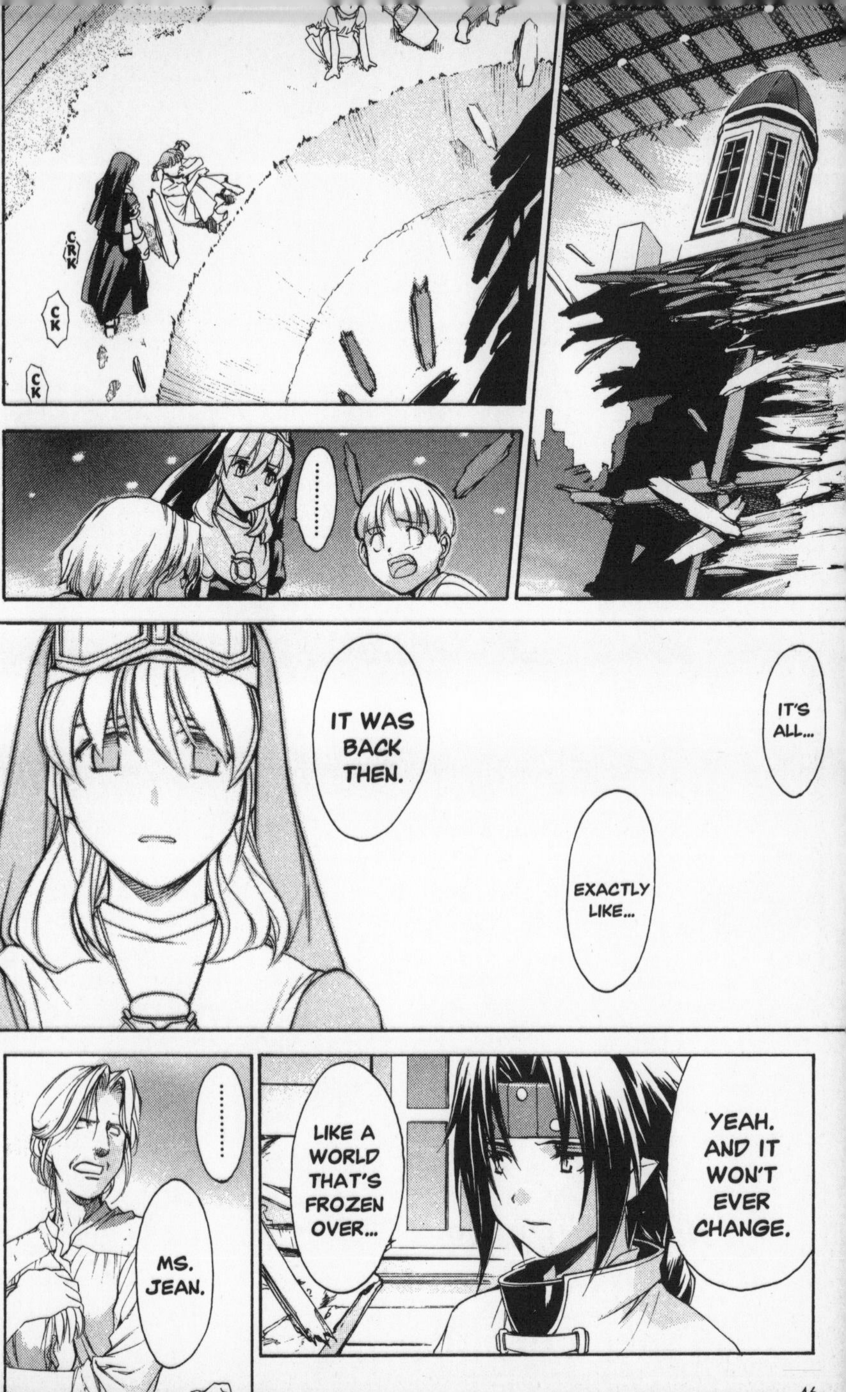
CRK
CK
CK
....
IT'S ALL...
EXACTLY LIKE...
IT WAS BACK THEN.
LIKE A WORLD THAT'S FROZEN OVER...
YEAH. AND IT WON'T EVER CHANGE.
....
MS. JEAN.

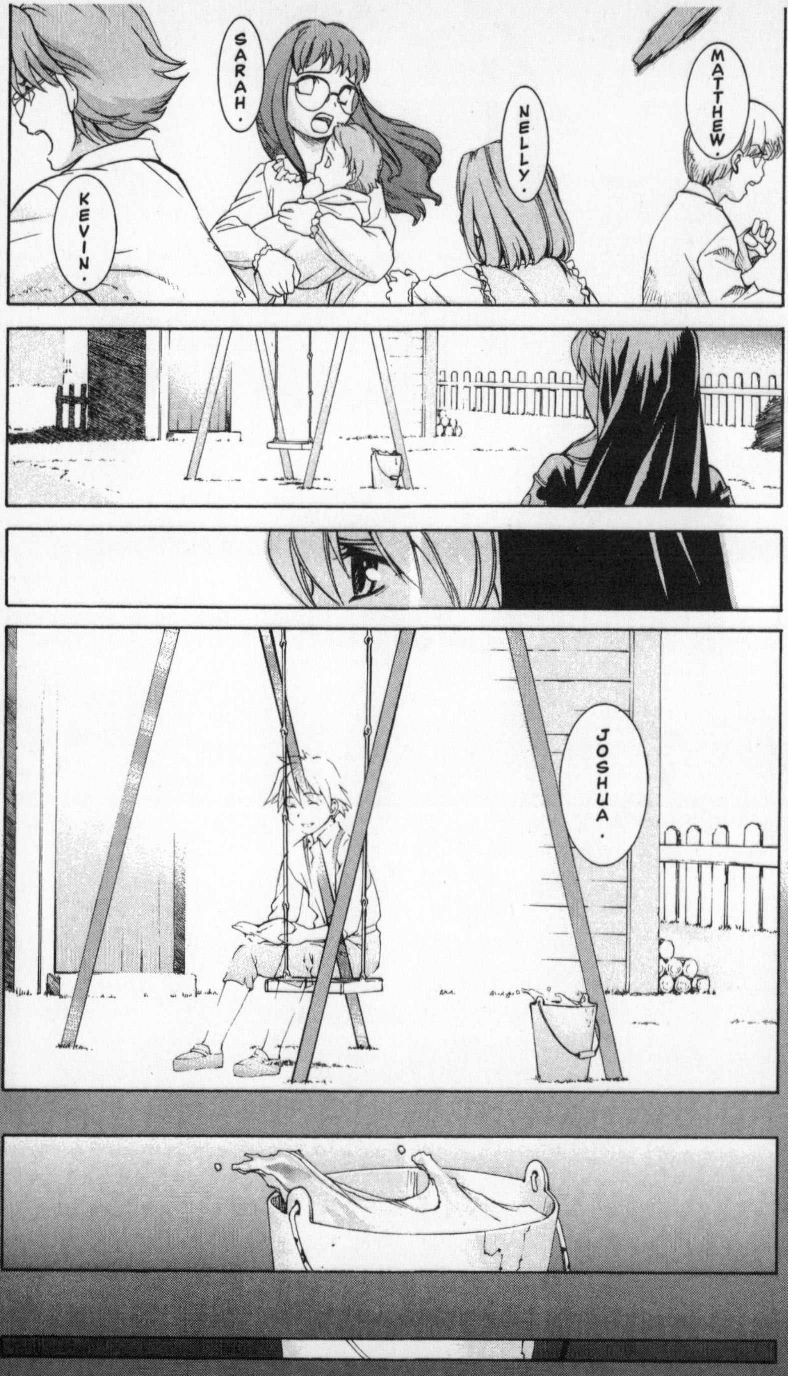
MATTHEW.
NELLY.
SARAH.
KEVIN.
JOSHUA.

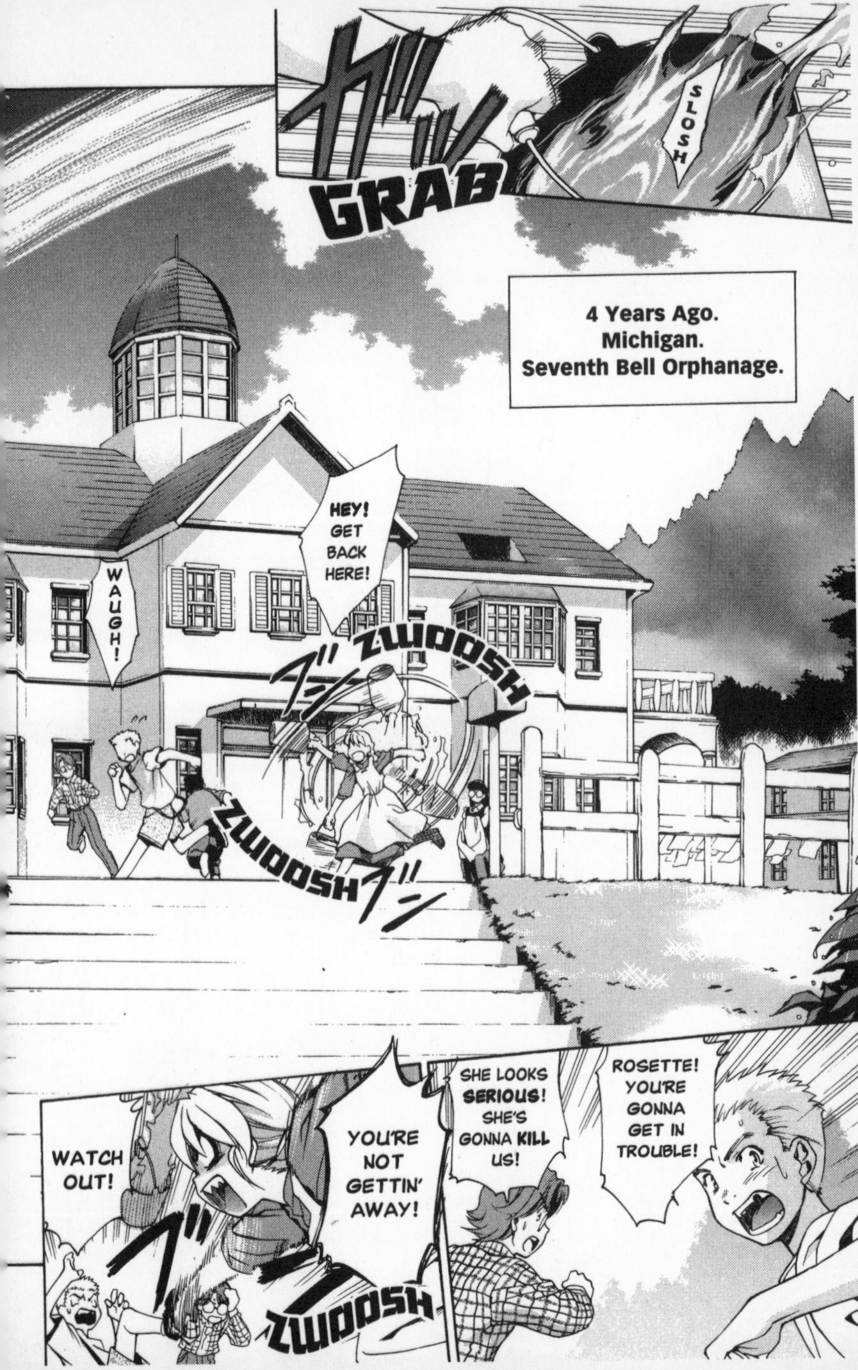
SLOSH
GRAB
4 Years Ago.
Michigan.
Seventh Bell Orphanage.
HEY! GET BACK HERE!
WAUGH!
ZWOOSH
ZWOOSH
ROSETTE! YOU'RE GONNA GET IN TROUBLE!
SHE LOOKS SERIOUS! SHE'S GONNA KILL US!
YOU'RE NOT GETTIN' AWAY!
WATCH OUT!
ZWOOSH

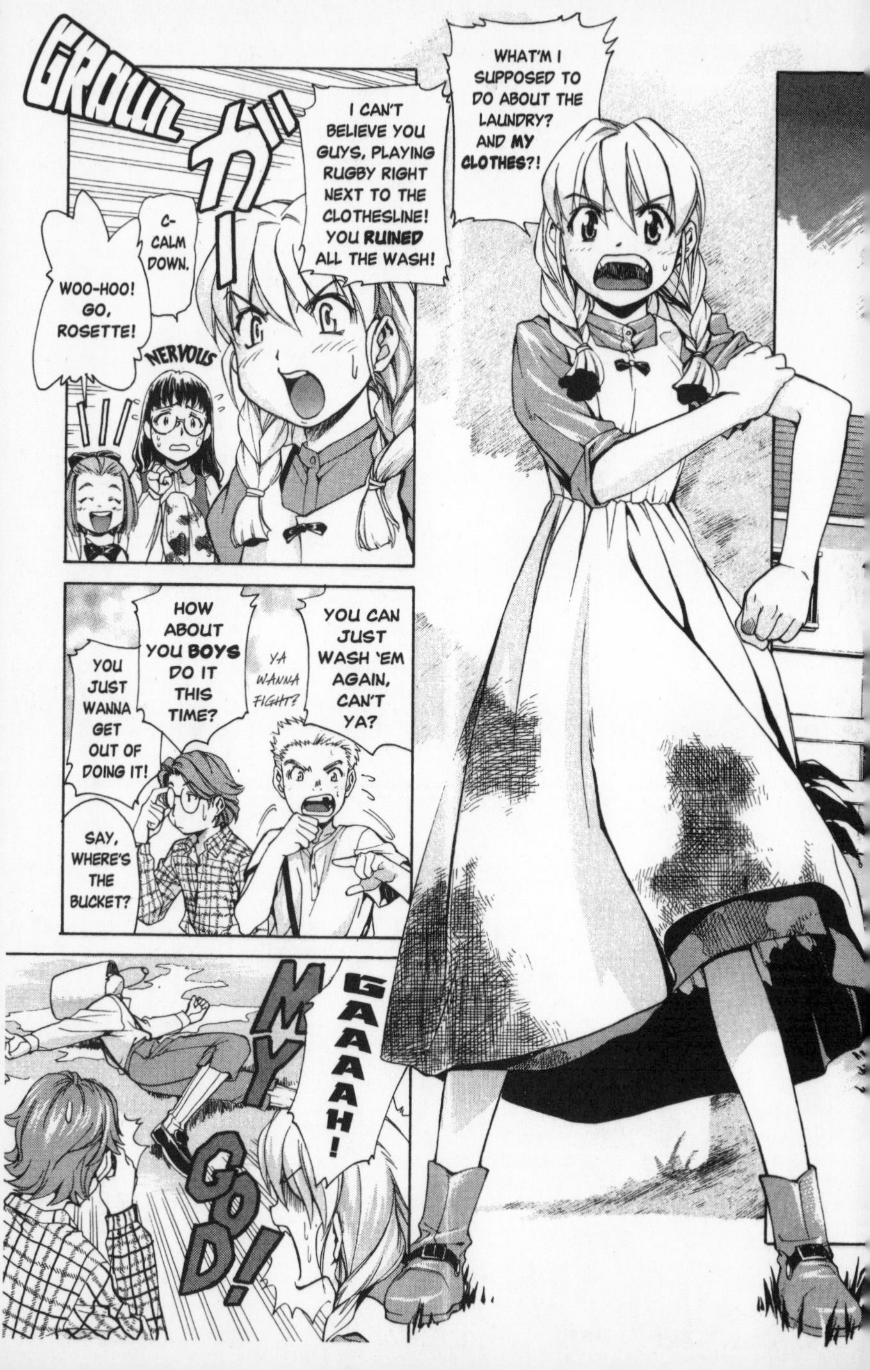
GROWL
I CAN'T BELIEVE YOU GUYS, PLAYING RUGBY RIGHT NEXT TO THE CLOTHESLINE! YOU **RUINED** ALL THE WASH!
C-CALM DOWN.
WOO-HOO! GO, ROSETTE!
NERVOUS
WHAT'M I SUPPOSED TO DO ABOUT THE LAUNDRY? AND **MY CLOTHES**?!
YOU CAN JUST WASH 'EM AGAIN, CAN'T YA?
YA WANNA FIGHT?
HOW ABOUT YOU **BOYS** DO IT THIS TIME?
YOU JUST WANNA GET OUT OF DOING IT!
SAY, WHERE'S THE BUCKET?
GAAAAAH!
MY GOD!

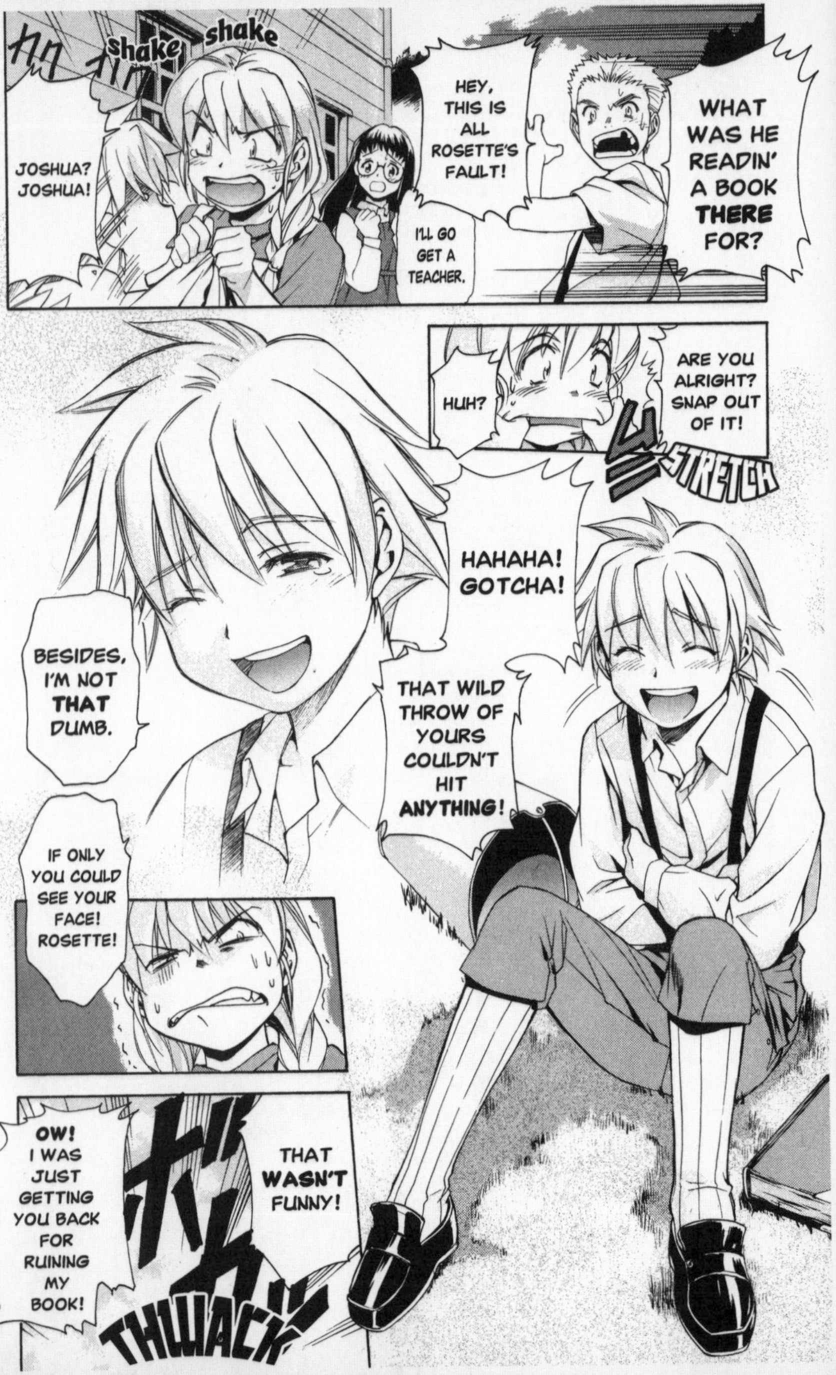
WHAT WAS HE READIN' A BOOK THERE FOR?
HEY, THIS IS ALL ROSETTE'S FAULT!
I'LL GO GET A TEACHER.
shake
shake
JOSHUA? JOSHUA!
ARE YOU ALRIGHT? SNAP OUT OF IT!
HUH?
STRETCH
HAHAHA! GOTCHA!
THAT WILD THROW OF YOURS COULDN'T HIT ANYTHING!
BESIDES, I'M NOT THAT DUMB.
IF ONLY YOU COULD SEE YOUR FACE! ROSETTE!
THAT WASN'T FUNNY!
OW! I WAS JUST GETTING YOU BACK FOR RUINING MY BOOK!
THWACK

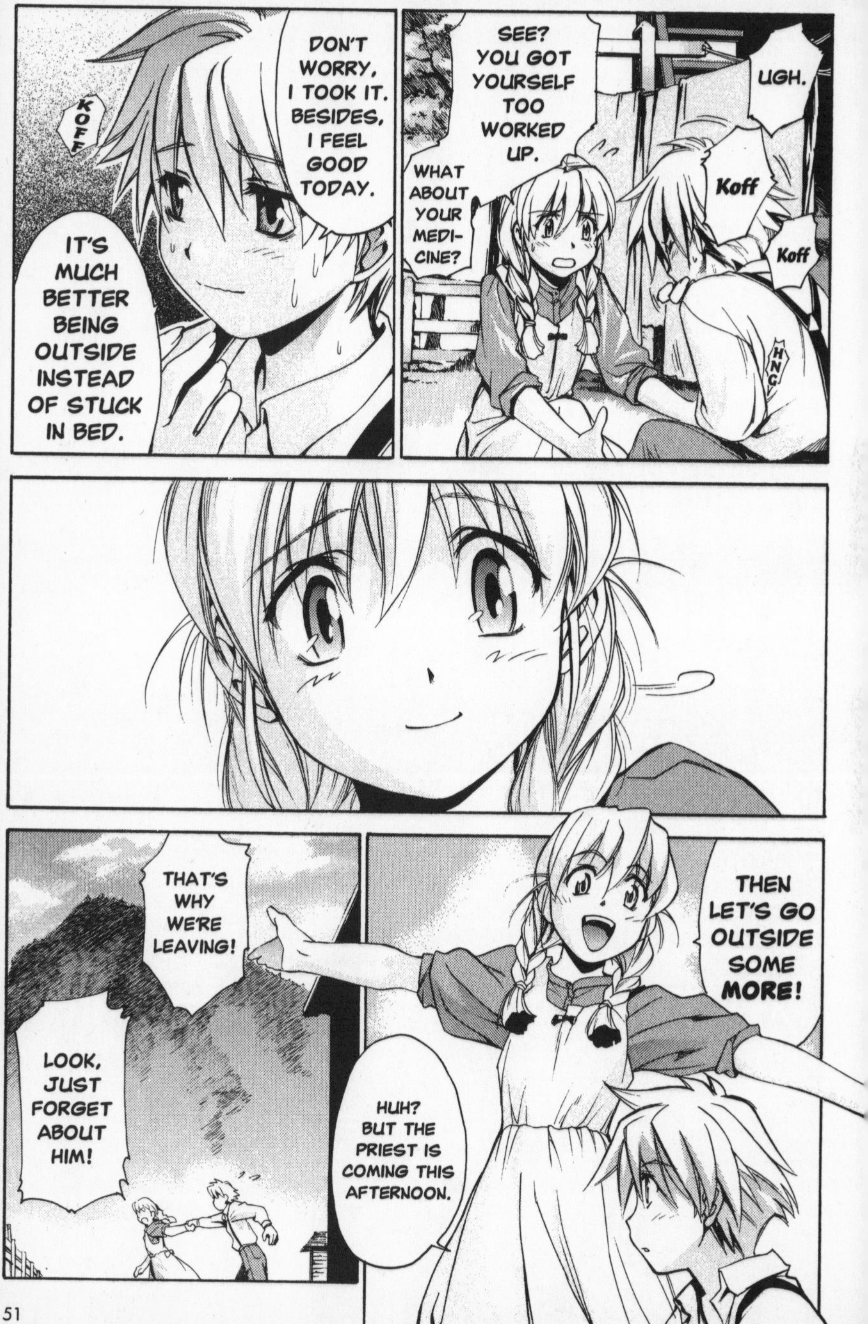
SEE? YOU GOT YOURSELF TOO WORKED UP.
UGH.
Koff
Koff
HNG
WHAT ABOUT YOUR MEDI-CINE?
DON'T WORRY, I TOOK IT. BESIDES, I FEEL GOOD TODAY.
KOFF
IT'S MUCH BETTER BEING OUTSIDE INSTEAD OF STUCK IN BED.
THEN LET'S GO OUTSIDE SOME MORE!
HUH? BUT THE PRIEST IS COMING THIS AFTERNOON.
THAT'S WHY WE'RE LEAVING!
LOOK, JUST FORGET ABOUT HIM!

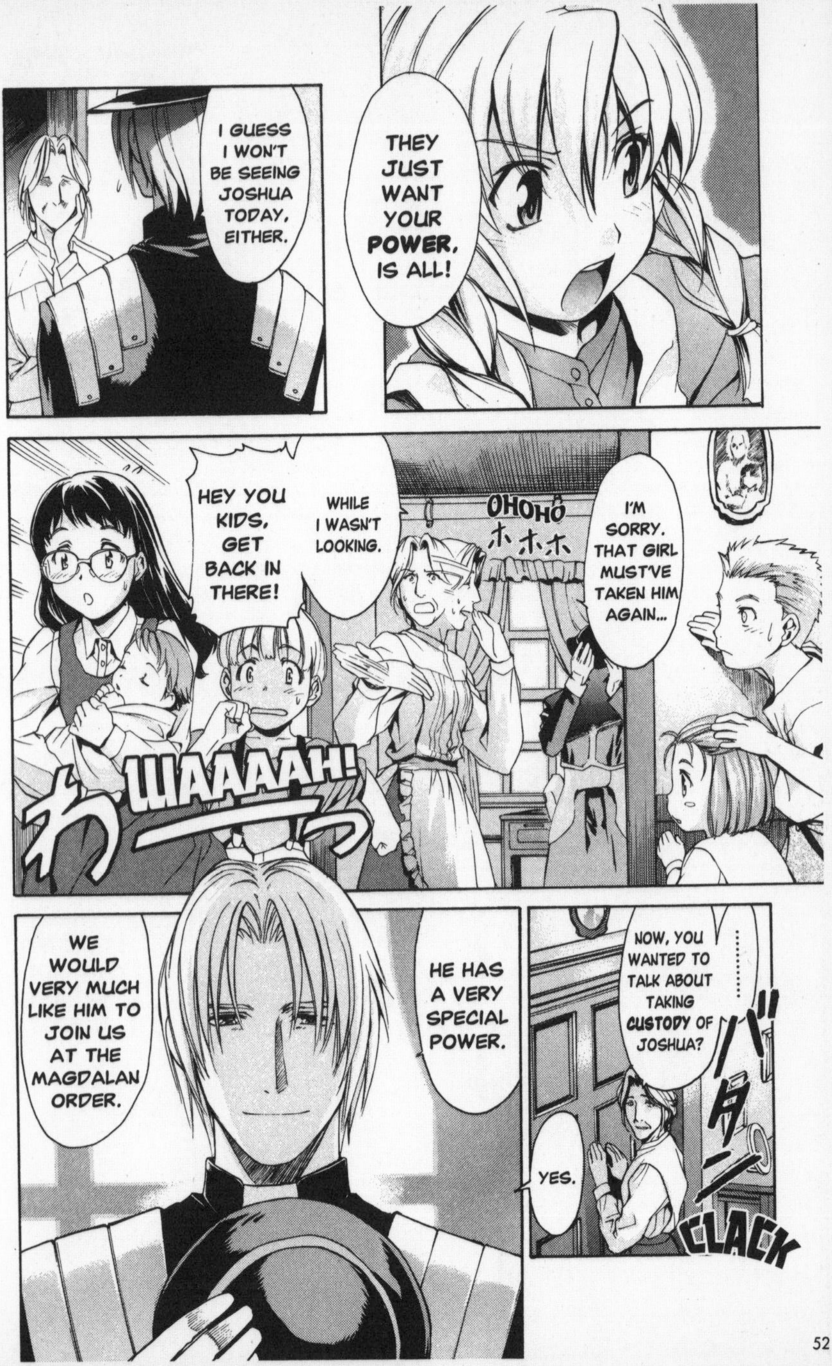
THEY JUST WANT YOUR POWER, IS ALL!
I GUESS I WON'T BE SEEING JOSHUA TODAY, EITHER.
I'M SORRY. THAT GIRL MUST'VE TAKEN HIM AGAIN...
OHOHO
WHILE I WASN'T LOOKING.
HEY YOU KIDS, GET BACK IN THERE!
WAAAAAH!
NOW, YOU WANTED TO TALK ABOUT TAKING CUSTODY OF JOSHUA?
......
YES.
CLACK
HE HAS A VERY SPECIAL POWER.
WE WOULD VERY MUCH LIKE HIM TO JOIN US AT THE MAGDALAN ORDER.

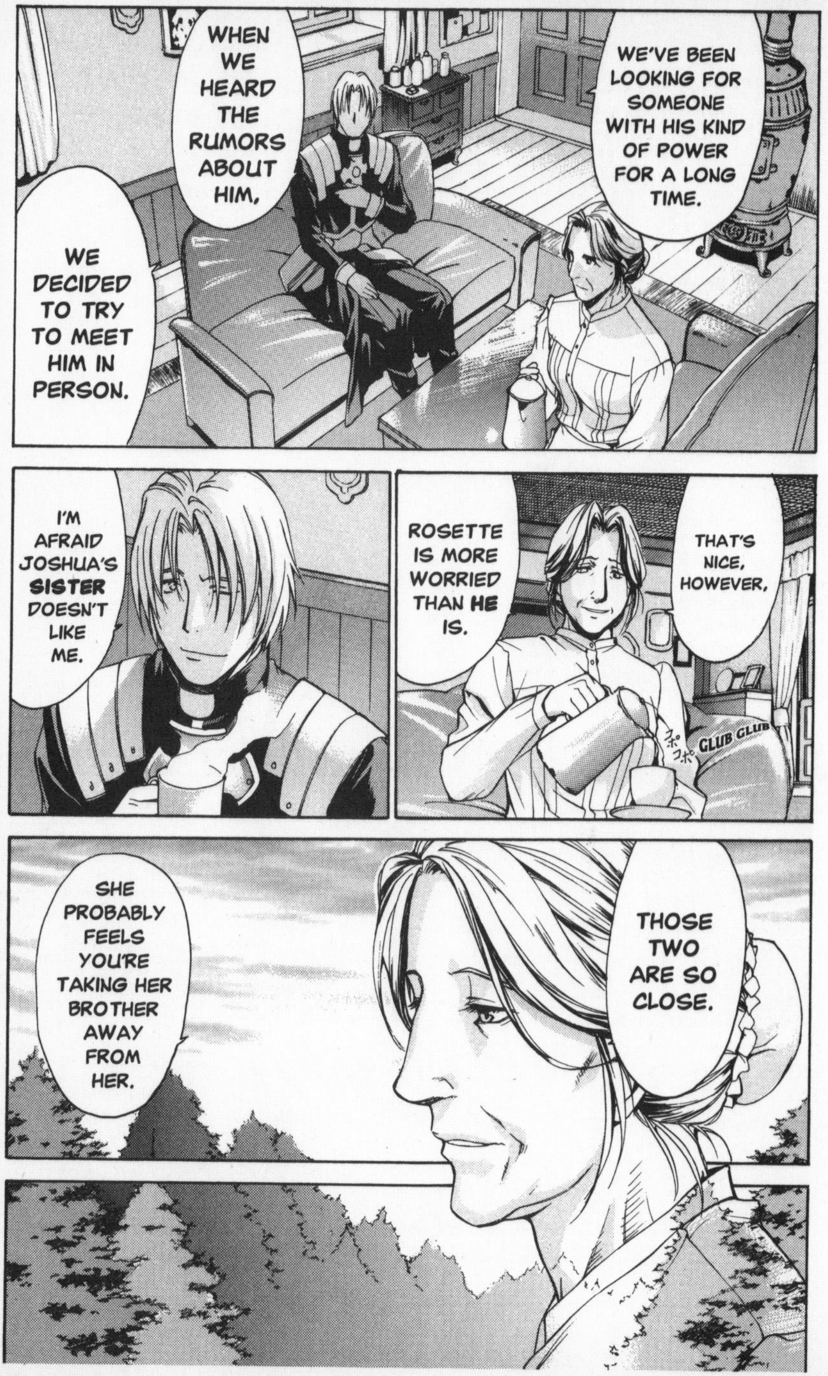
WE'VE BEEN LOOKING FOR SOMEONE WITH HIS KIND OF POWER FOR A LONG TIME.
WHEN WE HEARD THE RUMORS ABOUT HIM,
WE DECIDED TO TRY TO MEET HIM IN PERSON.
THAT'S NICE, HOWEVER,
ROSETTE IS MORE WORRIED THAN **HE** IS.
フポフポ
GLUB GLUB
I'M AFRAID JOSHUA'S **SISTER** DOESN'T LIKE ME.
THOSE TWO ARE SO CLOSE.
SHE PROBABLY FEELS YOU'RE TAKING HER BROTHER AWAY FROM HER.

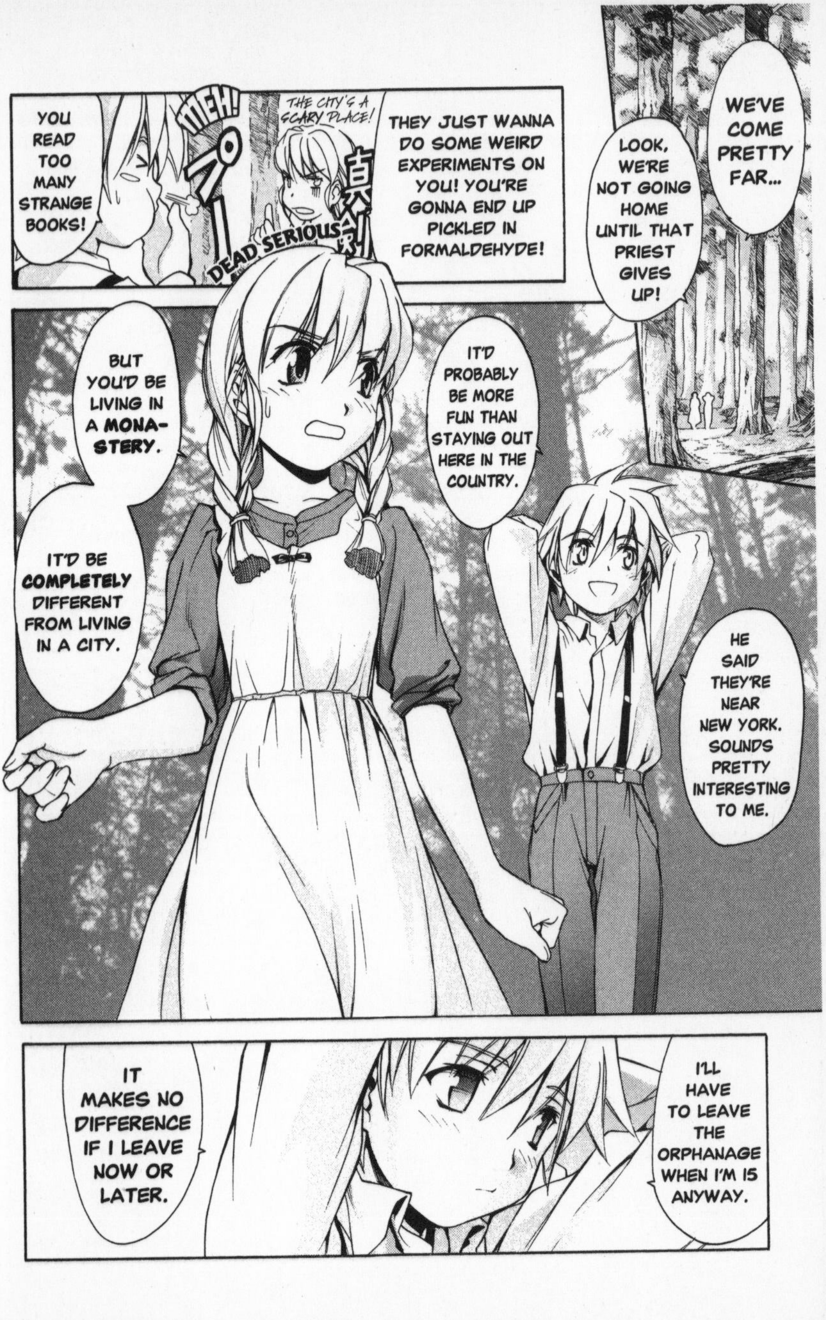
WE'VE COME PRETTY FAR...
LOOK, WE'RE NOT GOING HOME UNTIL THAT PRIEST GIVES UP!
THEY JUST WANNA DO SOME WEIRD EXPERIMENTS ON YOU! YOU'RE GONNA END UP PICKLED IN FORMALDEHYDE!
THE CITY'S A SCARY PLACE!
DEAD SERIOUS
MEH!
YOU READ TOO MANY STRANGE BOOKS!
IT'D PROBABLY BE MORE FUN THAN STAYING OUT HERE IN THE COUNTRY.
HE SAID THEY'RE NEAR NEW YORK. SOUNDS PRETTY INTERESTING TO ME.
BUT YOU'D BE LIVING IN A **MONASTERY**.
IT'D BE **COMPLETELY** DIFFERENT FROM LIVING IN A CITY.
I'LL HAVE TO LEAVE THE ORPHANAGE WHEN I'M 15 ANYWAY.
IT MAKES NO DIFFERENCE IF I LEAVE NOW OR LATER.

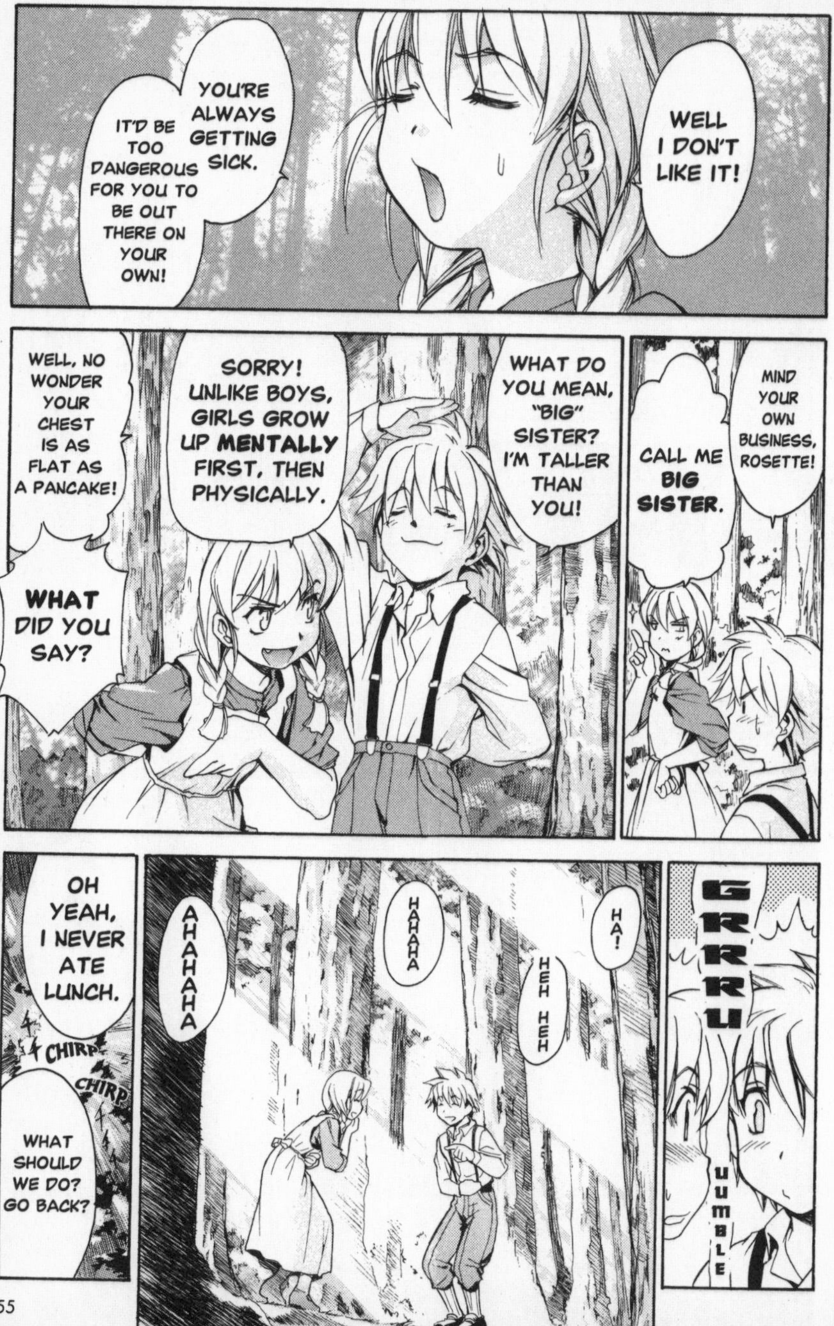
WELL I DON'T LIKE IT!
YOU'RE ALWAYS GETTING SICK.
IT'D BE TOO DANGEROUS FOR YOU TO BE OUT THERE ON YOUR OWN!
MIND YOUR OWN BUSINESS, ROSETTE!
CALL ME **BIG SISTER**.
WHAT DO YOU MEAN, "BIG" SISTER? I'M TALLER THAN YOU!
SORRY! UNLIKE BOYS, GIRLS GROW UP **MENTALLY** FIRST, THEN PHYSICALLY.
WELL, NO WONDER YOUR CHEST IS AS FLAT AS A PANCAKE!
WHAT DID YOU SAY?
GRRRU
UUMBLE
HA!
HEH HEH
HAHAHA
AHAHAHA
OH YEAH, I NEVER ATE LUNCH.
CHIRP
CHIRP
WHAT SHOULD WE DO? GO BACK?

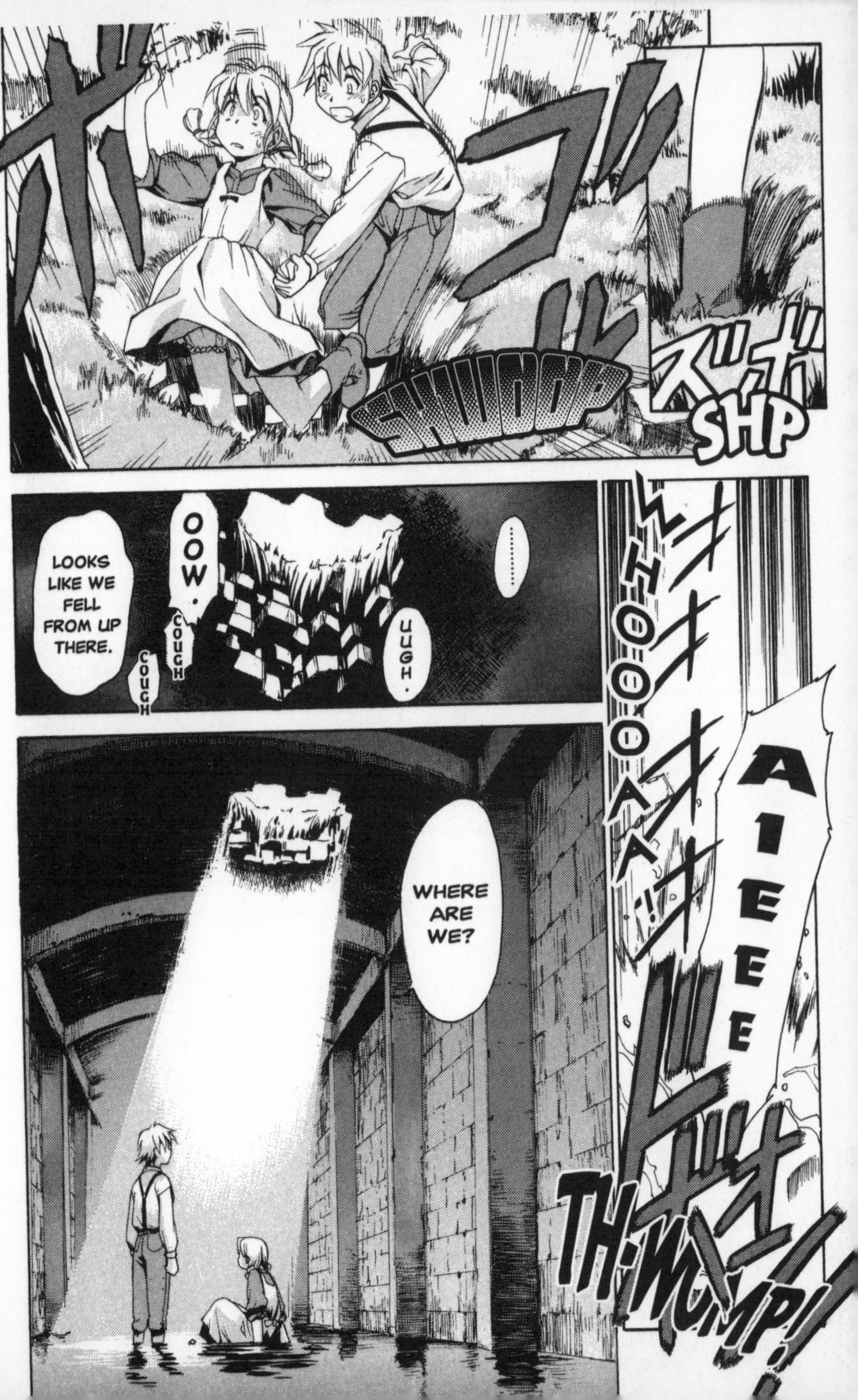
SHWOOP
SHP
WHOOOOAA!!
AIEEEE
THWUMP!
......
UUGH.
OOW.
COUGH
COUGH
LOOKS LIKE WE FELL FROM UP THERE.
WHERE ARE WE?

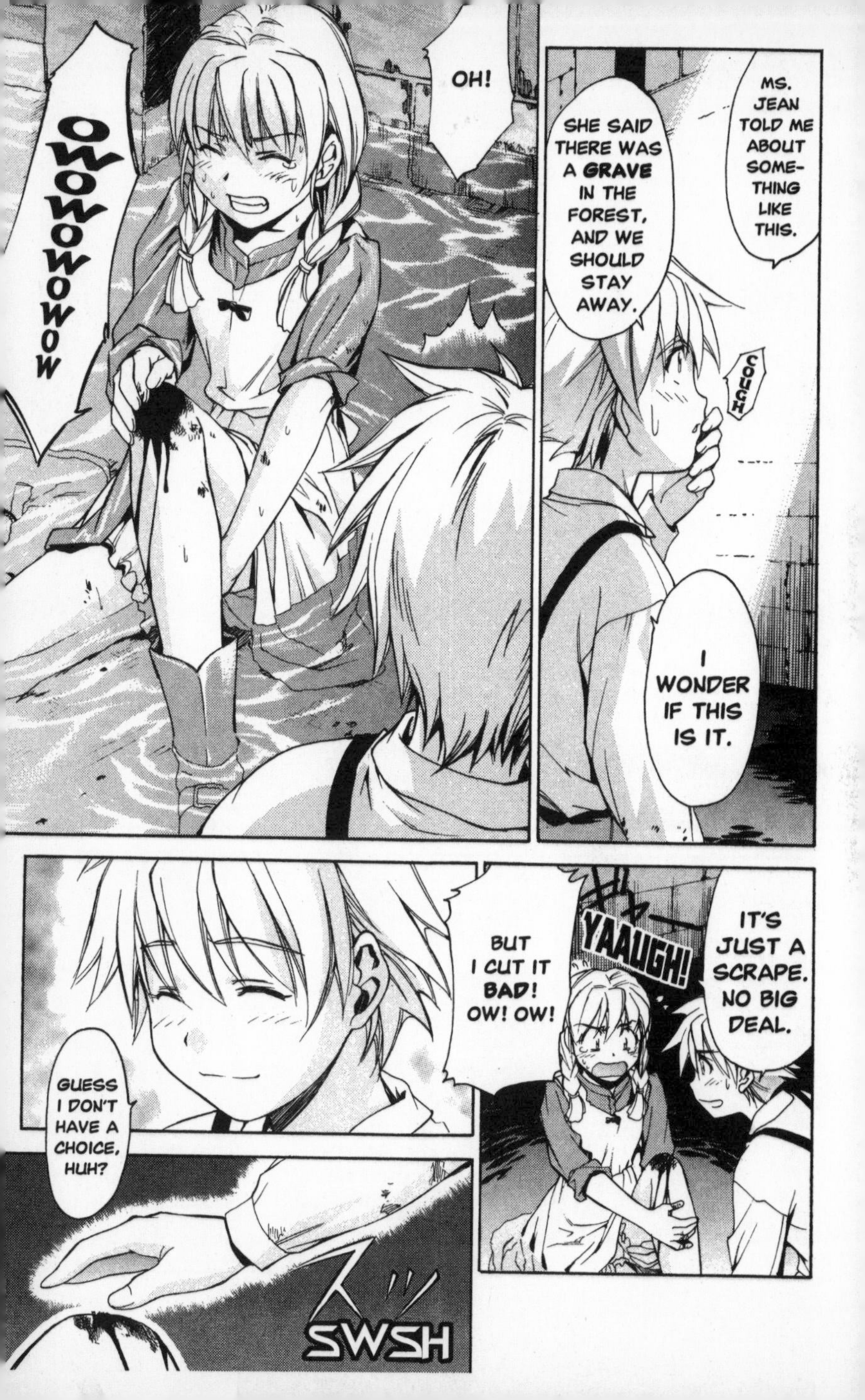
MS. JEAN TOLD ME ABOUT SOMETHING LIKE THIS.
SHE SAID THERE WAS A **GRAVE** IN THE FOREST, AND WE SHOULD STAY AWAY.
COUGH
I WONDER IF THIS IS IT.
OH!
OWOWOWOWOWOW
IT'S JUST A SCRAPE. NO BIG DEAL.
YAAUGH!
BUT I CUT IT **BAD**! OW! OW!
GUESS I DON'T HAVE A CHOICE, HUH?
SWSH

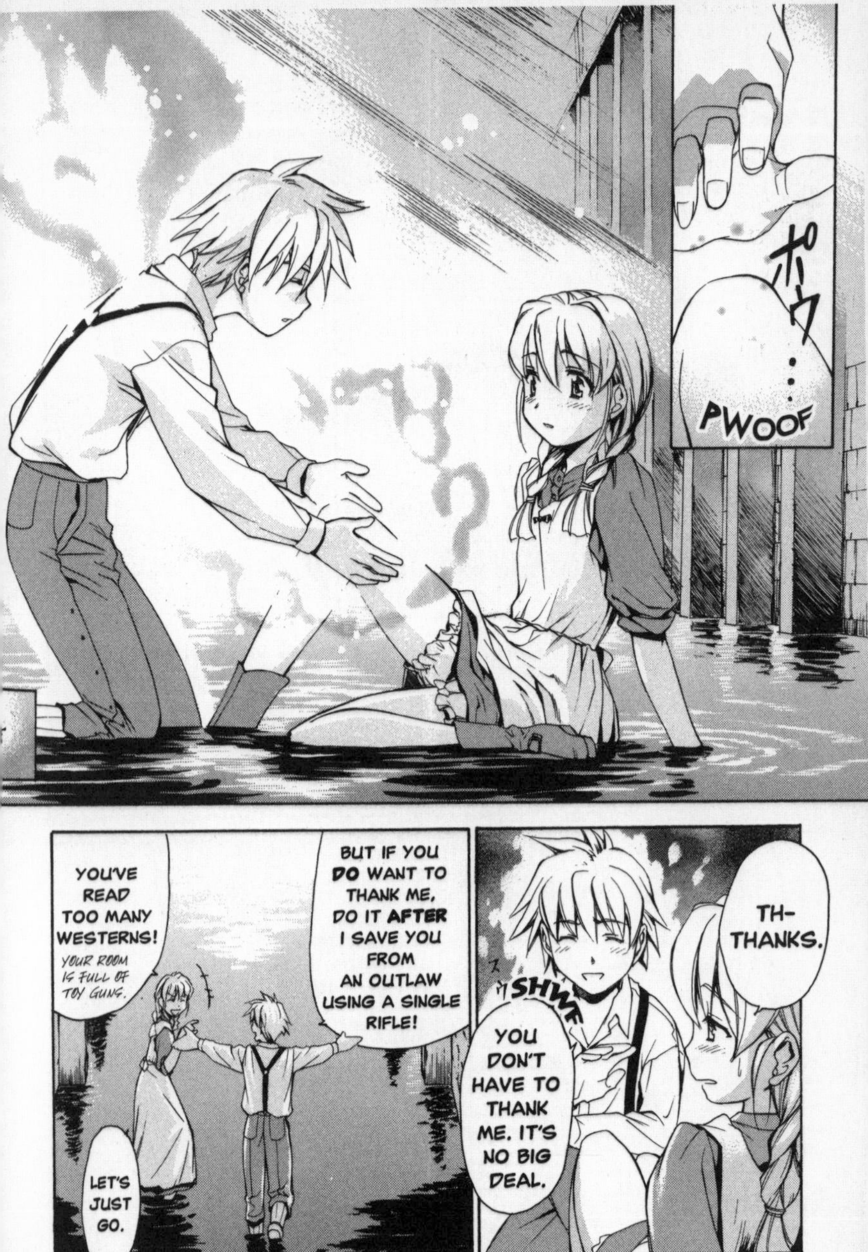
ポウ…
PWOOF
TH- THANKS.
SHWF
YOU DON'T HAVE TO THANK ME. IT'S NO BIG DEAL.
BUT IF YOU DO WANT TO THANK ME, DO IT AFTER I SAVE YOU FROM AN OUTLAW USING A SINGLE RIFLE!
YOU'VE READ TOO MANY WESTERNS!
YOUR ROOM IS FULL OF TOY GUNS.
LET'S JUST GO.

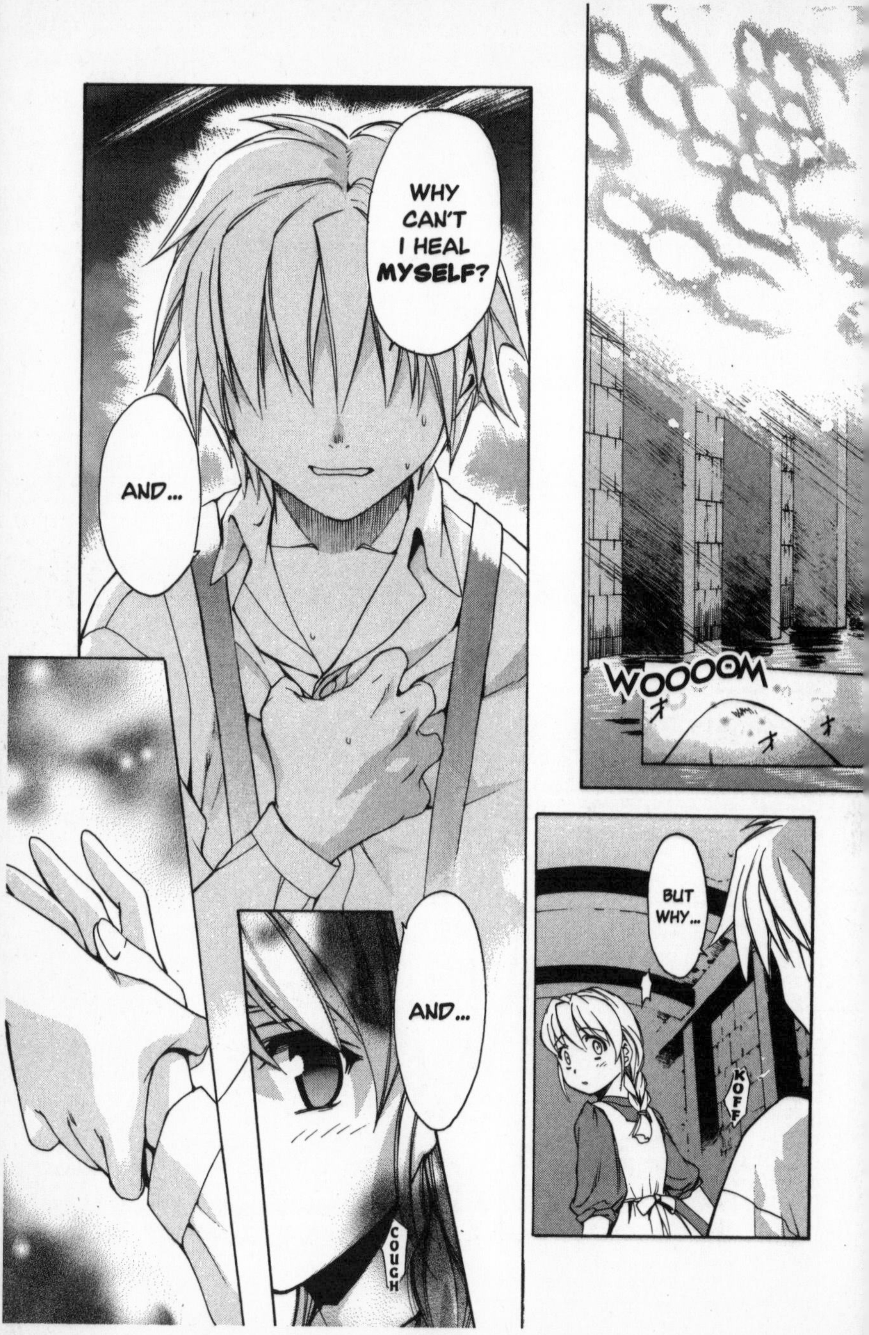
WOOOOM
BUT WHY...
KOFF
WHY CAN'T I HEAL MYSELF?
AND...
AND...
COUGH

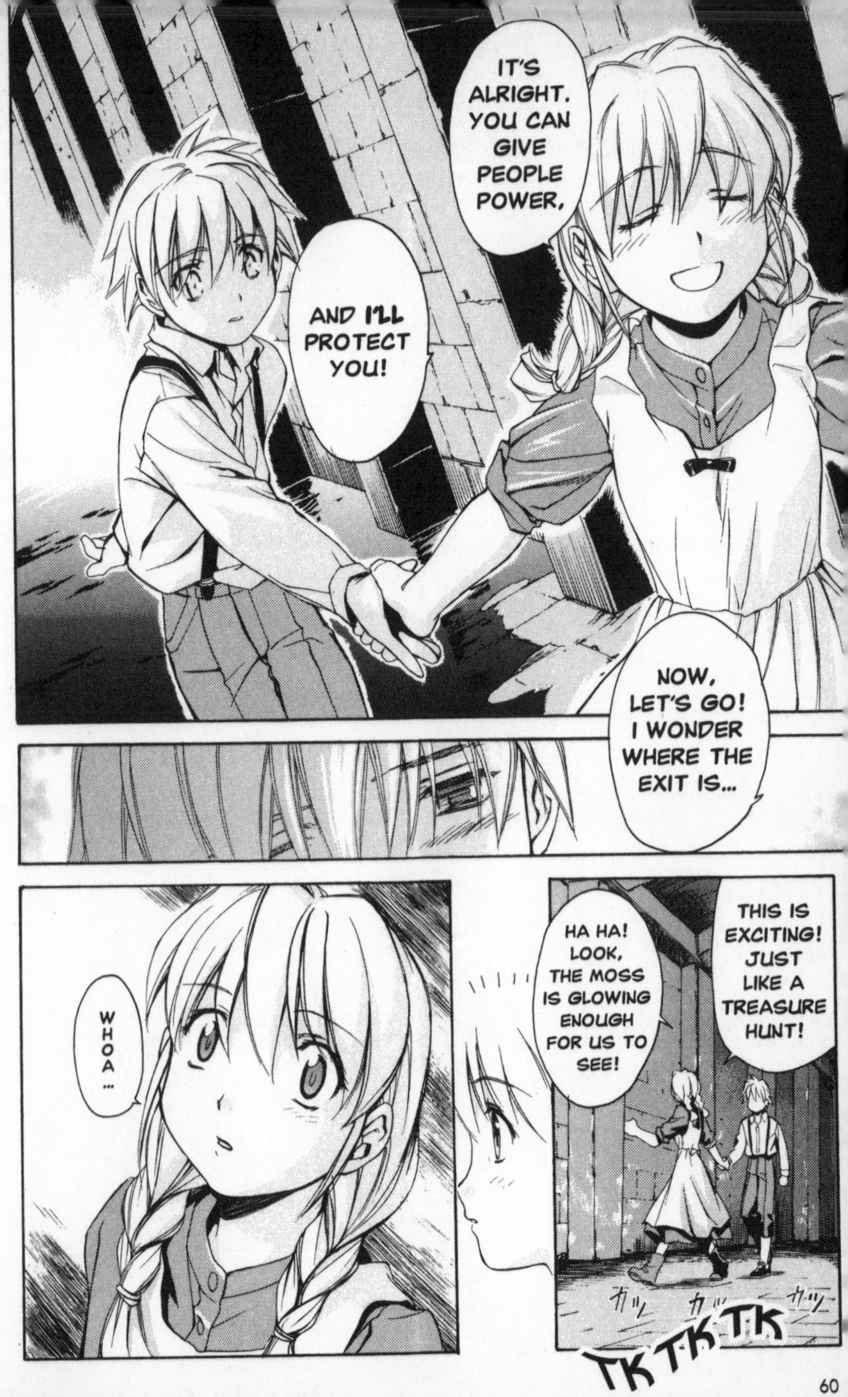
IT'S ALRIGHT. YOU CAN GIVE PEOPLE POWER,
AND I'LL PROTECT YOU!
NOW, LET'S GO! I WONDER WHERE THE EXIT IS...
THIS IS EXCITING! JUST LIKE A TREASURE HUNT!
HA HA! LOOK, THE MOSS IS GLOWING ENOUGH FOR US TO SEE!
TK TK TK
WHOA...

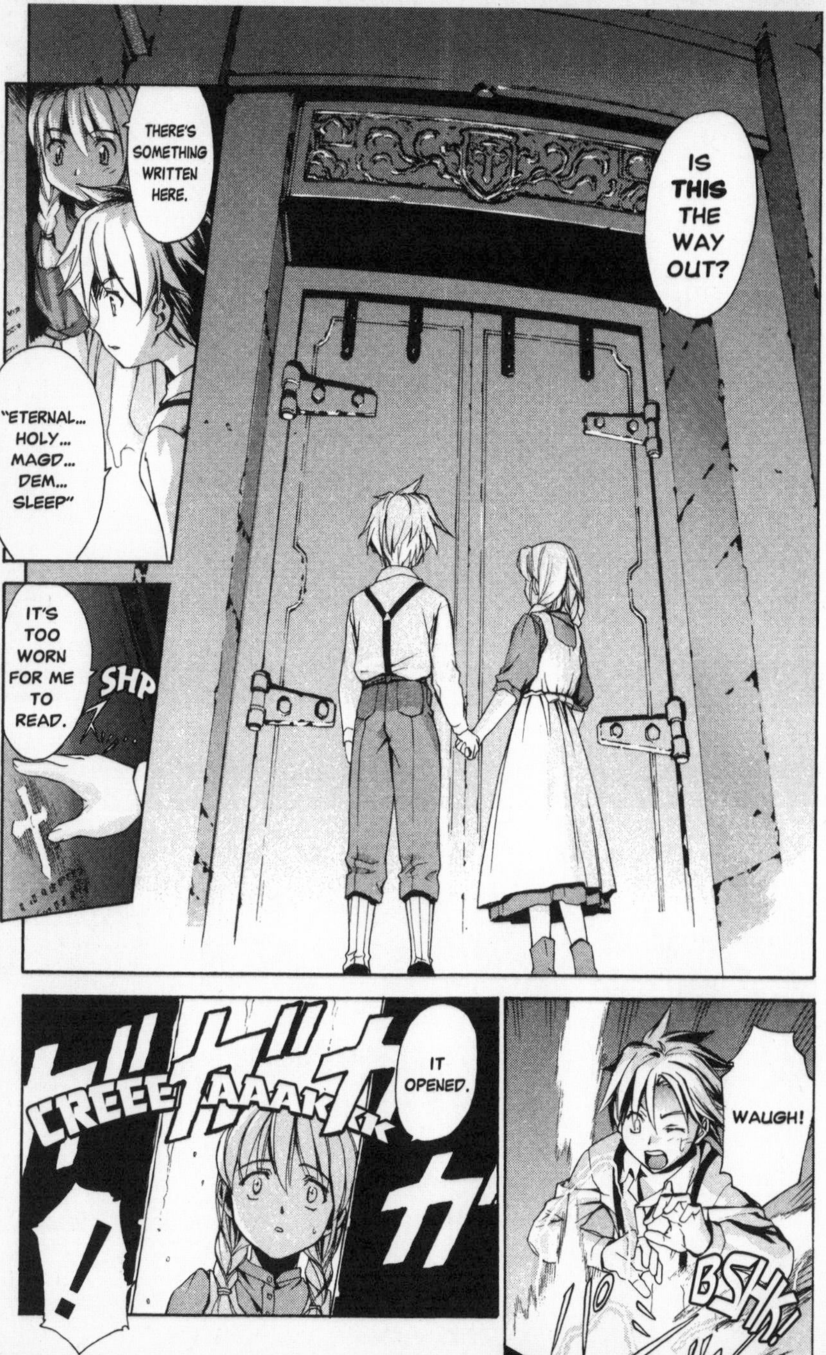
IS THIS THE WAY OUT?
THERE'S SOMETHING WRITTEN HERE.
"ETERNAL... HOLY... MAGD... DEM... SLEEP"
IT'S TOO WORN FOR ME TO READ.
SHP
CREEEAAAKKK
IT OPENED.
!
WAUGH!
BSHK!

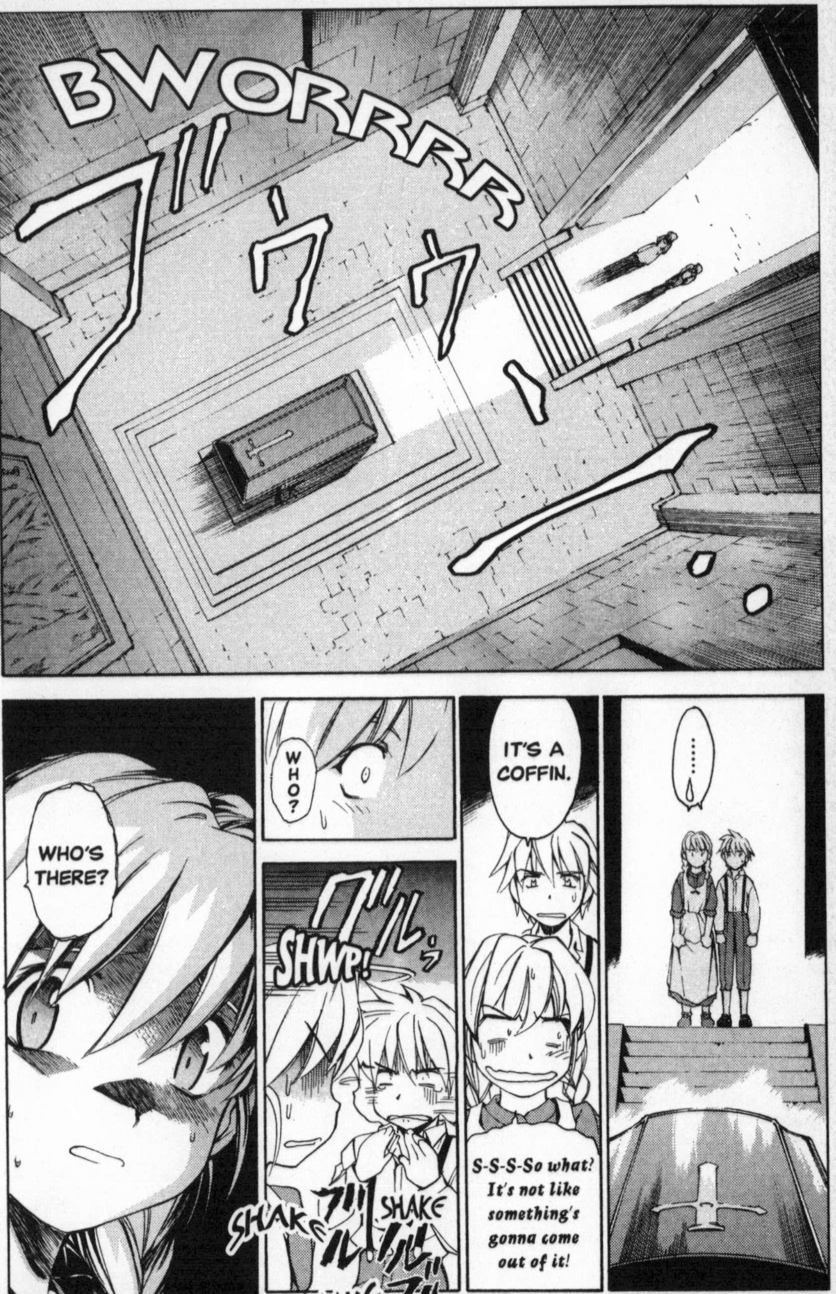

BWORRRR
......
IT'S A COFFIN.
S-S-S-So what? It's not like something's gonna come out of it!
WHO?
SHWP!
SHAKE
SHAKE
SHAKE
WHO'S THERE?

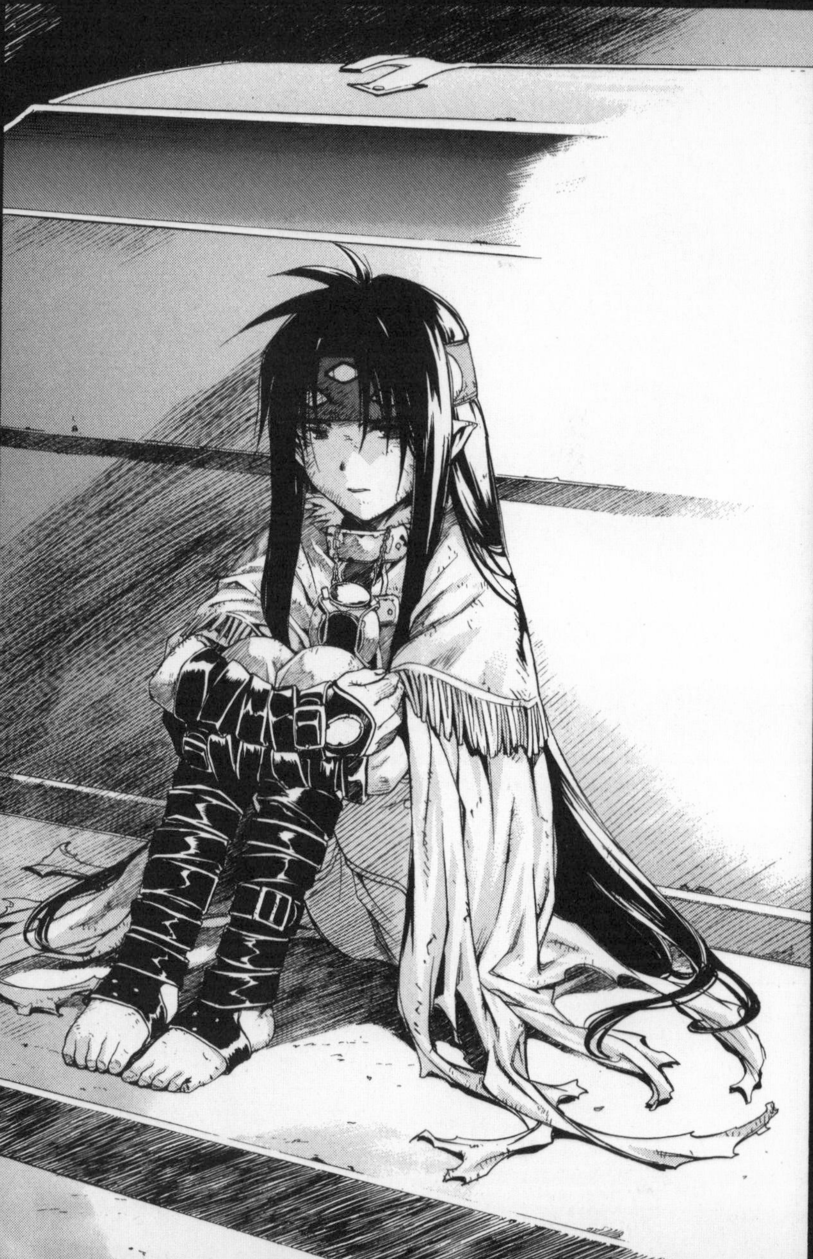

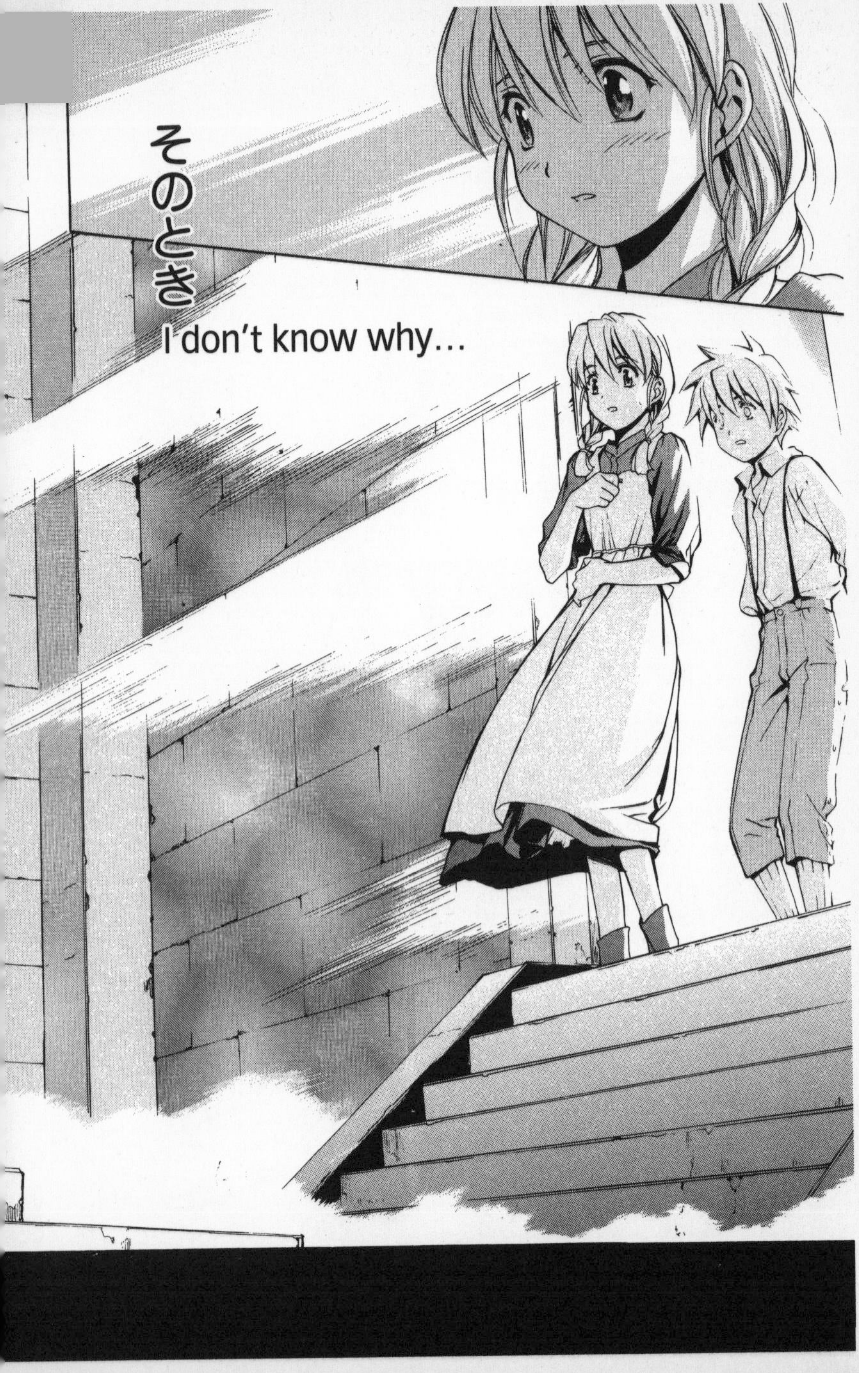
そのとき
I don't know why…

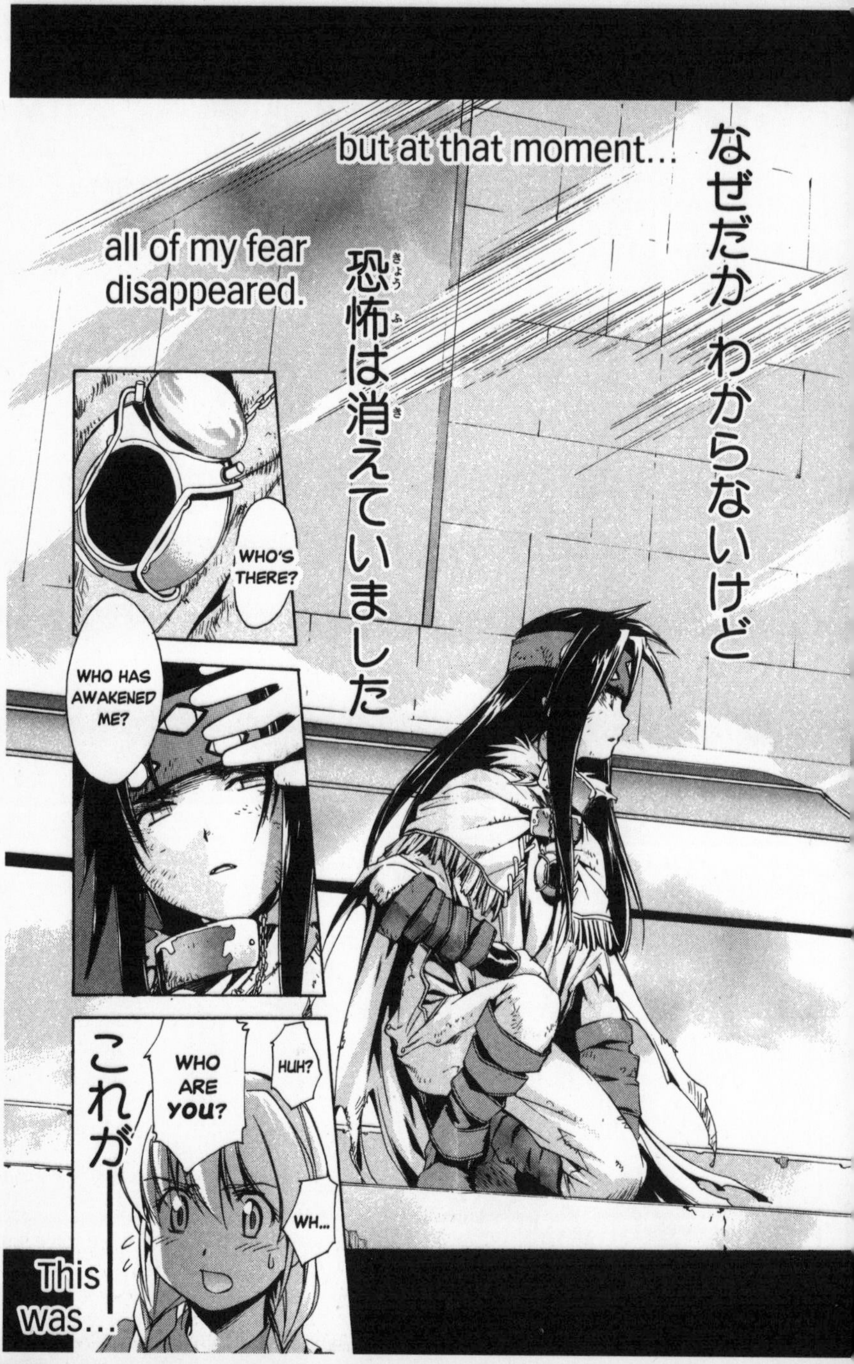
なぜだか わからないけど
but at that moment...
恐怖は消えていました
all of my fear disappeared.
WHO'S THERE?
WHO HAS AWAKENED ME?
HUH?
WHO ARE YOU?
WH...
これが――
This was...

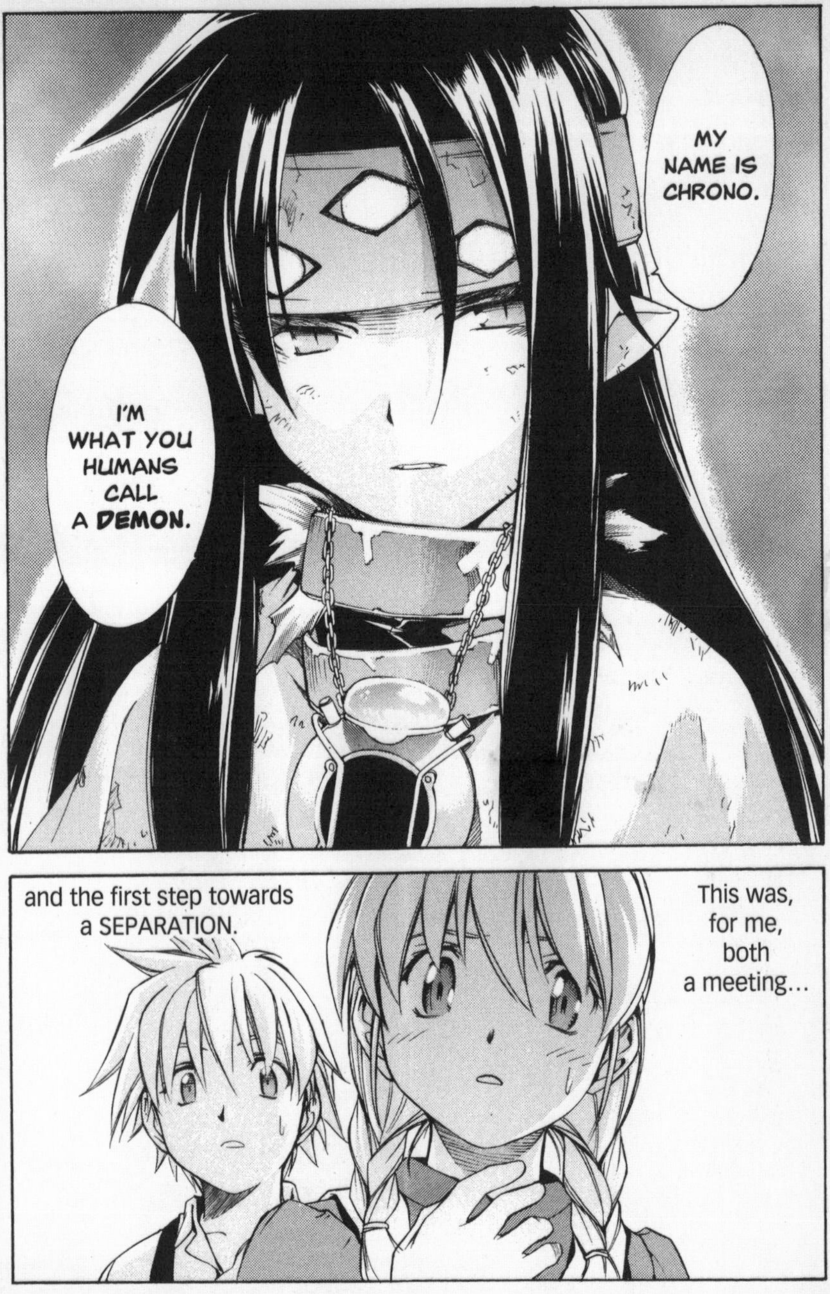
MY NAME IS CHRONO.
I'M WHAT YOU HUMANS CALL A **DEMON**.
This was, for me, both a meeting...
and the first step towards a SEPARATION.

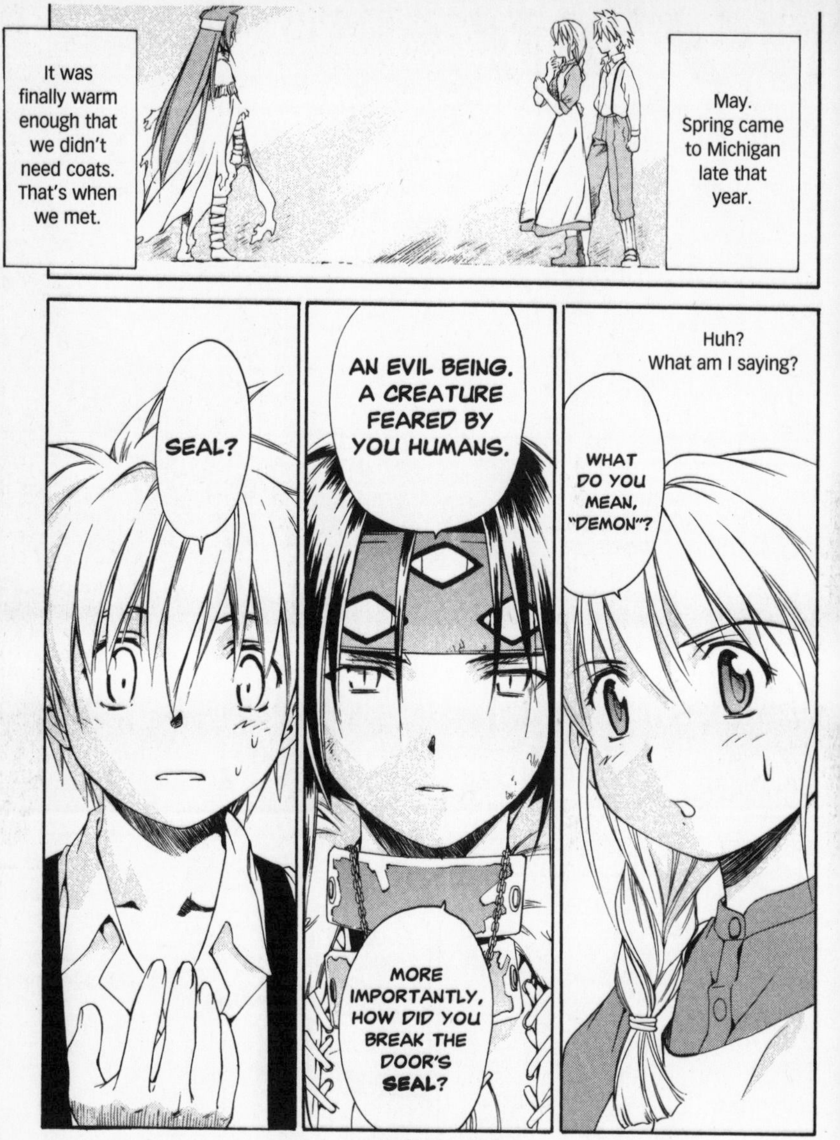
May.
Spring came to Michigan late that year.
It was finally warm enough that we didn't need coats. That's when we met.
Huh? What am I saying?
WHAT DO YOU MEAN, "DEMON"?
AN EVIL BEING. A CREATURE FEARED BY YOU HUMANS.
MORE IMPORTANTLY, HOW DID YOU BREAK THE DOOR'S SEAL?
SEAL?

ACT 10
「二人の選択」
Two Decisions

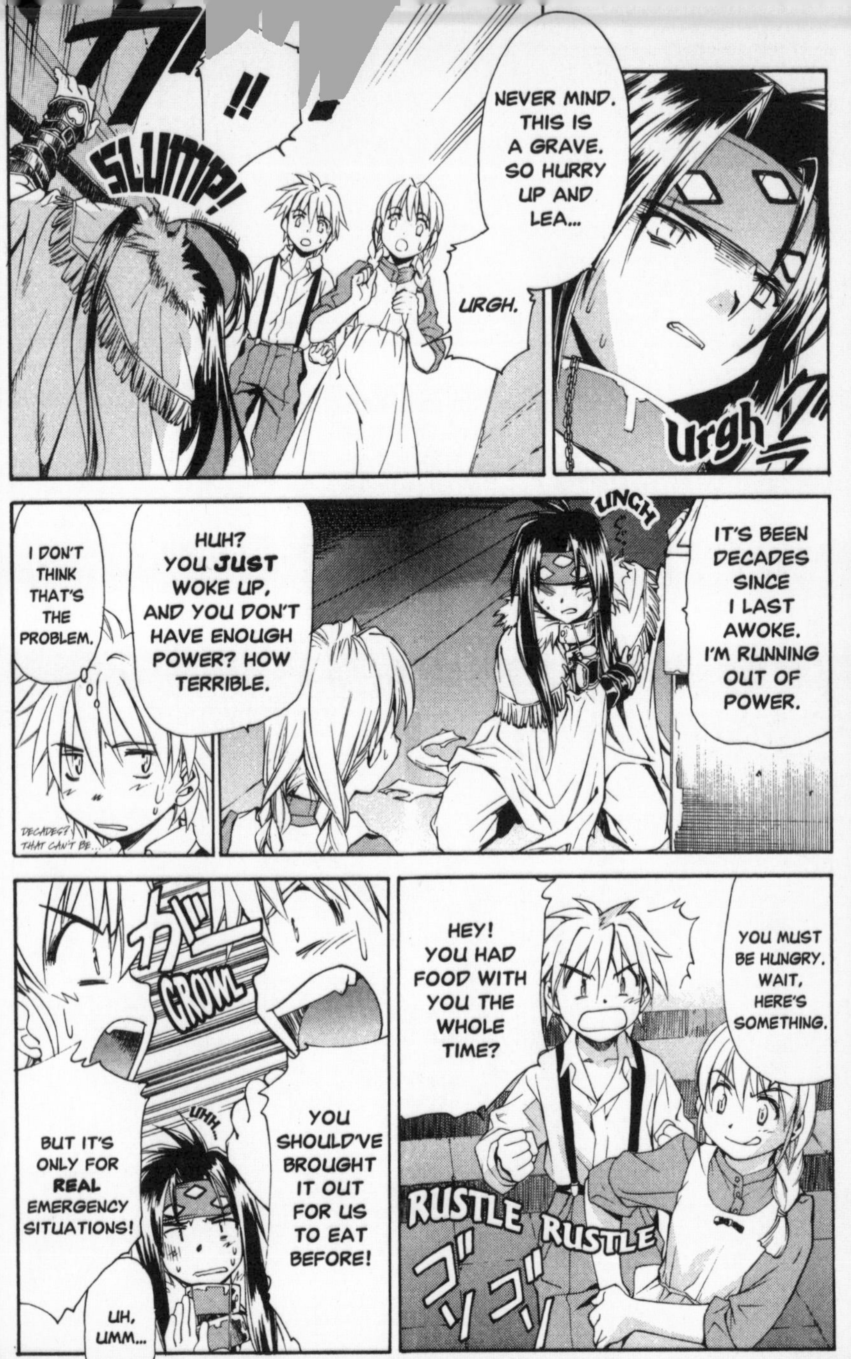

NEVER MIND. THIS IS A GRAVE. SO HURRY UP AND LEA...
URGH.
Urgh
SLUMP!
!!
IT'S BEEN DECADES SINCE I LAST AWOKE. I'M RUNNING OUT OF POWER.
UNGH
HUH? YOU JUST WOKE UP, AND YOU DON'T HAVE ENOUGH POWER? HOW TERRIBLE.
I DON'T THINK THAT'S THE PROBLEM.
DECADES? THAT CAN'T BE...
YOU MUST BE HUNGRY. WAIT, HERE'S SOMETHING.
HEY! YOU HAD FOOD WITH YOU THE WHOLE TIME?
RUSTLE RUSTLE
GROWL
YOU SHOULD'VE BROUGHT IT OUT FOR US TO EAT BEFORE!
BUT IT'S ONLY FOR REAL EMERGENCY SITUATIONS!
UHH...
UH, UMM...

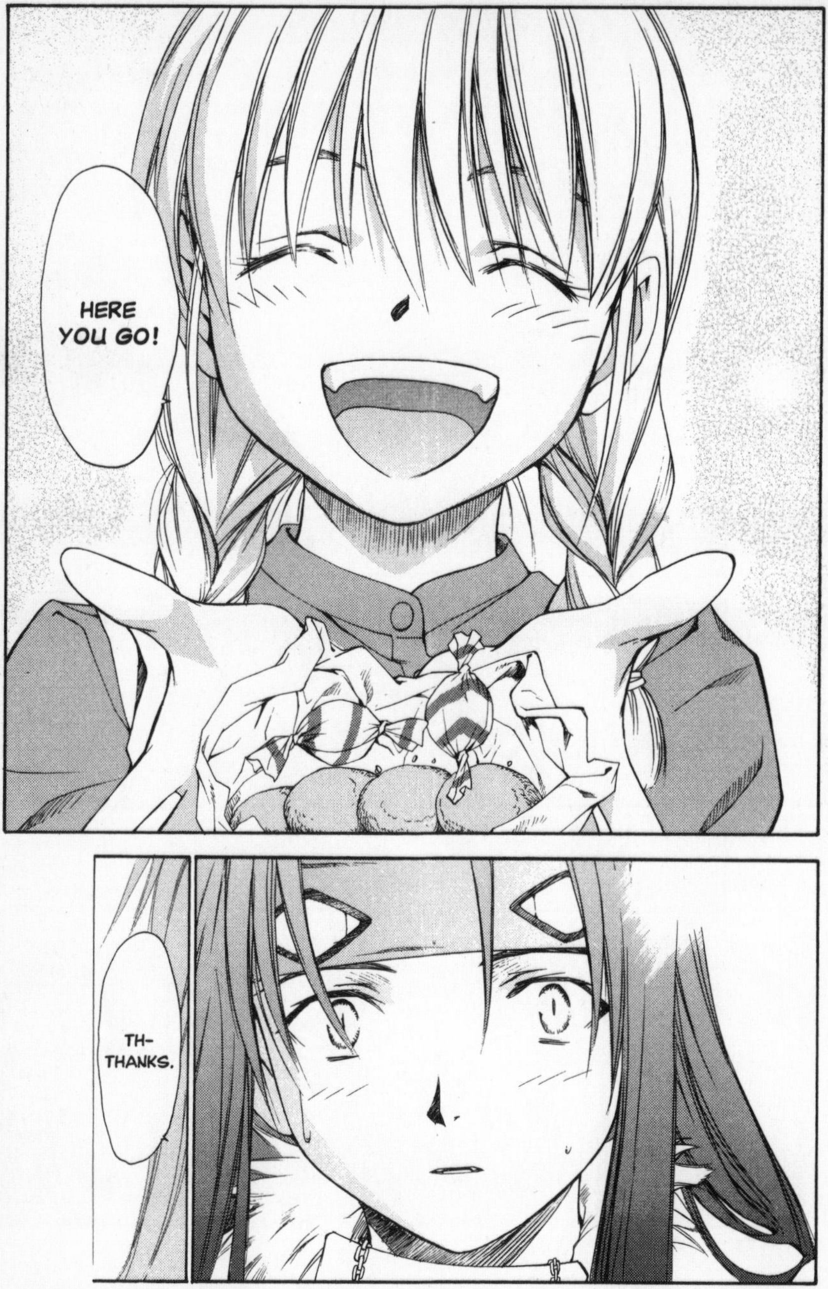
HERE YOU GO!
TH- THANKS.

That was the beginning.

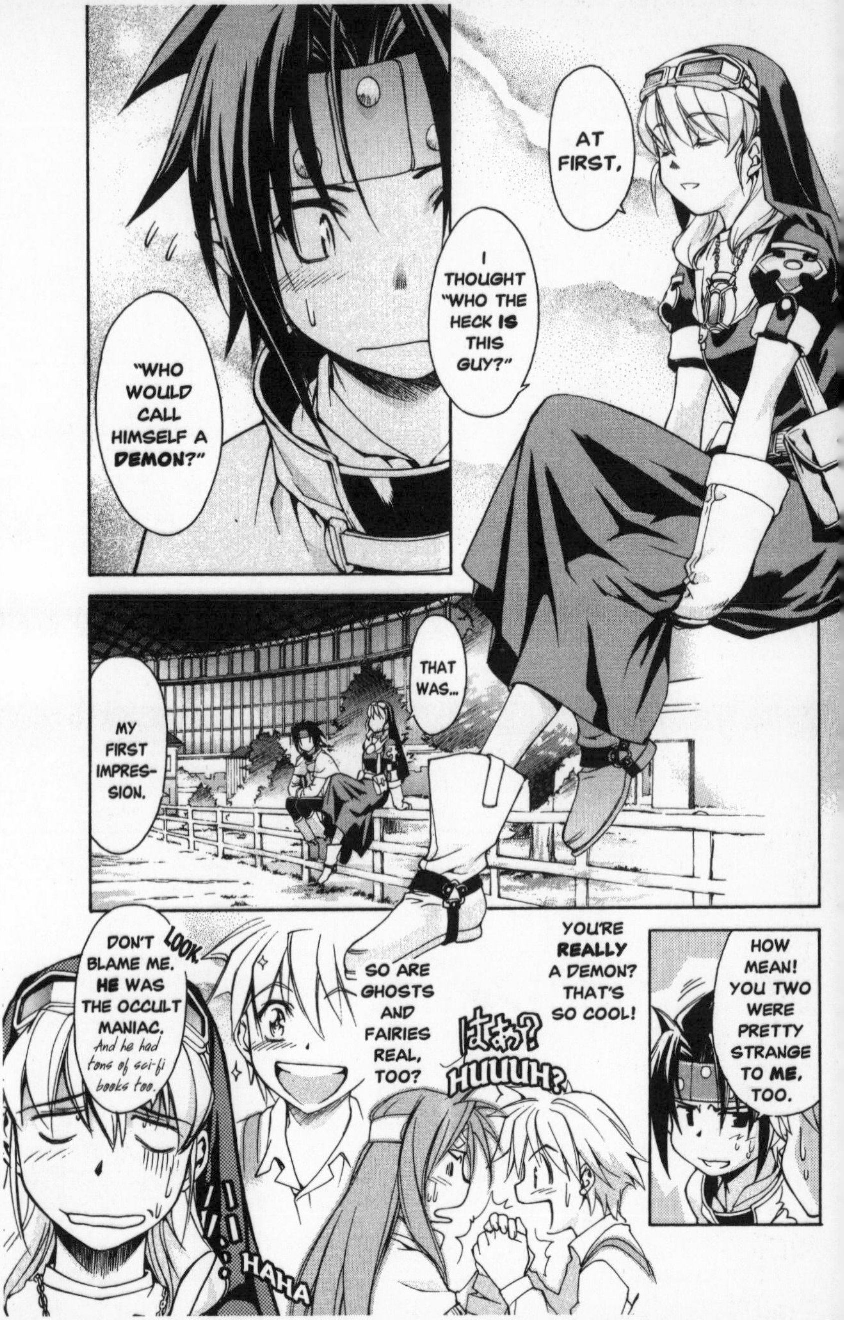
AT FIRST,
I THOUGHT "WHO THE HECK IS THIS GUY?"
"WHO WOULD CALL HIMSELF A DEMON?"
THAT WAS...
MY FIRST IMPRESSION.
HOW MEAN! YOU TWO WERE PRETTY STRANGE TO ME, TOO.
YOU'RE REALLY A DEMON? THAT'S SO COOL!
はあ?
HUUUH?
SO ARE GHOSTS AND FAIRIES REAL, TOO?
LOOK.
DON'T BLAME ME. HE WAS THE OCCULT MANIAC.
And he had tons of sci-fi books too.
HAHA

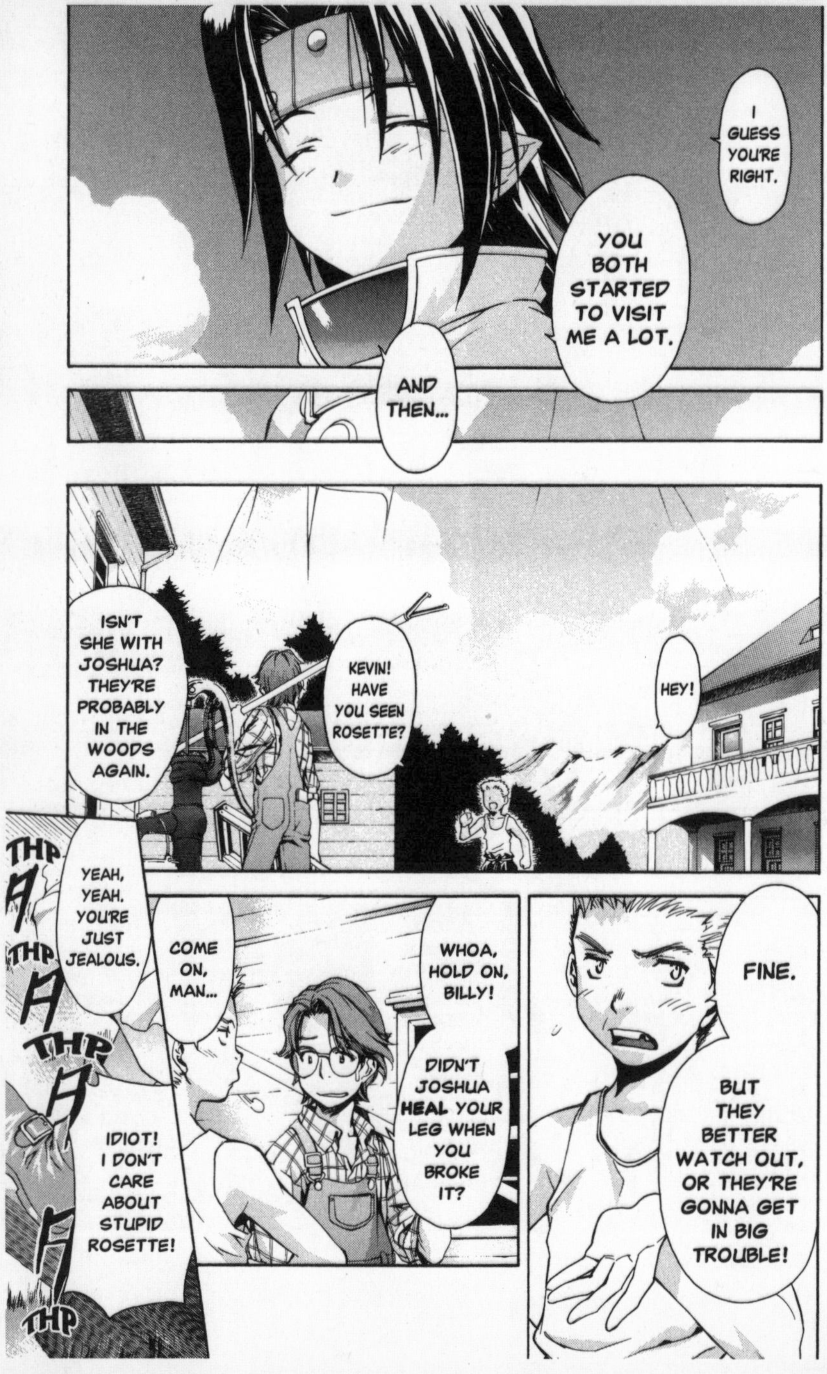

I GUESS YOU'RE RIGHT.
YOU BOTH STARTED TO VISIT ME A LOT.
AND THEN...
HEY!
KEVIN! HAVE YOU SEEN ROSETTE?
ISN'T SHE WITH JOSHUA? THEY'RE PROBABLY IN THE WOODS AGAIN.
FINE.
BUT THEY BETTER WATCH OUT, OR THEY'RE GONNA GET IN BIG TROUBLE!
WHOA, HOLD ON, BILLY!
DIDN'T JOSHUA **HEAL** YOUR LEG WHEN YOU BROKE IT?
COME ON, MAN...
YEAH, YEAH. YOU'RE JUST JEALOUS.
IDIOT! I DON'T CARE ABOUT STUPID ROSETTE!
THP
THP
THP
THP

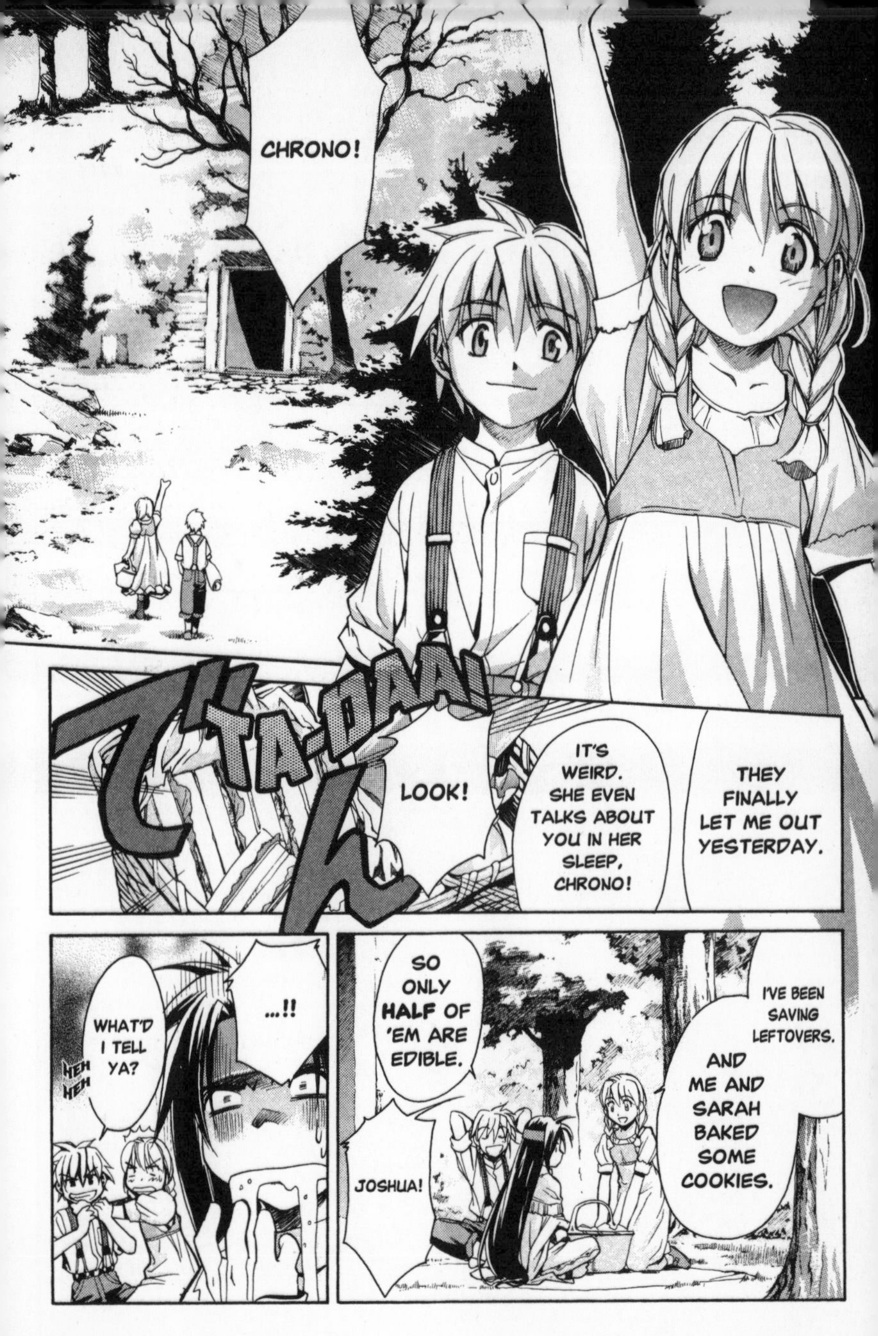
CHRONO!
THEY FINALLY LET ME OUT YESTERDAY.
IT'S WEIRD. SHE EVEN TALKS ABOUT YOU IN HER SLEEP, CHRONO!
LOOK!
TA-DAA!
I'VE BEEN SAVING LEFTOVERS.
AND ME AND SARAH BAKED SOME COOKIES.
SO ONLY HALF OF 'EM ARE EDIBLE.
JOSHUA!
...!!
WHAT'D I TELL YA?
HEH HEH

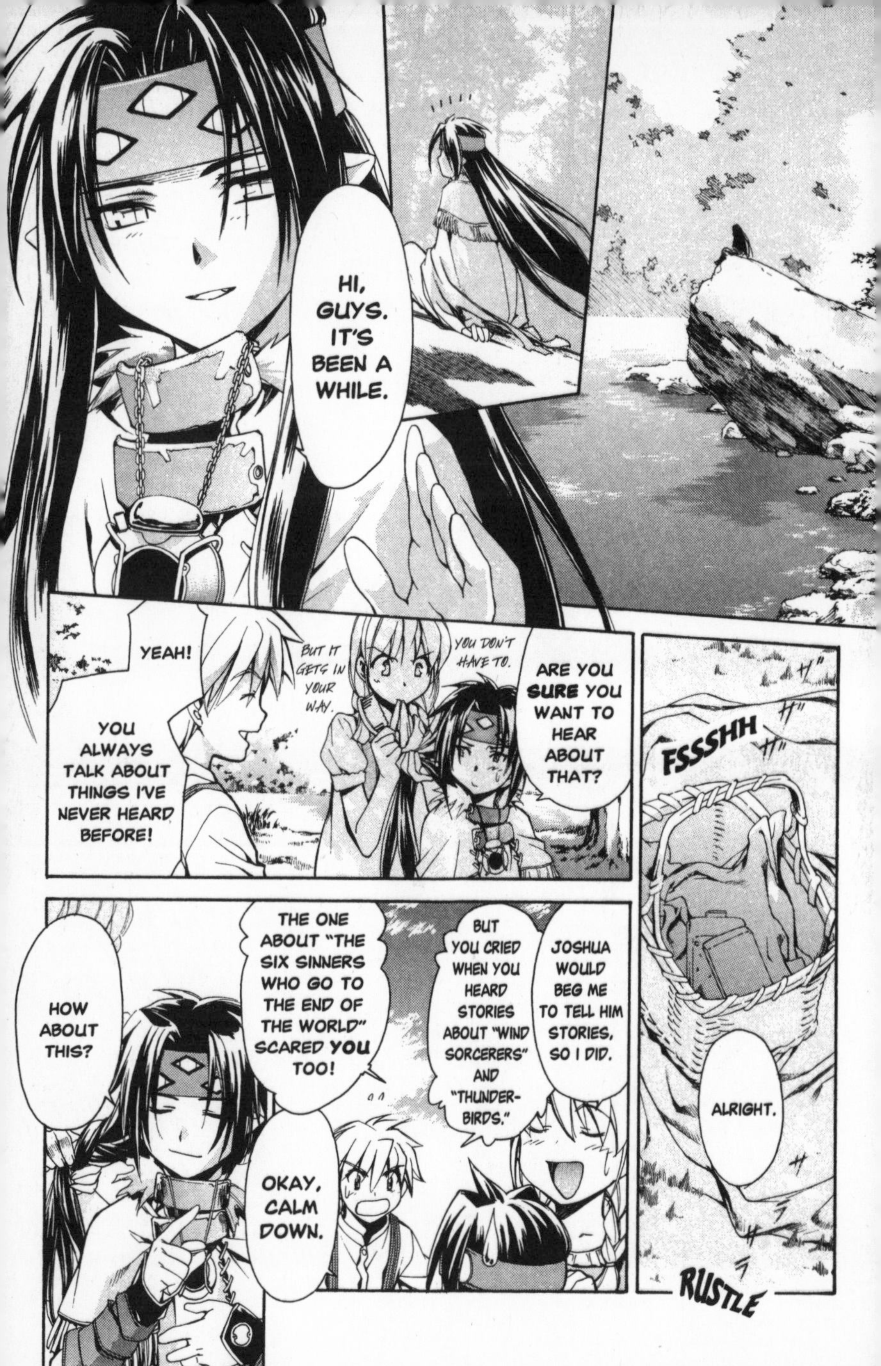
HI, GUYS. IT'S BEEN A WHILE.
ARE YOU SURE YOU WANT TO HEAR ABOUT THAT?
YOU DON'T HAVE TO.
BUT IT GETS IN YOUR WAY.
YEAH!
YOU ALWAYS TALK ABOUT THINGS I'VE NEVER HEARD BEFORE!
FSSSHH
ALRIGHT.
RUSTLE
JOSHUA WOULD BEG ME TO TELL HIM STORIES, SO I DID.
BUT YOU CRIED WHEN YOU HEARD STORIES ABOUT "WIND SORCERERS" AND "THUNDER-BIRDS."
THE ONE ABOUT "THE SIX SINNERS WHO GO TO THE END OF THE WORLD" SCARED YOU TOO!
OKAY, CALM DOWN.
HOW ABOUT THIS?

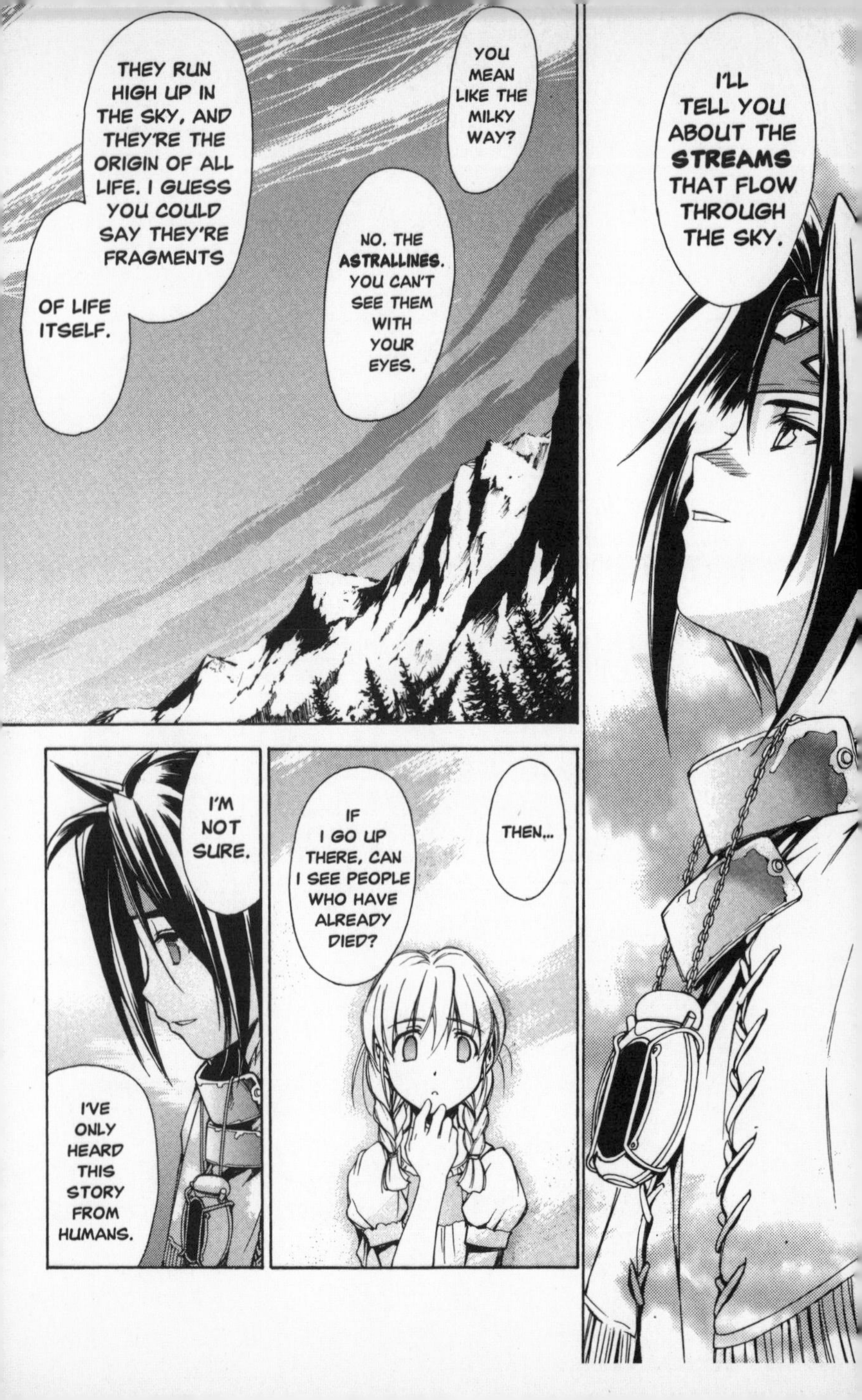
I'LL TELL YOU ABOUT THE STREAMS THAT FLOW THROUGH THE SKY.
YOU MEAN LIKE THE MILKY WAY?
NO. THE ASTRALLINES. YOU CAN'T SEE THEM WITH YOUR EYES.
THEY RUN HIGH UP IN THE SKY, AND THEY'RE THE ORIGIN OF ALL LIFE. I GUESS YOU COULD SAY THEY'RE FRAGMENTS
OF LIFE ITSELF.
THEN...
IF I GO UP THERE, CAN I SEE PEOPLE WHO HAVE ALREADY DIED?
I'M NOT SURE.
I'VE ONLY HEARD THIS STORY FROM HUMANS.

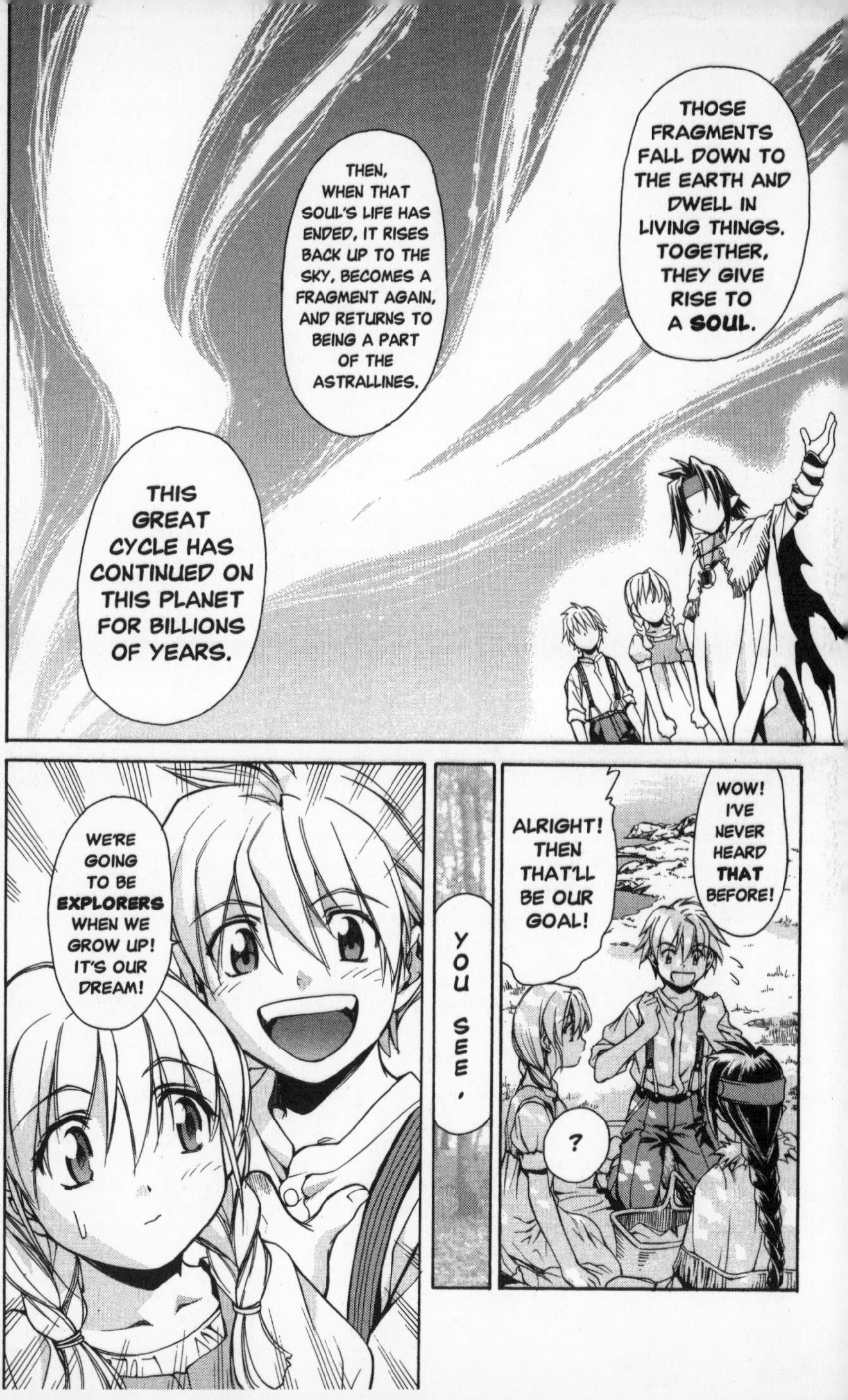
THOSE FRAGMENTS FALL DOWN TO THE EARTH AND DWELL IN LIVING THINGS. TOGETHER, THEY GIVE RISE TO A **SOUL**.
THEN, WHEN THAT SOUL'S LIFE HAS ENDED, IT RISES BACK UP TO THE SKY, BECOMES A FRAGMENT AGAIN, AND RETURNS TO BEING A PART OF THE ASTRALLINES.
THIS GREAT CYCLE HAS CONTINUED ON THIS PLANET FOR BILLIONS OF YEARS.
WOW! I'VE NEVER HEARD **THAT** BEFORE!
ALRIGHT! THEN THAT'LL BE OUR GOAL!
?
YOU SEE,
WE'RE GOING TO BE **EXPLORERS** WHEN WE GROW UP! IT'S OUR DREAM!

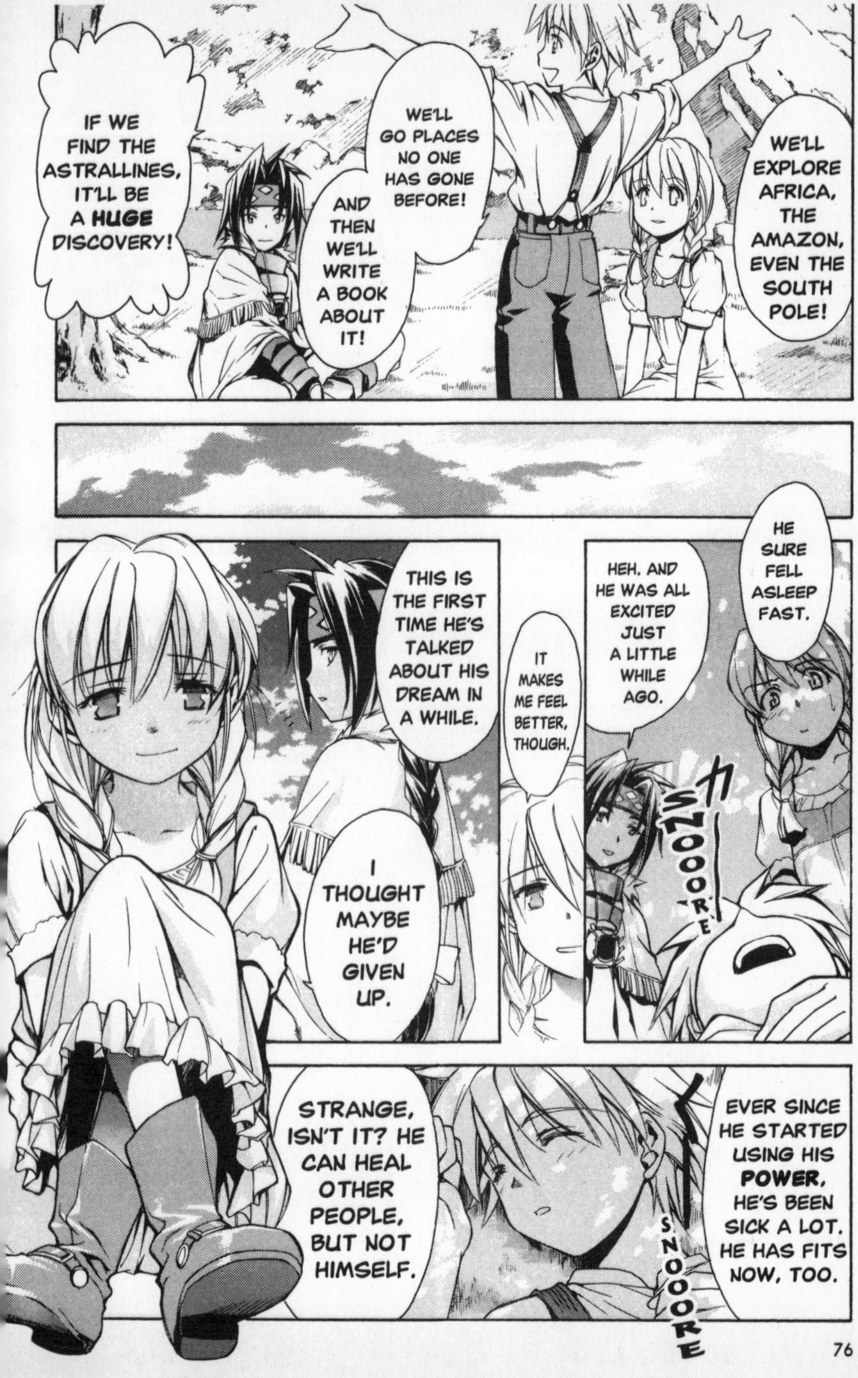

WE'LL EXPLORE AFRICA, THE AMAZON, EVEN THE SOUTH POLE!
WE'LL GO PLACES NO ONE HAS GONE BEFORE!
AND THEN WE'LL WRITE A BOOK ABOUT IT!
IF WE FIND THE ASTRALLINES, IT'LL BE A HUGE DISCOVERY!
HE SURE FELL ASLEEP FAST.
HEH. AND HE WAS ALL EXCITED JUST A LITTLE WHILE AGO.
IT MAKES ME FEEL BETTER, THOUGH.
SNOOORE
THIS IS THE FIRST TIME HE'S TALKED ABOUT HIS DREAM IN A WHILE.
I THOUGHT MAYBE HE'D GIVEN UP.
EVER SINCE HE STARTED USING HIS POWER, HE'S BEEN SICK A LOT. HE HAS FITS NOW, TOO.
STRANGE, ISN'T IT? HE CAN HEAL OTHER PEOPLE, BUT NOT HIMSELF.
SNOOORE

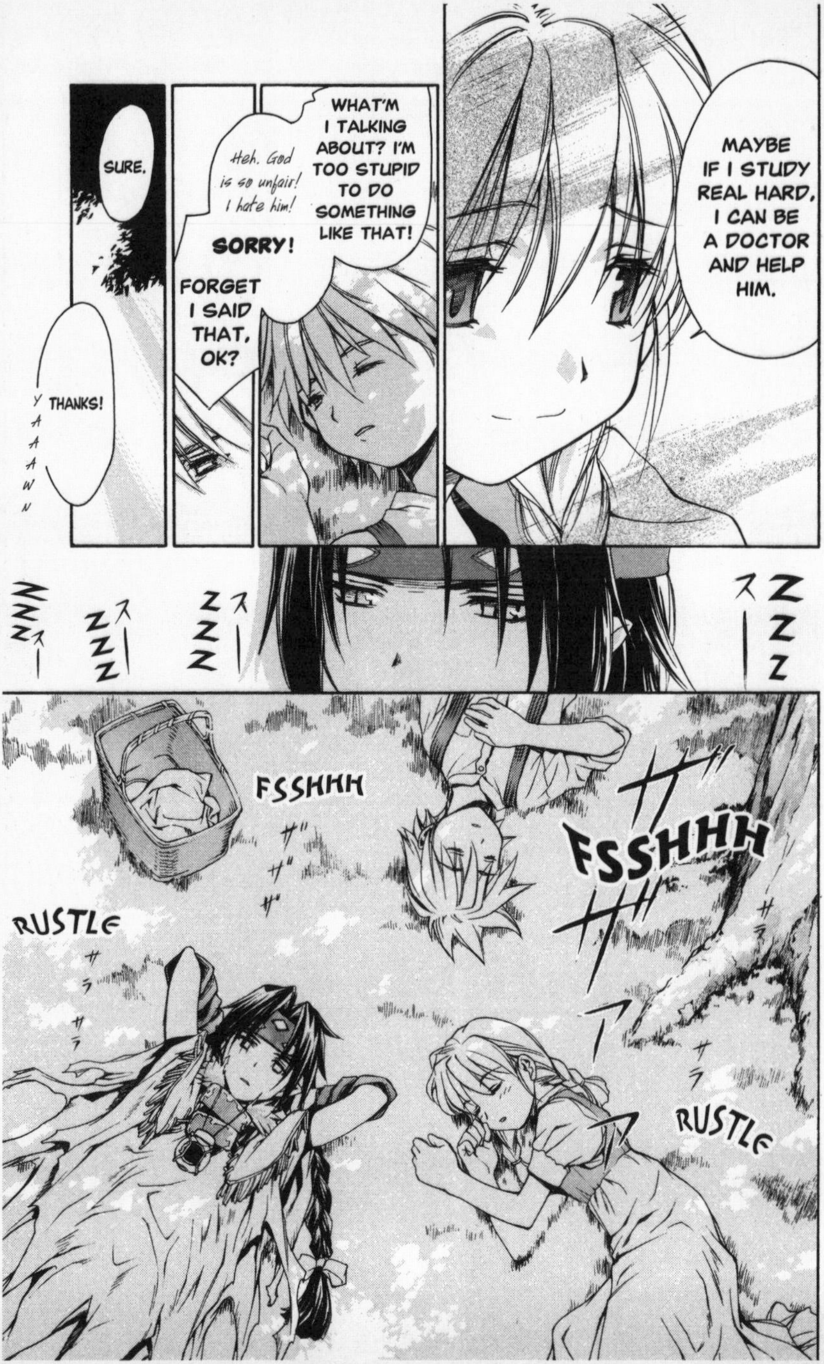
MAYBE IF I STUDY REAL HARD, I CAN BE A DOCTOR AND HELP HIM.
WHAT'M I TALKING ABOUT? I'M TOO STUPID TO DO SOMETHING LIKE THAT!
Heh. God is so unfair! I hate him!
SORRY!
FORGET I SAID THAT, OK?
SURE.
THANKS!
YAAAAWN
ZZZ
ZZZ
ZZZ
ZZZ
FSSHHH
FSSHHH
RUSTLE
RUSTLE

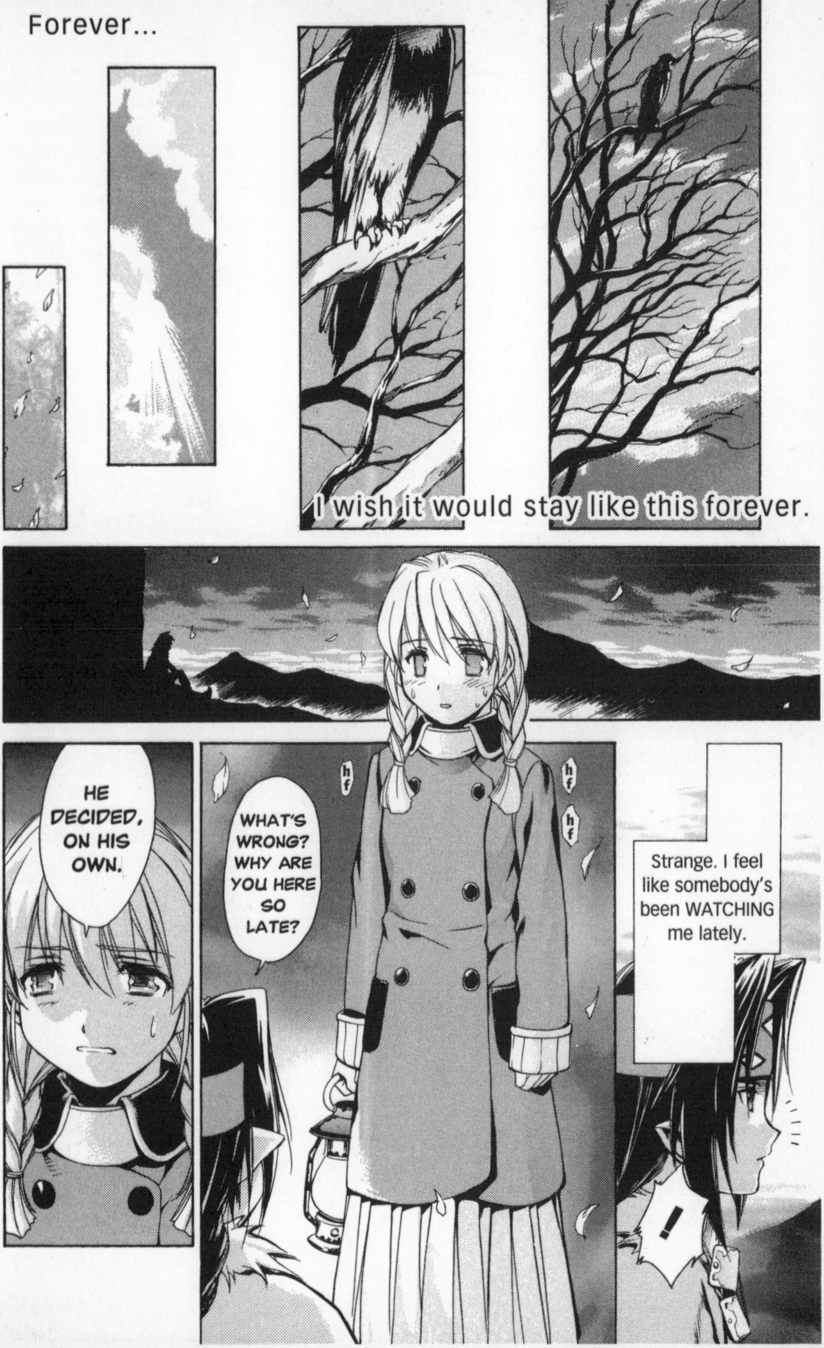
Forever...
I wish it would stay like this forever.
Strange. I feel like somebody's been WATCHING me lately.
!
hf hf hf
WHAT'S WRONG? WHY ARE YOU HERE SO LATE?
HE DECIDED, ON HIS OWN.

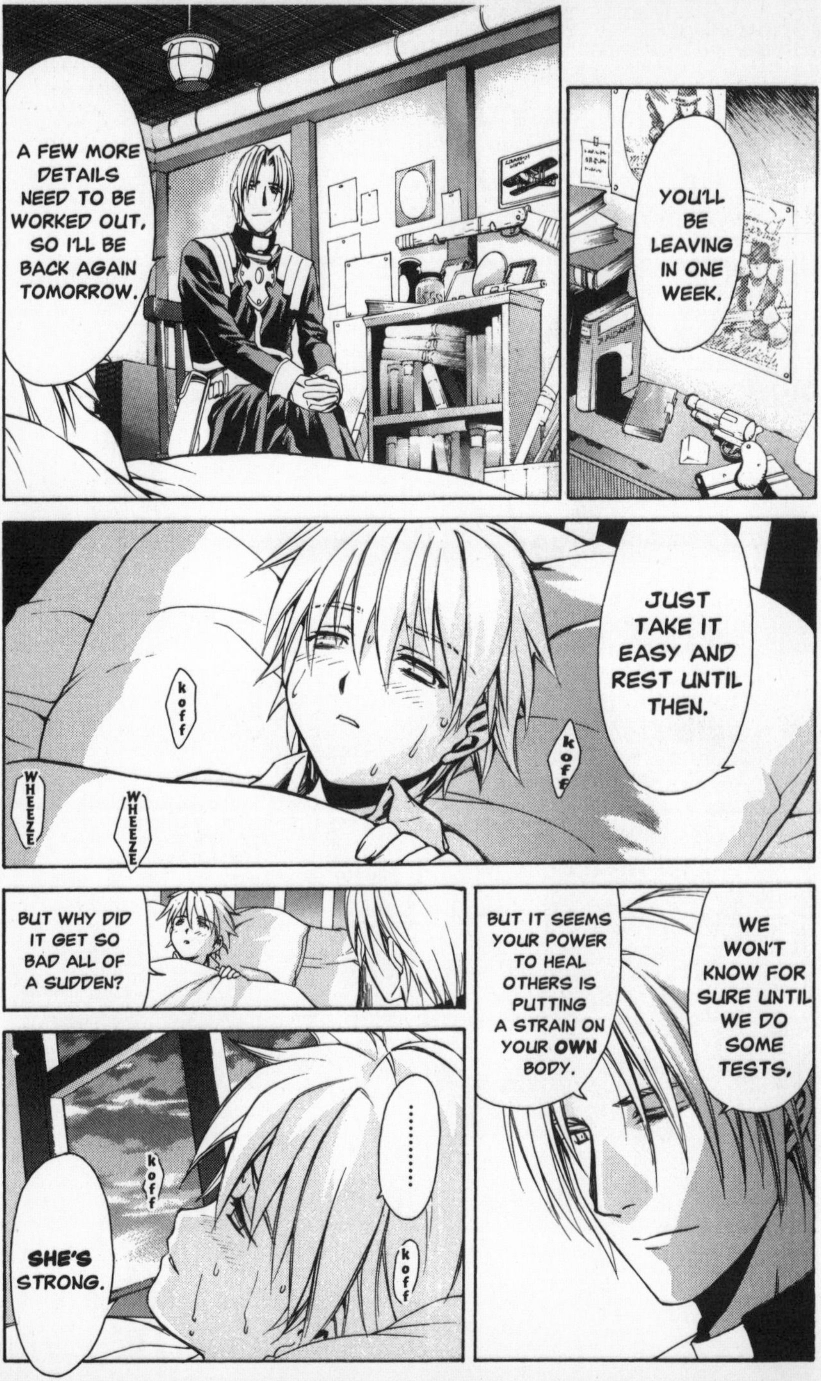
A FEW MORE DETAILS NEED TO BE WORKED OUT, SO I'LL BE BACK AGAIN TOMORROW.
YOU'LL BE LEAVING IN ONE WEEK.
JUST TAKE IT EASY AND REST UNTIL THEN.
koff
koff
WHEEZE
WHEEZE
BUT WHY DID IT GET SO BAD ALL OF A SUDDEN?
WE WON'T KNOW FOR SURE UNTIL WE DO SOME TESTS,
BUT IT SEEMS YOUR POWER TO HEAL OTHERS IS PUTTING A STRAIN ON YOUR **OWN** BODY.
....
koff
koff
SHE'S STRONG.

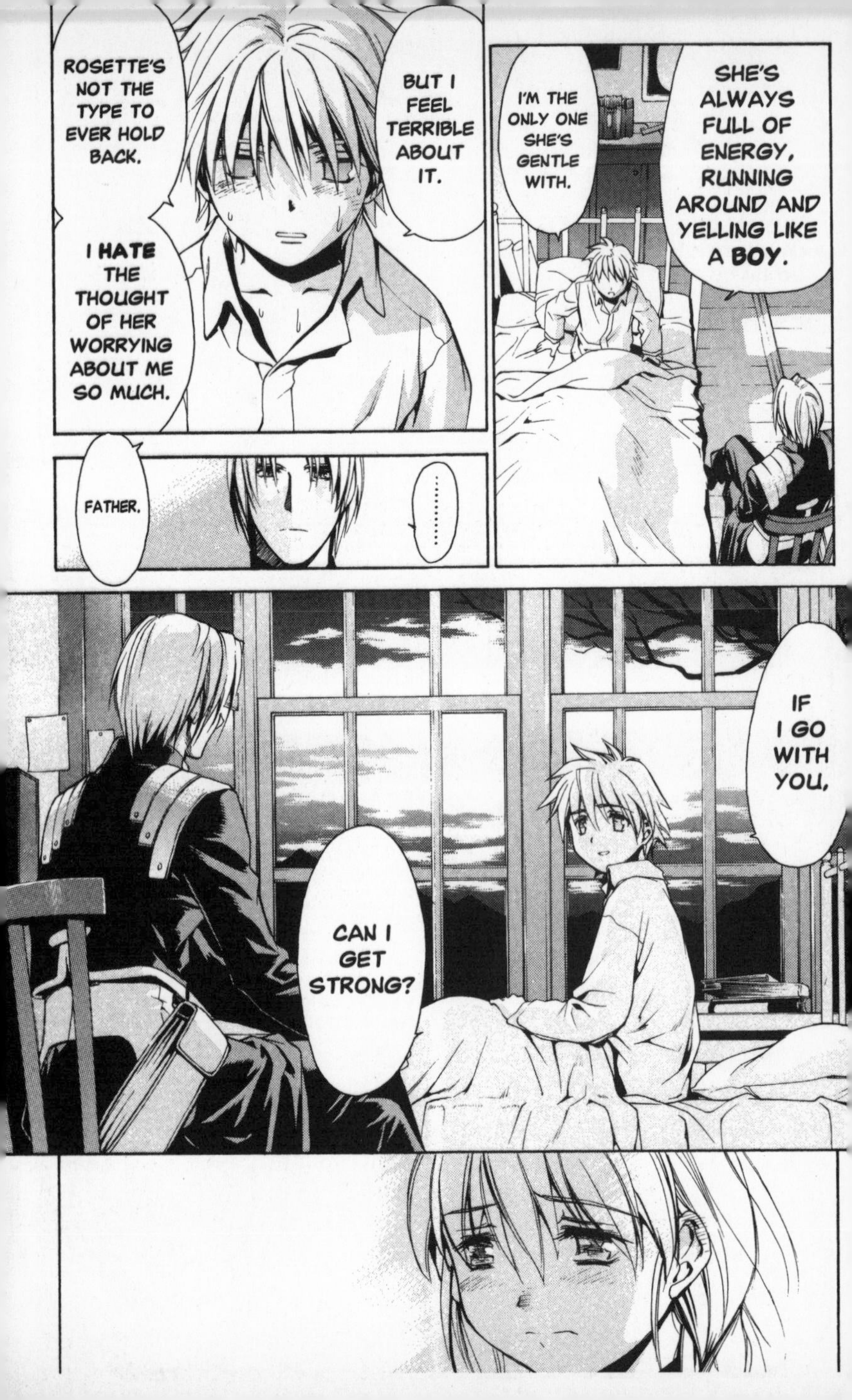
SHE'S ALWAYS FULL OF ENERGY, RUNNING AROUND AND YELLING LIKE A BOY.
I'M THE ONLY ONE SHE'S GENTLE WITH.
BUT I FEEL TERRIBLE ABOUT IT.
ROSETTE'S NOT THE TYPE TO EVER HOLD BACK.
I HATE THE THOUGHT OF HER WORRYING ABOUT ME SO MUCH.
......
FATHER.
IF I GO WITH YOU,
CAN I GET STRONG?

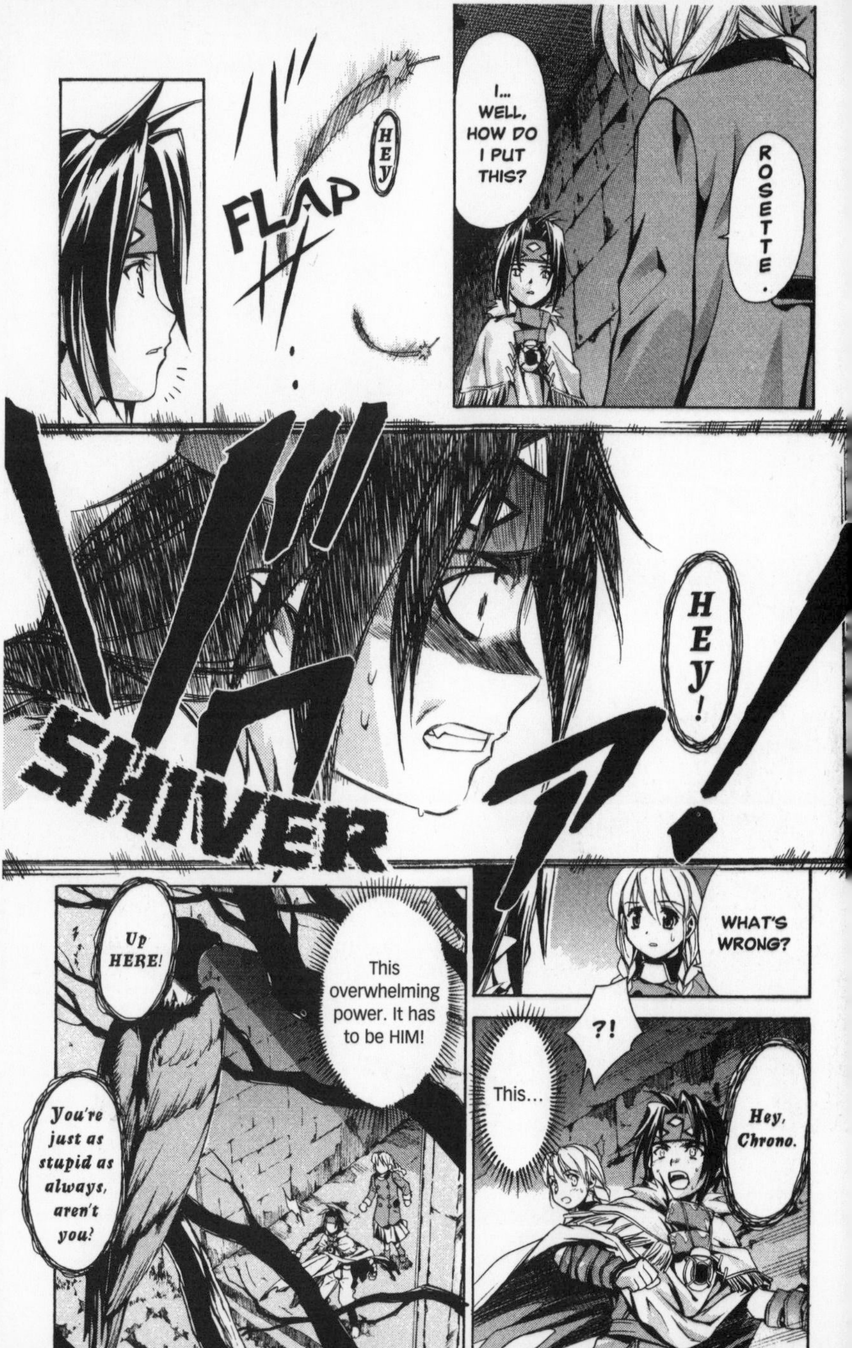
ROSETTE.
I... WELL, HOW DO I PUT THIS?
HEY
FLAP
HEY!
SHIVER
WHAT'S WRONG?
?!
Hey, Chrono.
This...
This overwhelming power. It has to be HIM!
Up HERE!
You're just as stupid as always, aren't you?

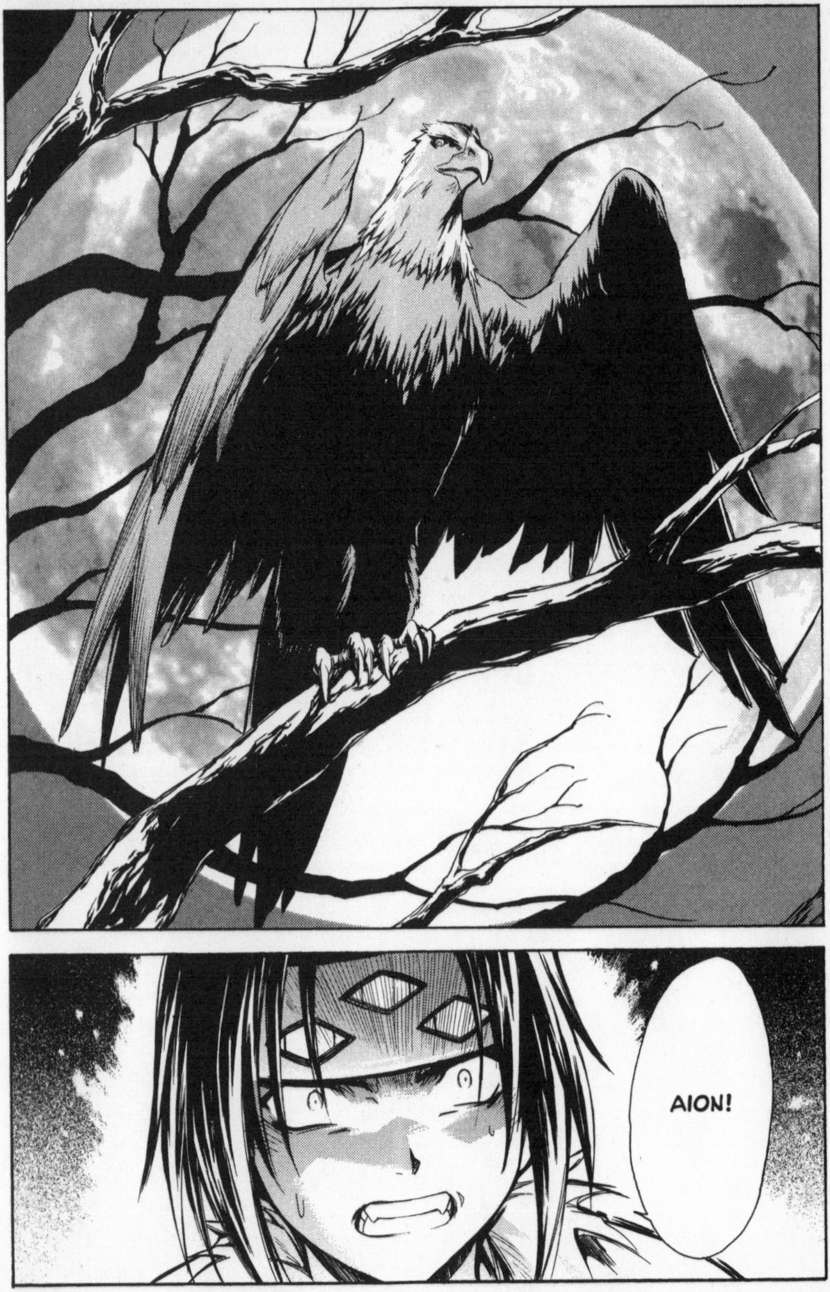
AION!

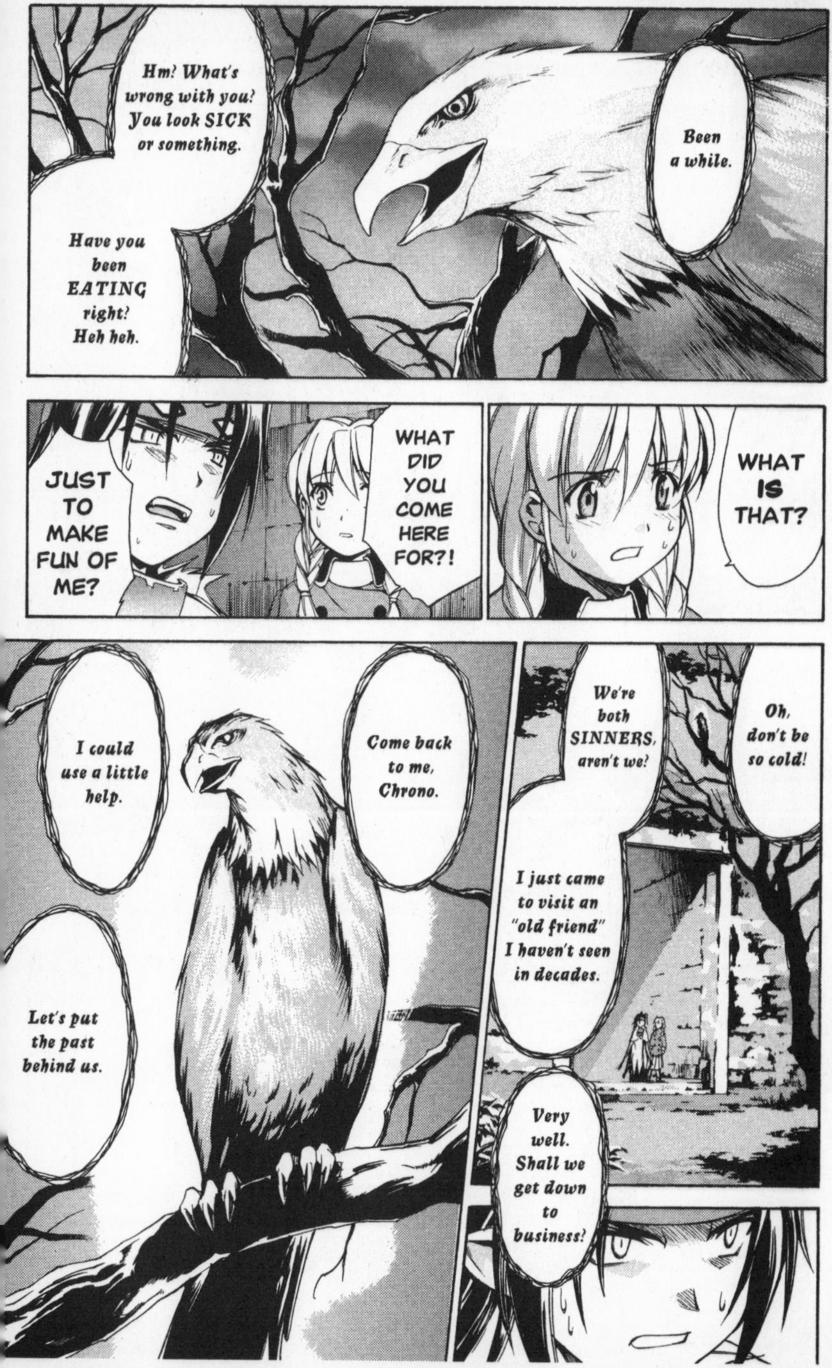

Been a while.
Hm? What's wrong with you? You look SICK or something.
Have you been EATING right? Heh heh.
WHAT IS THAT?
WHAT DID YOU COME HERE FOR?!
JUST TO MAKE FUN OF ME?
Oh, don't be so cold!
We're both SINNERS, aren't we?
I just came to visit an "old friend" I haven't seen in decades.
Very well. Shall we get down to business?
Come back to me, Chrono.
I could use a little help.
Let's put the past behind us.

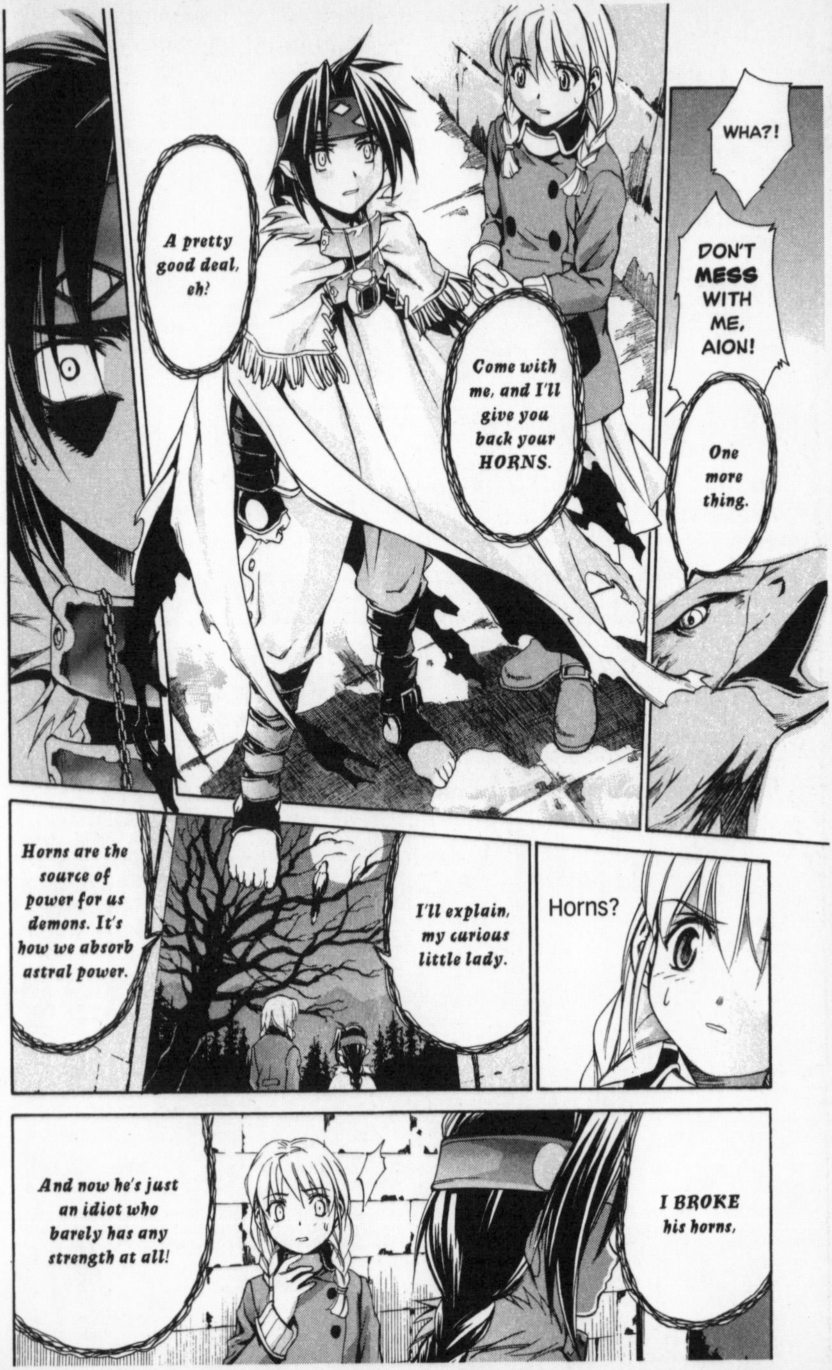
WHA?!
DON'T MESS WITH ME, AION!
One more thing.
Come with me, and I'll give you back your HORNS.
A pretty good deal, eh?
Horns?
I'll explain, my curious little lady.
Horns are the source of power for us demons. It's how we absorb astral power.
I BROKE his horns,
And now he's just an idiot who barely has any strength at all!

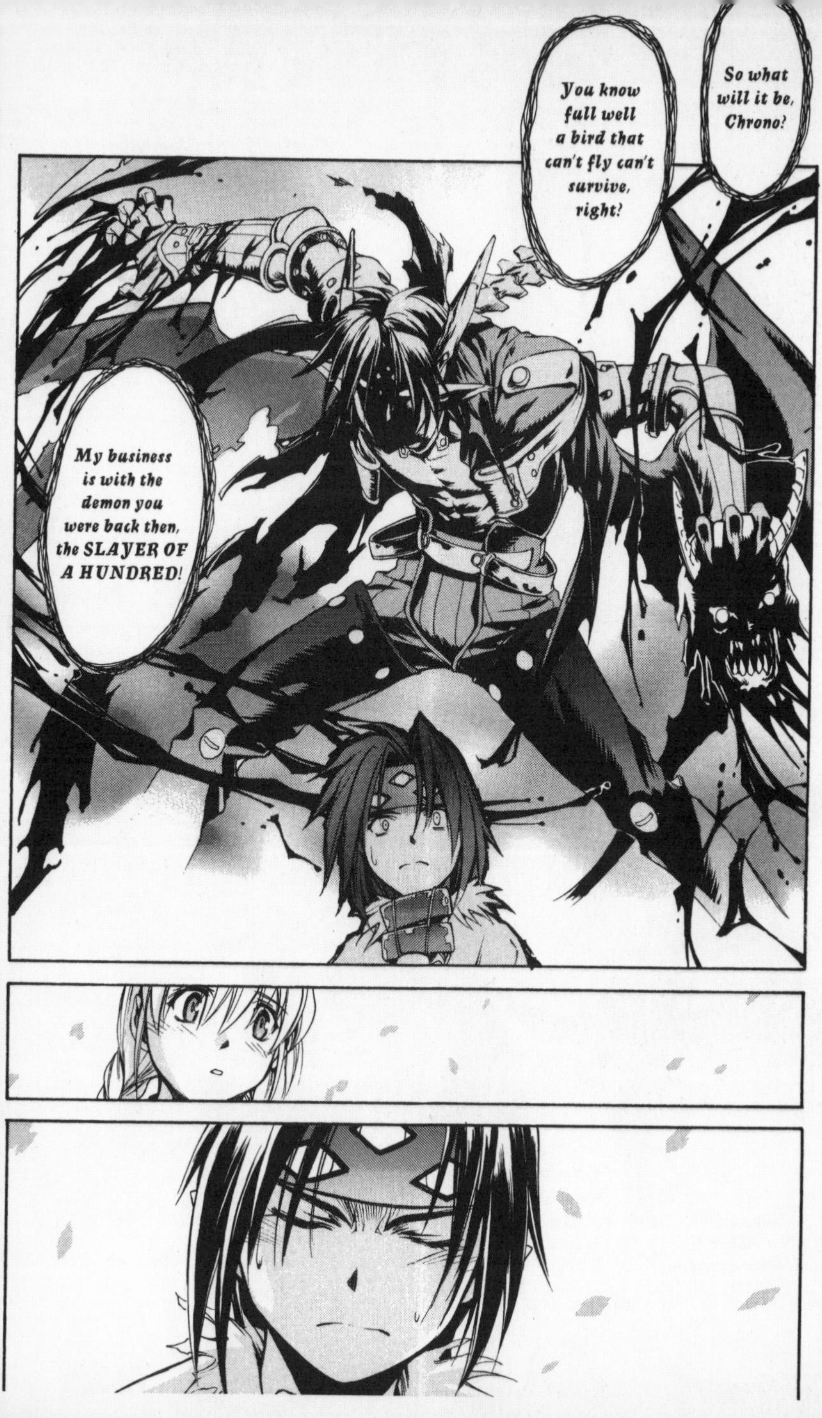
So what will it be, Chrono?
You know full well a bird that can't fly can't survive, right?
My business is with the demon you were back then, the SLAYER OF A HUNDRED!

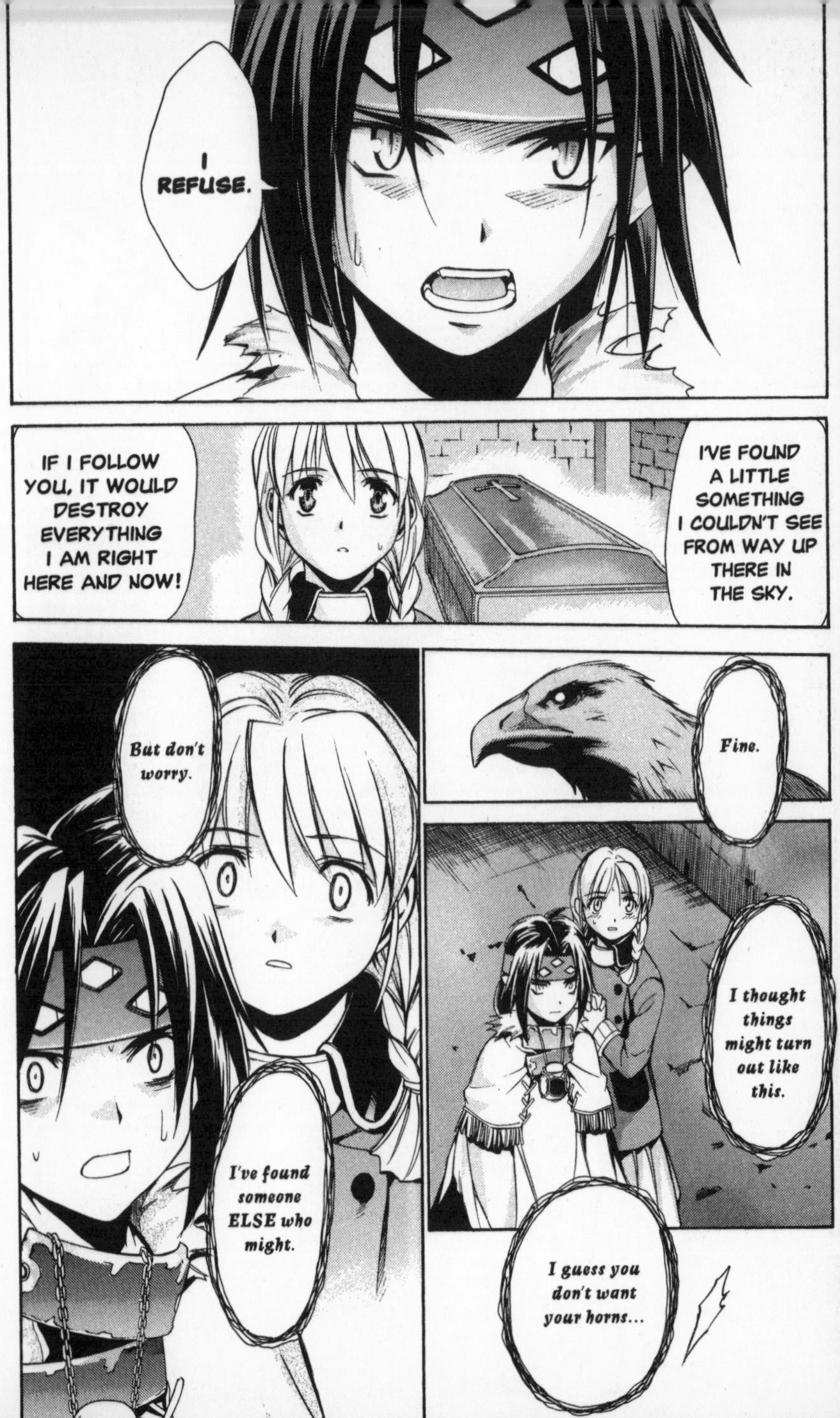
I REFUSE.
I'VE FOUND A LITTLE SOMETHING I COULDN'T SEE FROM WAY UP THERE IN THE SKY.
IF I FOLLOW YOU, IT WOULD DESTROY EVERYTHING I AM RIGHT HERE AND NOW!
Fine.
I thought things might turn out like this.
I guess you don't want your horns...
But don't worry.
I've found someone ELSE who might.

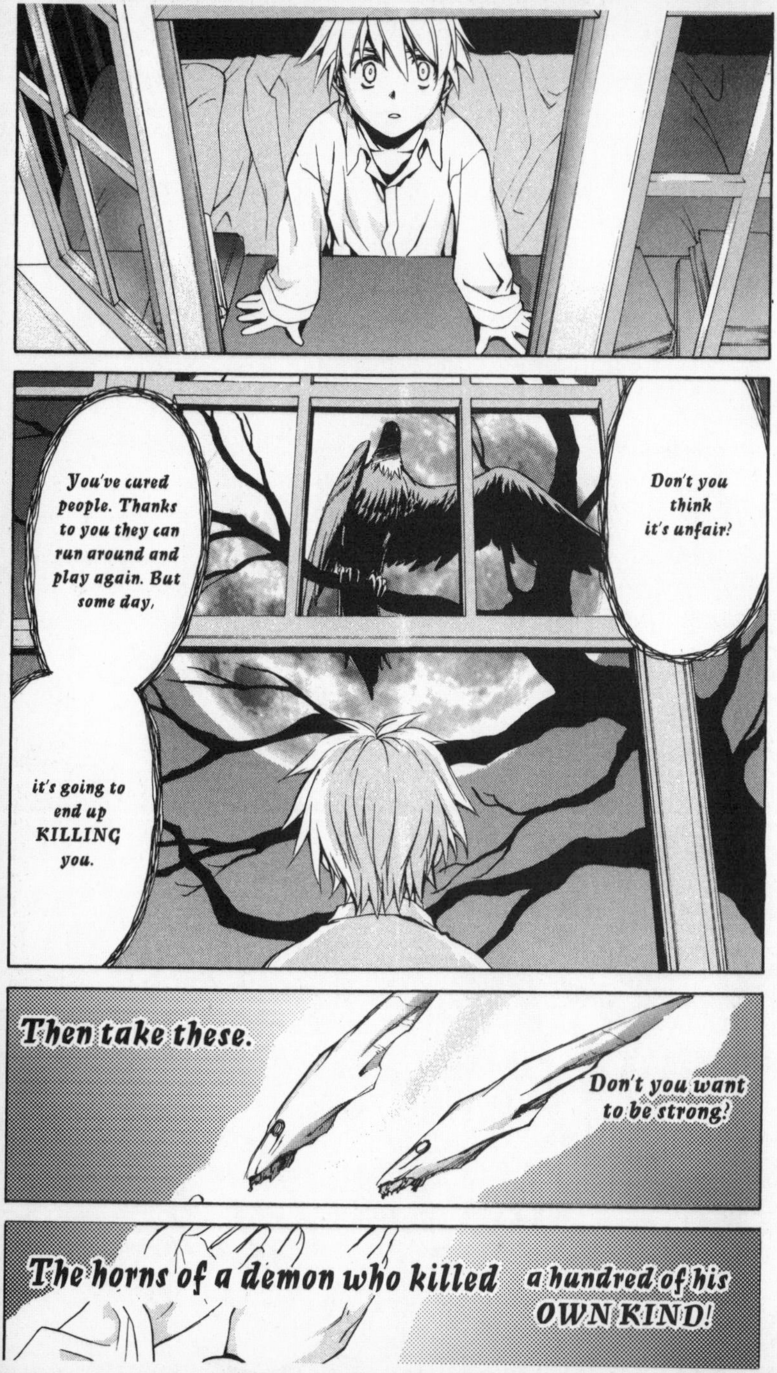
You've cured people. Thanks to you they can run around and play again. But some day,
it's going to end up KILLING you.
Don't you think it's unfair?
Then take these.
Don't you want to be strong?
The horns of a demon who killed
a hundred of his OWN KIND!

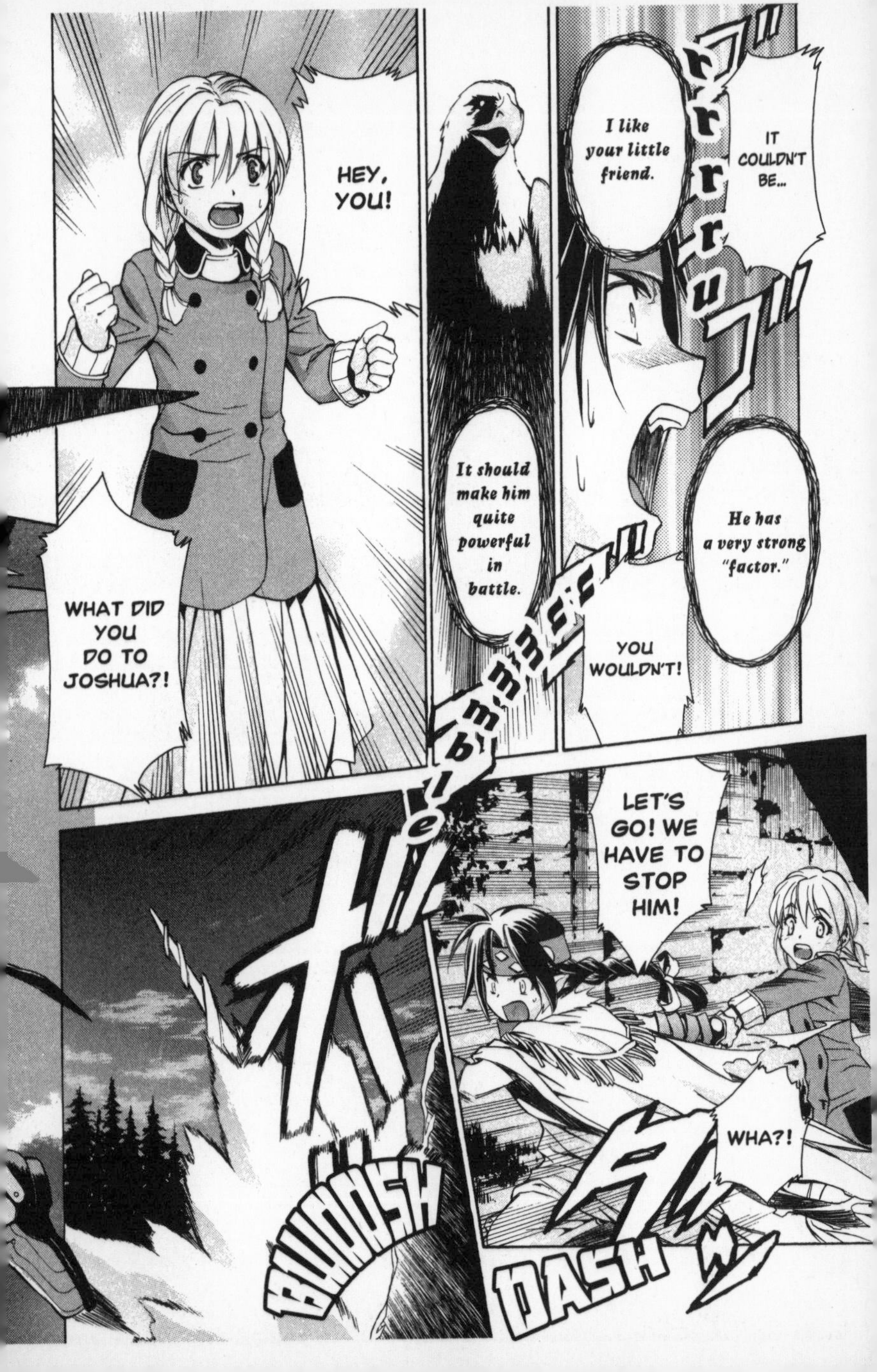
HEY, YOU!
WHAT DID YOU DO TO JOSHUA?!
I like your little friend.
IT COULDN'T BE...
rrru
He has a very strong "factor."
It should make him quite powerful in battle.
YOU WOULDN'T!
LET'S GO! WE HAVE TO STOP HIM!
WHA?!
BWOOSH
DASH

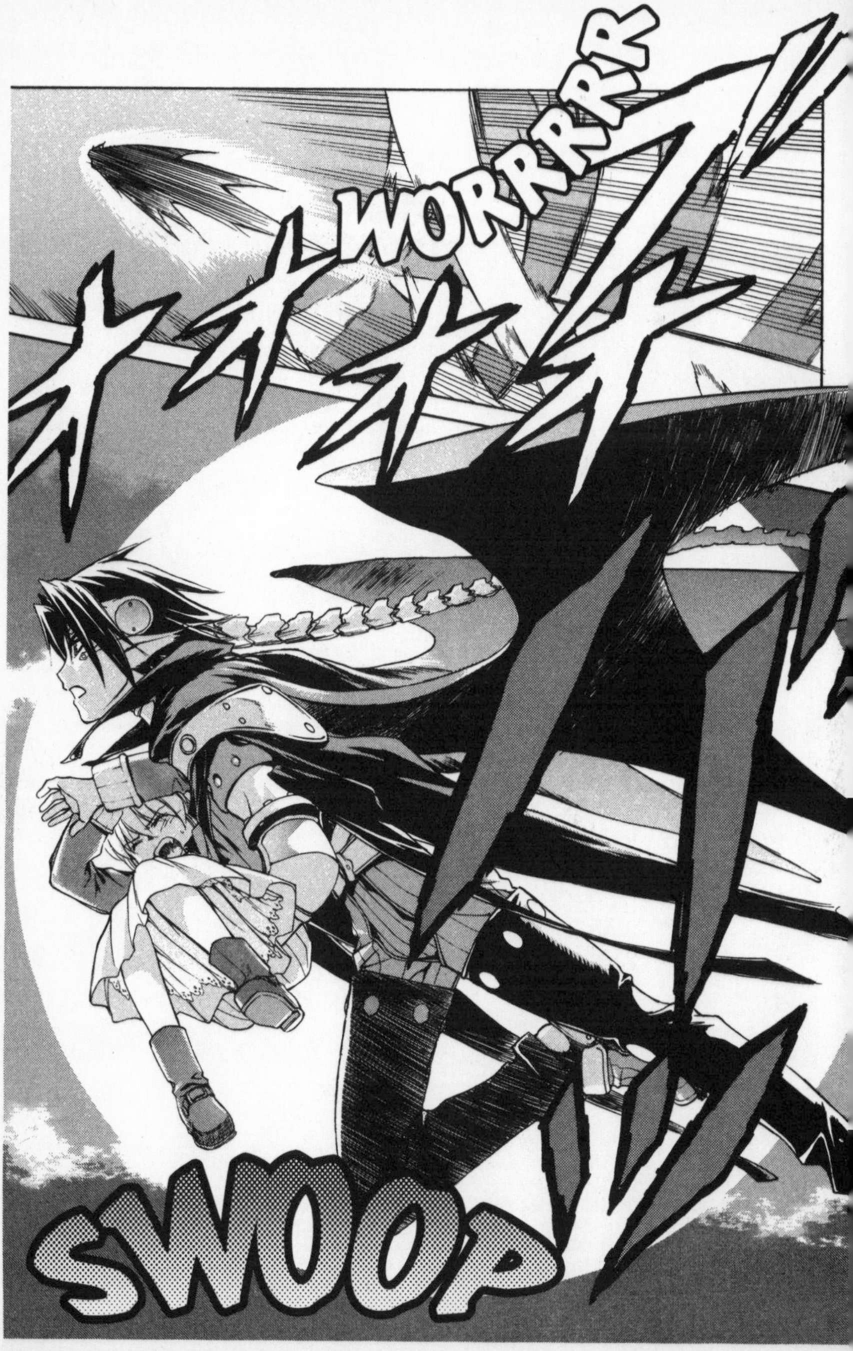
WORRRR
SWOOP

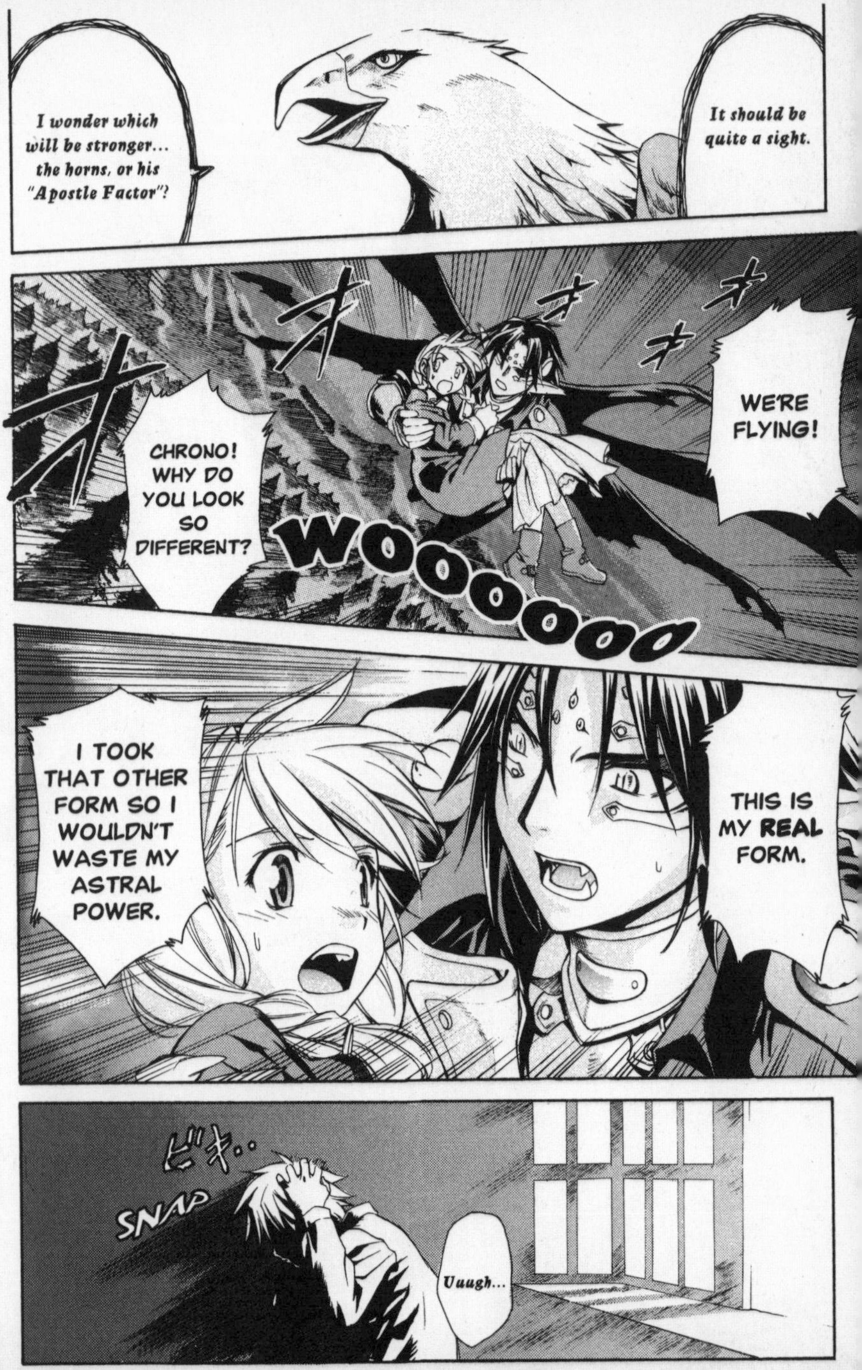
I wonder which will be stronger... the horns, or his "Apostle Factor"?
It should be quite a sight.
WE'RE FLYING!
CHRONO! WHY DO YOU LOOK SO DIFFERENT?
WOOOOOOO
THIS IS MY REAL FORM.
I TOOK THAT OTHER FORM SO I WOULDN'T WASTE MY ASTRAL POWER.
ビキ..
SNAP
Uuugh...

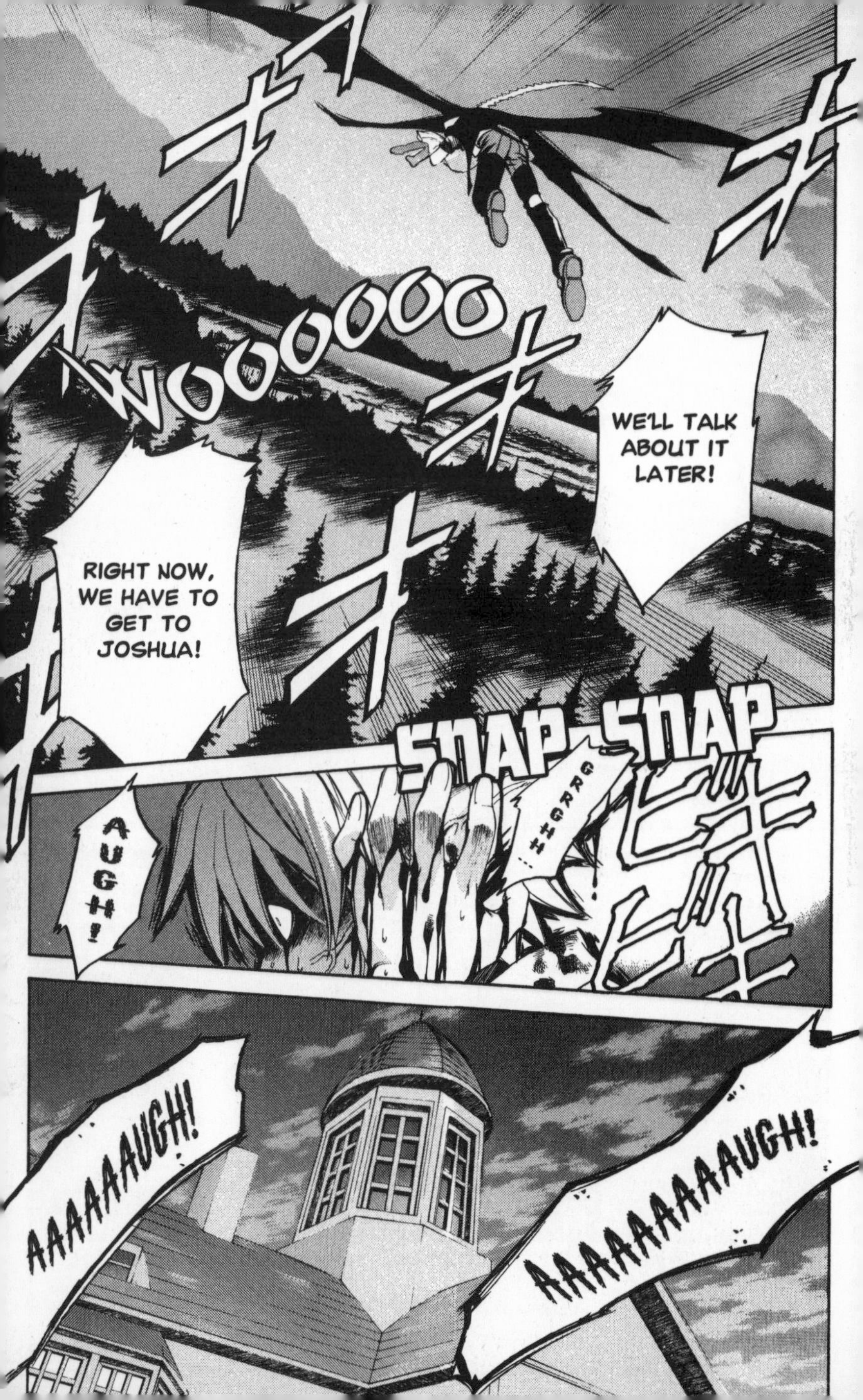
WOOOOOOO
WE'LL TALK ABOUT IT LATER!
RIGHT NOW, WE HAVE TO GET TO JOSHUA!
SNAP SNAP
GRRGHH!!
AUGH!
AAAAAAAAAUGH!
AAAAAAUGH!

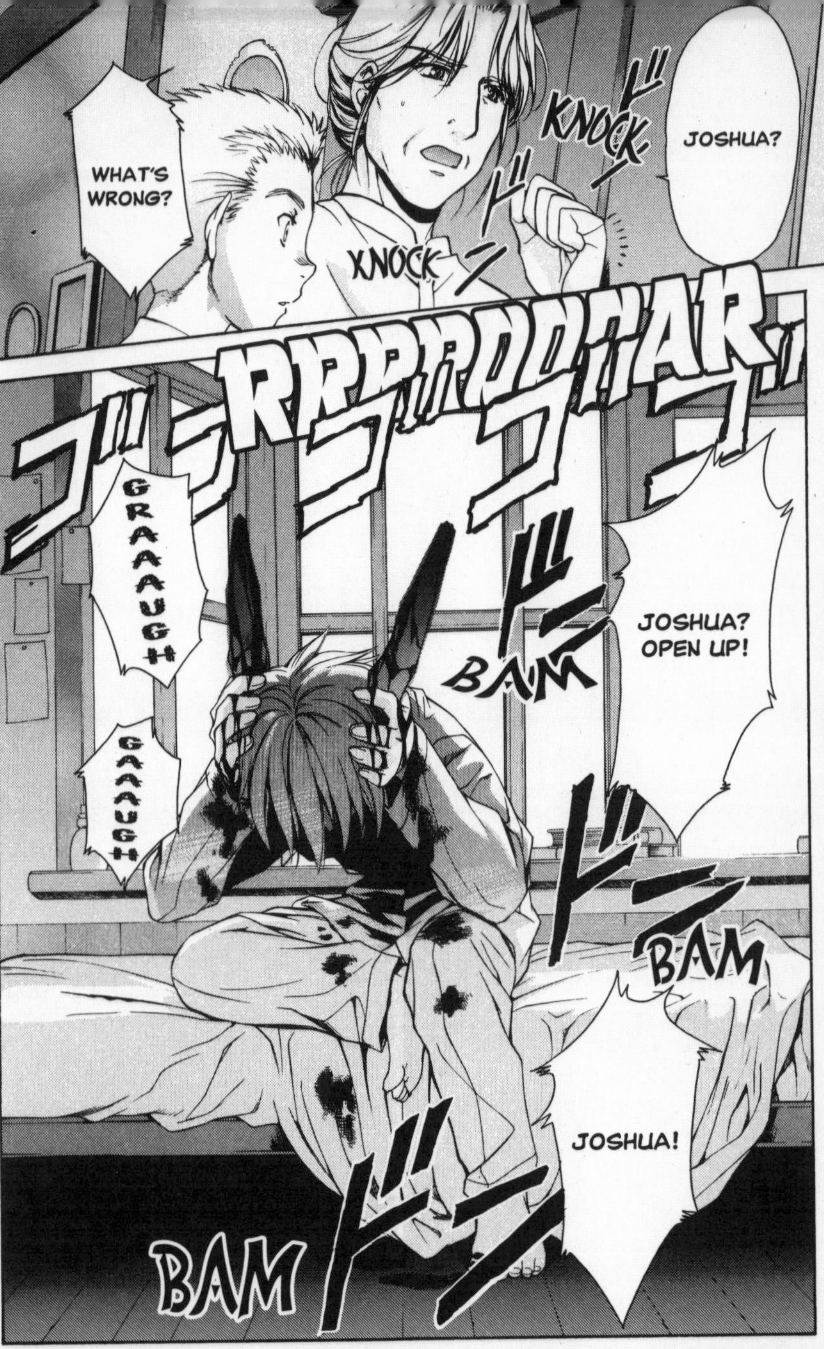
JOSHUA?
KNOCK
KNOCK
WHAT'S WRONG?
RRRROOOAR
JOSHUA? OPEN UP!
BAM
GRAAAAUGH
GAAAAUGH
BAM
JOSHUA!
BAM

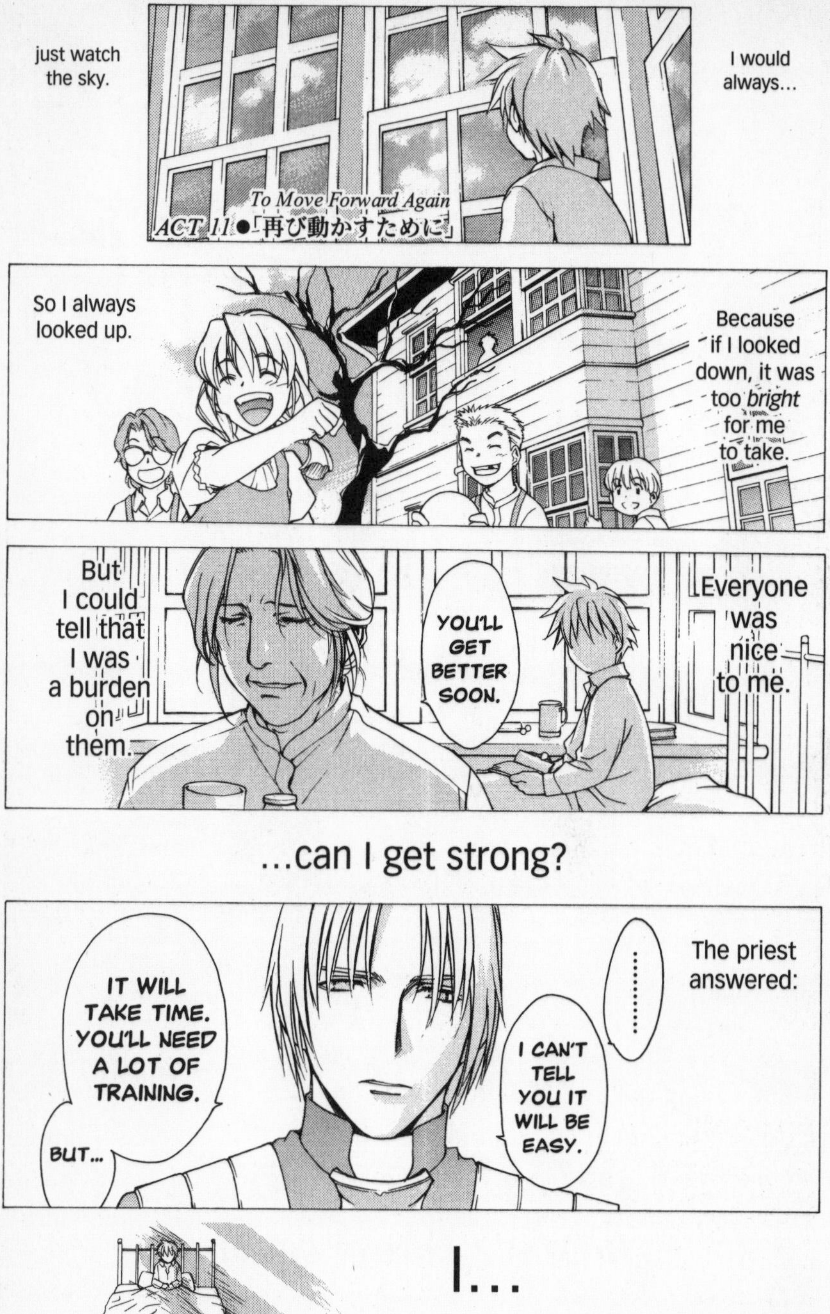
I would always...
just watch the sky.
To Move Forward Again
ACT 11●「再び動かすために」
Because if I looked down, it was too *bright* for me to take.
So I always looked up.
Everyone was nice to me.
YOU'LL GET BETTER SOON.
But I could tell that I was a burden on them.
...can I get strong?
The priest answered:
......
I CAN'T TELL YOU IT WILL BE EASY.
IT WILL TAKE TIME. YOU'LL NEED A LOT OF TRAINING.
BUT...
I...

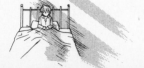

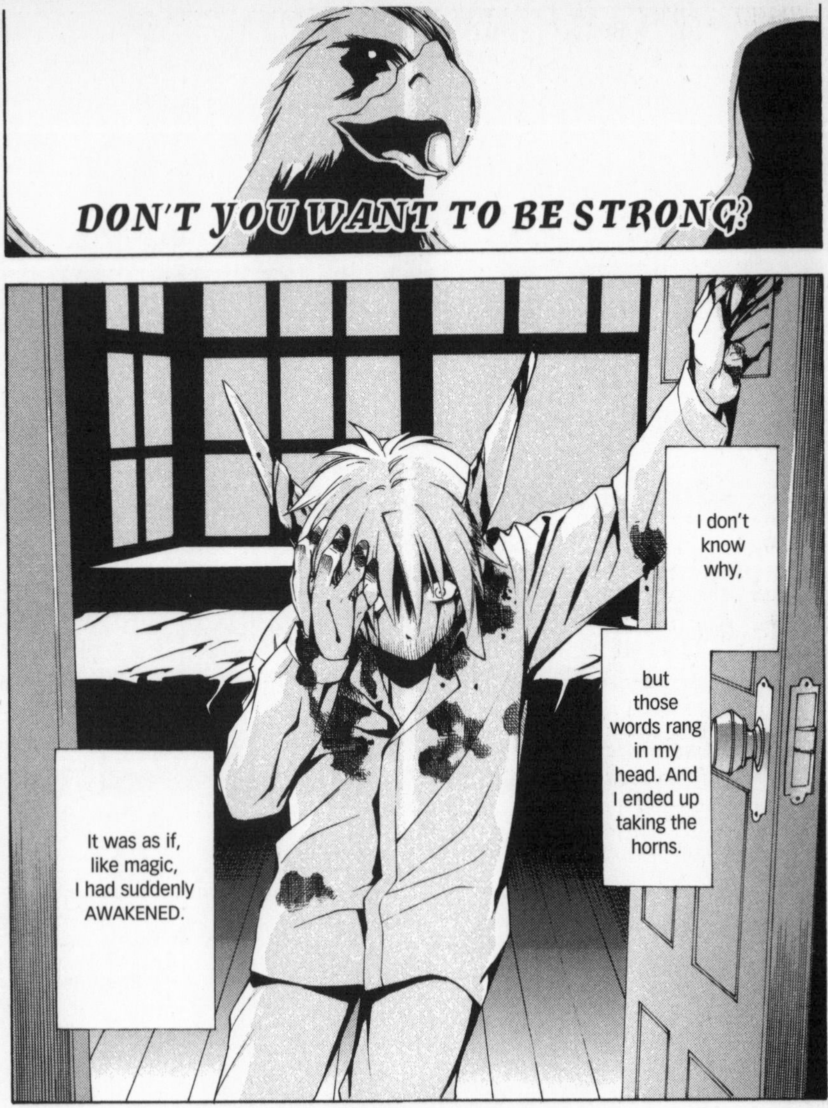
DON'T YOU WANT TO BE STRONG?
I don't know why,
but those words rang in my head. And I ended up taking the horns.
It was as if, like magic, I had suddenly AWAKENED.

ACT 11

「再び動かすために」

To Move Forward Again

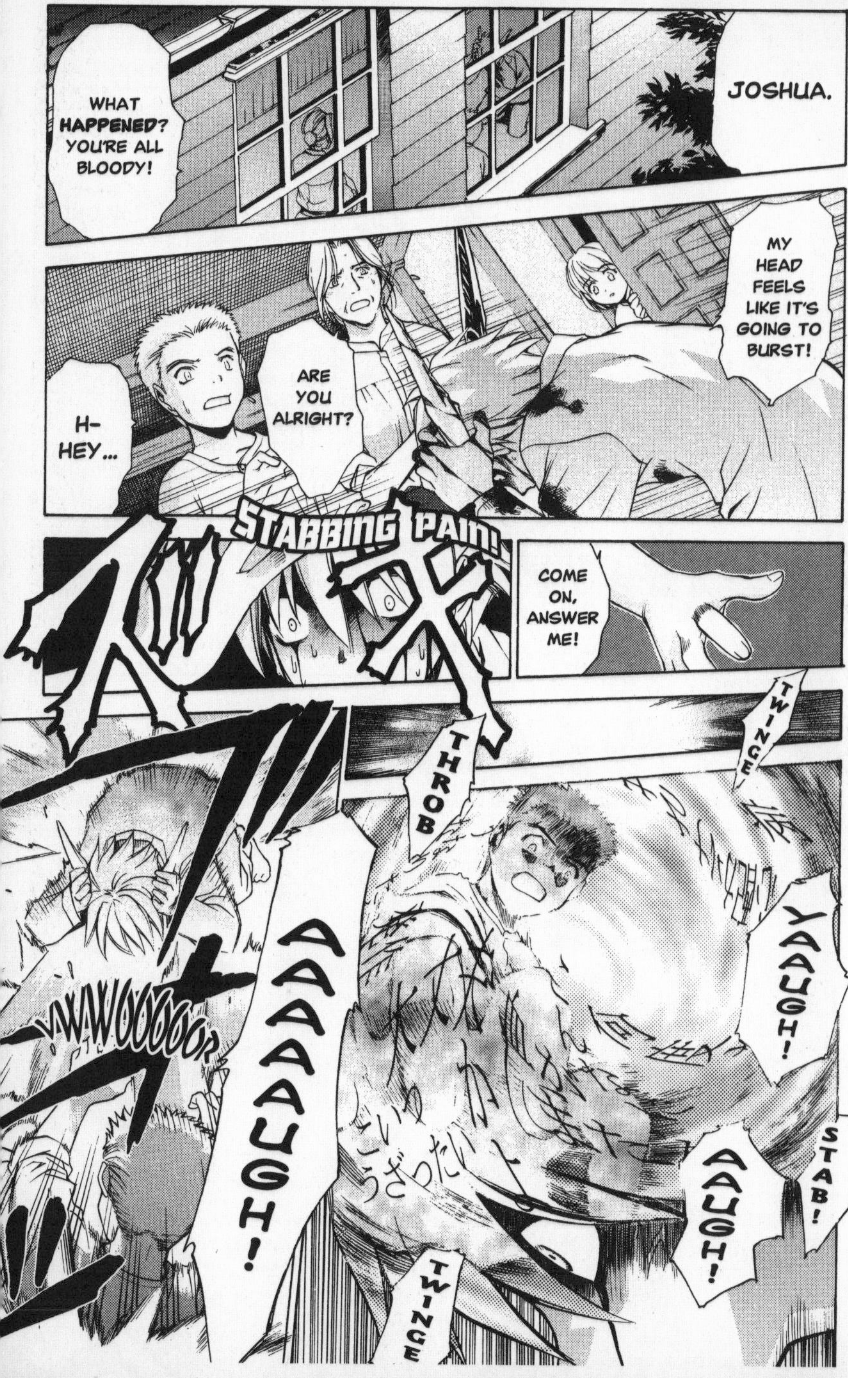
JOSHUA.
WHAT HAPPENED? YOU'RE ALL BLOODY!
MY HEAD FEELS LIKE IT'S GOING TO BURST!
ARE YOU ALRIGHT?
H- HEY...
COME ON, ANSWER ME!
STABBING PAIN!
TWINGE
THROB
YAAAUGH!
STAB!
AAUGH!
TWINGE
AAAAAAUGH!
WWOOOOOR

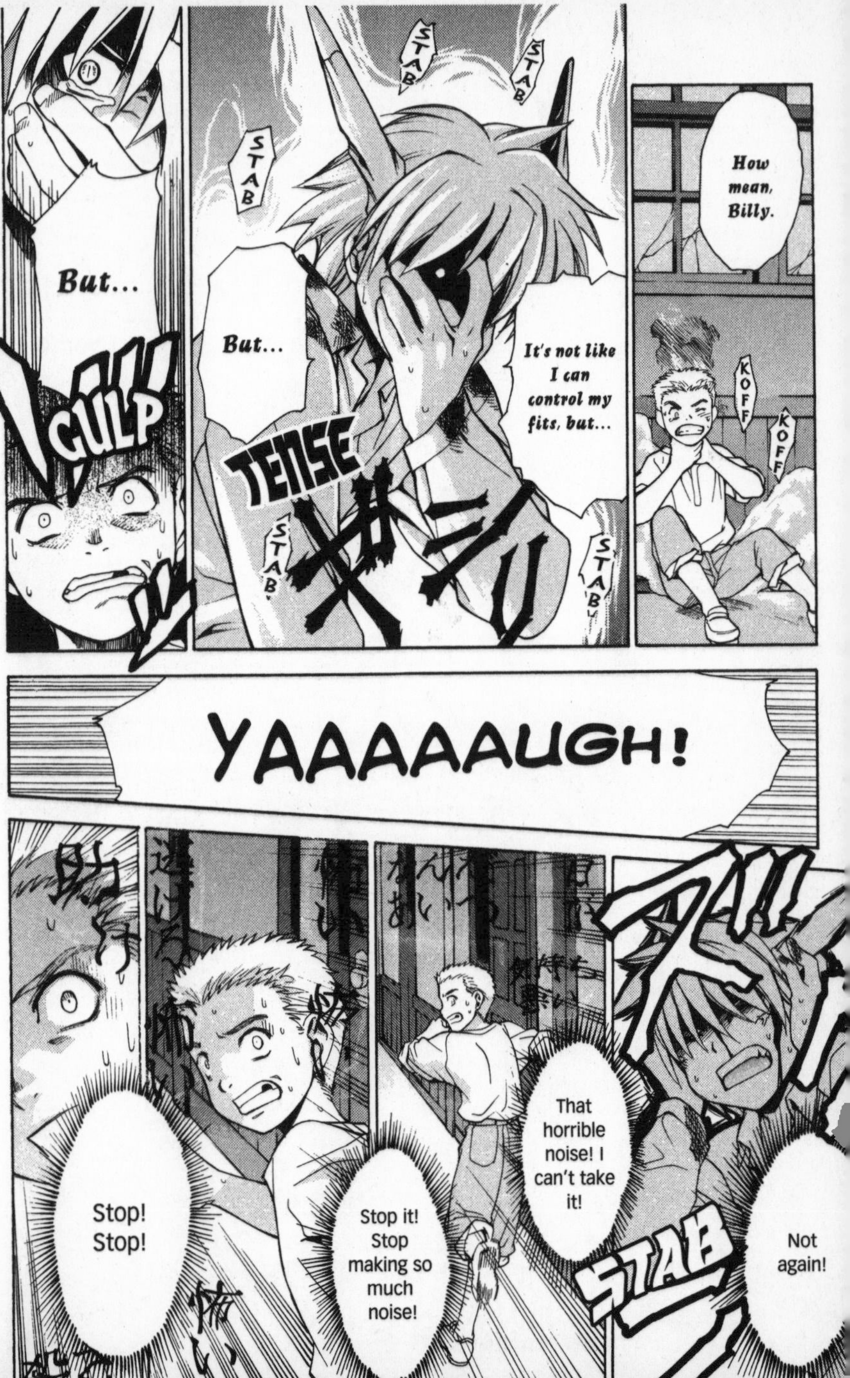

But...
GULP
STAB
STAB
STAB
But...
It's not like I can control my fits, but...
TENSE
STAB
STAB
How mean, Billy.
KOFF
KOFF
YAAAAAUGH!
Stop! Stop!
Stop it! Stop making so much noise!
That horrible noise! I can't take it!
STAB
Not again!

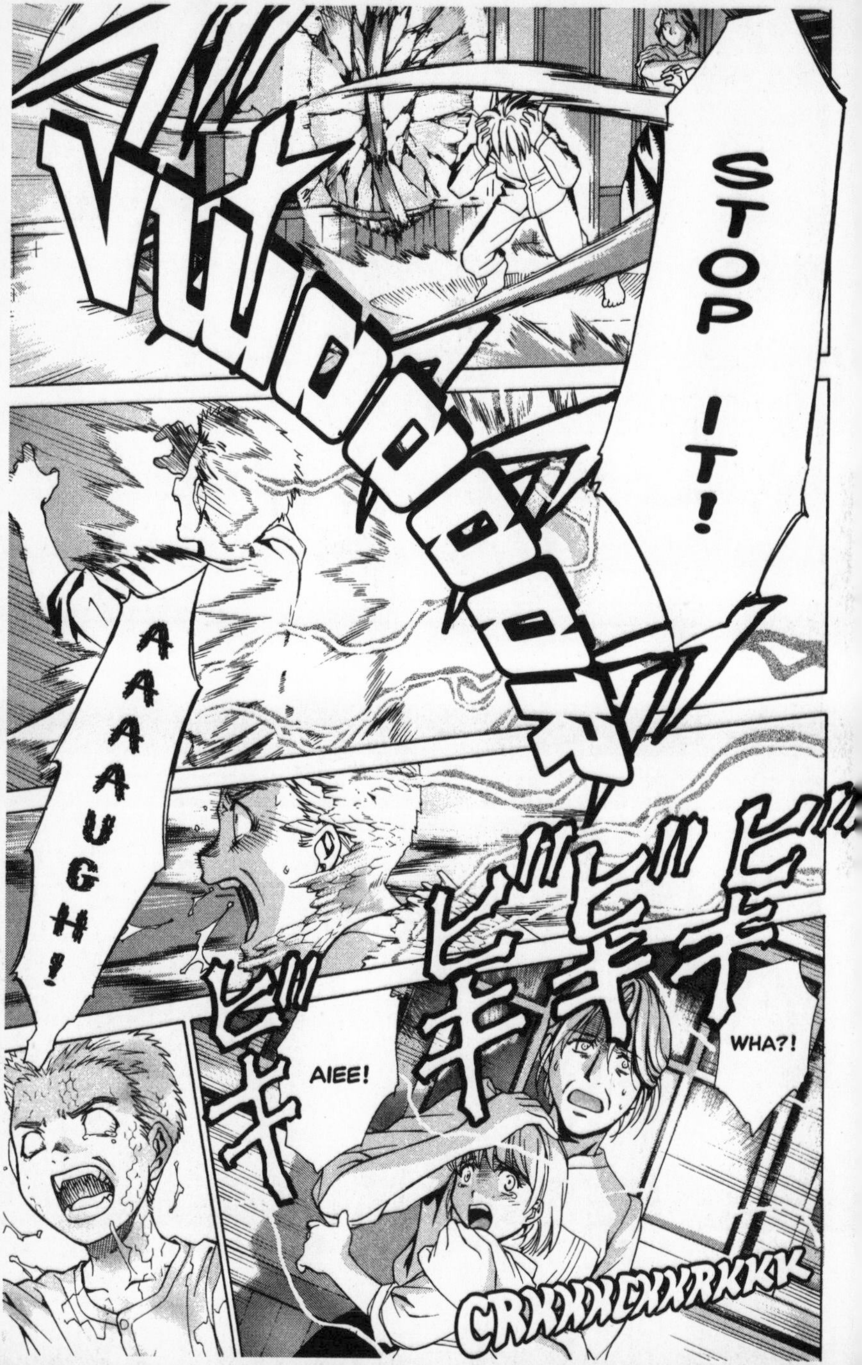
VUDOOOOR
STOP IT!
AAAAAUGH!
ビキビキビキ
WHA?!
AIEE!
CRAKKKCKKRKKK

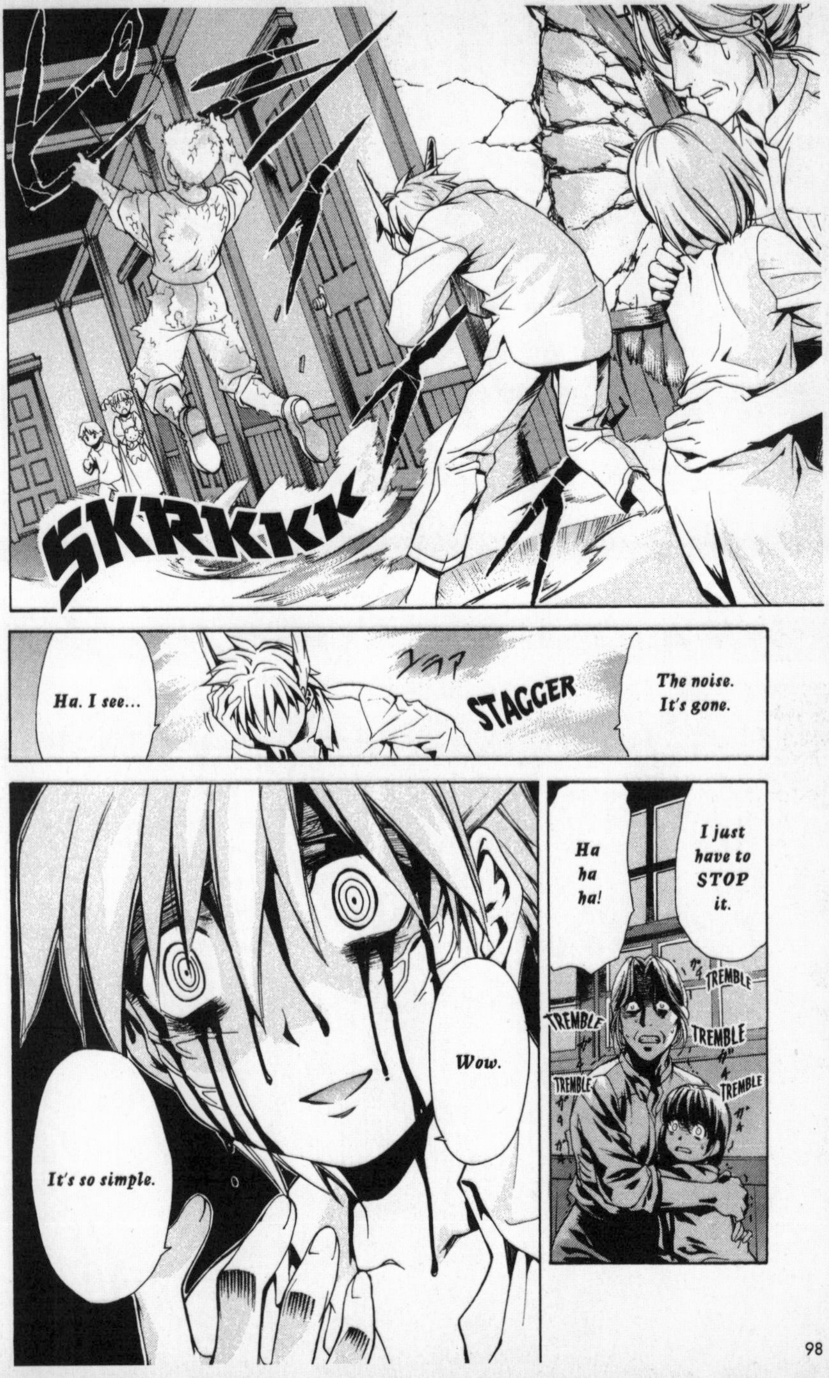
SKRKKK
The noise. It's gone.
STAGGER
Ha. I see...
I just have to STOP it.
Ha ha ha!
TREMBLE
TREMBLE
TREMBLE
TREMBLE
TREMBLE
Wow.
It's so simple.

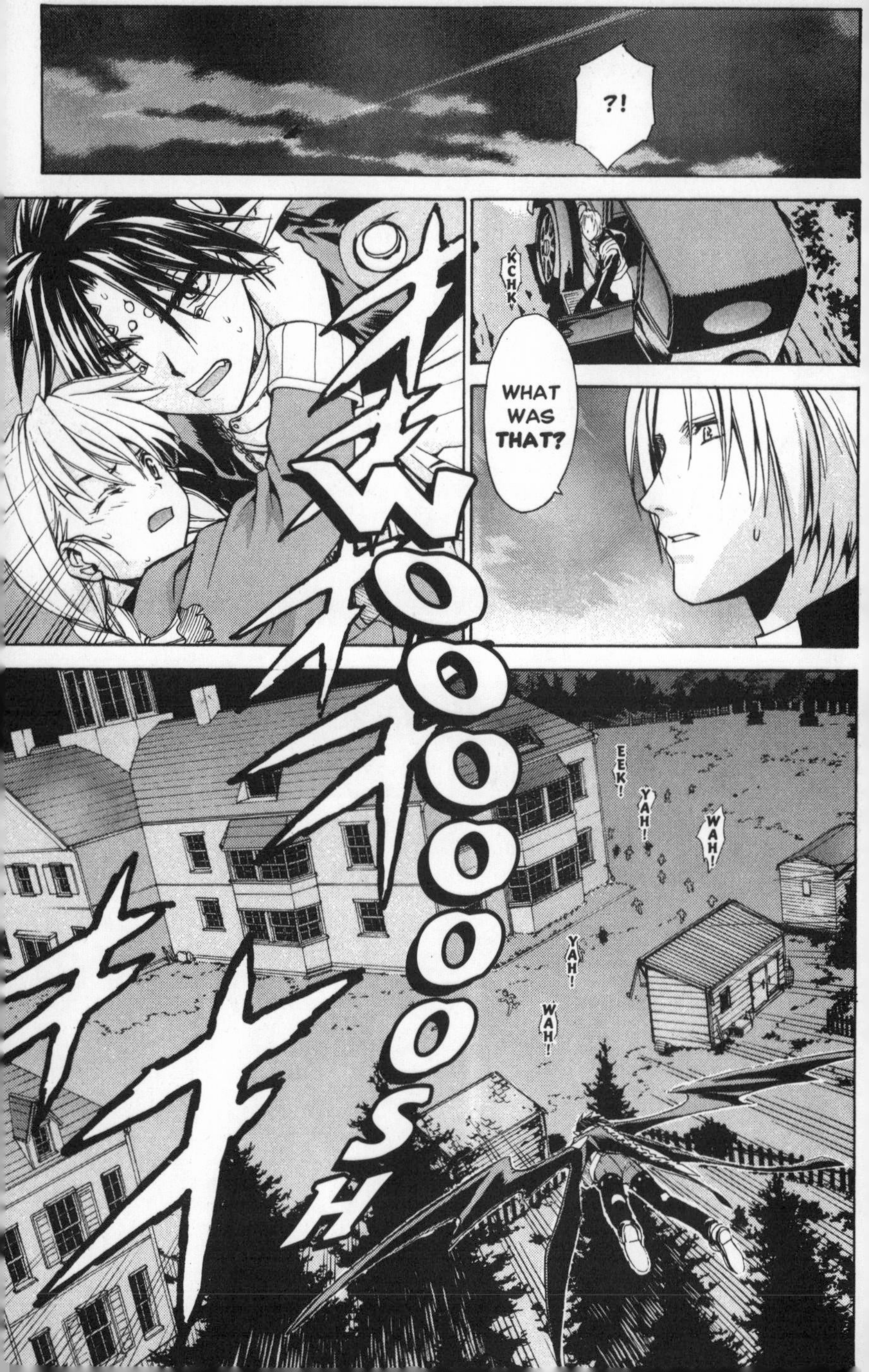
?!
KCHK
WHAT WAS THAT?
WOOOOOOOOSH
EEK!
YAH!
WAH!
YAH!
WAH!

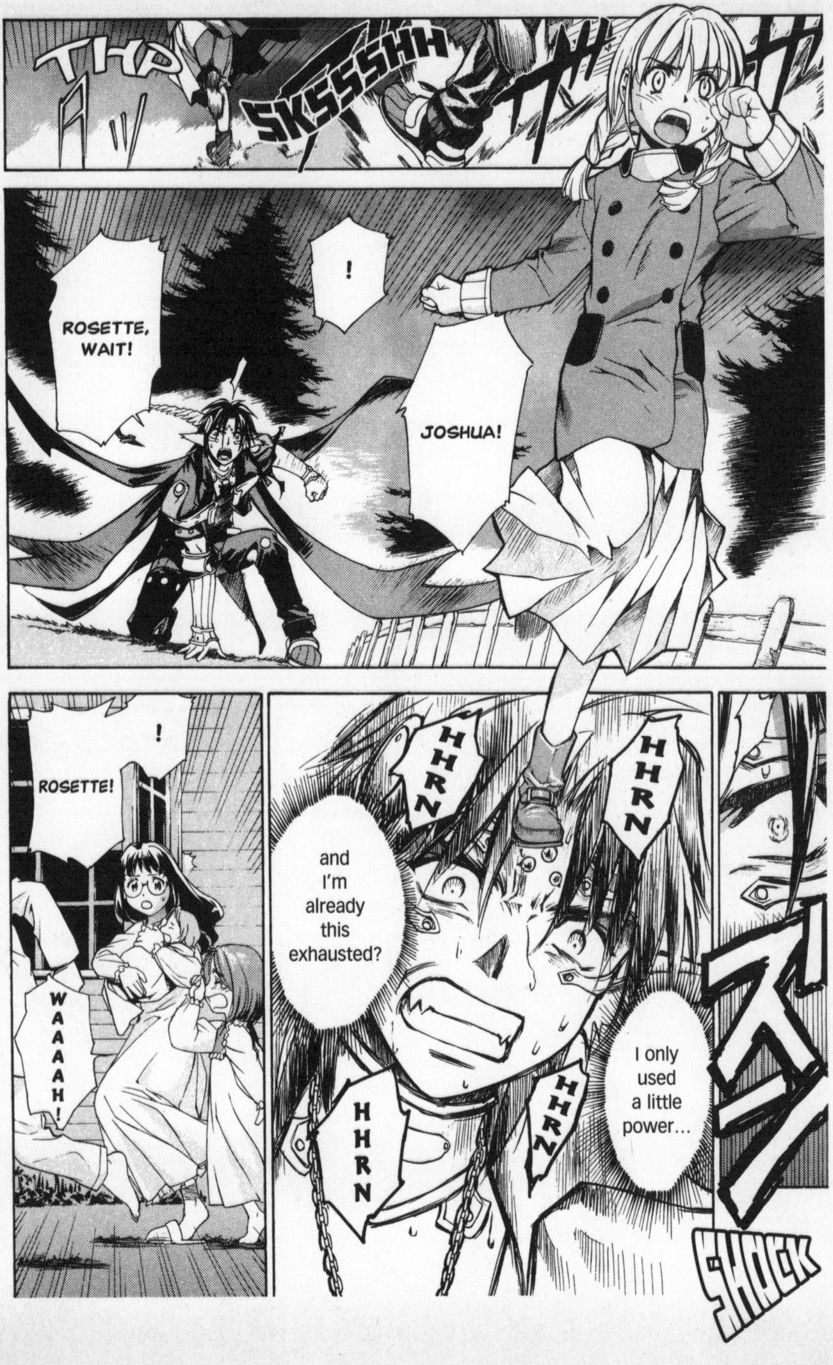
SKSSSHH
THP
JOSHUA!
!
ROSETTE, WAIT!
SHOCK
HHRN
HHRN
I only used a little power…
and I'm already this exhausted?
HHRN
HHRN
!
ROSETTE!
WAAAAAH!

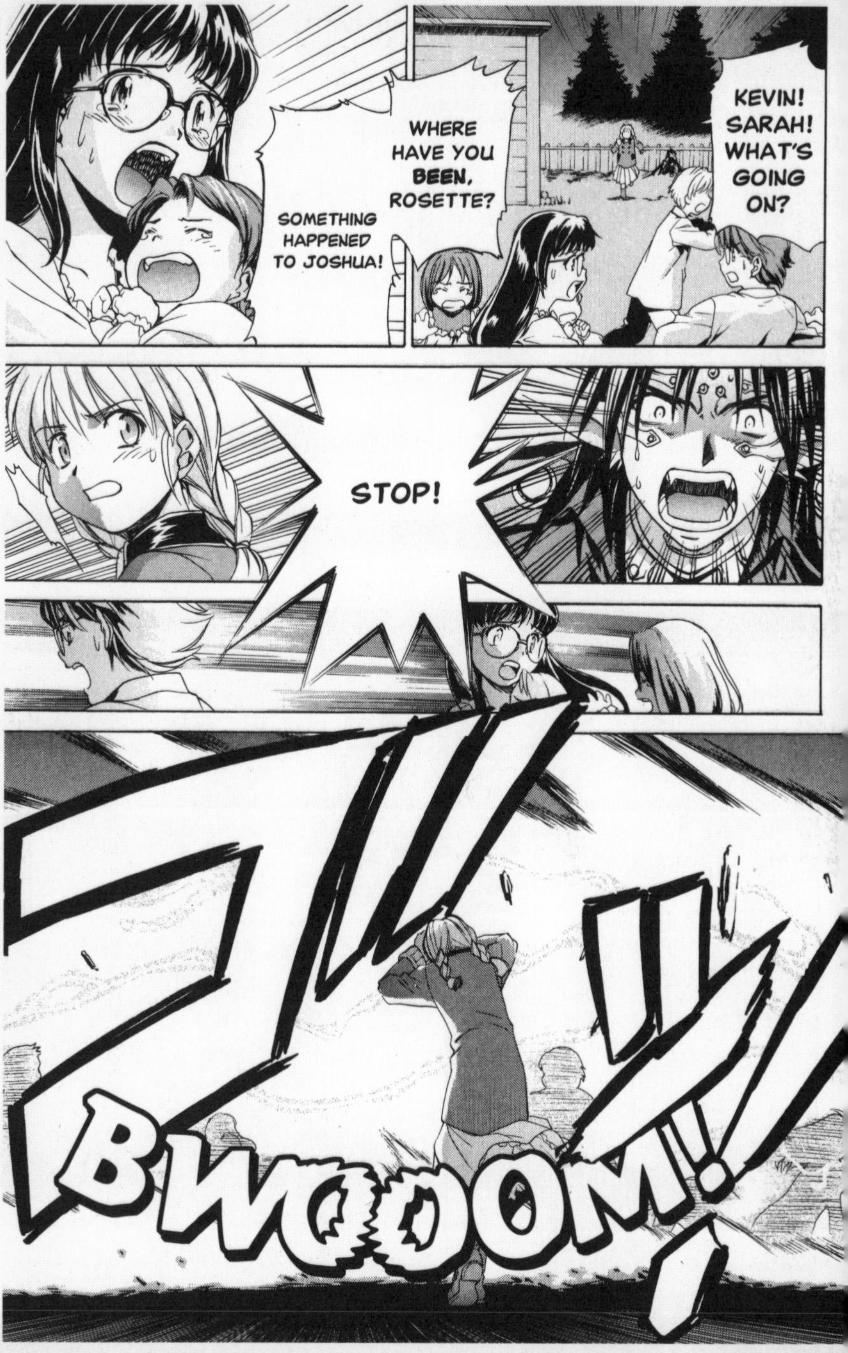
KEVIN! SARAH! WHAT'S GOING ON?
WHERE HAVE YOU BEEN, ROSETTE?
SOMETHING HAPPENED TO JOSHUA!
STOP!
BWOOOM!!

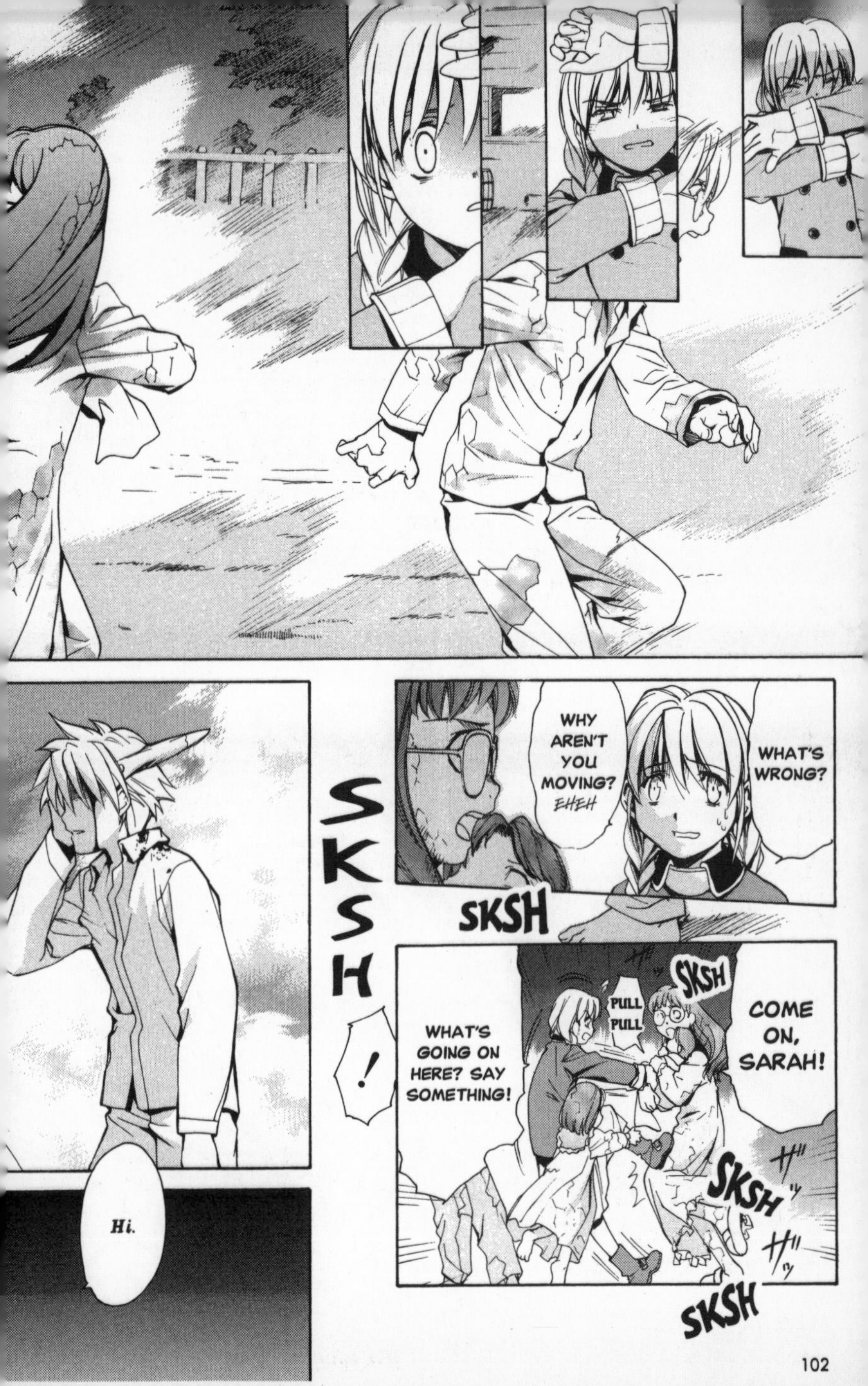
WHAT'S WRONG?
WHY AREN'T YOU MOVING?
EHEH
SKSH
COME ON, SARAH!
SKSH
PULL PULL
WHAT'S GOING ON HERE? SAY SOMETHING!
SKSH
SKSH
SKSH
!
Hi.

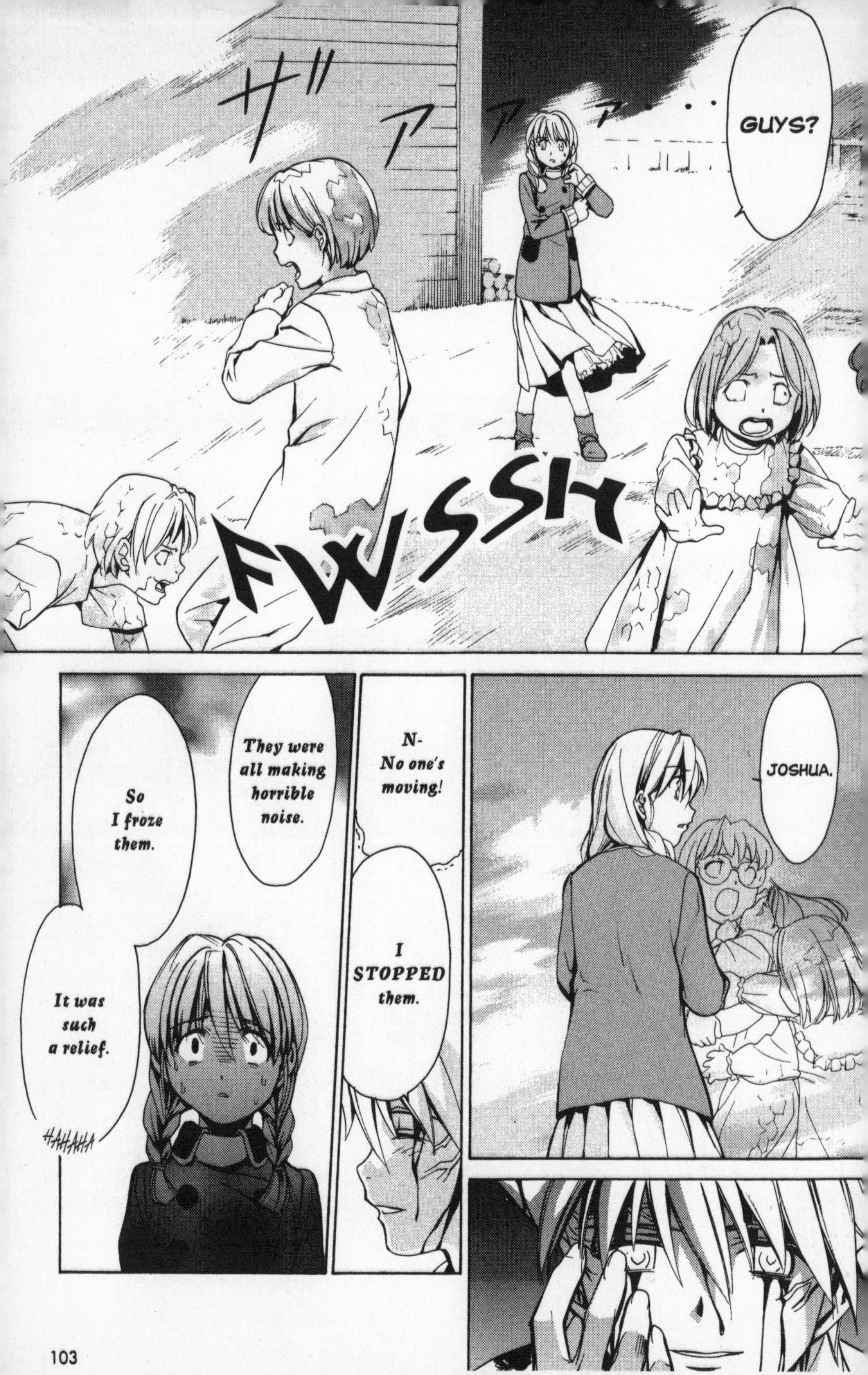
GUYS?
ザアアア・・
FWSSH
JOSHUA.
N-
No one's moving!
I STOPPED them.
They were all making horrible noise.
So I froze them.
It was such a relief.
HAHAHA

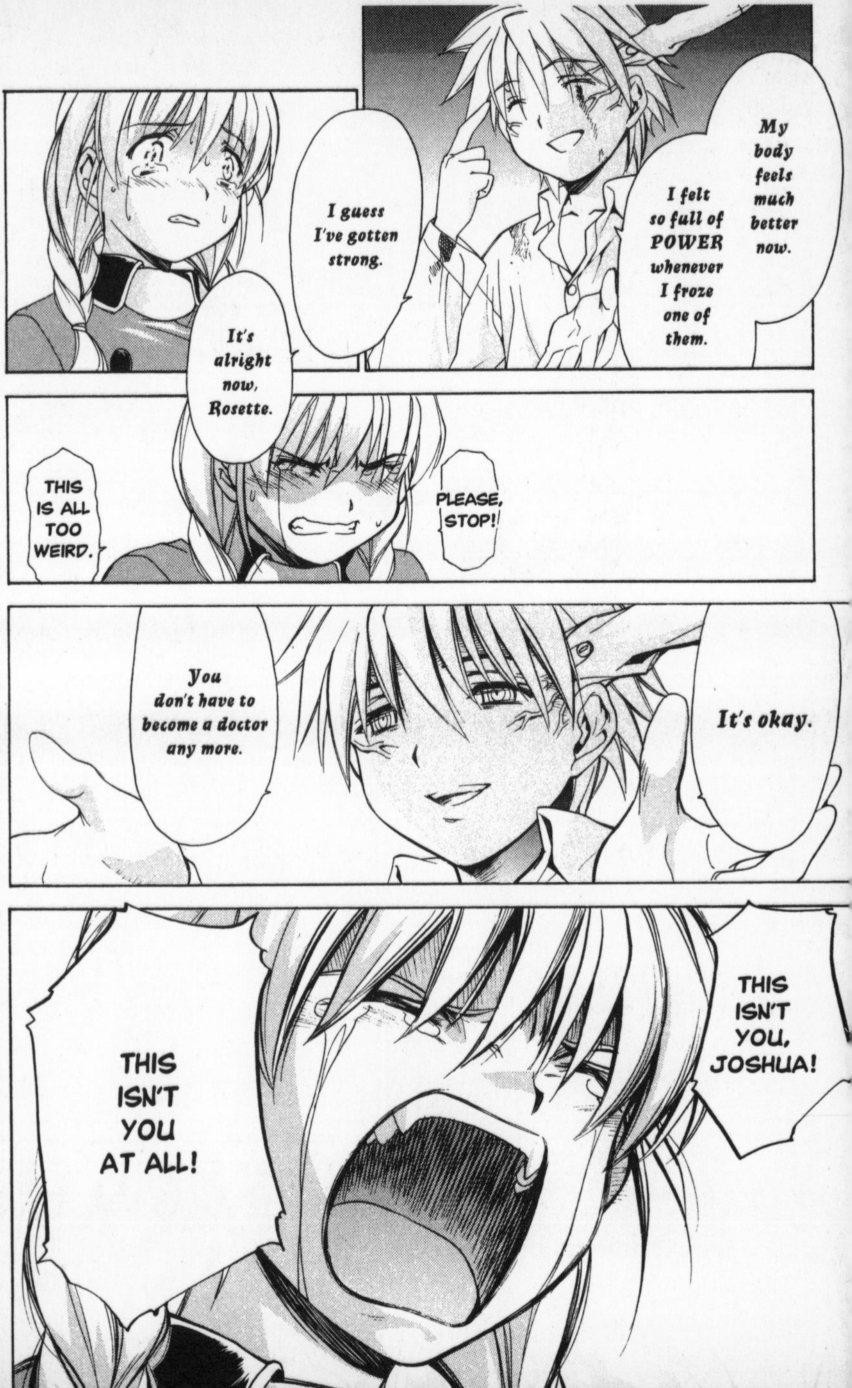
My body feels much better now.
I felt so full of POWER whenever I froze one of them.
I guess I've gotten strong.
It's alright now, Rosette.
PLEASE, STOP!
THIS IS ALL TOO WEIRD.
It's okay.
You don't have to become a doctor any more.
THIS ISN'T YOU, JOSHUA!
THIS ISN'T YOU AT ALL!

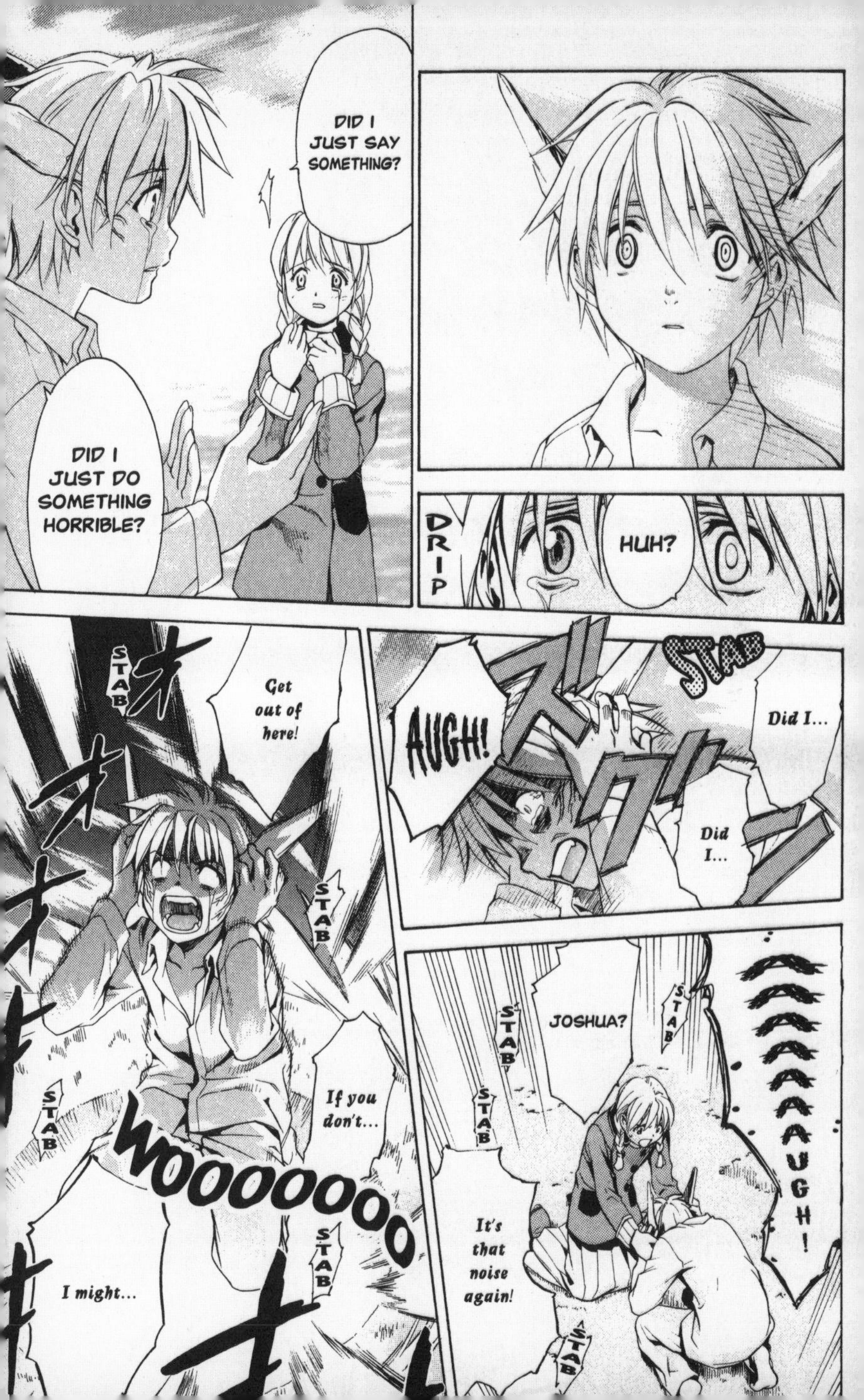

DRIP
HUH?
DID I JUST SAY SOMETHING?
DID I JUST DO SOMETHING HORRIBLE?
STAB
AUGH!
Did I...
Did I...
JOSHUA?
STAB
STAB
STAB
STAB
AAAAAAAAAUGH!
It's that noise again!
STAB
Get out of here!
STAB
STAB
If you don't...
STAB
WOOOOOOOO
STAB
I might...

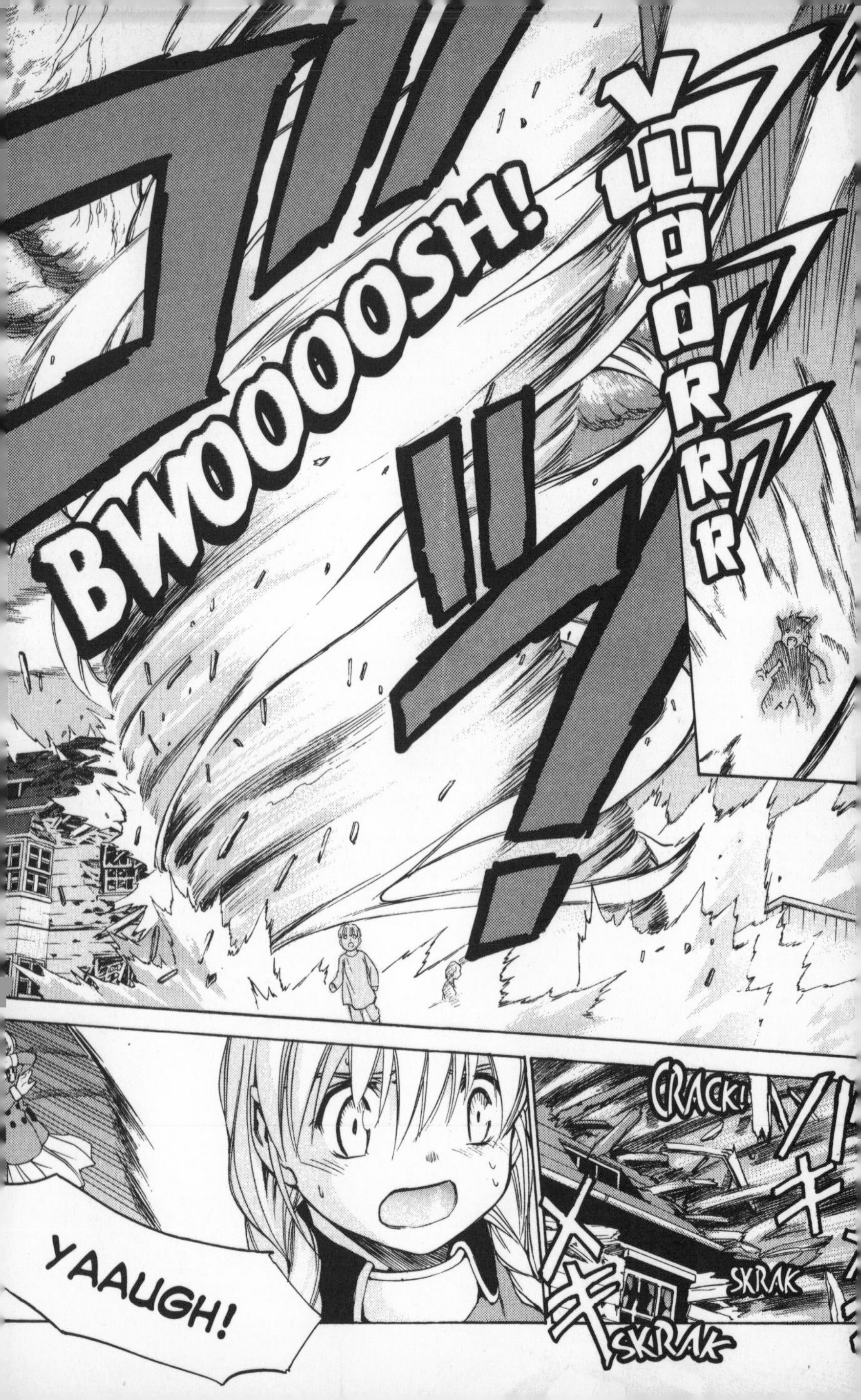

BWOOOOSH!!
WHOOORRR
CRACK!
YAAUGH!
SKRAK
SKRAK

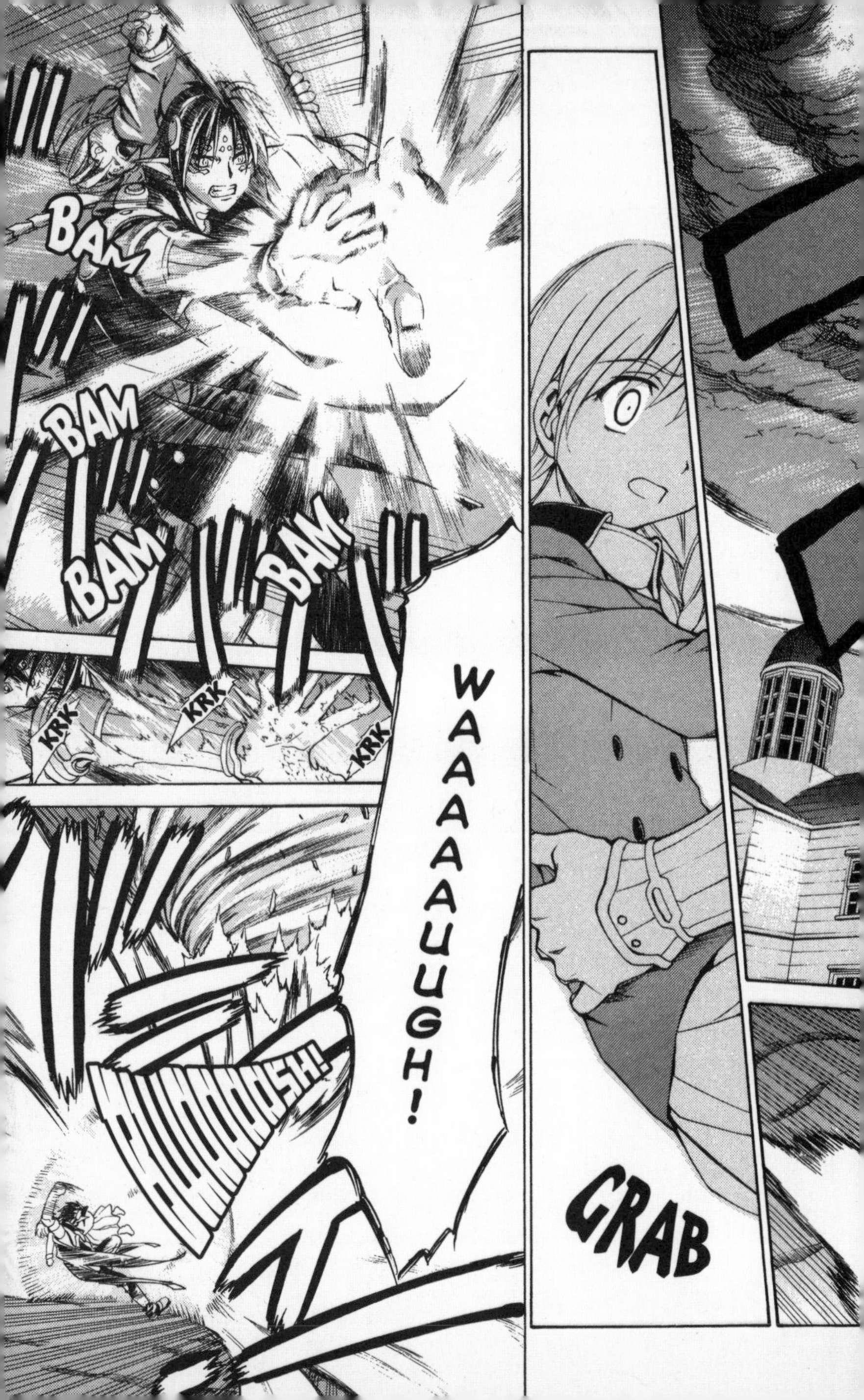
GRAB
BAM
BAM
BAM
BAM
KRK
KRK
KRK
WAAAAAUUGH!
FWOOOOSH!

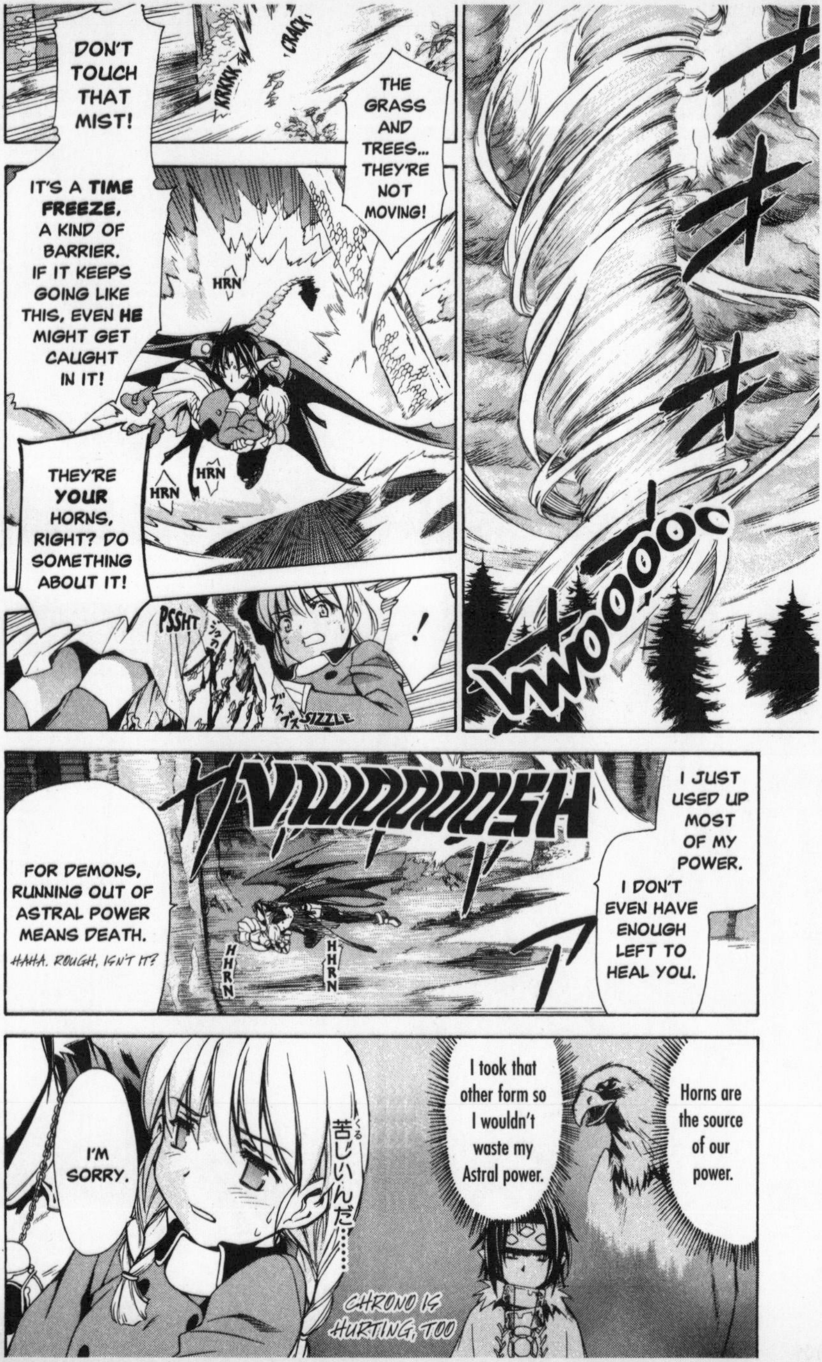

VWOOOOO
KRKKK
CRACK
DON'T TOUCH THAT MIST!
THE GRASS AND TREES... THEY'RE NOT MOVING!
IT'S A **TIME FREEZE**, A KIND OF BARRIER. IF IT KEEPS GOING LIKE THIS, EVEN **HE** MIGHT GET CAUGHT IN IT!
HRN
HRN
HRN
THEY'RE **YOUR** HORNS, RIGHT? DO SOMETHING ABOUT IT!
!
PSSHT
SIZZLE
VWOOOOOSH
I JUST USED UP MOST OF MY POWER.
I DON'T EVEN HAVE ENOUGH LEFT TO HEAL YOU.
FOR DEMONS, RUNNING OUT OF ASTRAL POWER MEANS DEATH.
HAHA. ROUGH, ISN'T IT?
HHRN
HHRN
Horns are the source of our power.
I took that other form so I wouldn't waste my Astral power.
苦しいんだ……
I'M SORRY.
CHRONO IS HURTING, TOO

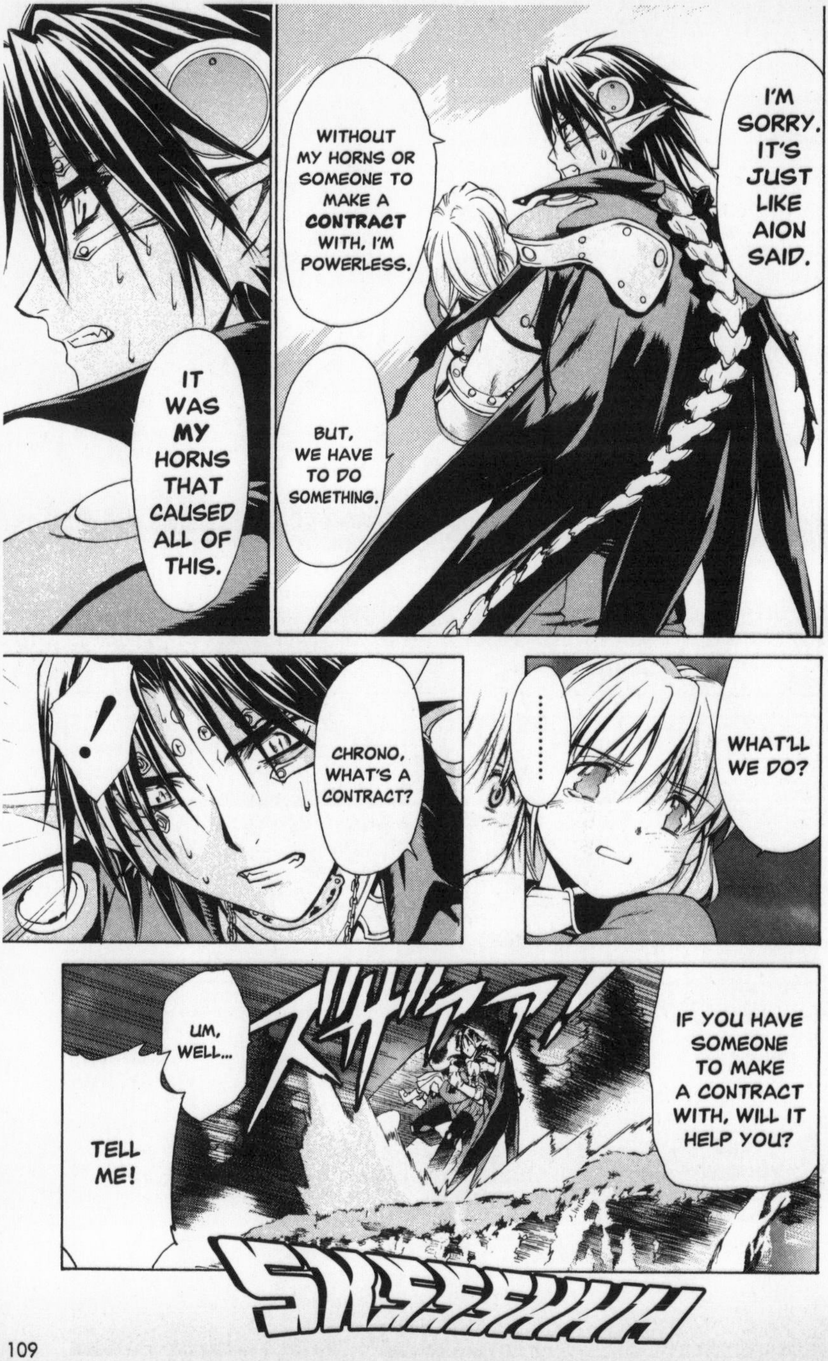
I'M SORRY. IT'S JUST LIKE AION SAID.
WITHOUT MY HORNS OR SOMEONE TO MAKE A **CONTRACT** WITH, I'M POWERLESS.
BUT, WE HAVE TO DO SOMETHING.
IT WAS **MY** HORNS THAT CAUSED ALL OF THIS.
WHAT'LL WE DO?
......
CHRONO, WHAT'S A CONTRACT?
!
IF YOU HAVE SOMEONE TO MAKE A CONTRACT WITH, WILL IT HELP YOU?
UM, WELL...
TELL ME!

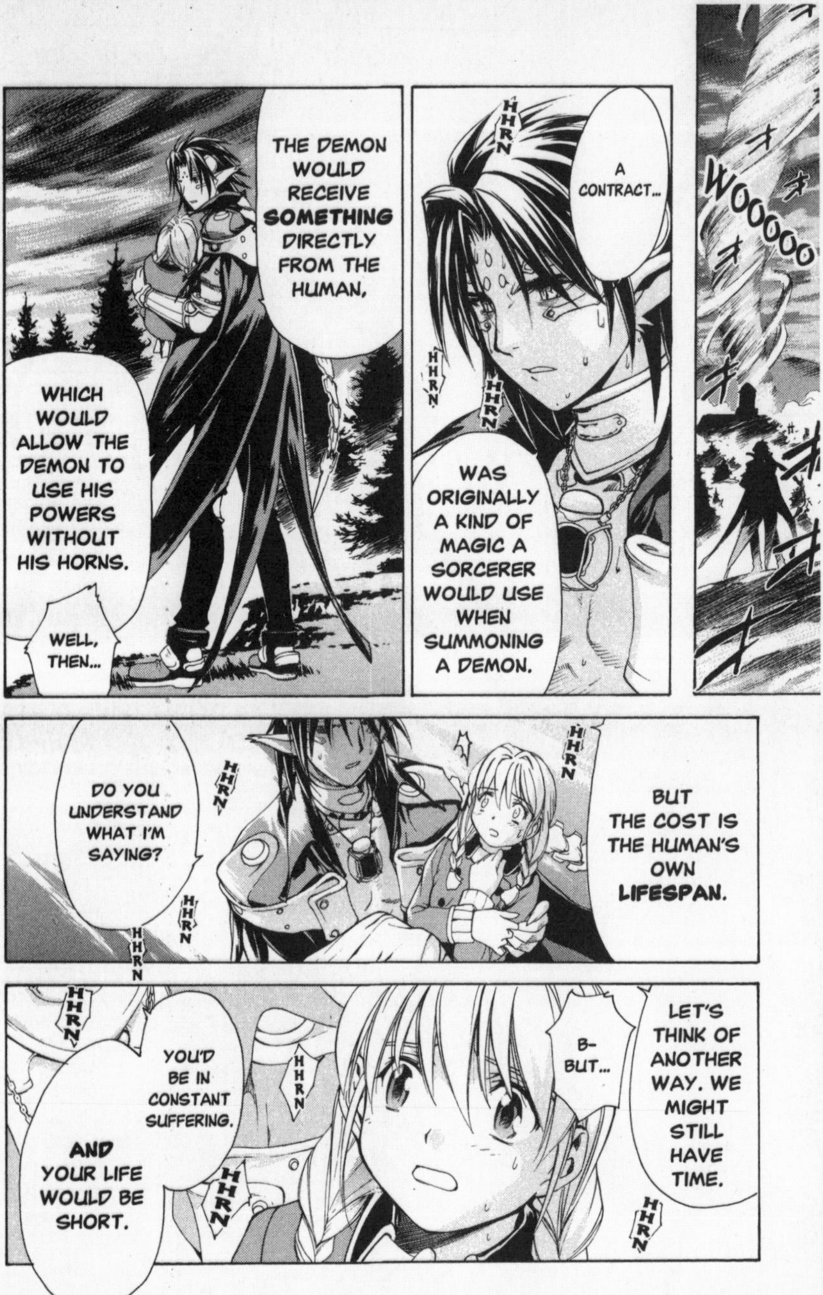
WOOOOOO
HHRN
A CONTRACT...
WAS ORIGINALLY A KIND OF MAGIC A SORCERER WOULD USE WHEN SUMMONING A DEMON.
HHRN
HHRN
THE DEMON WOULD RECEIVE SOMETHING DIRECTLY FROM THE HUMAN,
WHICH WOULD ALLOW THE DEMON TO USE HIS POWERS WITHOUT HIS HORNS.
WELL, THEN...
HHRN
BUT THE COST IS THE HUMAN'S OWN LIFESPAN.
HHRN
DO YOU UNDERSTAND WHAT I'M SAYING?
HHRN
HHRN
LET'S THINK OF ANOTHER WAY. WE MIGHT STILL HAVE TIME.
HHRN
B-BUT...
HHRN
YOU'D BE IN CONSTANT SUFFERING.
HHRN
AND YOUR LIFE WOULD BE SHORT.
HHRN

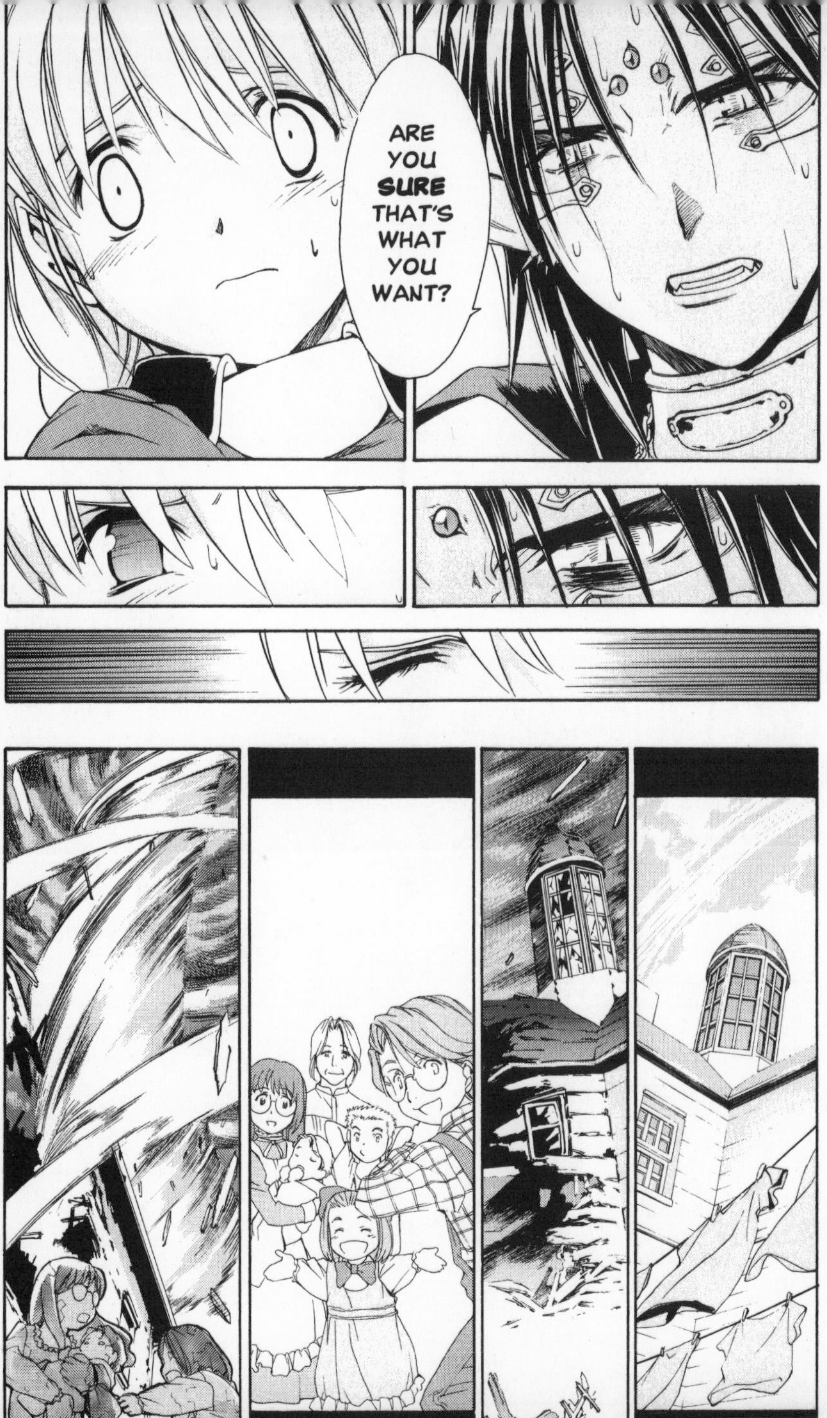
ARE YOU SURE THAT'S WHAT YOU WANT?

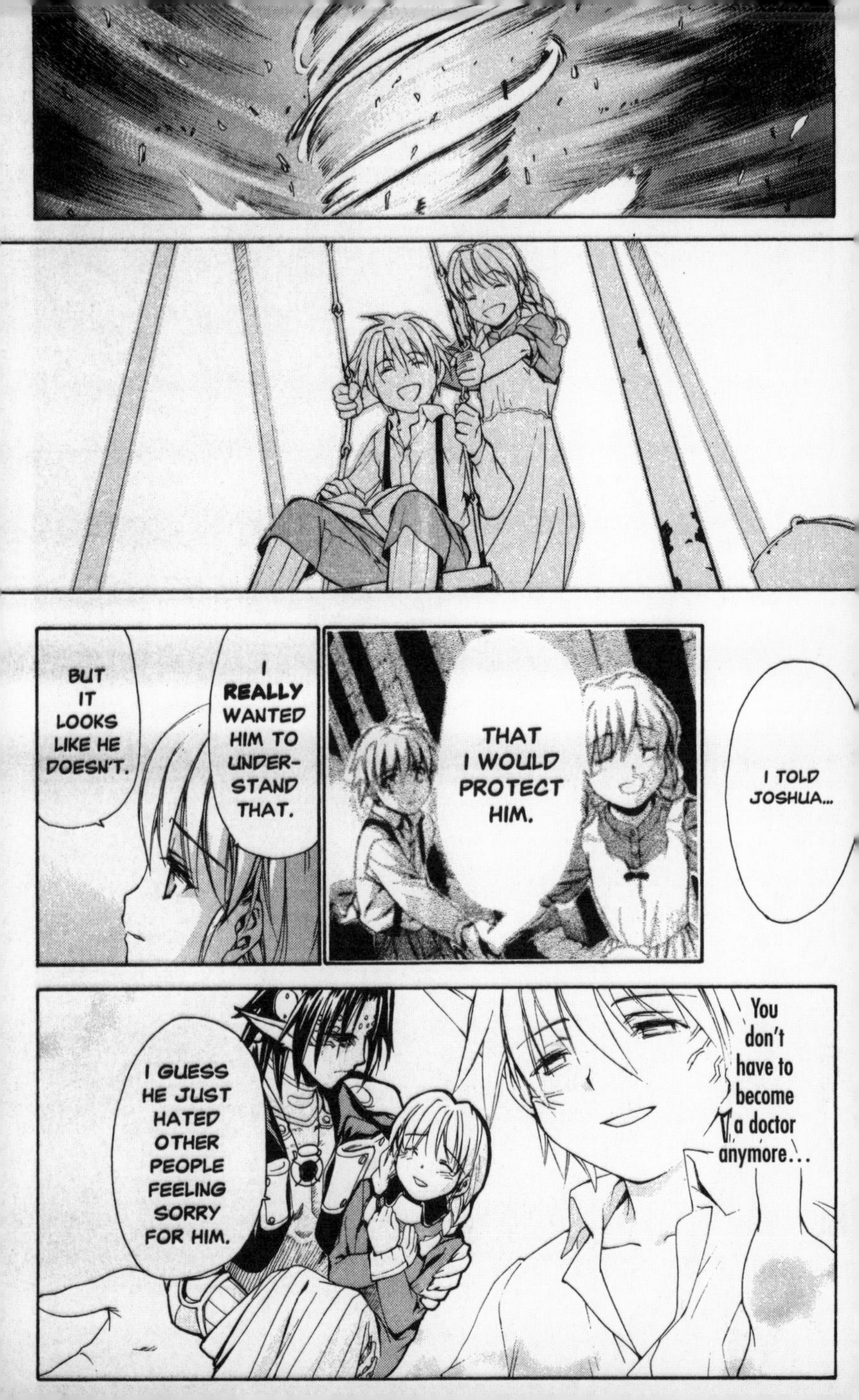
I TOLD JOSHUA...
THAT I WOULD PROTECT HIM.
I REALLY WANTED HIM TO UNDER-STAND THAT.
BUT IT LOOKS LIKE HE DOESN'T.
You don't have to become a doctor anymore...
I GUESS HE JUST HATED OTHER PEOPLE FEELING SORRY FOR HIM.

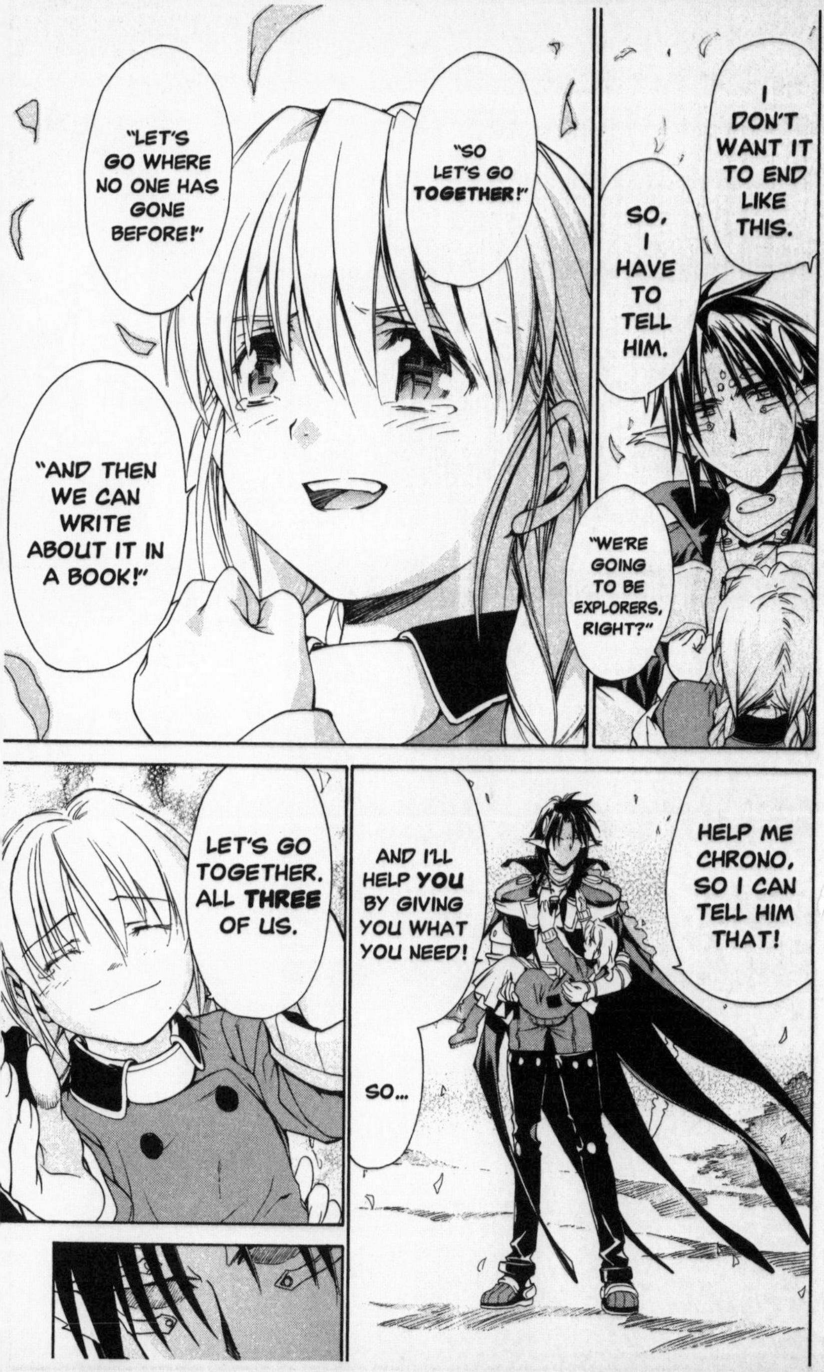
I DON'T WANT IT TO END LIKE THIS.
SO, I HAVE TO TELL HIM.
"WE'RE GOING TO BE EXPLORERS, RIGHT?"
"SO LET'S GO TOGETHER!"
"LET'S GO WHERE NO ONE HAS GONE BEFORE!"
"AND THEN WE CAN WRITE ABOUT IT IN A BOOK!"
HELP ME CHRONO, SO I CAN TELL HIM THAT!
AND I'LL HELP YOU BY GIVING YOU WHAT YOU NEED!
SO...
LET'S GO TOGETHER. ALL THREE OF US.

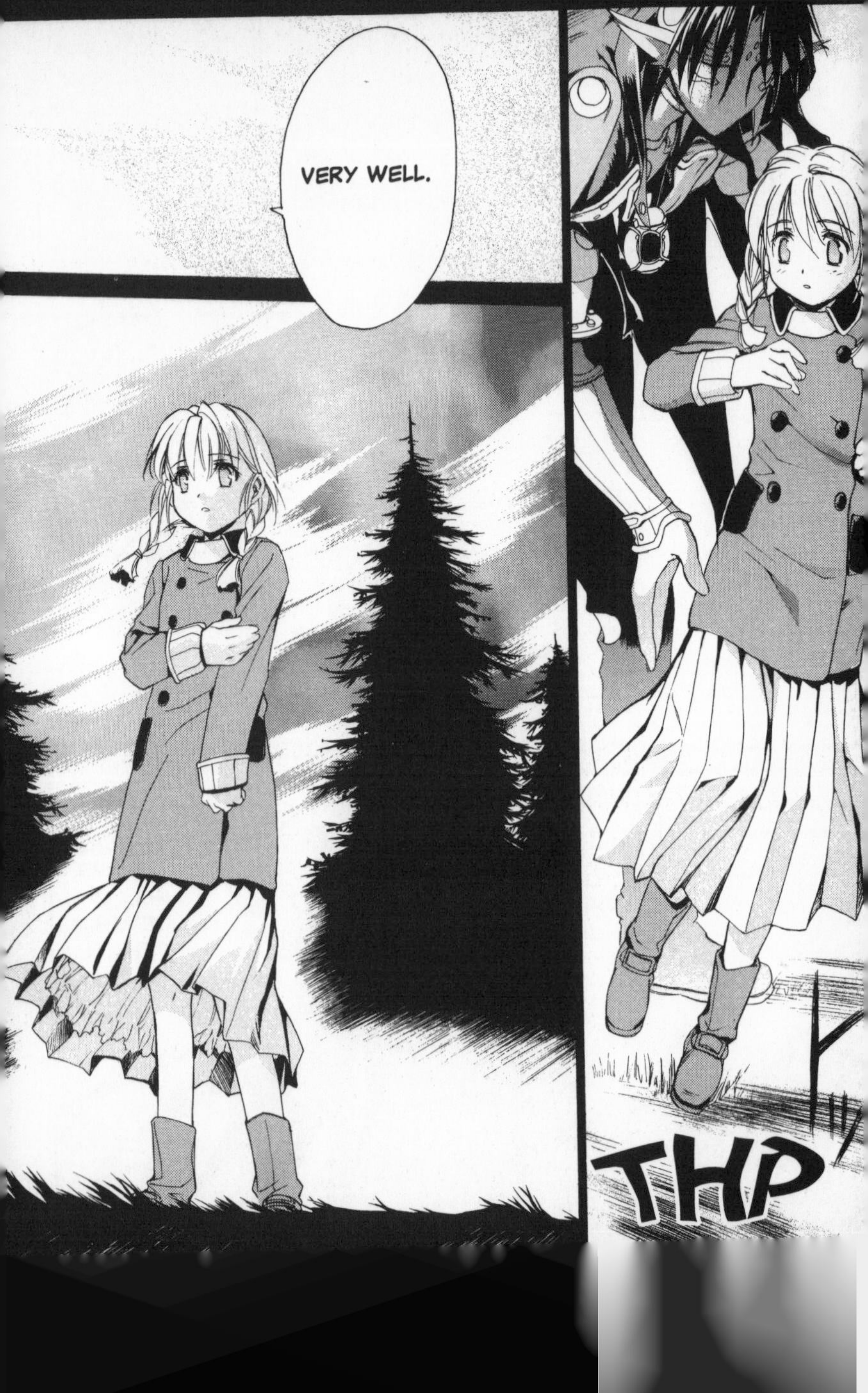
THP
VERY WELL.

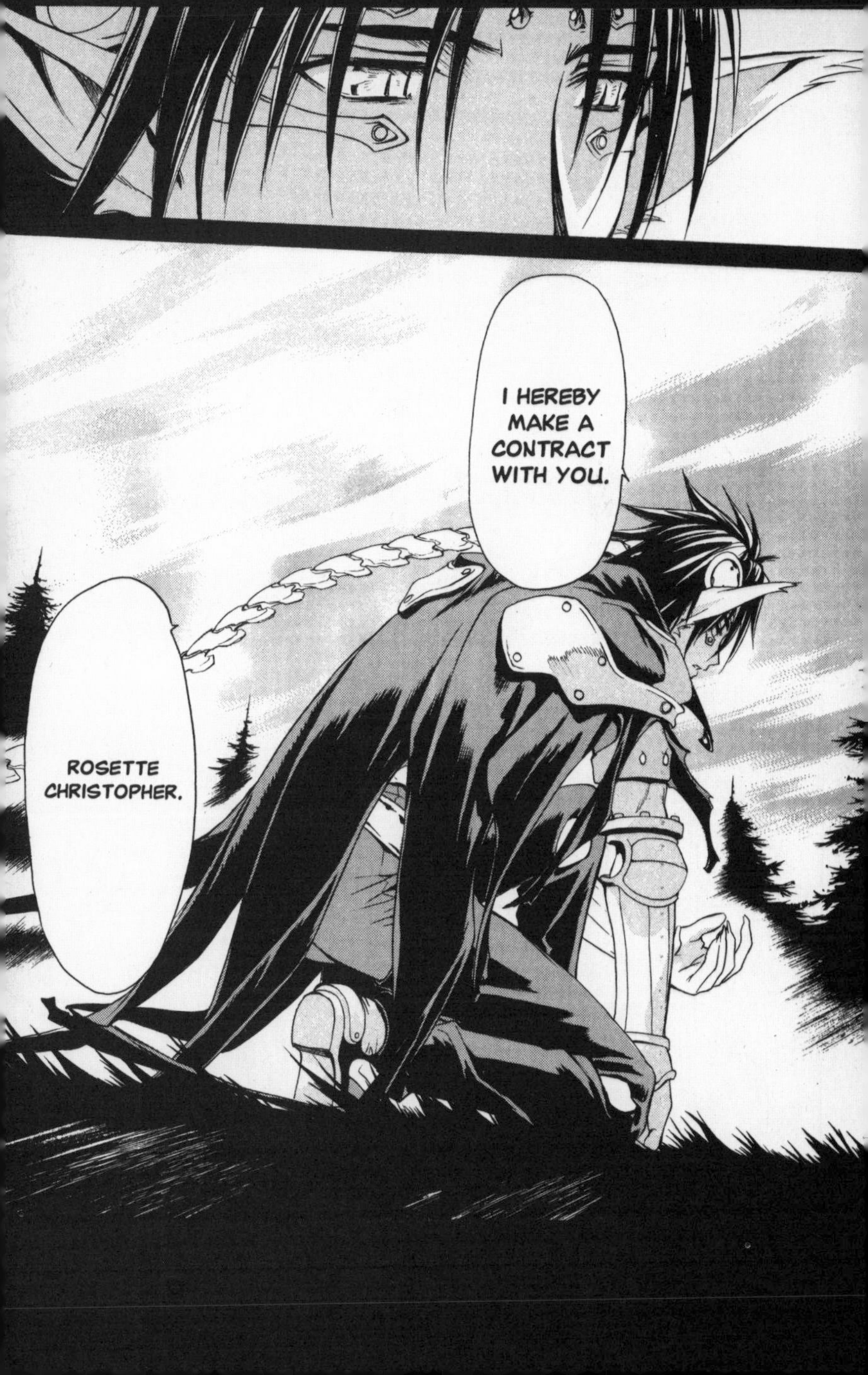
I HEREBY MAKE A CONTRACT WITH YOU.
ROSETTE CHRISTOPHER.

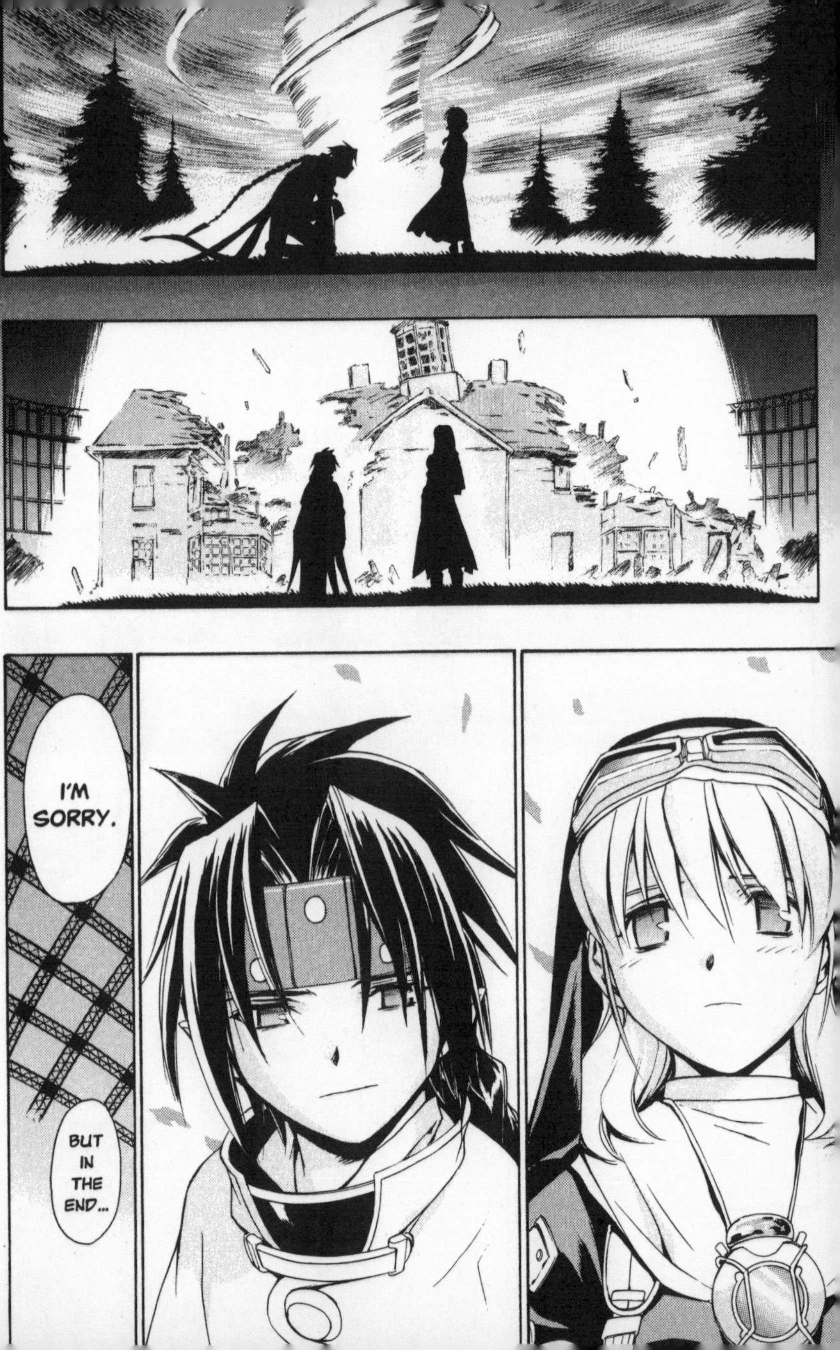
I'M SORRY.
BUT IN THE END...

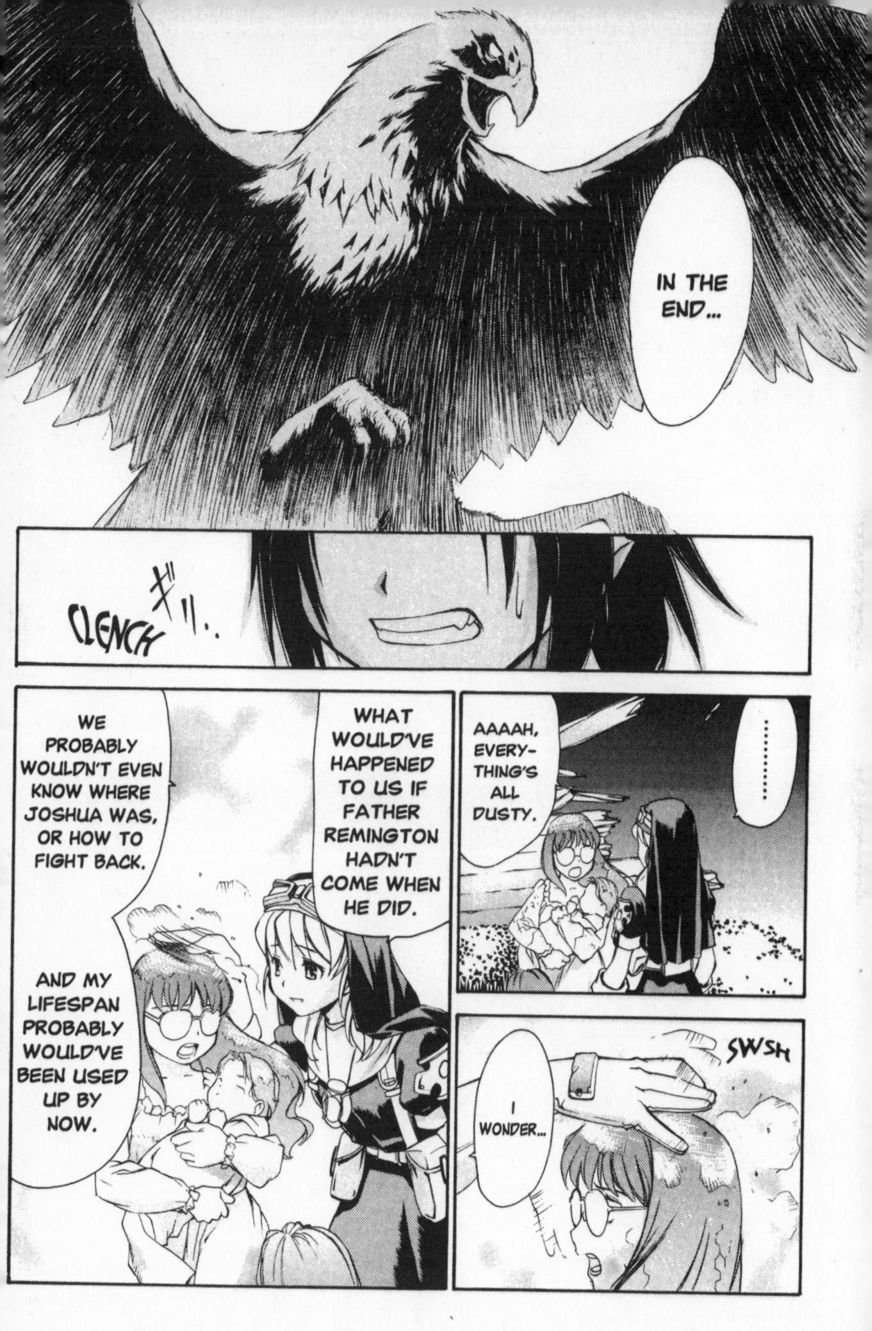
IN THE END...
CLENCH
ギッ..
AAAAH, EVERY-THING'S ALL DUSTY.
....
WHAT WOULD'VE HAPPENED TO US IF FATHER REMINGTON HADN'T COME WHEN HE DID.
WE PROBABLY WOULDN'T EVEN KNOW WHERE JOSHUA WAS, OR HOW TO FIGHT BACK.
AND MY LIFESPAN PROBABLY WOULD'VE BEEN USED UP BY NOW.
SWSH
I WONDER...

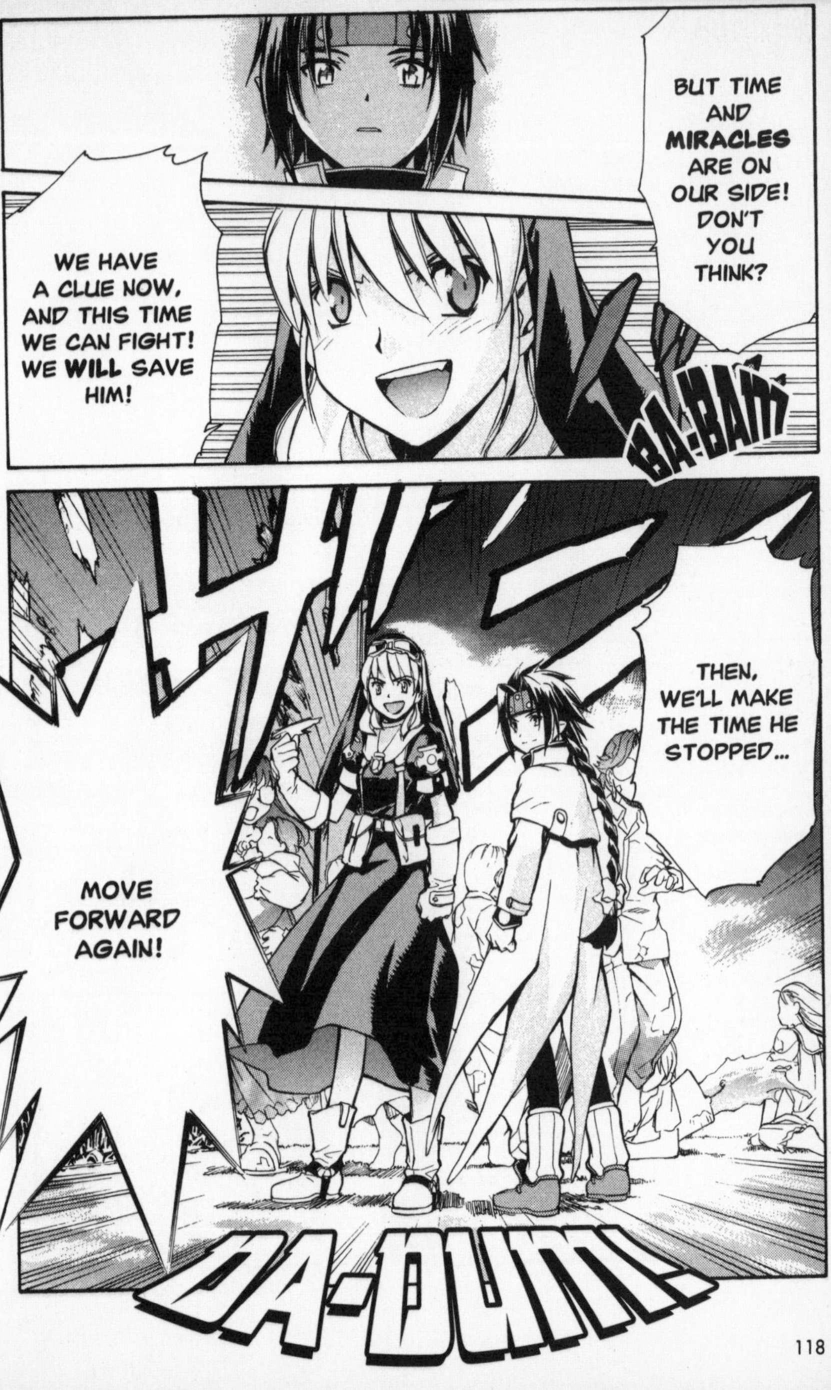
BUT TIME AND MIRACLES ARE ON OUR SIDE! DON'T YOU THINK?
WE HAVE A CLUE NOW, AND THIS TIME WE CAN FIGHT! WE WILL SAVE HIM!
BA-BAM!
THEN, WE'LL MAKE THE TIME HE STOPPED...
MOVE FORWARD AGAIN!
BA-DUM!

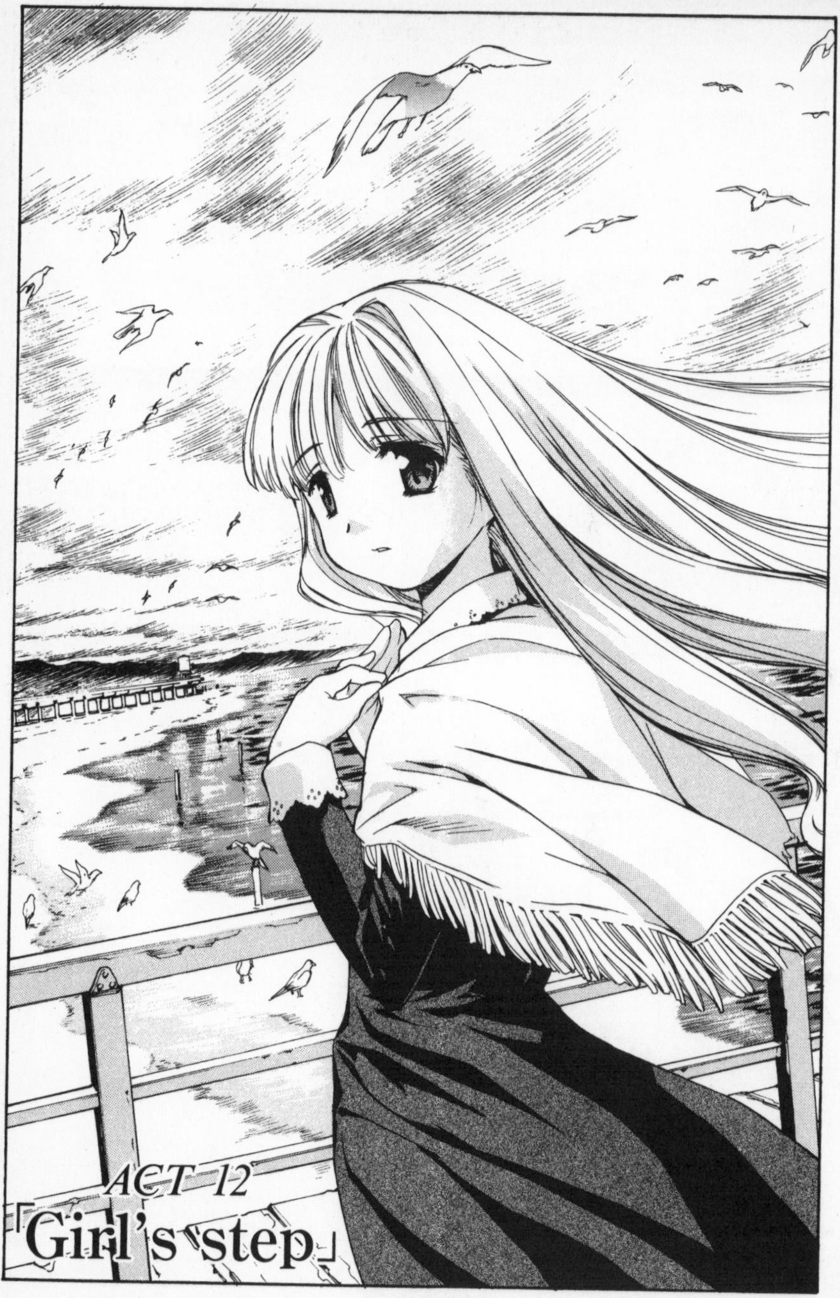
ACT 12
「Girl's step」

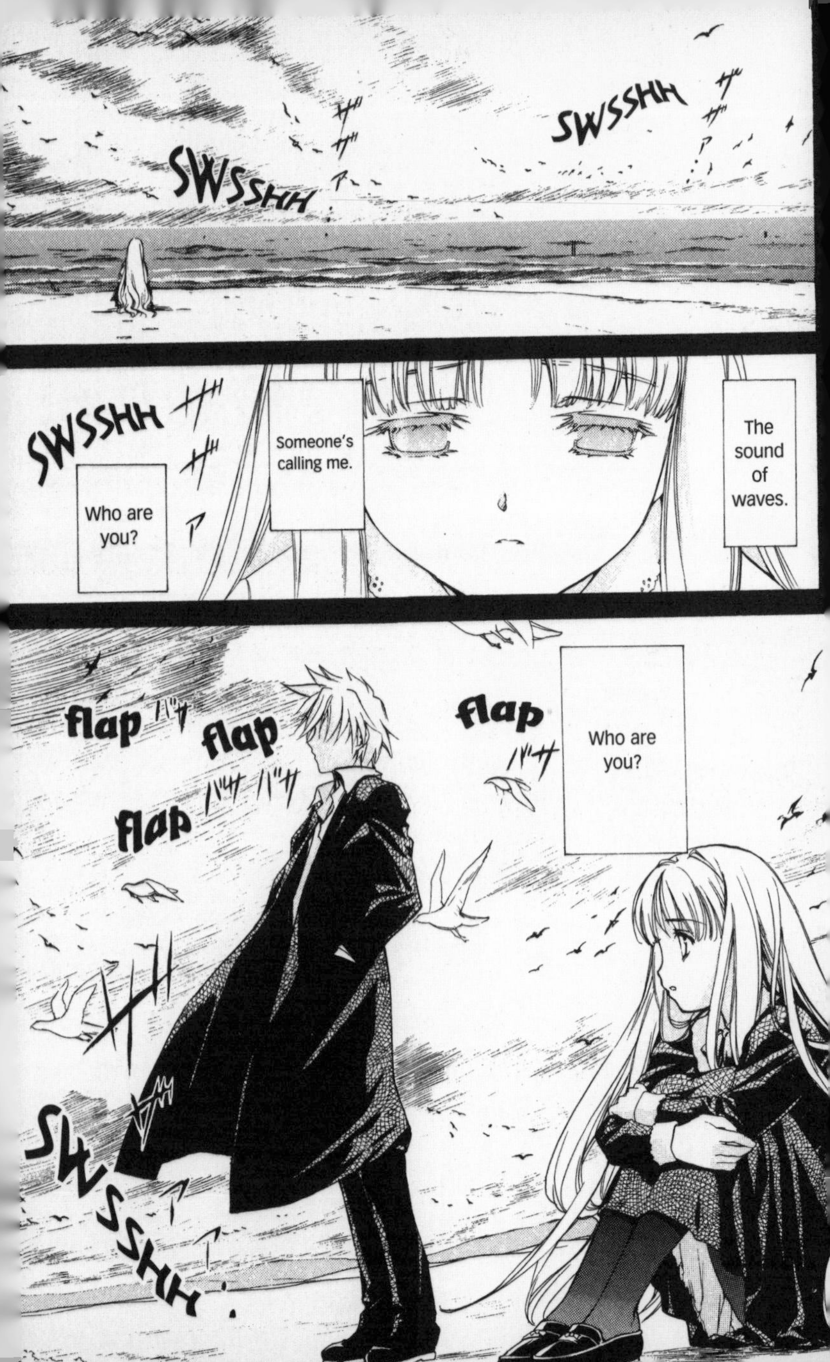
SWSSHH
SWSSHH
The sound of waves.
Someone's calling me.
SWSSHH
Who are you?
Who are you?
flap
flap
flap
flap
SWSSHH

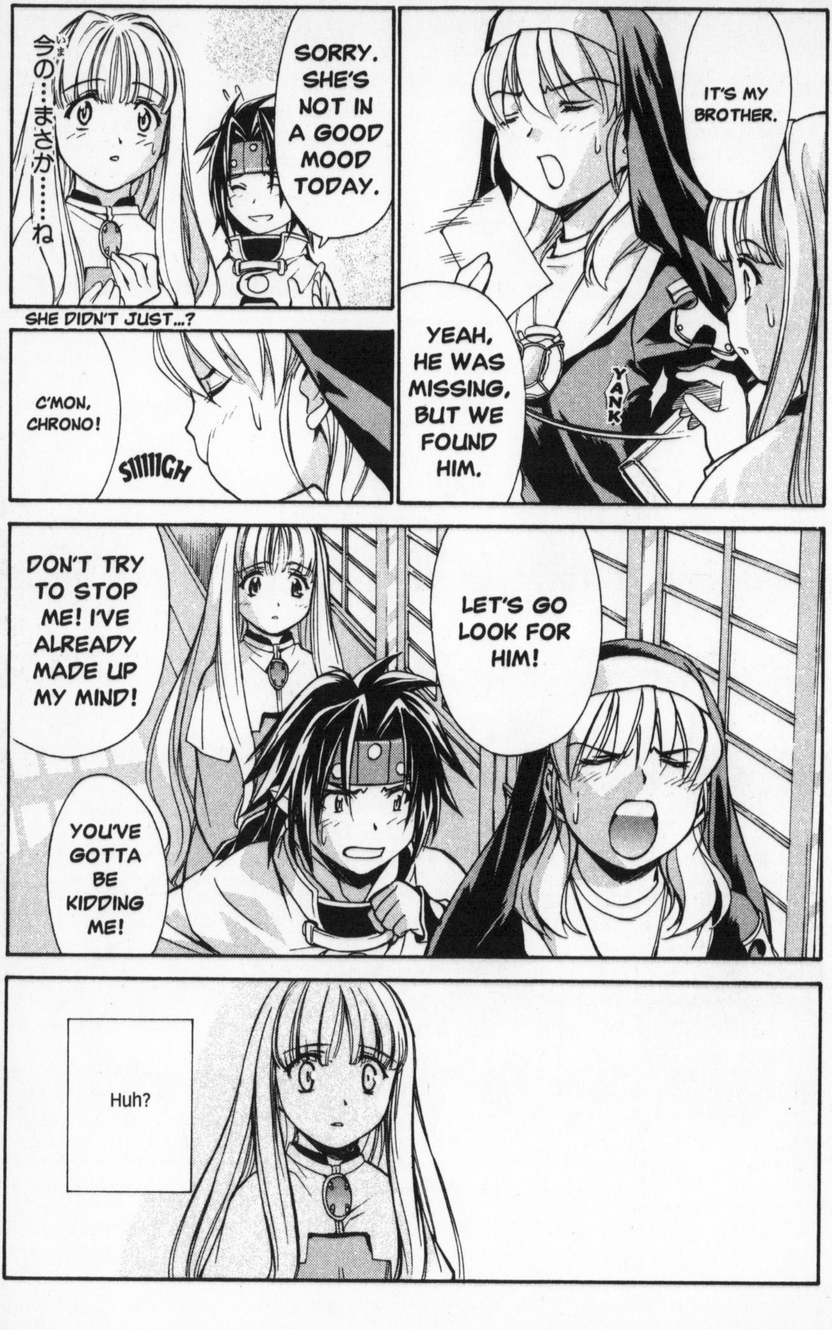
IT'S MY BROTHER.
YEAH, HE WAS MISSING, BUT WE FOUND HIM.
YANK
SORRY. SHE'S NOT IN A GOOD MOOD TODAY.
今の…まさか……ね
SHE DIDN'T JUST...?
C'MON, CHRONO!
SIIIIGH
LET'S GO LOOK FOR HIM!
DON'T TRY TO STOP ME! I'VE ALREADY MADE UP MY MIND!
YOU'VE GOTTA BE KIDDING ME!
Huh?

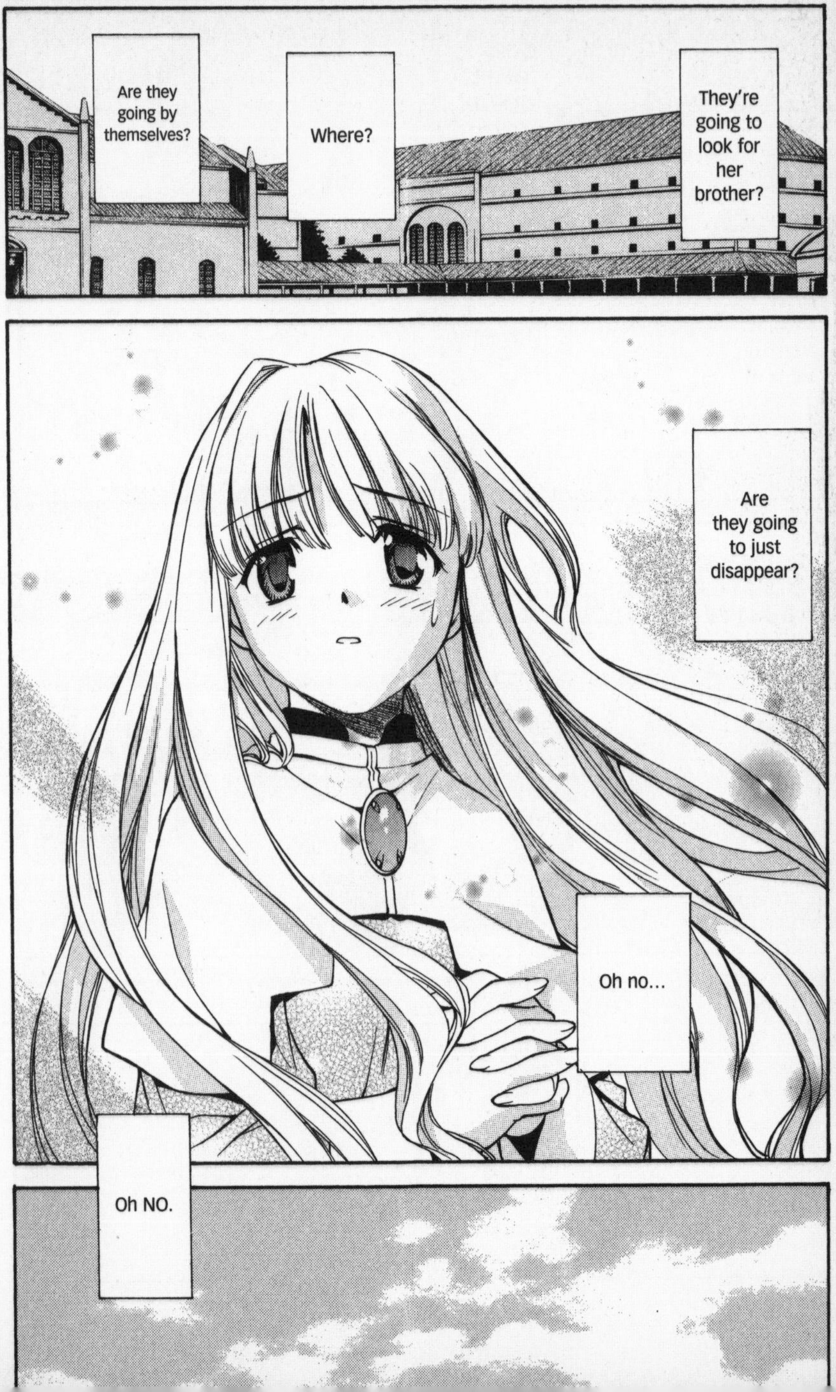
They're going to look for her brother?
Where?
Are they going by themselves?
Are they going to just disappear?
Oh no...
Oh NO.

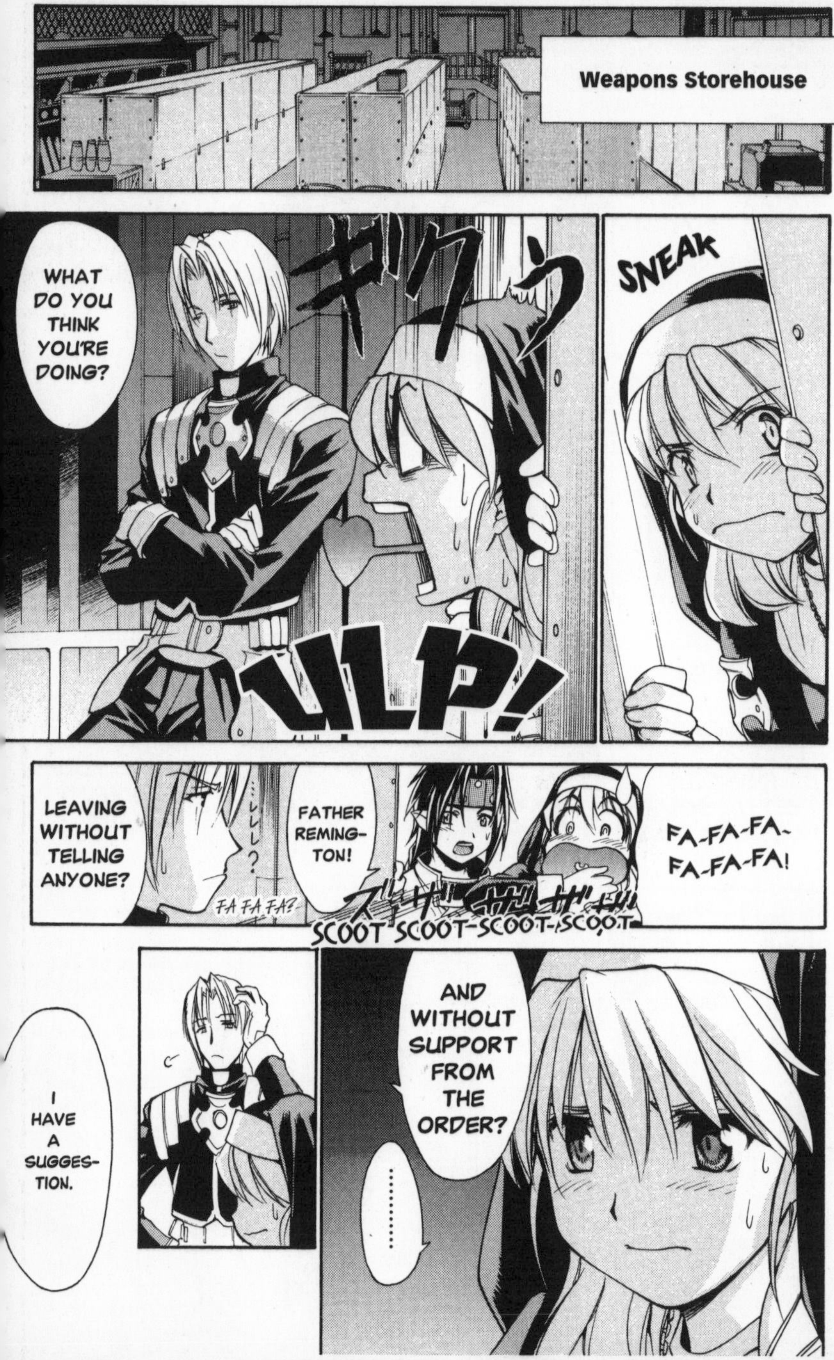
Weapons Storehouse
SNEAK
WHAT DO YOU THINK YOU'RE DOING?
ULP!
FA-FA-FA-FA-FA-FA!
FATHER REMING-TON!
FA FA FA?
LEAVING WITHOUT TELLING ANYONE?
SCOOT SCOOT-SCOOT-SCOOT
AND WITHOUT SUPPORT FROM THE ORDER?
....
I HAVE A SUGGES-TION.

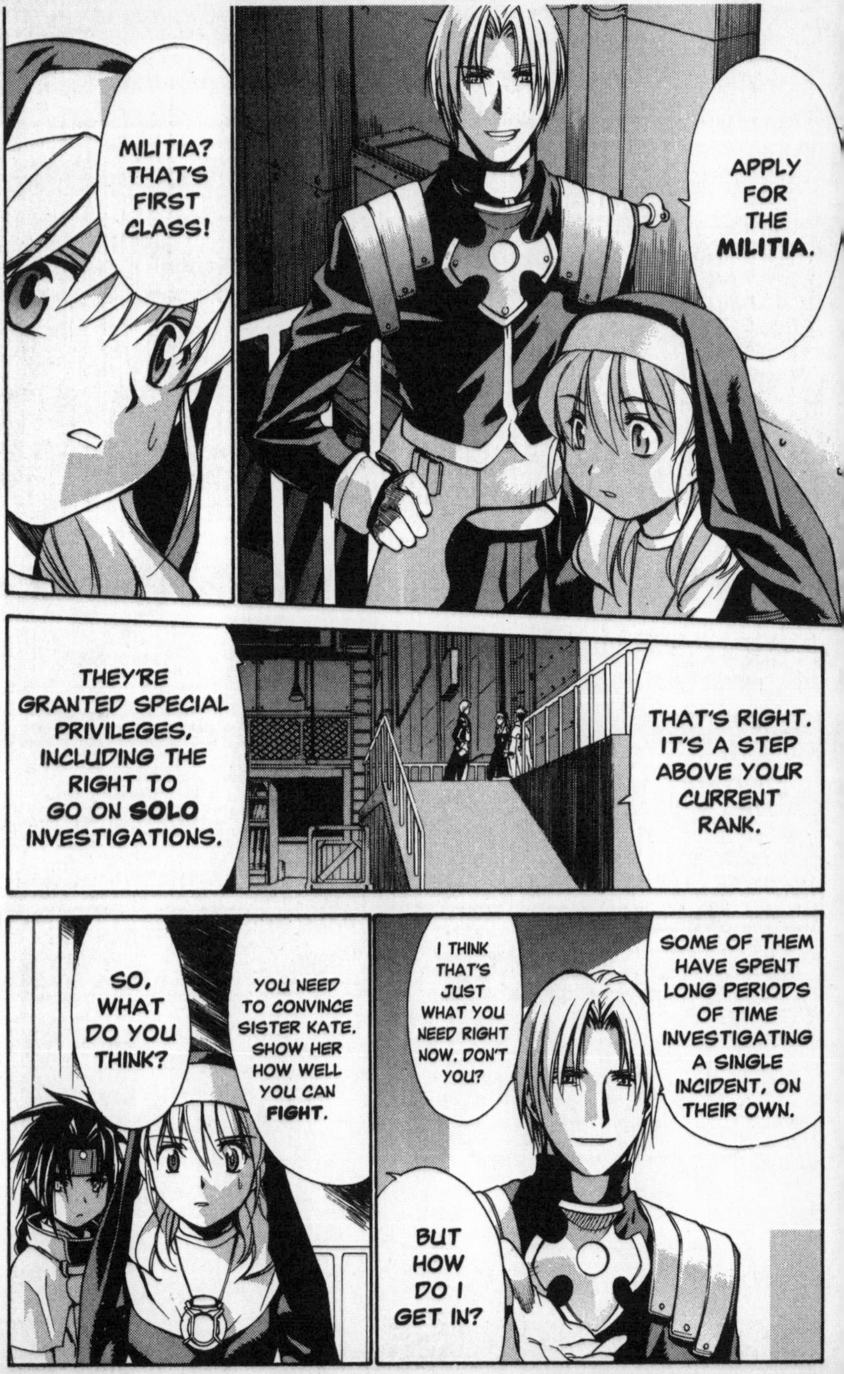
APPLY FOR THE MILITIA.
MILITIA? THAT'S FIRST CLASS!
THAT'S RIGHT. IT'S A STEP ABOVE YOUR CURRENT RANK.
THEY'RE GRANTED SPECIAL PRIVILEGES, INCLUDING THE RIGHT TO GO ON SOLO INVESTIGATIONS.
SOME OF THEM HAVE SPENT LONG PERIODS OF TIME INVESTIGATING A SINGLE INCIDENT, ON THEIR OWN.
I THINK THAT'S JUST WHAT YOU NEED RIGHT NOW. DON'T YOU?
BUT HOW DO I GET IN?
YOU NEED TO CONVINCE SISTER KATE. SHOW HER HOW WELL YOU CAN FIGHT.
SO, WHAT DO YOU THINK?

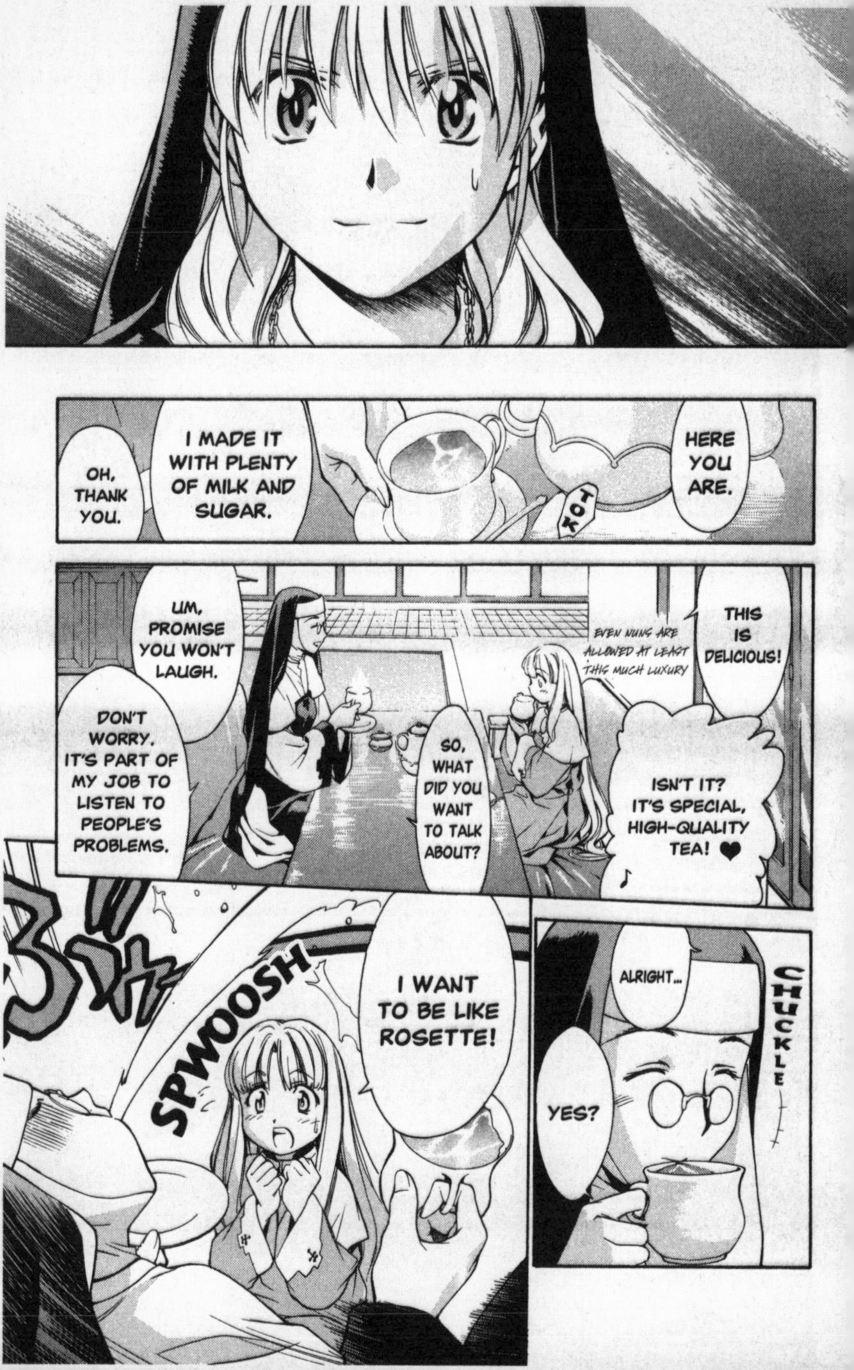
HERE YOU ARE.
TOK
I MADE IT WITH PLENTY OF MILK AND SUGAR.
OH, THANK YOU.
THIS IS DELICIOUS!
EVEN NUNS ARE ALLOWED AT LEAST THIS MUCH LUXURY
ISN'T IT? IT'S SPECIAL, HIGH-QUALITY TEA! ❤
SO, WHAT DID YOU WANT TO TALK ABOUT?
UM, PROMISE YOU WON'T LAUGH.
DON'T WORRY. IT'S PART OF MY JOB TO LISTEN TO PEOPLE'S PROBLEMS.
CHUCKLE
ALRIGHT...
YES?
I WANT TO BE LIKE ROSETTE!
SPWOOSH

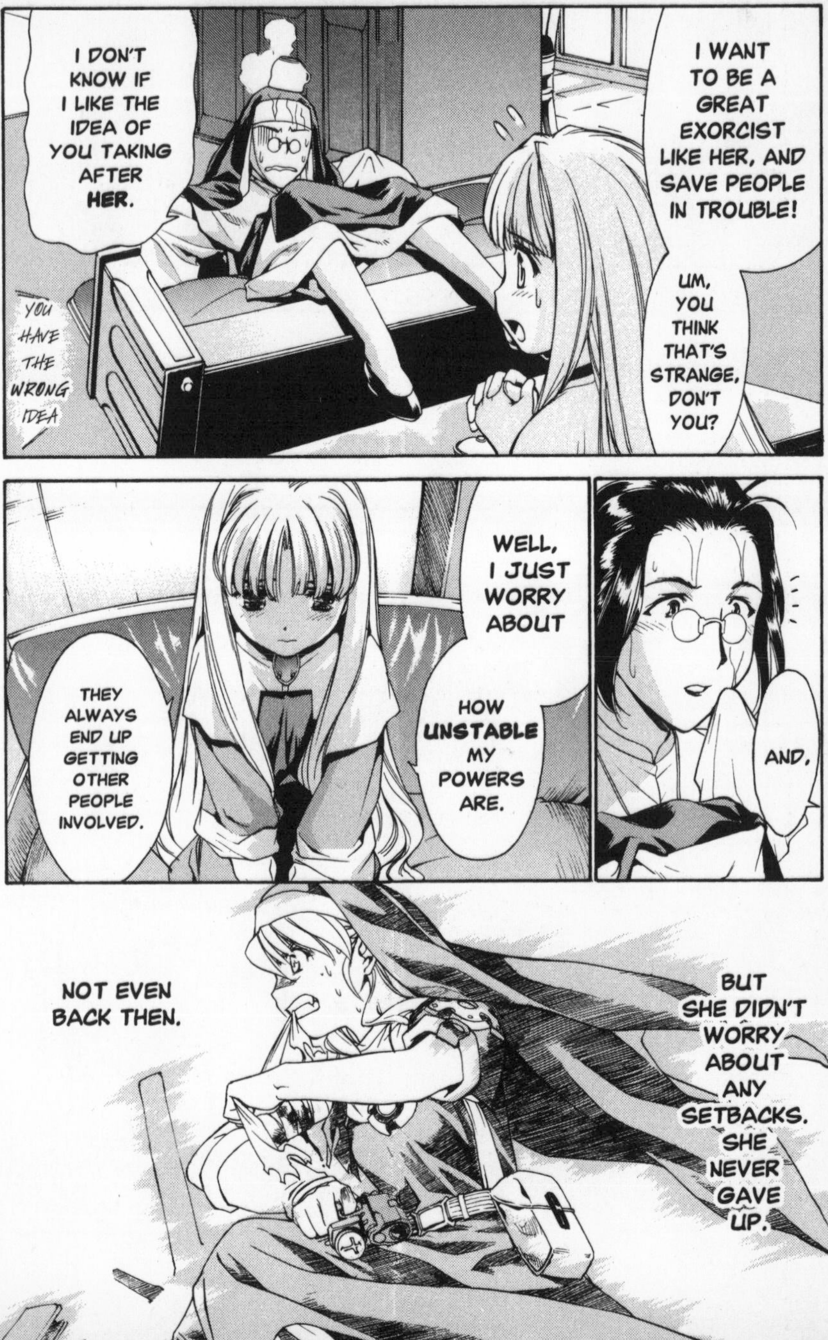
I WANT TO BE A GREAT EXORCIST LIKE HER, AND SAVE PEOPLE IN TROUBLE!
UM, YOU THINK THAT'S STRANGE, DON'T YOU?
I DON'T KNOW IF I LIKE THE IDEA OF YOU TAKING AFTER **HER**.
YOU HAVE THE WRONG IDEA
AND,
WELL, I JUST WORRY ABOUT
HOW **UNSTABLE** MY POWERS ARE.
THEY ALWAYS END UP GETTING OTHER PEOPLE INVOLVED.
BUT SHE DIDN'T WORRY ABOUT ANY SETBACKS. SHE NEVER GAVE UP.
NOT EVEN BACK THEN.

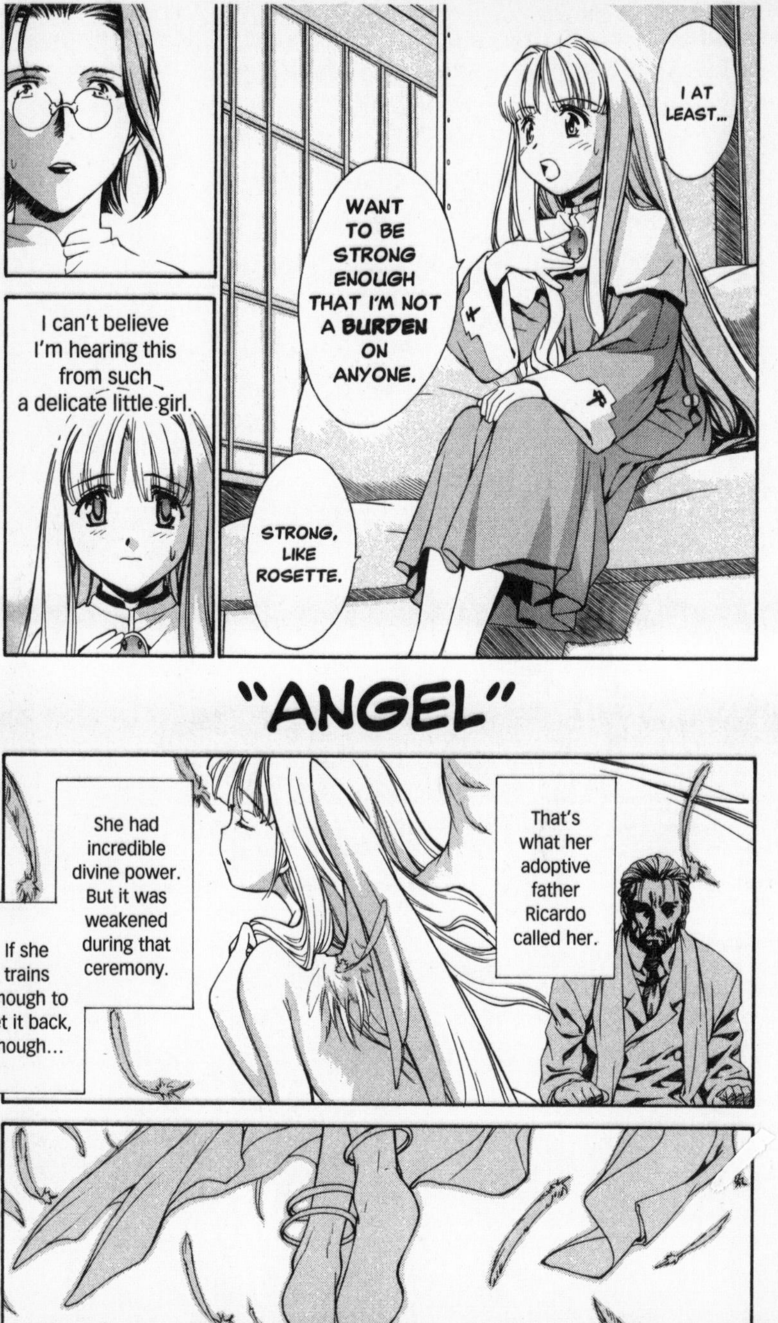
I AT LEAST...
WANT TO BE STRONG ENOUGH THAT I'M NOT A BURDEN ON ANYONE.
STRONG, LIKE ROSETTE.
I can't believe I'm hearing this from such a delicate little girl.
"ANGEL"
That's what her adoptive father Ricardo called her.
She had incredible divine power. But it was weakened during that ceremony.
If she trains enough to get it back, though...

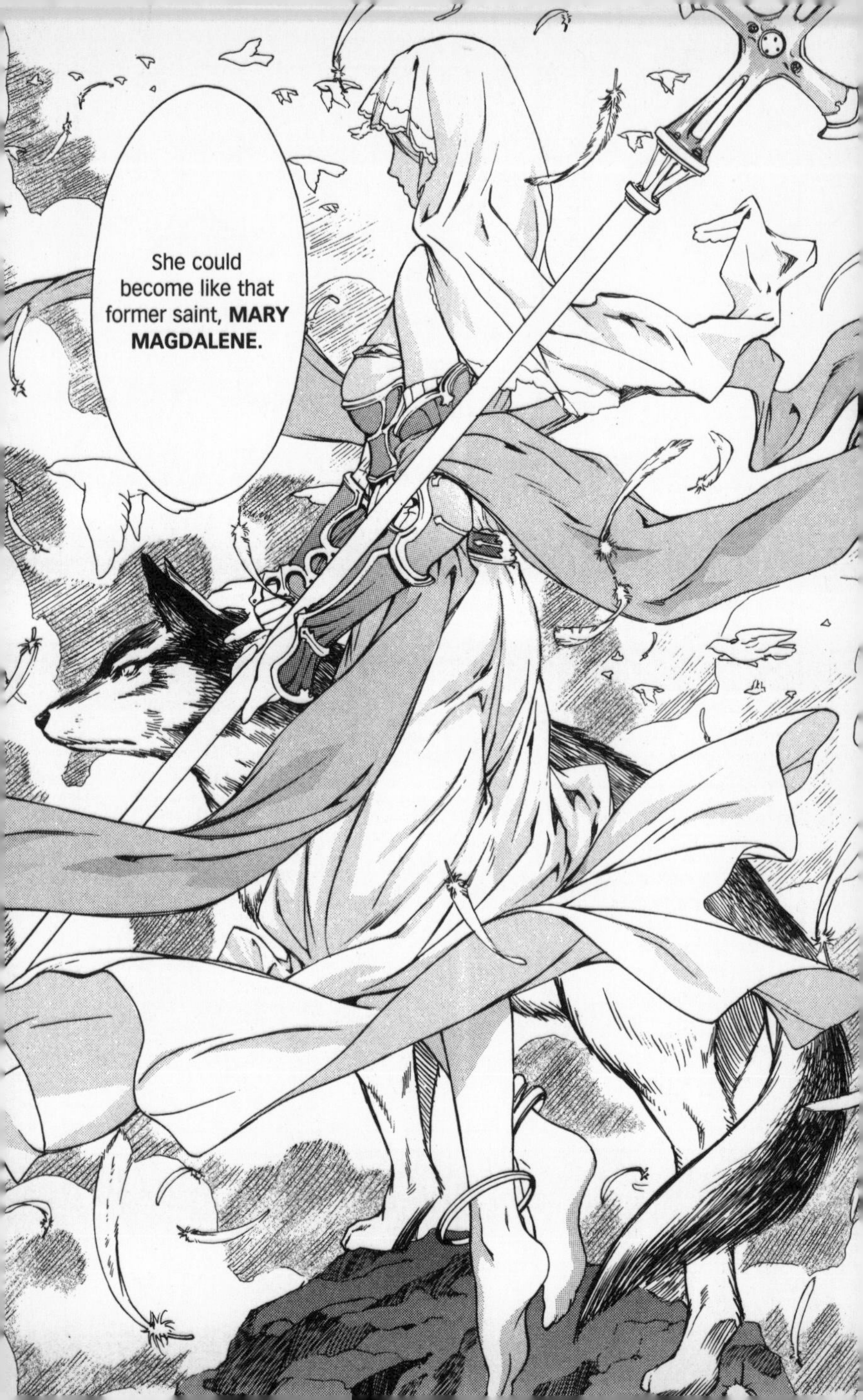
She could become like that former saint, MARY MAGDALENE.

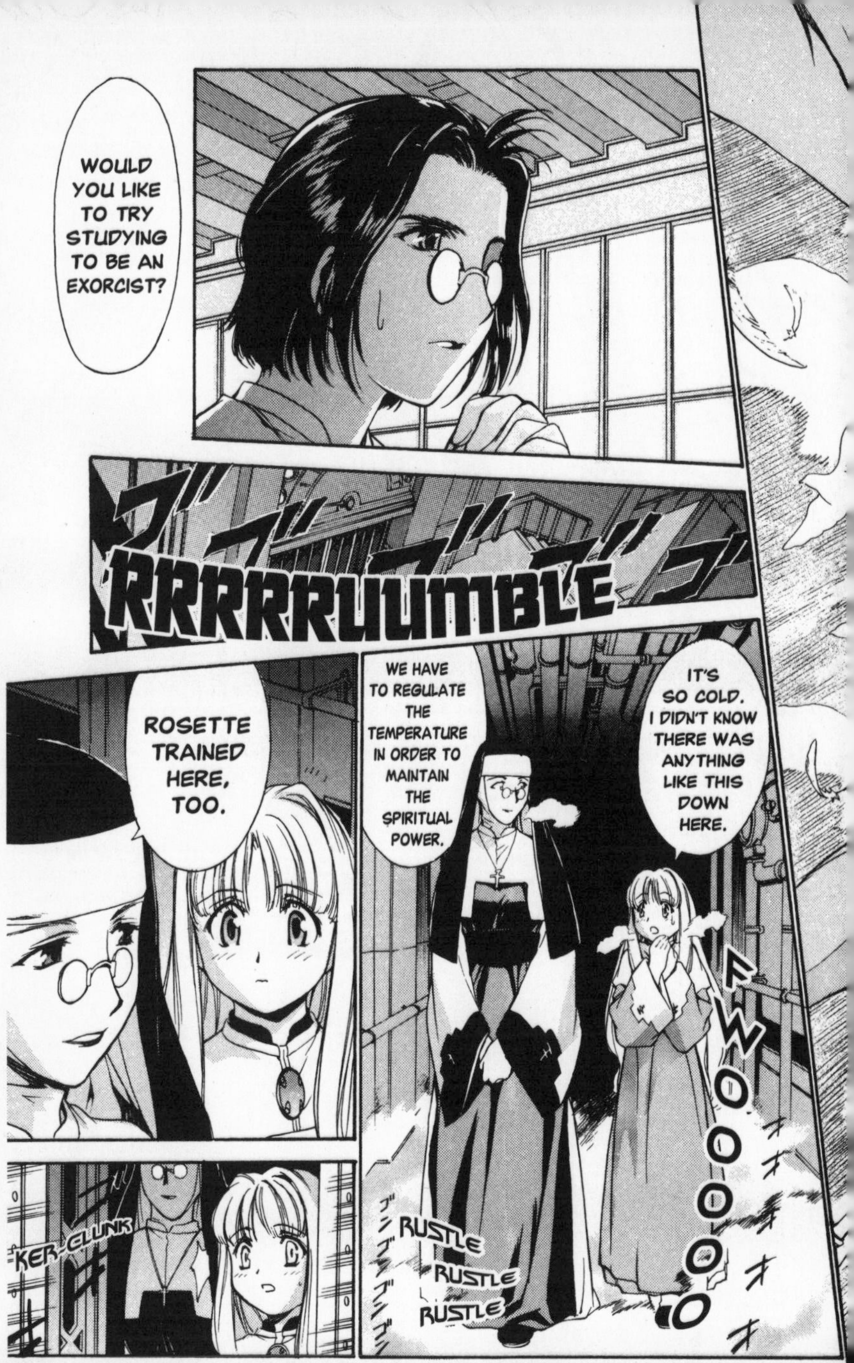
WOULD YOU LIKE TO TRY STUDYING TO BE AN EXORCIST?
RRRRRUUMBLE
IT'S SO COLD. I DIDN'T KNOW THERE WAS ANYTHING LIKE THIS DOWN HERE.
WE HAVE TO REGULATE THE TEMPERATURE IN ORDER TO MAINTAIN THE SPIRITUAL POWER.
FWOOOOOO
RUSTLE RUSTLE RUSTLE
ROSETTE TRAINED HERE, TOO.
KER-CLUNK

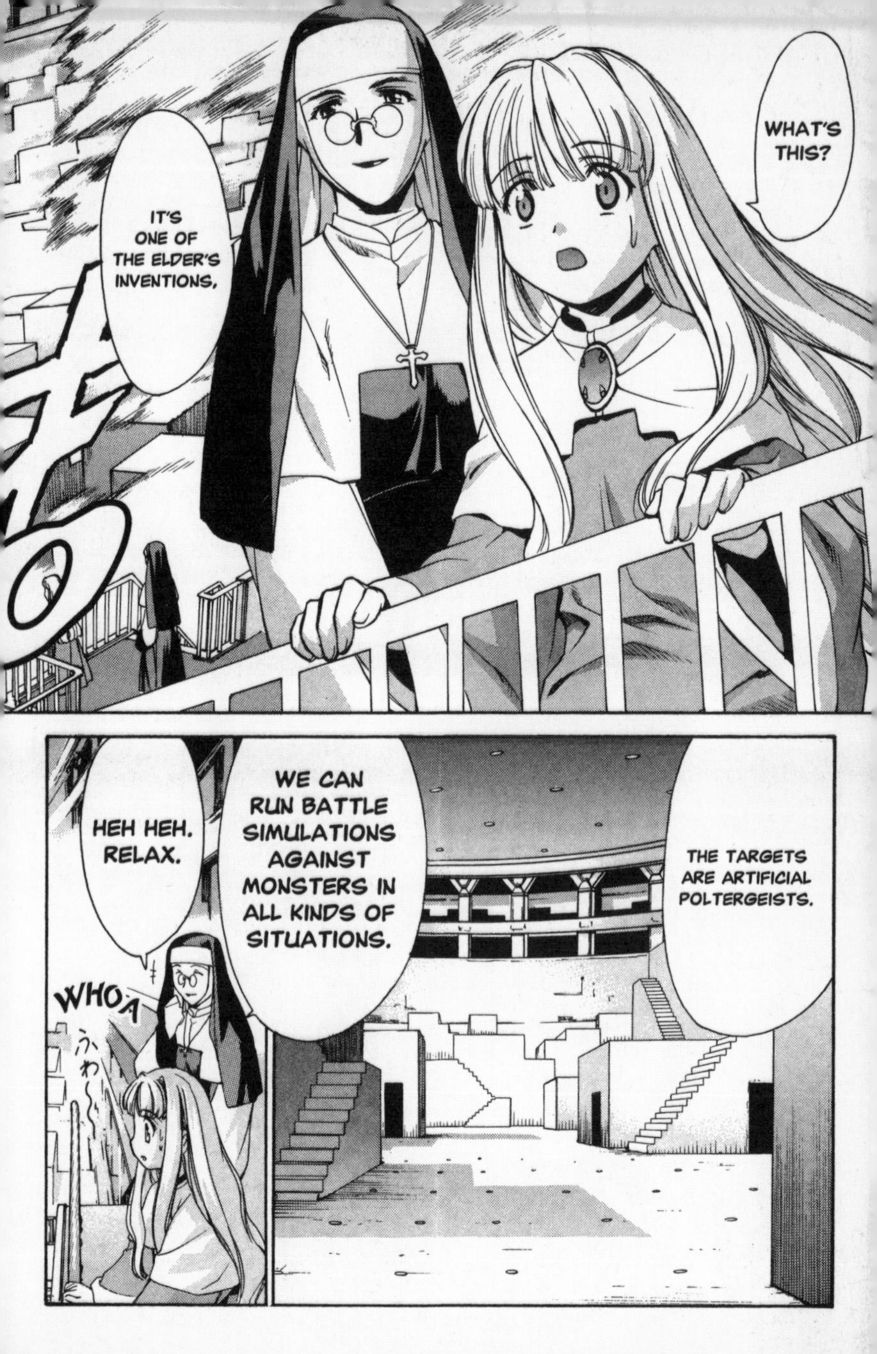
WHAT'S THIS?
IT'S ONE OF THE ELDER'S INVENTIONS,
THE TARGETS ARE ARTIFICIAL POLTERGEISTS.
WE CAN RUN BATTLE SIMULATIONS AGAINST MONSTERS IN ALL KINDS OF SITUATIONS.
HEH HEH. RELAX.
WHOA
ふわ～

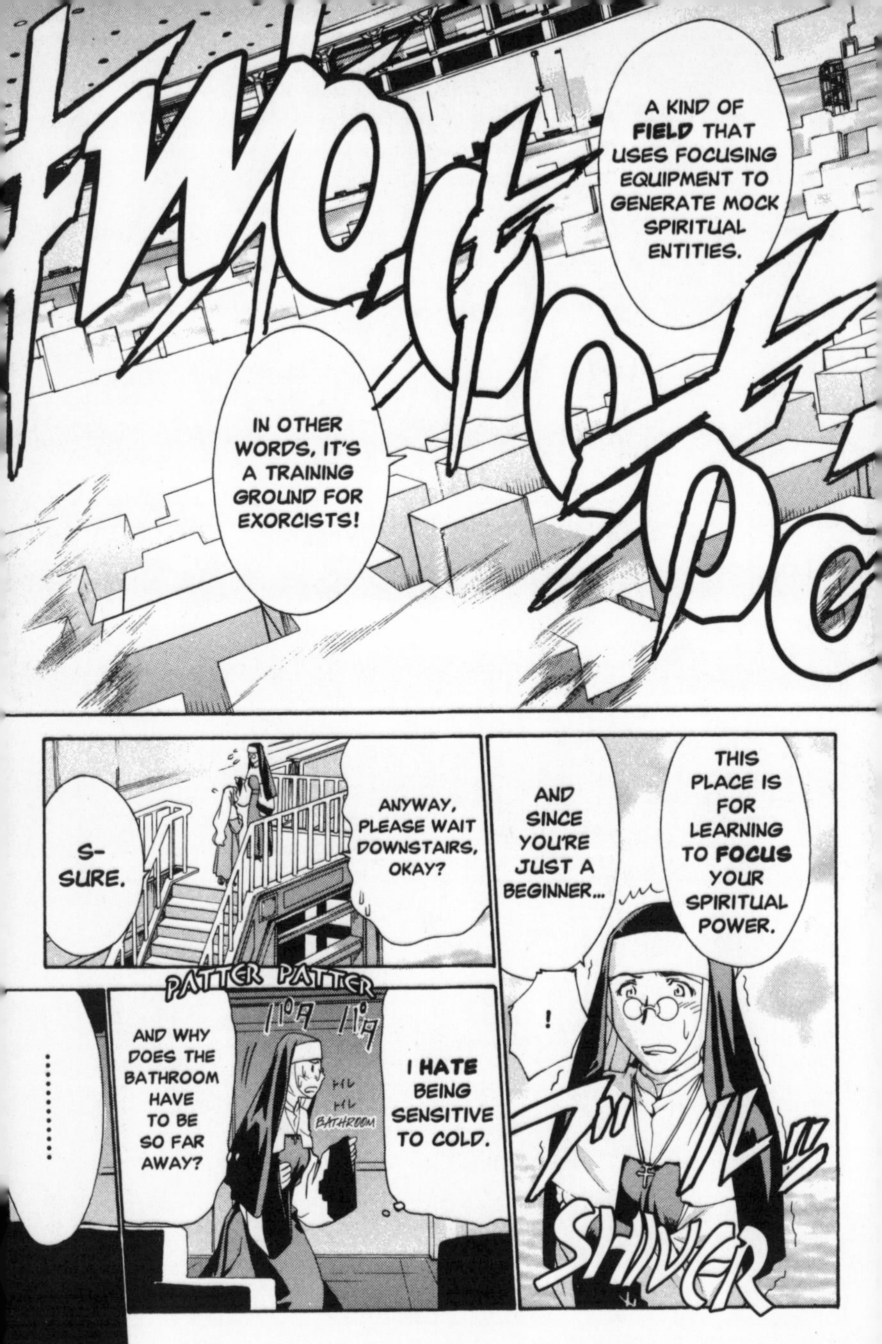
A KIND OF FIELD THAT USES FOCUSING EQUIPMENT TO GENERATE MOCK SPIRITUAL ENTITIES.
IN OTHER WORDS, IT'S A TRAINING GROUND FOR EXORCISTS!
THIS PLACE IS FOR LEARNING TO FOCUS YOUR SPIRITUAL POWER.
AND SINCE YOU'RE JUST A BEGINNER...
ANYWAY, PLEASE WAIT DOWNSTAIRS, OKAY?
S-SURE.
!
SHIVER
I HATE BEING SENSITIVE TO COLD.
PATTER PATTER
BATHROOM
AND WHY DOES THE BATHROOM HAVE TO BE SO FAR AWAY?
....

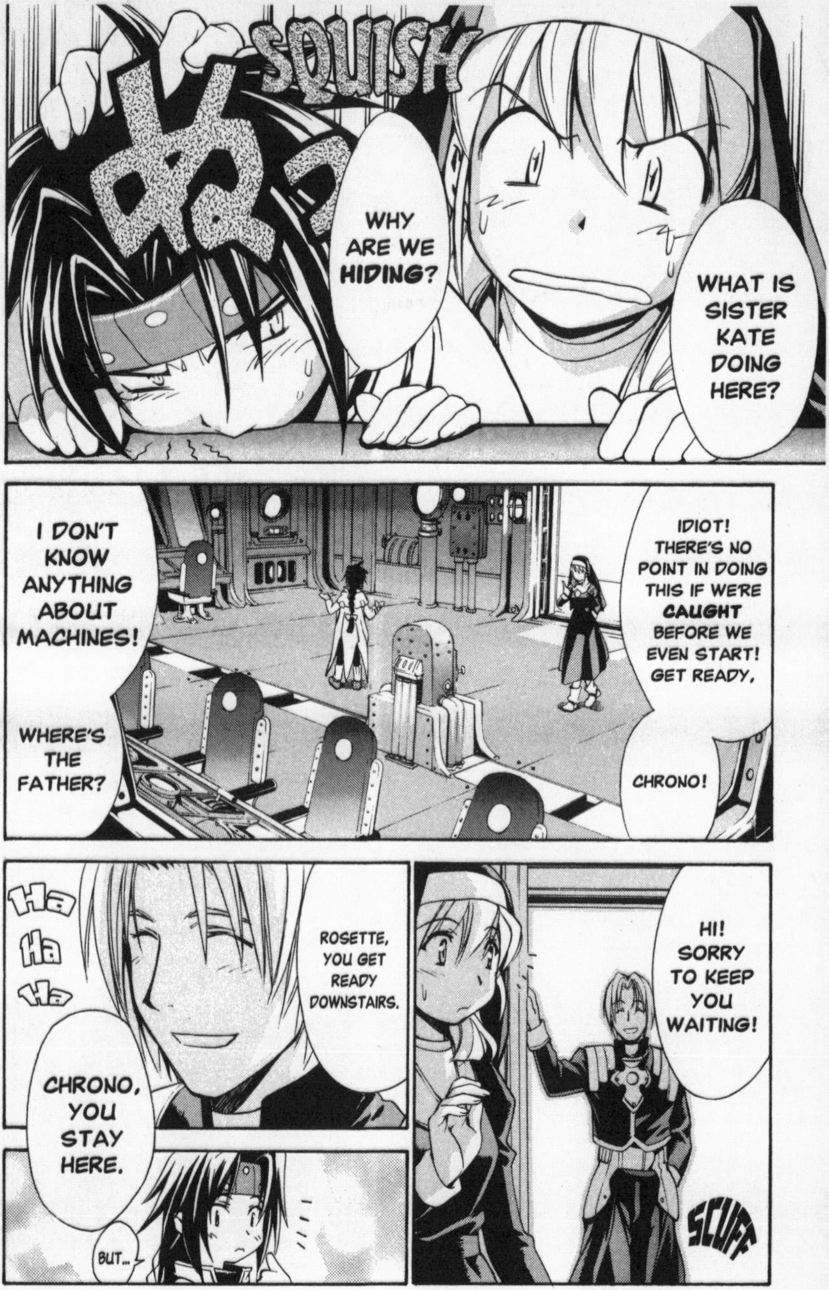
SQUISH
WHAT IS SISTER KATE DOING HERE?
WHY ARE WE HIDING?
IDIOT! THERE'S NO POINT IN DOING THIS IF WE'RE CAUGHT BEFORE WE EVEN START! GET READY,
CHRONO!
I DON'T KNOW ANYTHING ABOUT MACHINES!
WHERE'S THE FATHER?
HI! SORRY TO KEEP YOU WAITING!
SCUFF
Ha Ha Ha
ROSETTE, YOU GET READY DOWNSTAIRS.
CHRONO, YOU STAY HERE.
BUT...

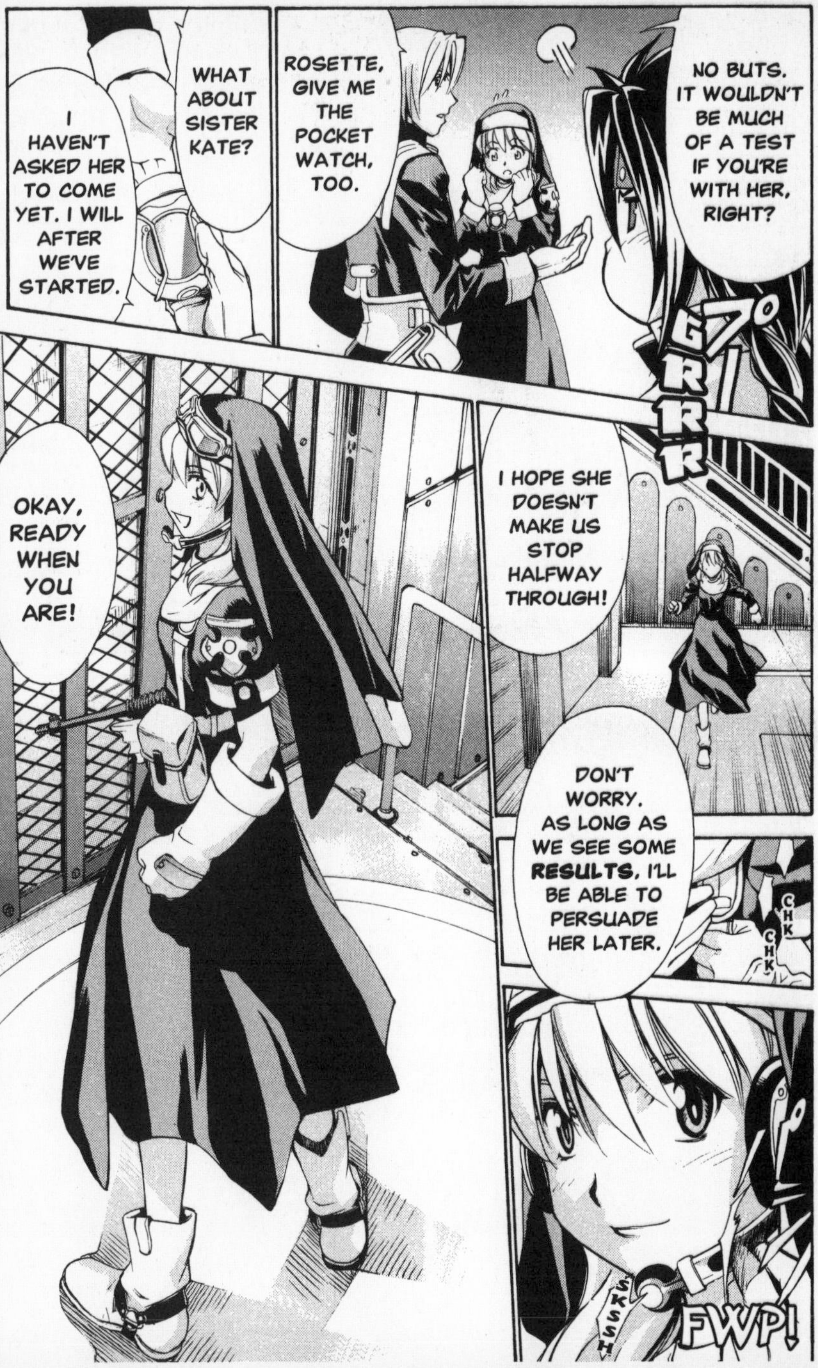

WHAT ABOUT SISTER KATE?
I HAVEN'T ASKED HER TO COME YET. I WILL AFTER WE'VE STARTED.
ROSETTE, GIVE ME THE POCKET WATCH, TOO.
NO BUTS. IT WOULDN'T BE MUCH OF A TEST IF YOU'RE WITH HER, RIGHT?
GRRR
OKAY, READY WHEN YOU ARE!
I HOPE SHE DOESN'T MAKE US STOP HALFWAY THROUGH!
DON'T WORRY. AS LONG AS WE SEE SOME **RESULTS**, I'LL BE ABLE TO PERSUADE HER LATER.
CHK CHK
SKSSH
FWP!

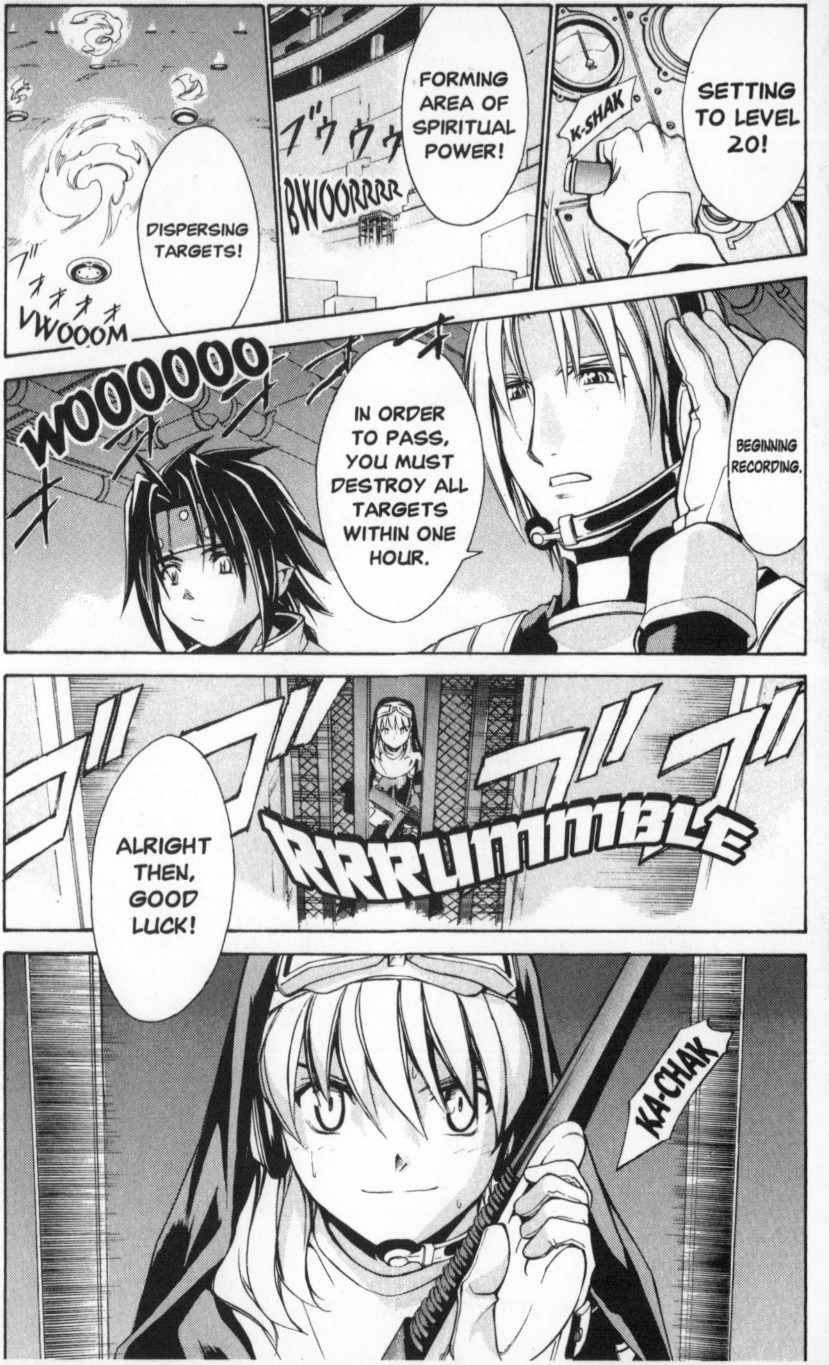
SETTING TO LEVEL 20!
K-SHAK
FORMING AREA OF SPIRITUAL POWER!
BWOORRRR
DISPERSING TARGETS!
VWOOOM
BEGINNING RECORDING.
IN ORDER TO PASS, YOU MUST DESTROY ALL TARGETS WITHIN ONE HOUR.
WOOOOOO
RRRUMMMBLE
ALRIGHT THEN, GOOD LUCK!
KA-CHAK

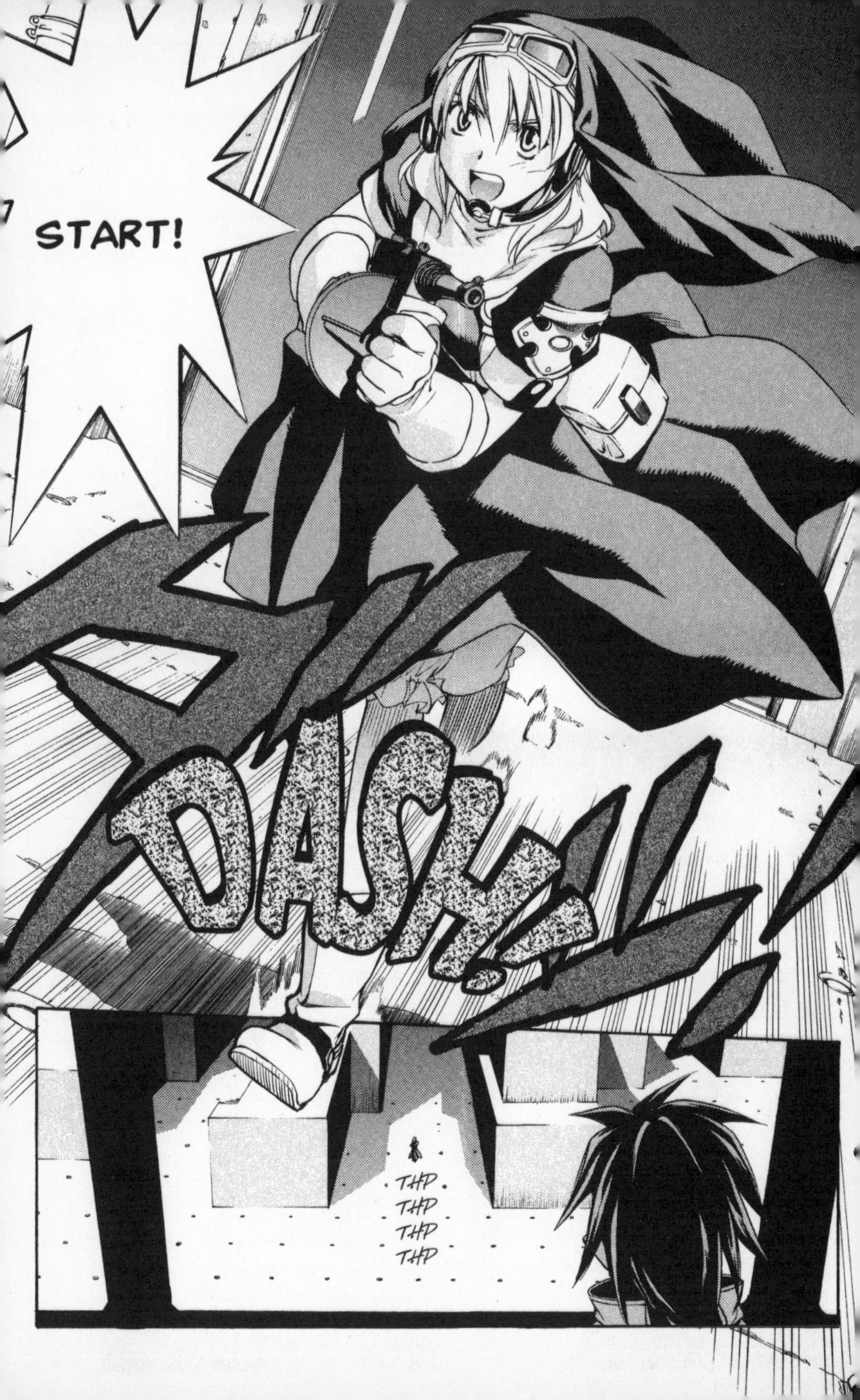
START!
DASH!!
THP
THP
THP
THP

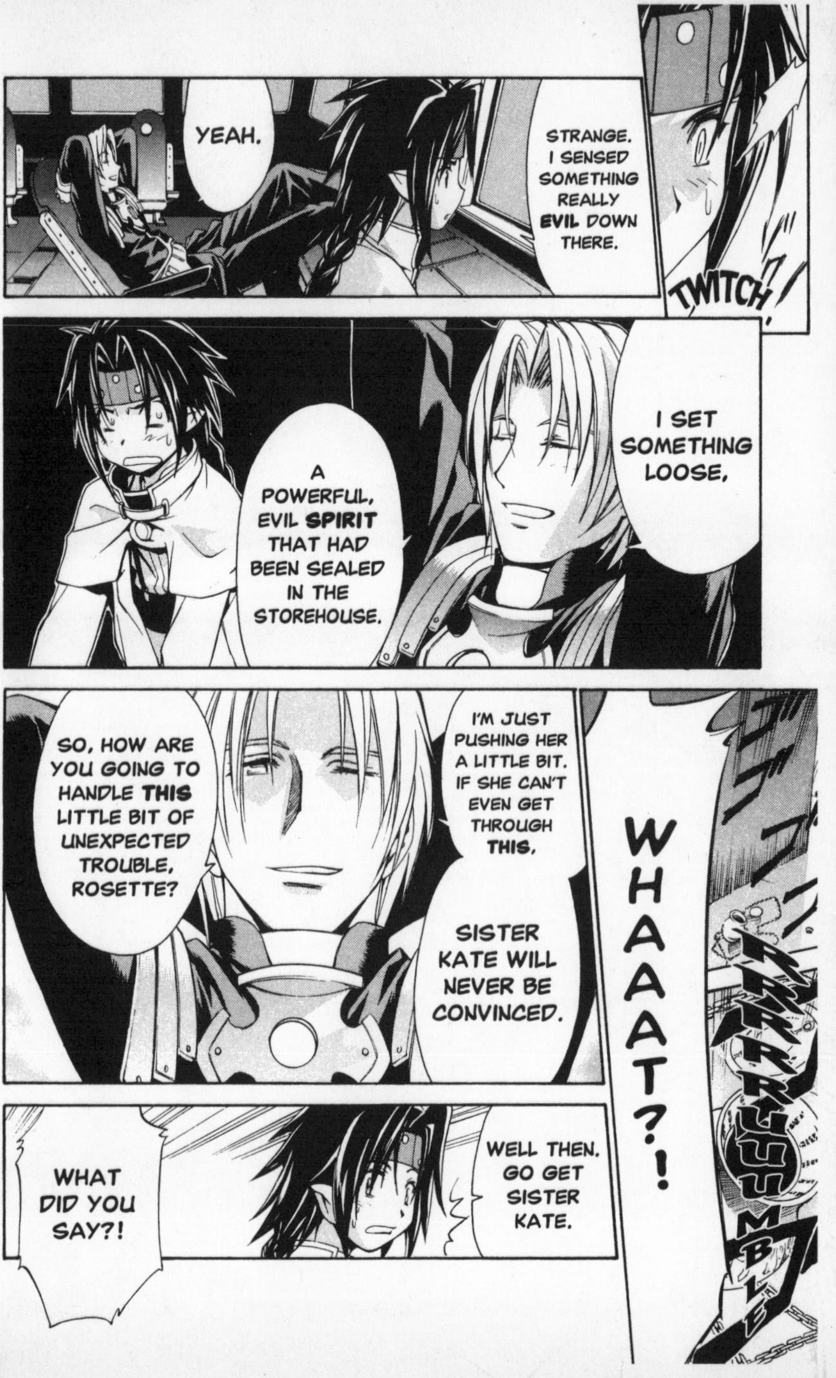
TWITCH?!
STRANGE. I SENSED SOMETHING REALLY EVIL DOWN THERE.
YEAH.
I SET SOMETHING LOOSE,
A POWERFUL, EVIL SPIRIT THAT HAD BEEN SEALED IN THE STOREHOUSE.
WHAAAT?!
RRRRRUUUMBLE
I'M JUST PUSHING HER A LITTLE BIT. IF SHE CAN'T EVEN GET THROUGH THIS,
SISTER KATE WILL NEVER BE CONVINCED.
SO, HOW ARE YOU GOING TO HANDLE THIS LITTLE BIT OF UNEXPECTED TROUBLE, ROSETTE?
WELL THEN. GO GET SISTER KATE.
WHAT DID YOU SAY?!

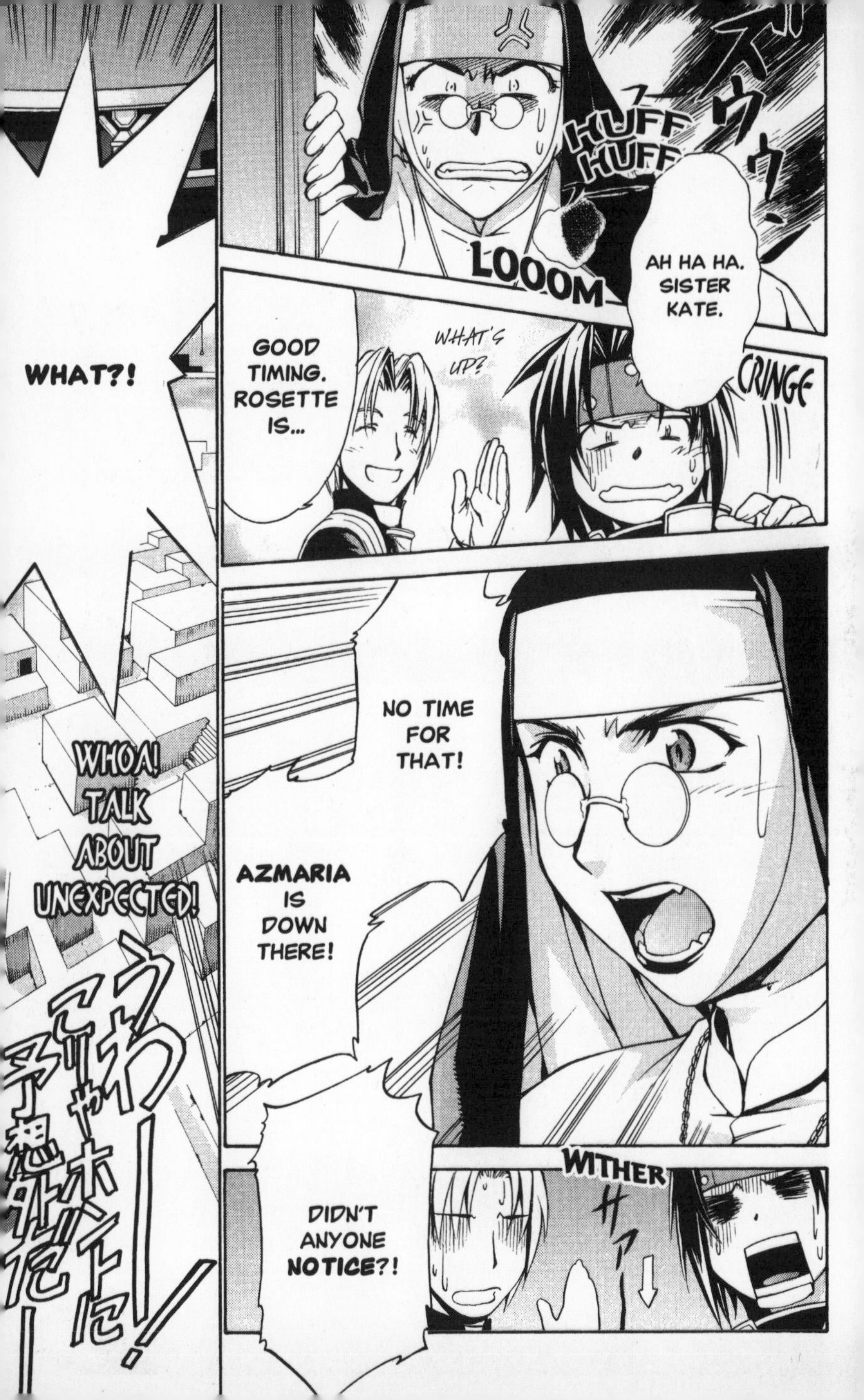
HUFF HUFF
LOOOM
AH HA HA. SISTER KATE.
CRINGE
WHAT'S UP?
GOOD TIMING. ROSETTE IS...
NO TIME FOR THAT!
AZMARIA IS DOWN THERE!
WITHER
DIDN'T ANYONE NOTICE?!
WHAT?!
WHOA! TALK ABOUT UNEXPECTED!
うわー！こりゃホントに予想外だー！

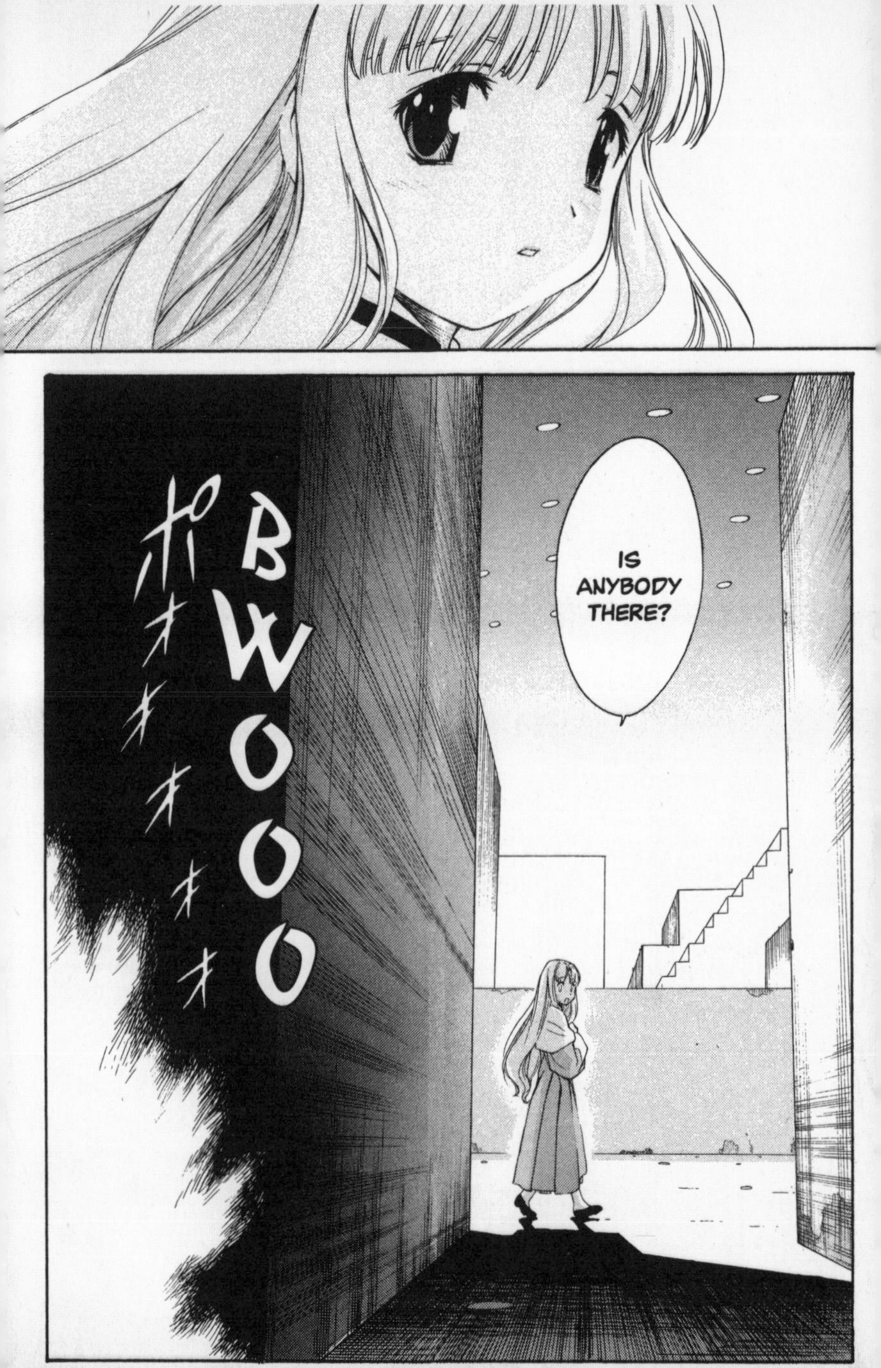
IS ANYBODY THERE?
BWOOO
ポオオオオオ

ACT 13
「駆け抜ける竜巻」
Raging Tornado

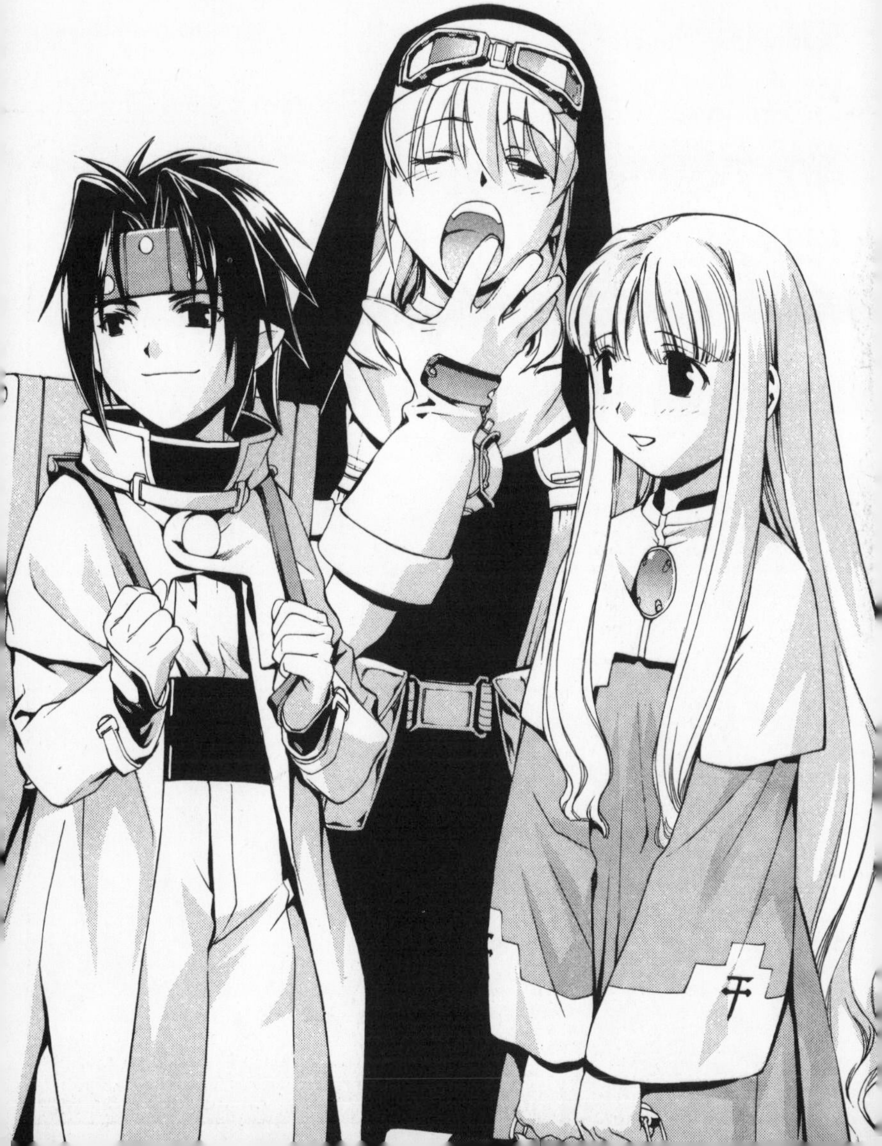

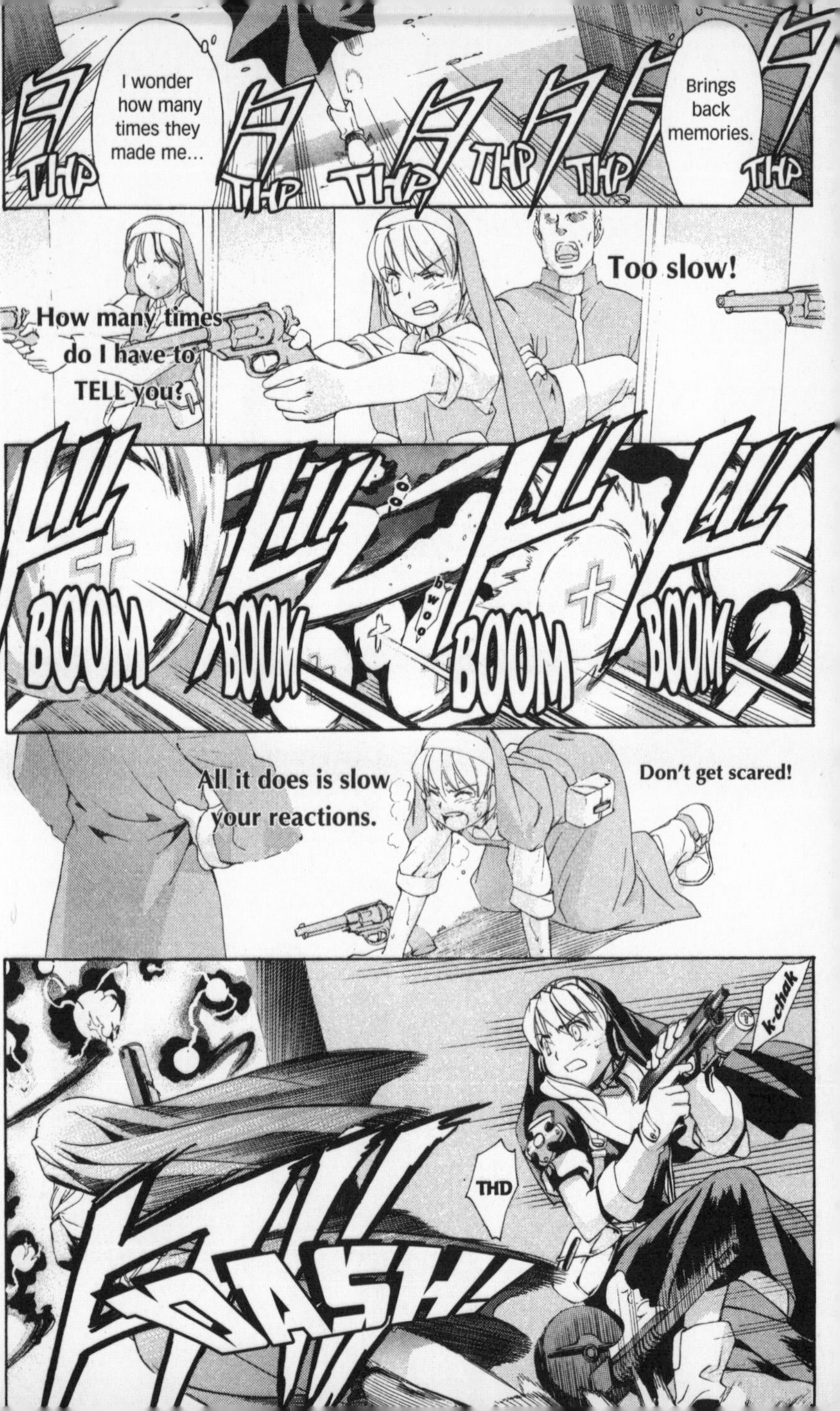
Brings back memories.
THP
THP
THP
THP
THP
THP
I wonder how many times they made me...
Too slow!
How many times do I have to TELL you?
BOOM
BOOM
bwoo
BOOM
BOOM
Don't get scared!
All it does is slow your reactions.
k-chak
THD
DASH!

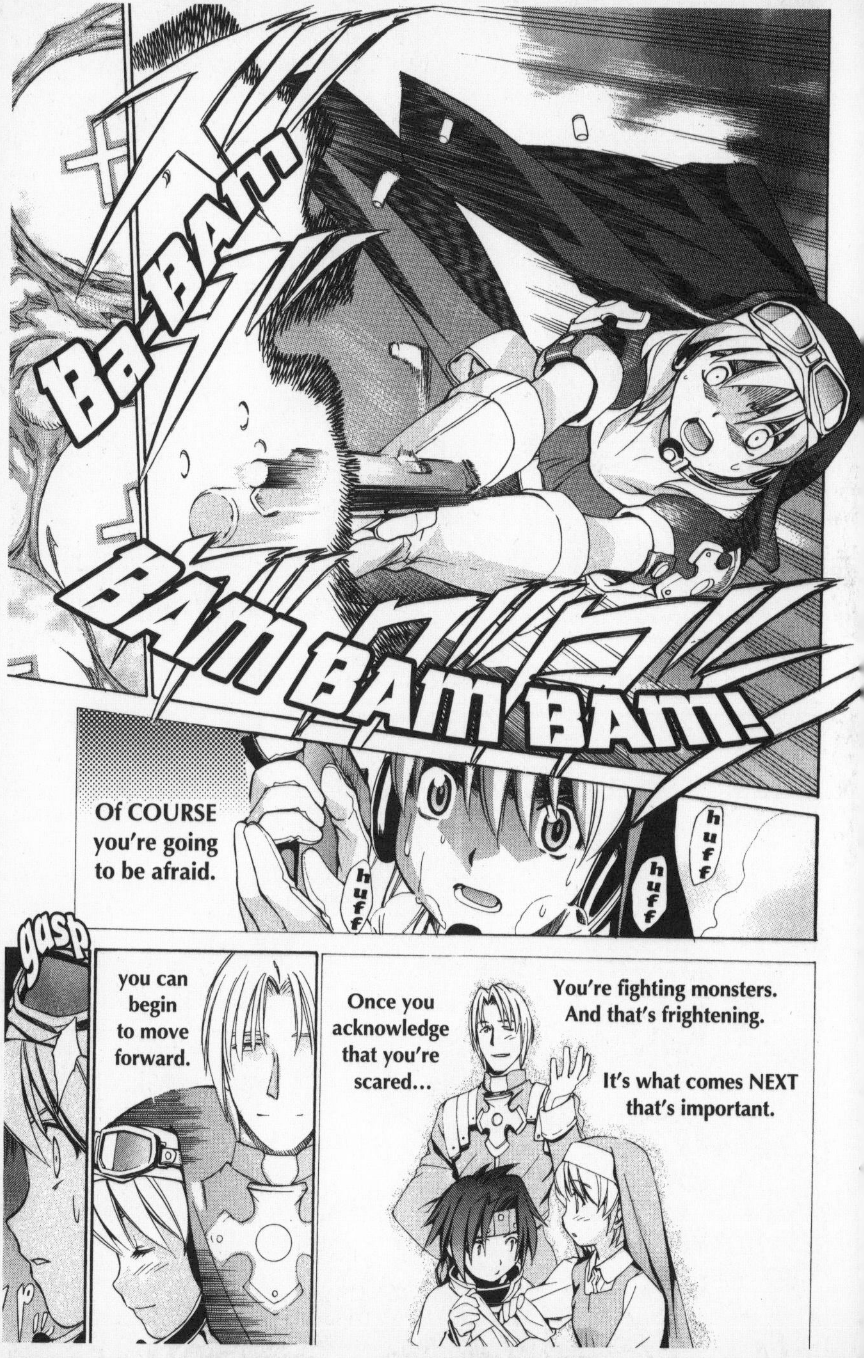
Ba-BAM
BAM BAM BAM!
Of COURSE you're going to be afraid.
huff
huff
huff
You're fighting monsters. And that's frightening.
It's what comes NEXT that's important.
Once you acknowledge that you're scared...
you can begin to move forward.
gasp

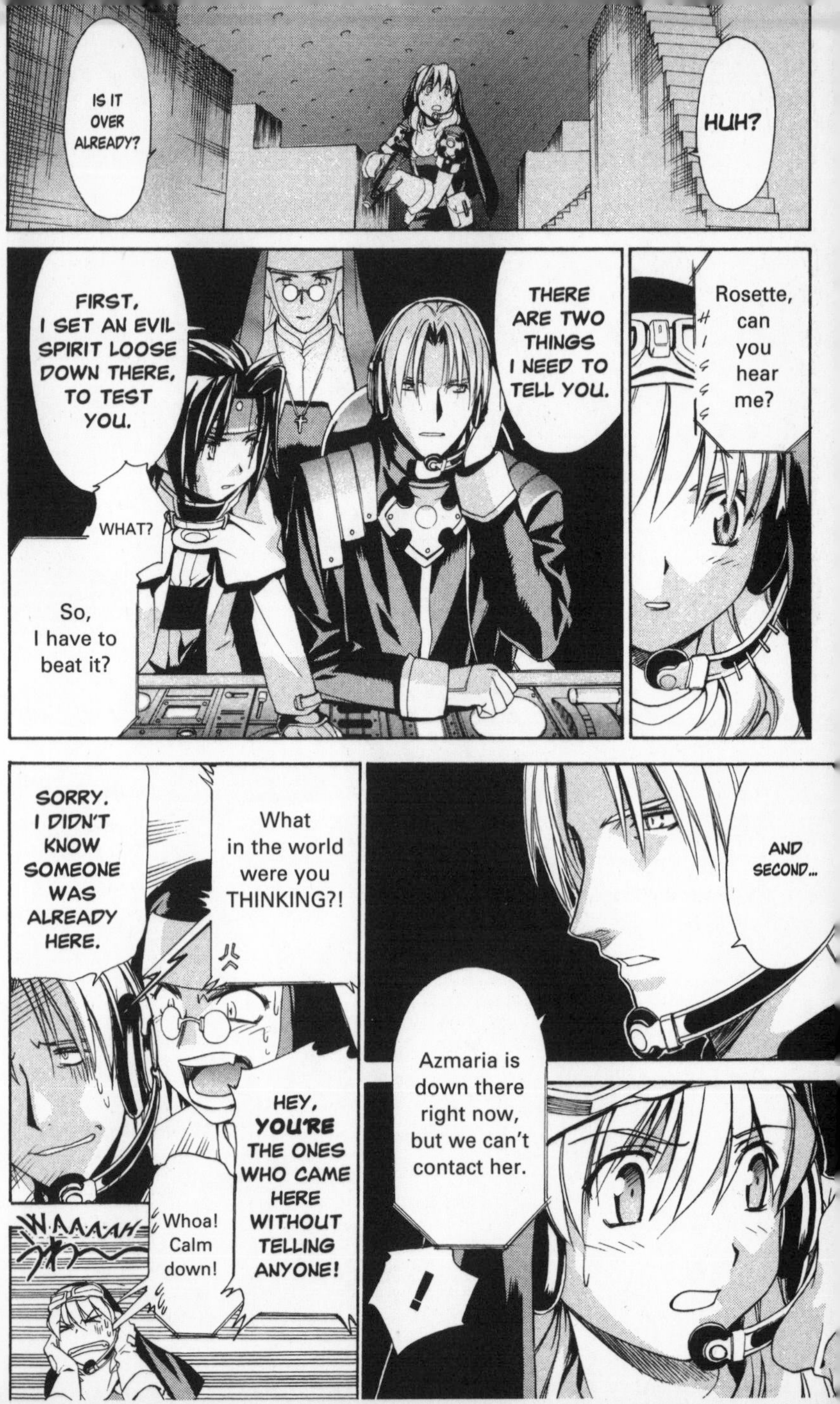

HUH?
IS IT OVER ALREADY?
Rosette, can you hear me?
THERE ARE TWO THINGS I NEED TO TELL YOU.
FIRST, I SET AN EVIL SPIRIT LOOSE DOWN THERE, TO TEST YOU.
WHAT?
So, I have to beat it?
AND SECOND...
Azmaria is down there right now, but we can't contact her.
!
What in the world were you THINKING?!
SORRY. I DIDN'T KNOW SOMEONE WAS ALREADY HERE.
HEY, YOU'RE THE ONES WHO CAME HERE WITHOUT TELLING ANYONE!
Whoa! Calm down!
WAAAAH

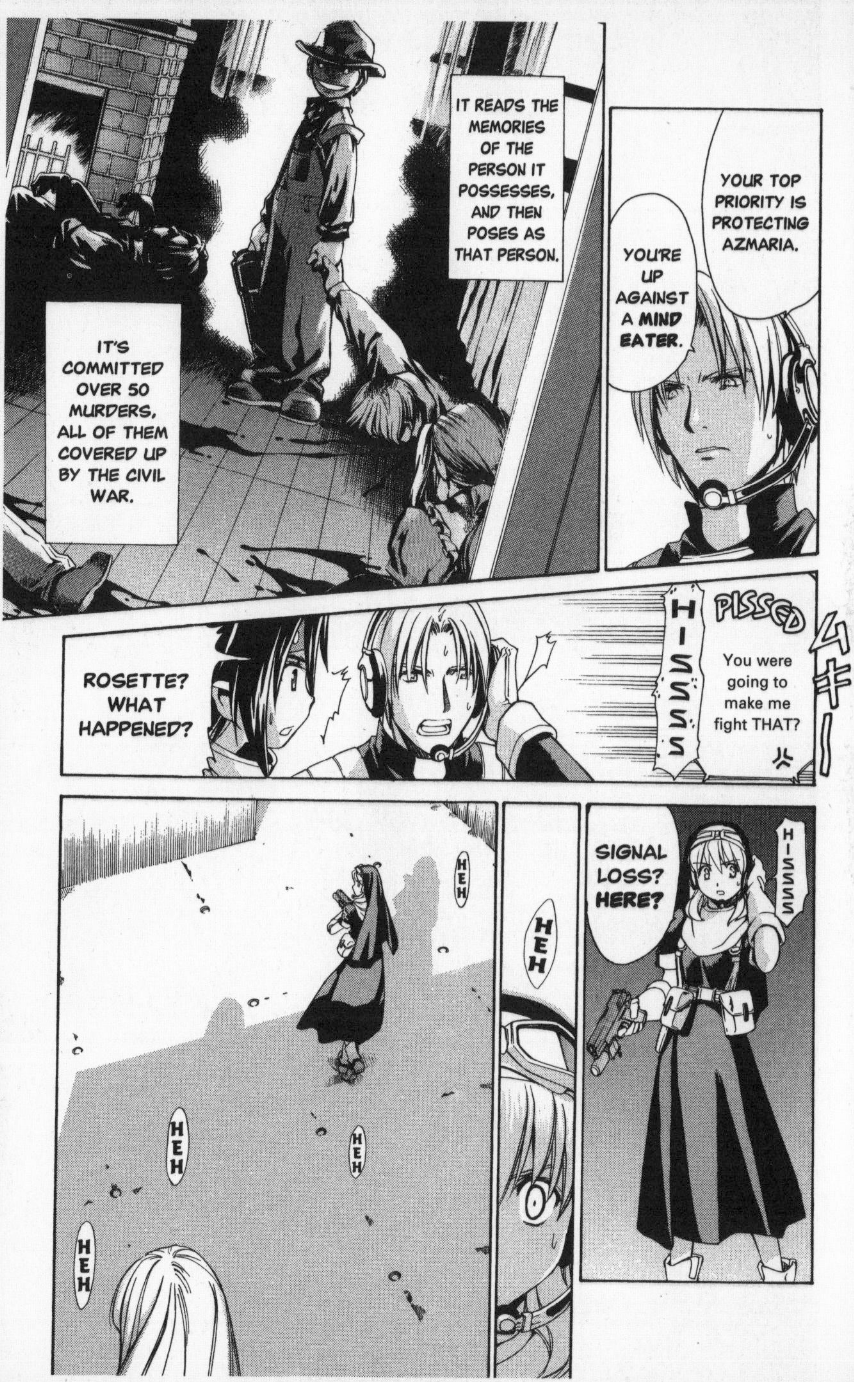
YOUR TOP PRIORITY IS PROTECTING AZMARIA.
YOU'RE UP AGAINST A MIND EATER.
IT READS THE MEMORIES OF THE PERSON IT POSSESSES, AND THEN POSES AS THAT PERSON.
IT'S COMMITTED OVER 50 MURDERS, ALL OF THEM COVERED UP BY THE CIVIL WAR.
ムキー
PISSED
You were going to make me fight THAT?
HISSS
ROSETTE? WHAT HAPPENED?
HISSSS
SIGNAL LOSS? HERE?
HEH
HEH
HEH
HEH
HEH
HEH

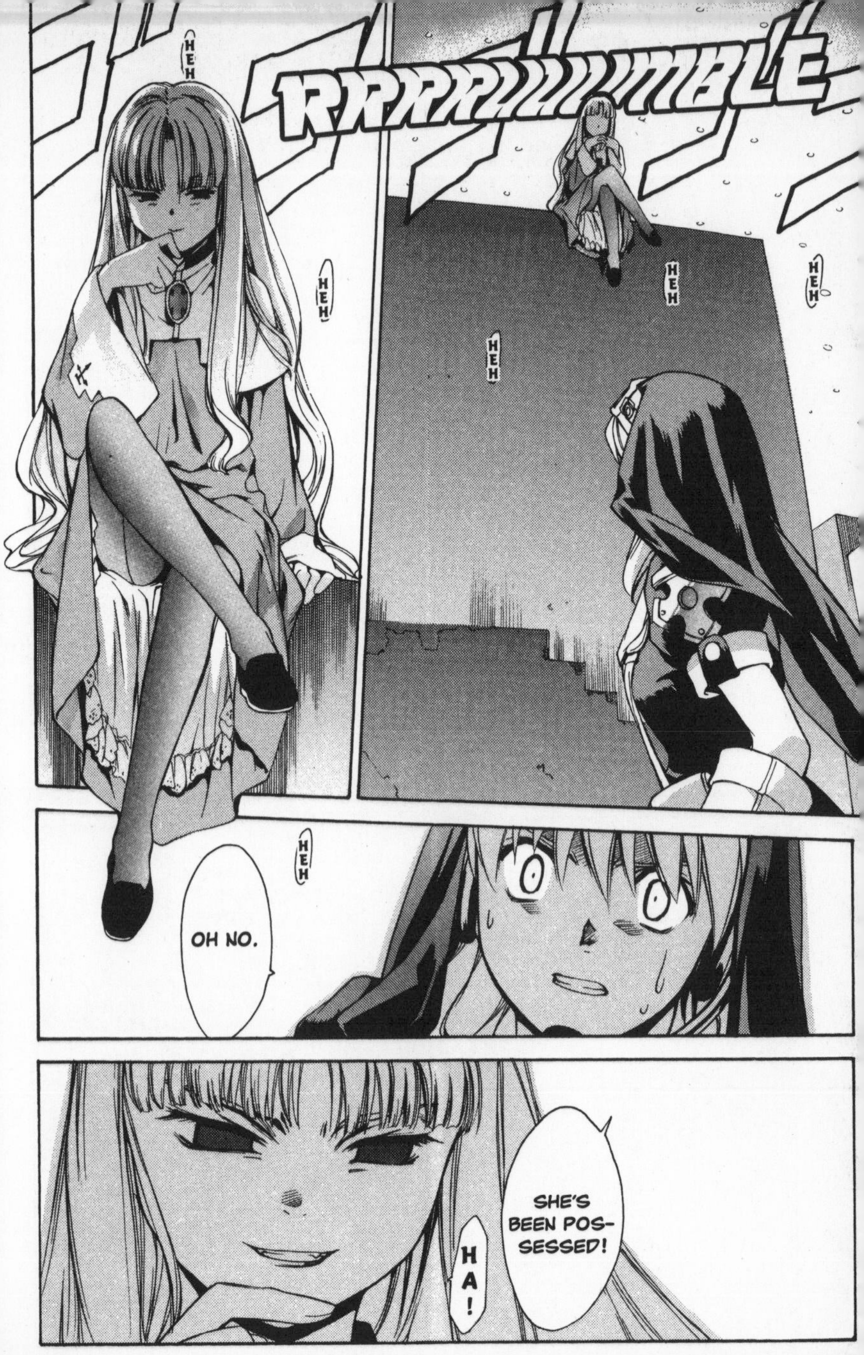
RRRRUUUMBLE
HEH
HEH
HEH
HEH
HEH
HEH
OH NO.
SHE'S BEEN POS-SESSED!
HA!

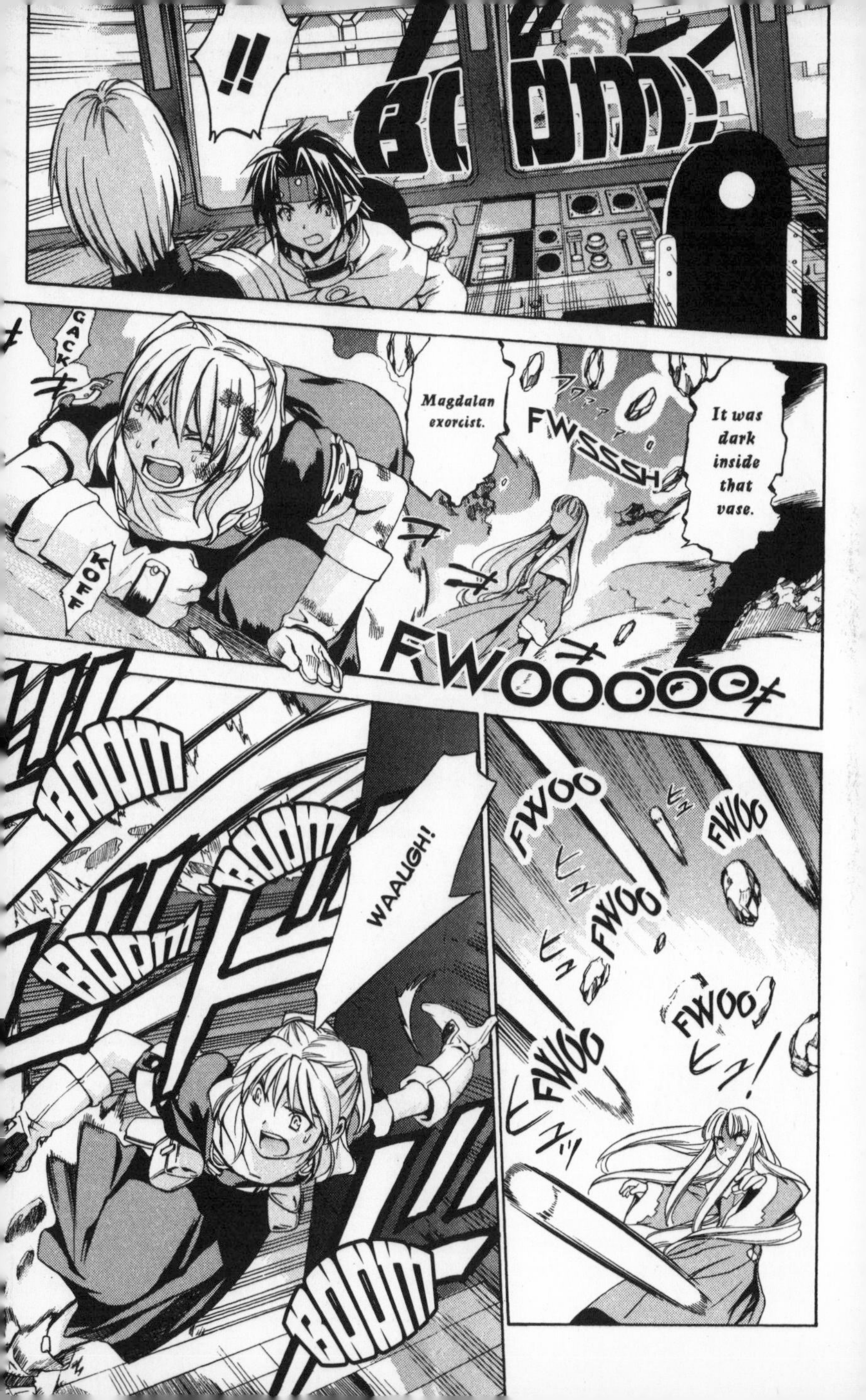

!!
BOOM!
It was dark inside that vase.
FWSSSH
Magdalan exorcist.
GACK
KOFF
FWOOOOOF
FWOO
FWOO
FWOO
FWOO
FWOO
WAAUGH!
BOOM
BOOM
BOOM
BOOM

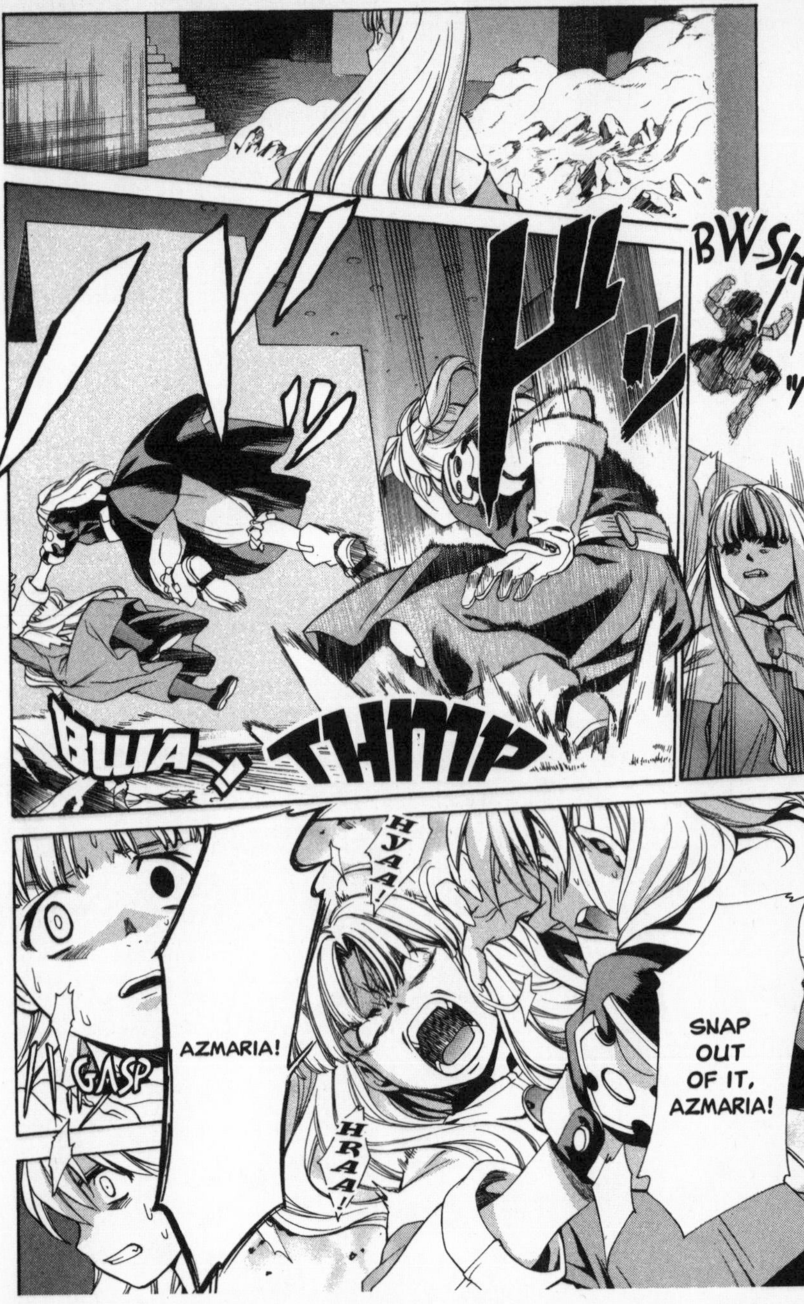
BW-SHY
THMP
BWUA—!
SNAP OUT OF IT, AZMARIA!
HYAA!
HRAA!
AZMARIA!
GASP

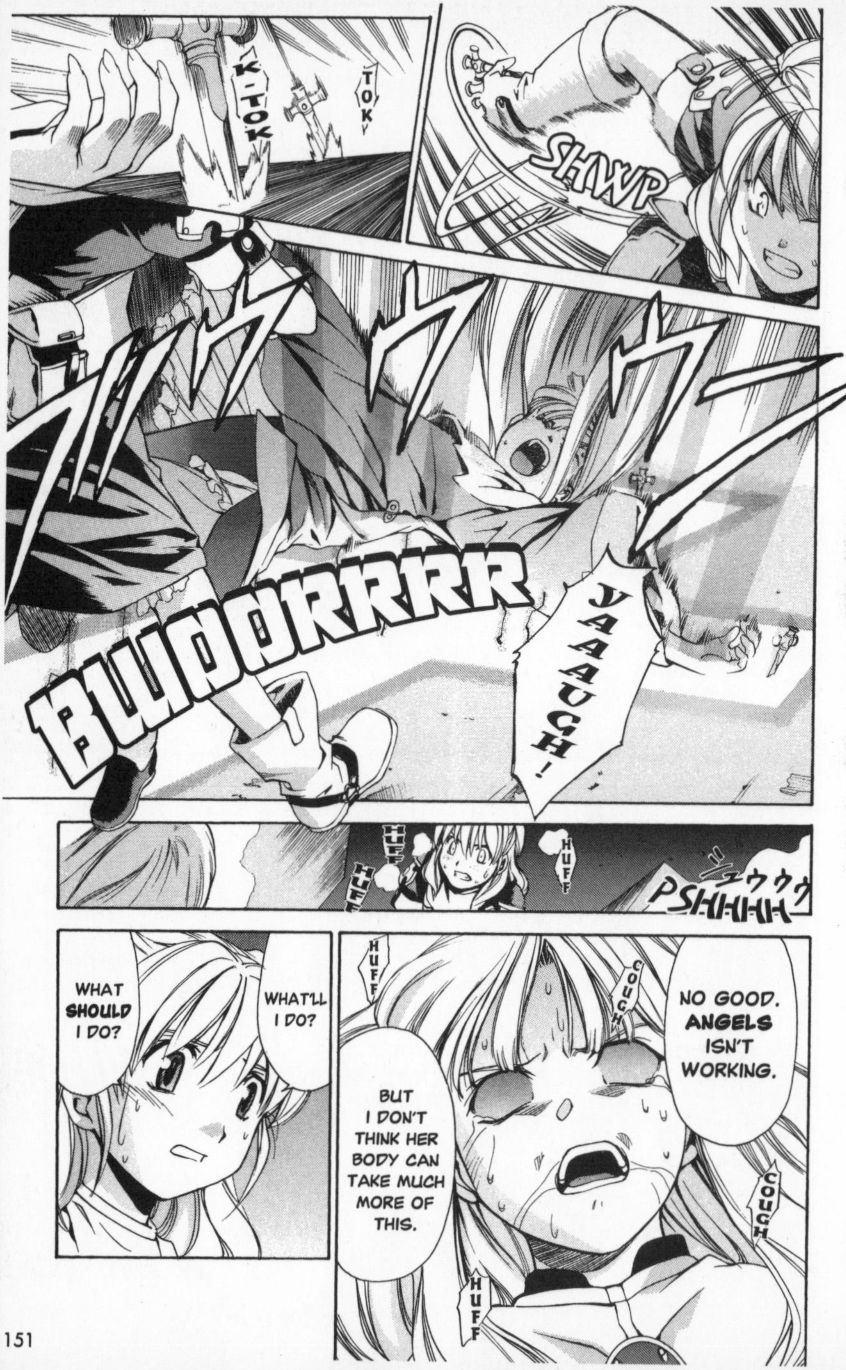
SHWP
TOK
K-TOK
BUDDRRRRR
YAAAUCH!
HUFF
HUFF
HUFF
ジュウウウ
PSHHHHH
NO GOOD. ANGELS ISN'T WORKING.
COUGH
BUT I DON'T THINK HER BODY CAN TAKE MUCH MORE OF THIS.
COUGH
HUFF
HUFF
WHAT'LL I DO?
WHAT SHOULD I DO?

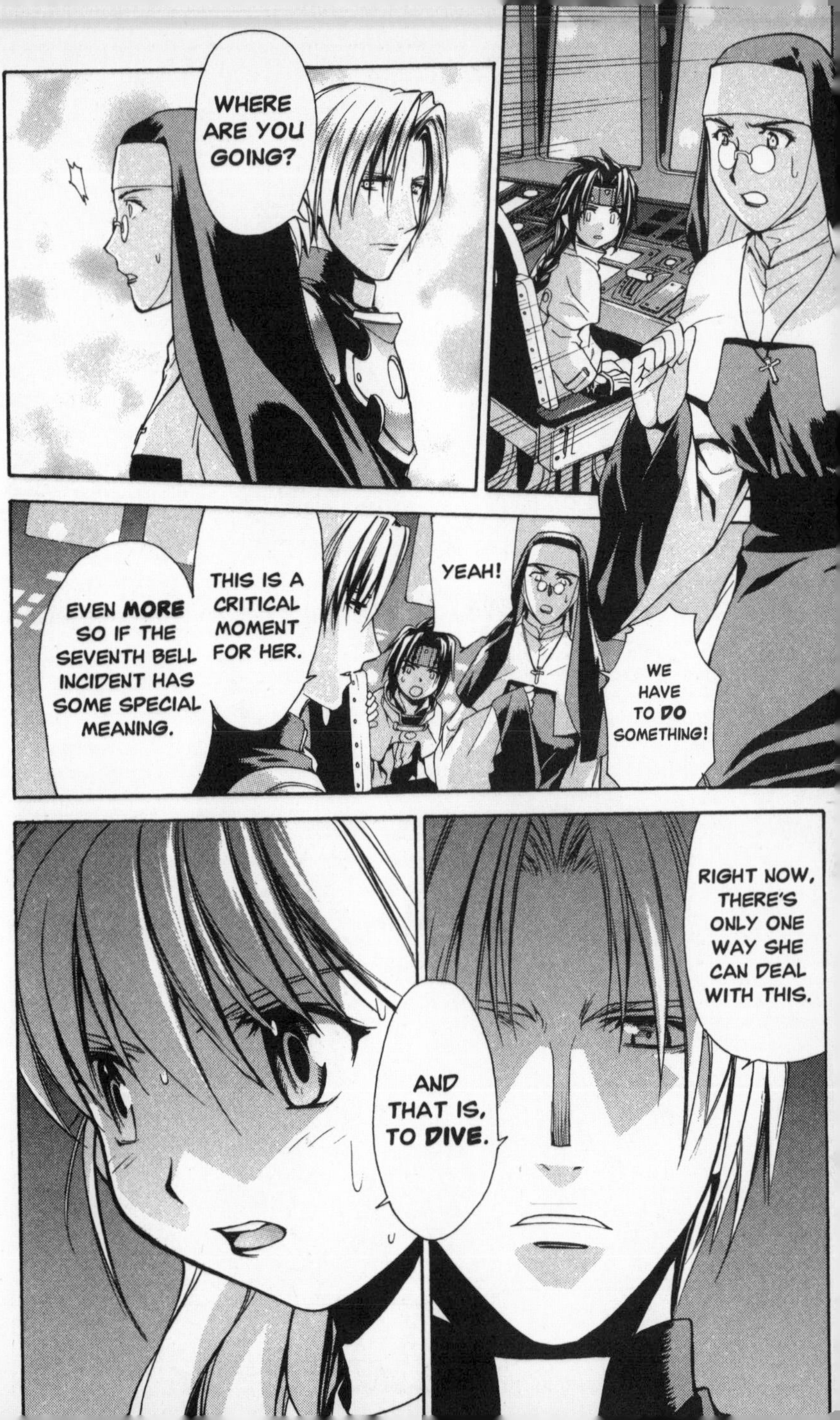
WHERE ARE YOU GOING?
WE HAVE TO DO SOMETHING!
YEAH!
THIS IS A CRITICAL MOMENT FOR HER.
EVEN MORE SO IF THE SEVENTH BELL INCIDENT HAS SOME SPECIAL MEANING.
RIGHT NOW, THERE'S ONLY ONE WAY SHE CAN DEAL WITH THIS.
AND THAT IS, TO DIVE.

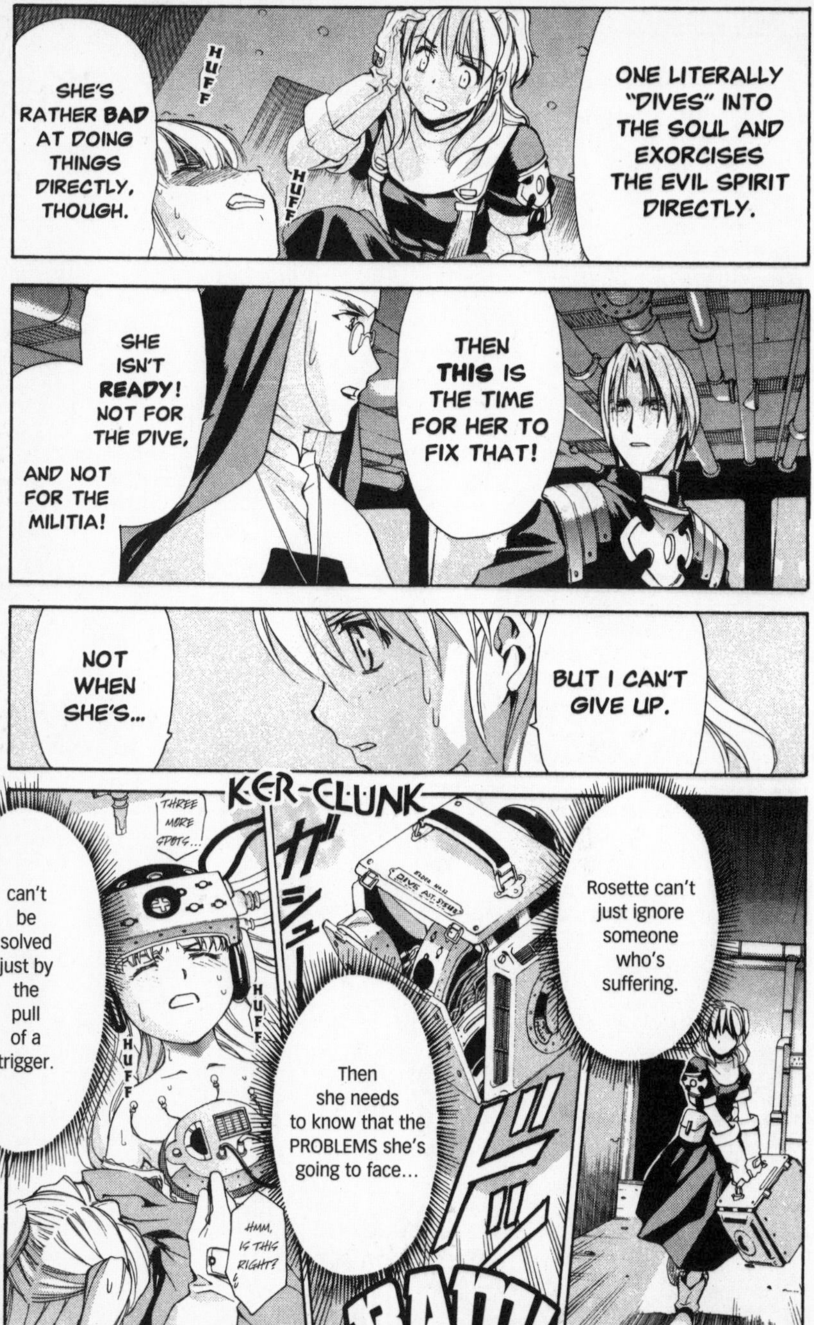

ONE LITERALLY "DIVES" INTO THE SOUL AND EXORCISES THE EVIL SPIRIT DIRECTLY.
HUFF
HUFF
SHE'S RATHER BAD AT DOING THINGS DIRECTLY, THOUGH.
SHE ISN'T READY! NOT FOR THE DIVE,
AND NOT FOR THE MILITIA!
THEN THIS IS THE TIME FOR HER TO FIX THAT!
NOT WHEN SHE'S...
BUT I CAN'T GIVE UP.
KER-CLUNK
THREE MORE SPOTS...
Rosette can't just ignore someone who's suffering.
Then she needs to know that the PROBLEMS she's going to face...
can't be solved just by the pull of a trigger.
HUFF
HUFF
HMM, IS THIS RIGHT?
BAM!

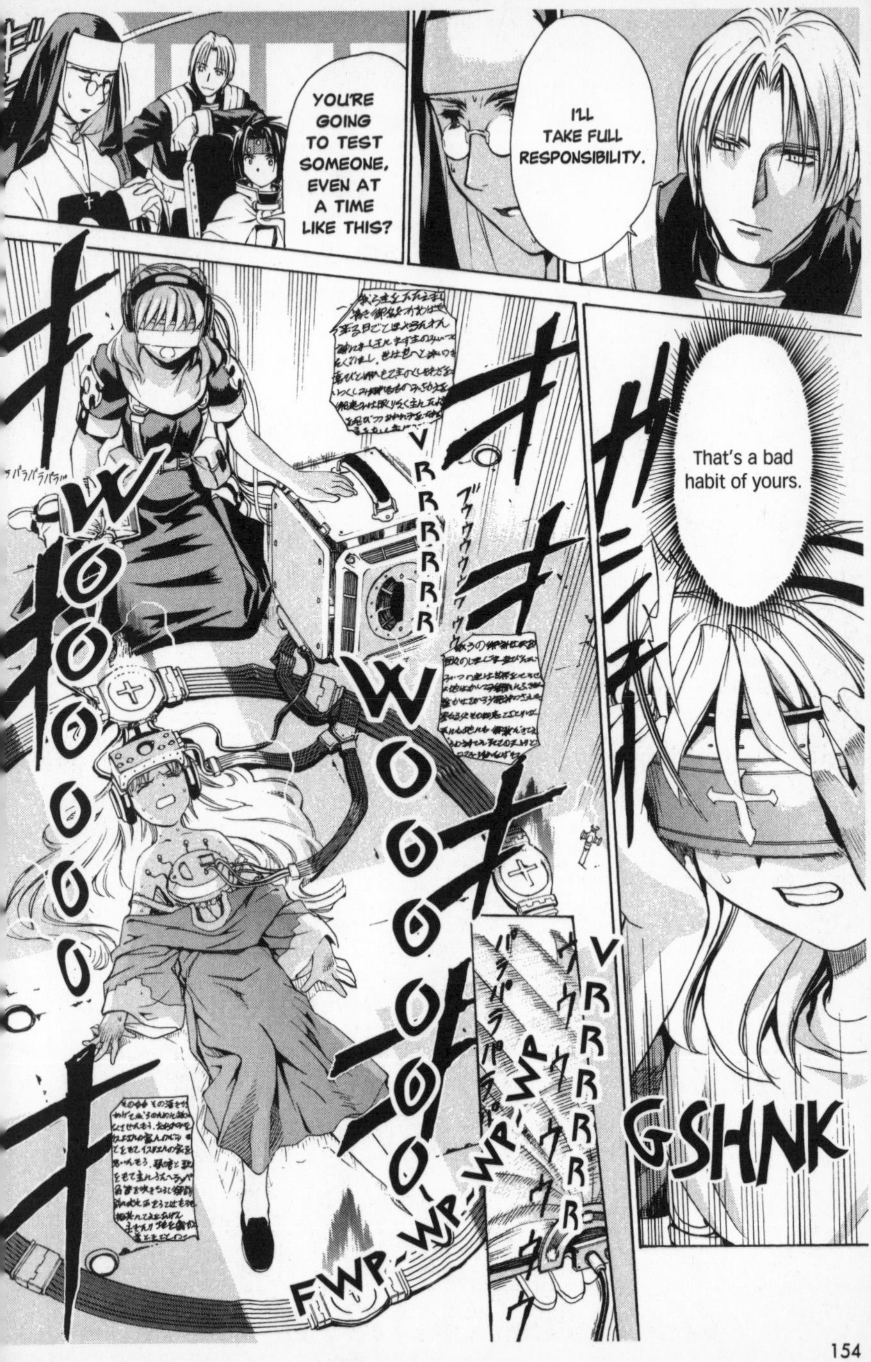
I'LL TAKE FULL RESPONSIBILITY.
YOU'RE GOING TO TEST SOMEONE, EVEN AT A TIME LIKE THIS?
That's a bad habit of yours.
GSHNK
VRRRRRR
VRRRRR
WOOOO-OOO-OO
FWP-WP-WP-WP
WOOOOOOOO

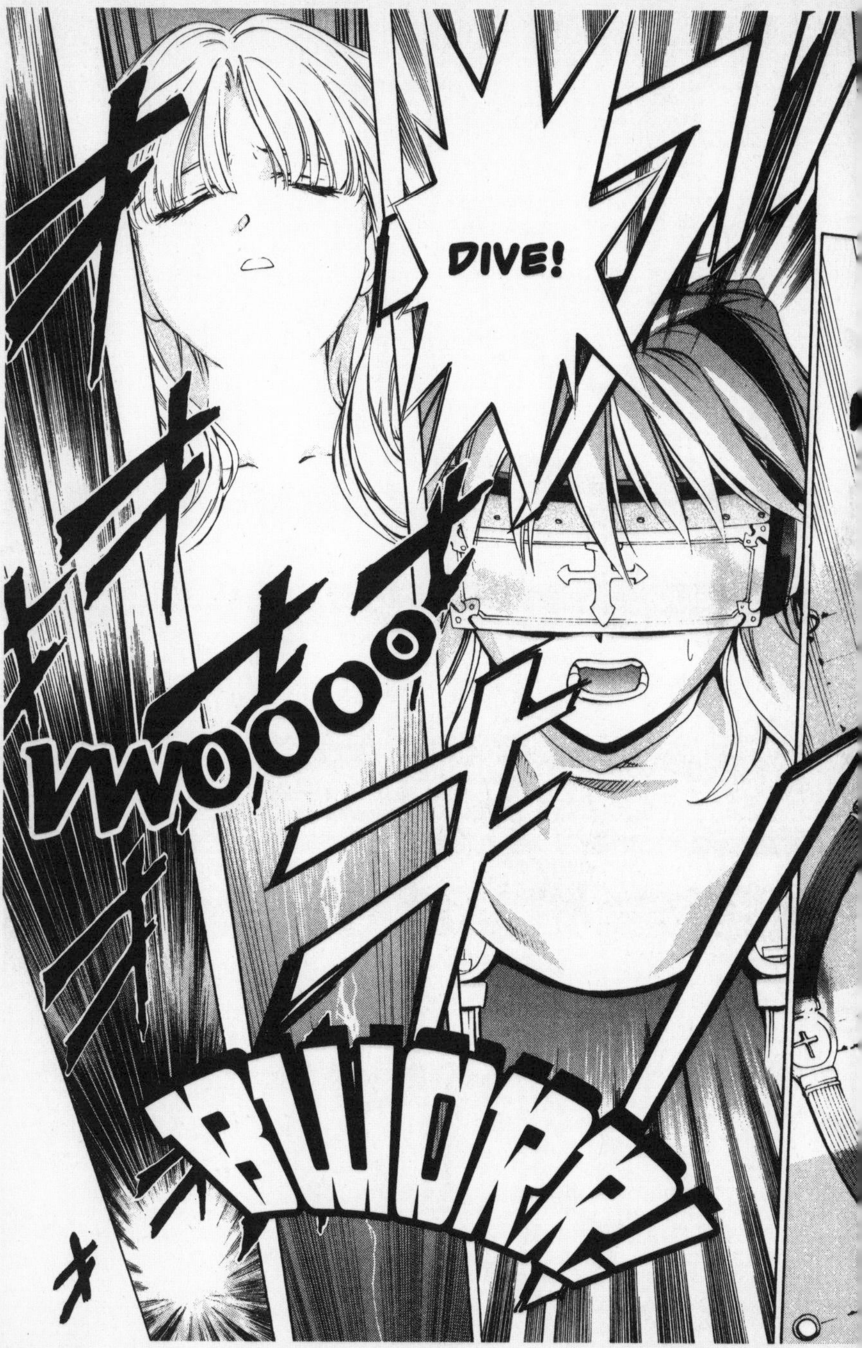
DIVE!
VWOOOOO
BUORR!

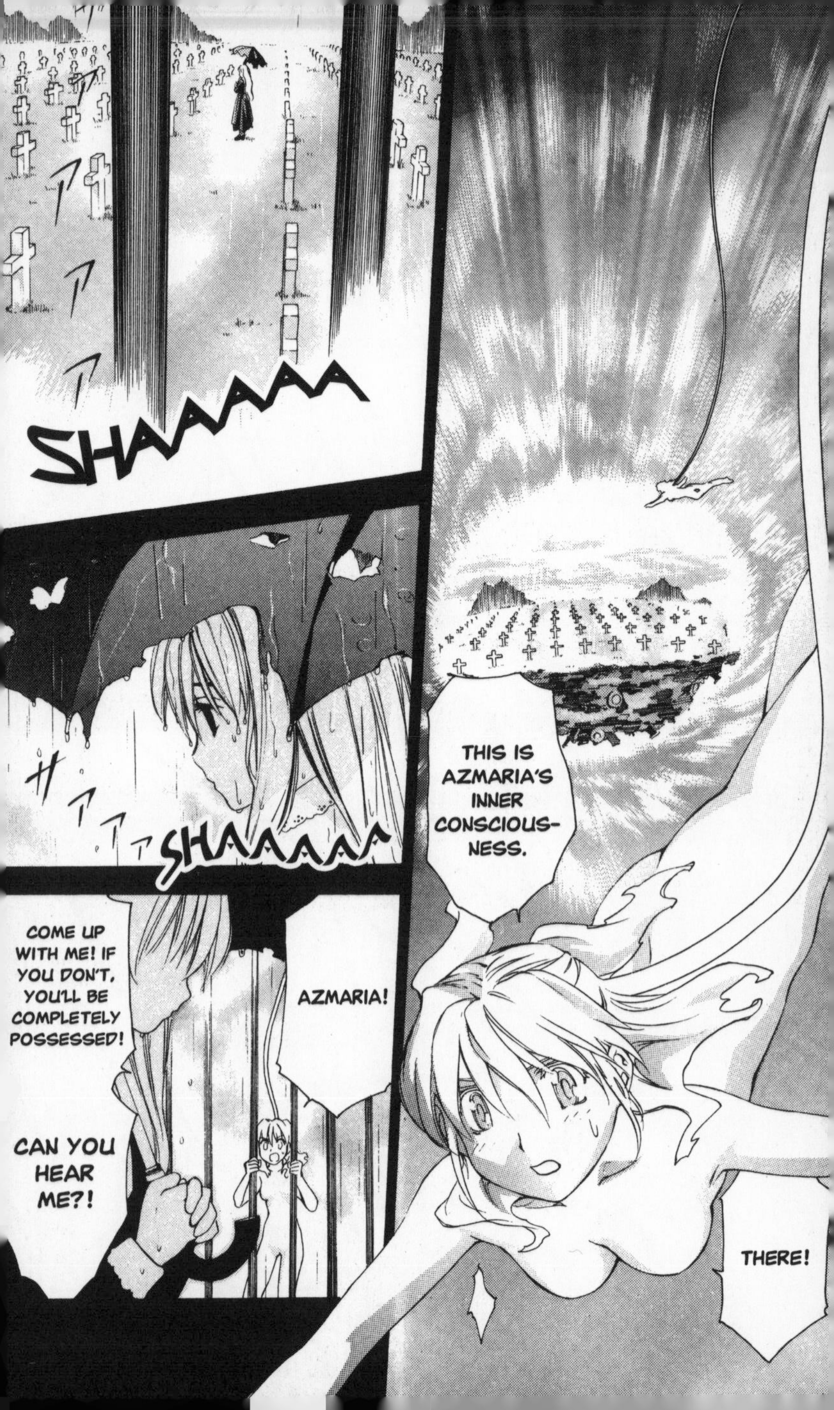

THIS IS AZMARIA'S INNER CONSCIOUS-NESS.
THERE!
SHAAAAA
SHAAAAAA
AZMARIA!
COME UP WITH ME! IF YOU DON'T, YOU'LL BE COMPLETELY POSSESSED!
CAN YOU HEAR ME?!

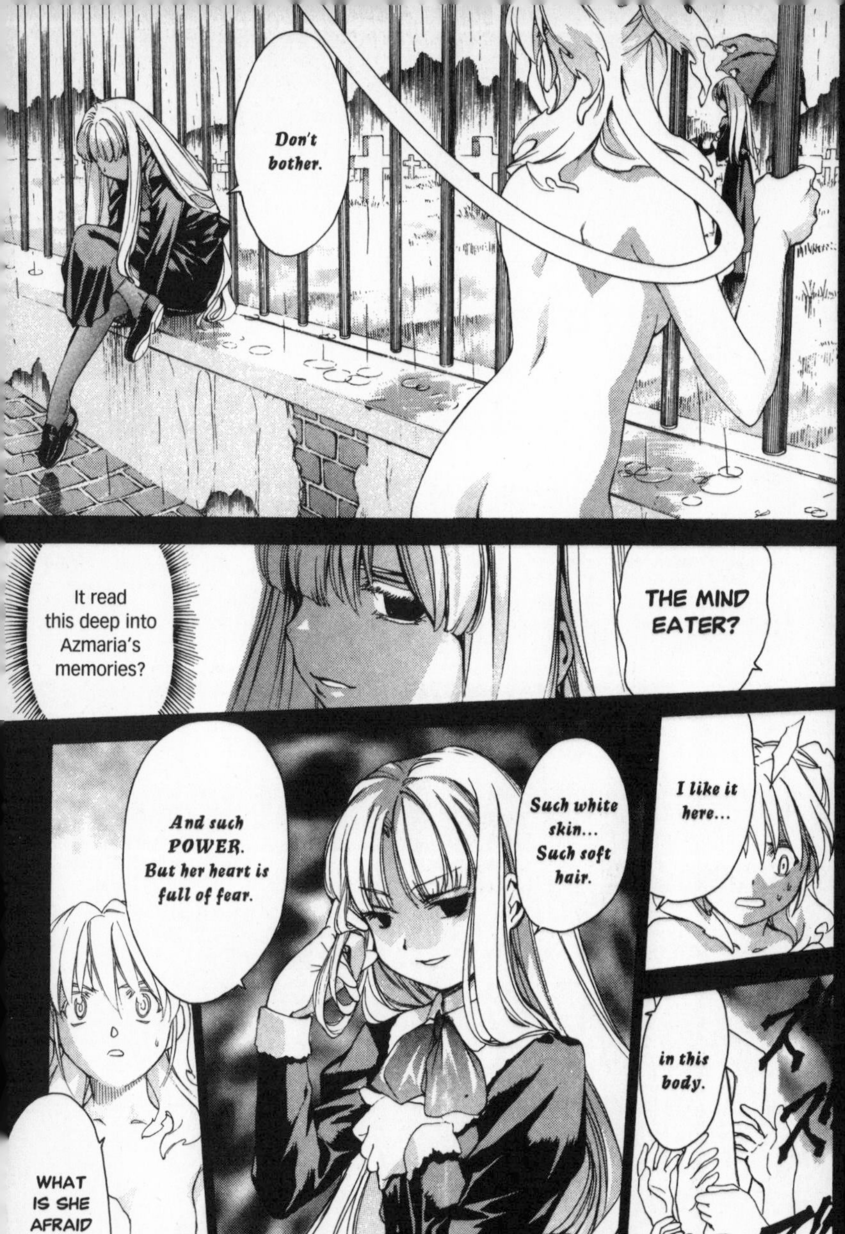
Don't bother.
THE MIND EATER?
It read this deep into Azmaria's memories?
I like it here...
in this body.
Such white skin... Such soft hair.
And such POWER. But her heart is full of fear.
WHAT IS SHE AFRAID OF?

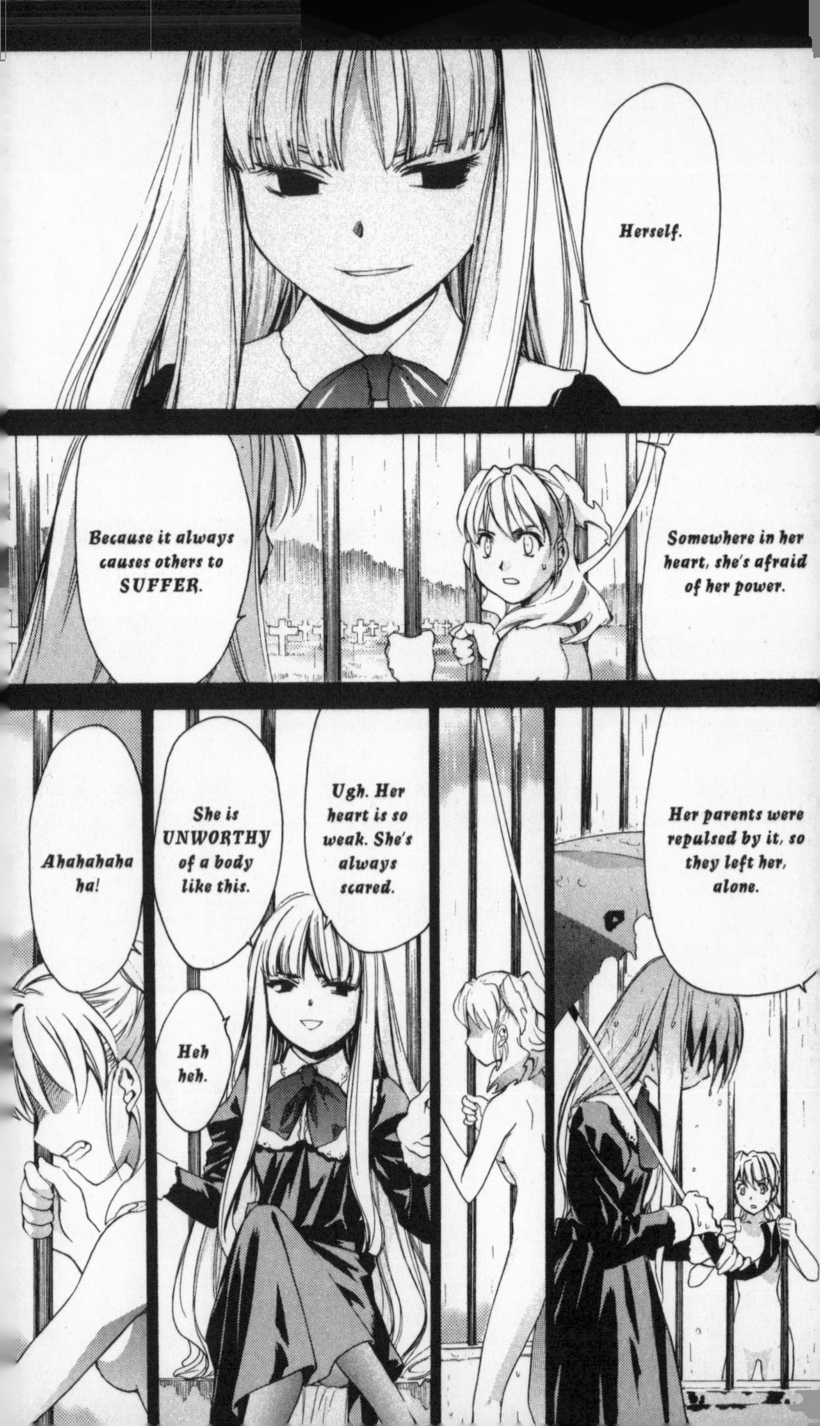
Herself.
Somewhere in her heart, she's afraid of her power.
Because it always causes others to SUFFER.
Her parents were repulsed by it, so they left her, alone.
Ugh. Her heart is so weak. She's always scared.
She is UNWORTHY of a body like this.
Heh heh.
Ahahahaha ha!

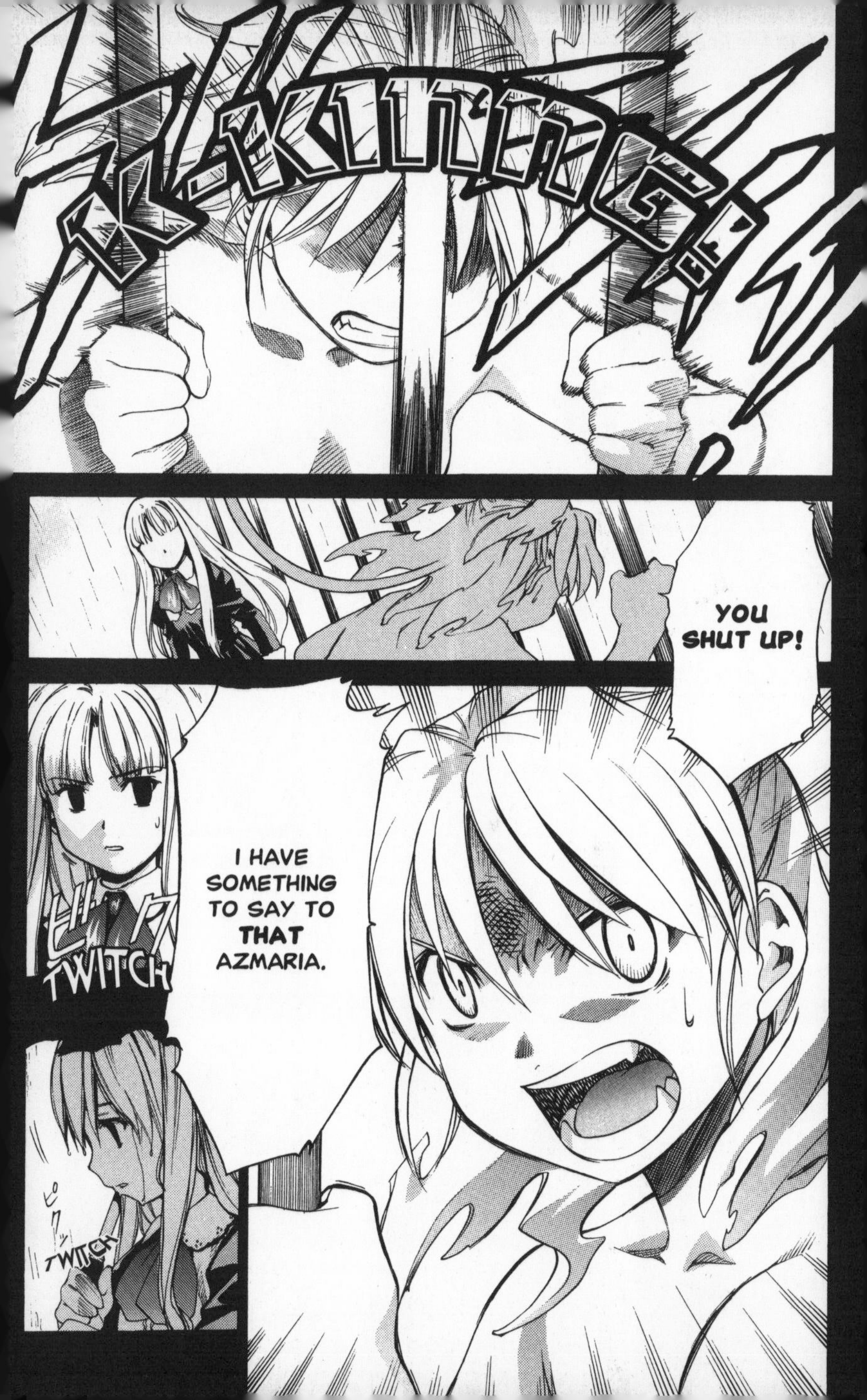
YOU SHUT UP!
I HAVE SOMETHING TO SAY TO **THAT** AZMARIA.
TWITCH
TWITCH

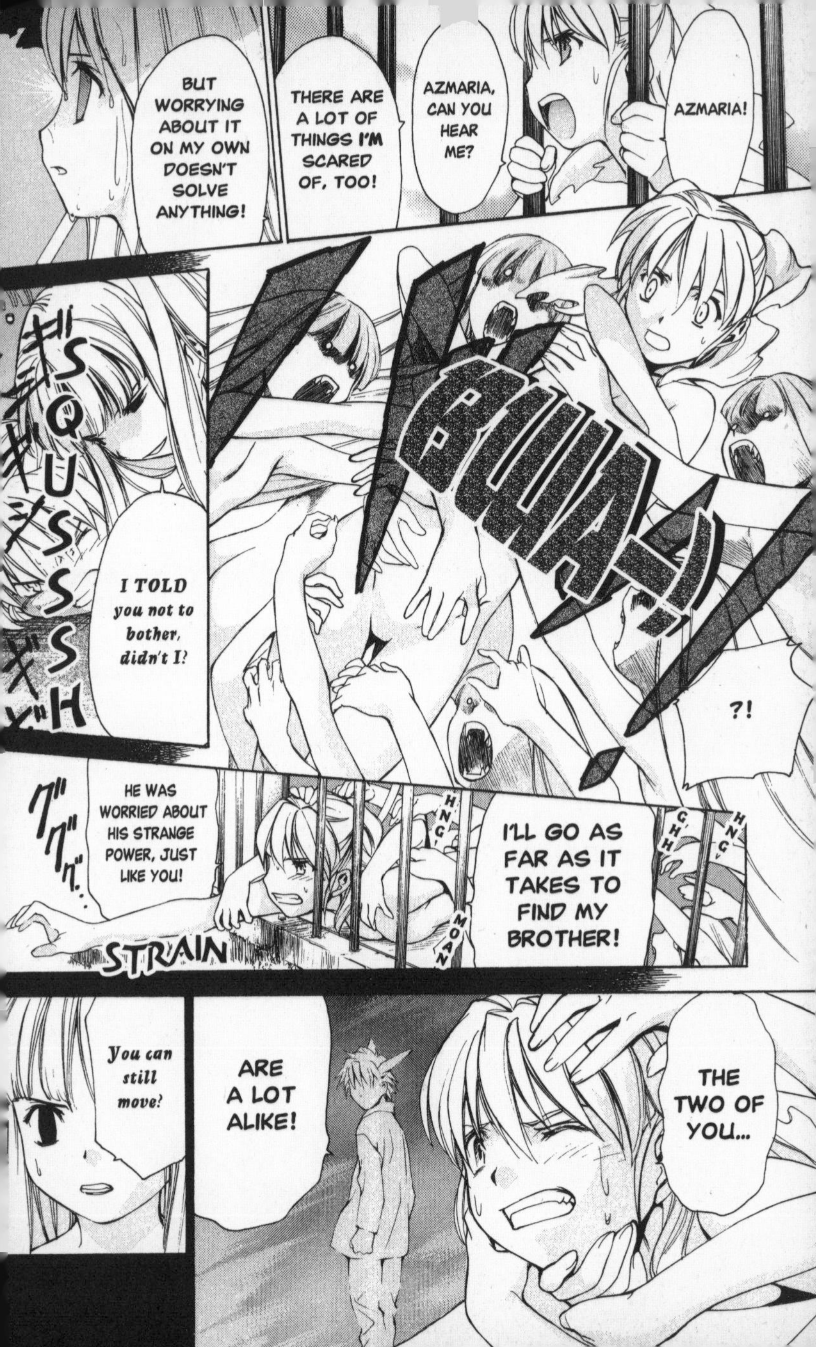
AZMARIA!
AZMARIA, CAN YOU HEAR ME?
THERE ARE A LOT OF THINGS I'M SCARED OF, TOO!
BUT WORRYING ABOUT IT ON MY OWN DOESN'T SOLVE ANYTHING!
?!
I TOLD you not to bother, didn't I?
SQUSSSH
HNG
GHH
I'LL GO AS FAR AS IT TAKES TO FIND MY BROTHER!
HNG
MOAN
HE WAS WORRIED ABOUT HIS STRANGE POWER, JUST LIKE YOU!
STRAIN
THE TWO OF YOU...
ARE A LOT ALIKE!
You can still move?

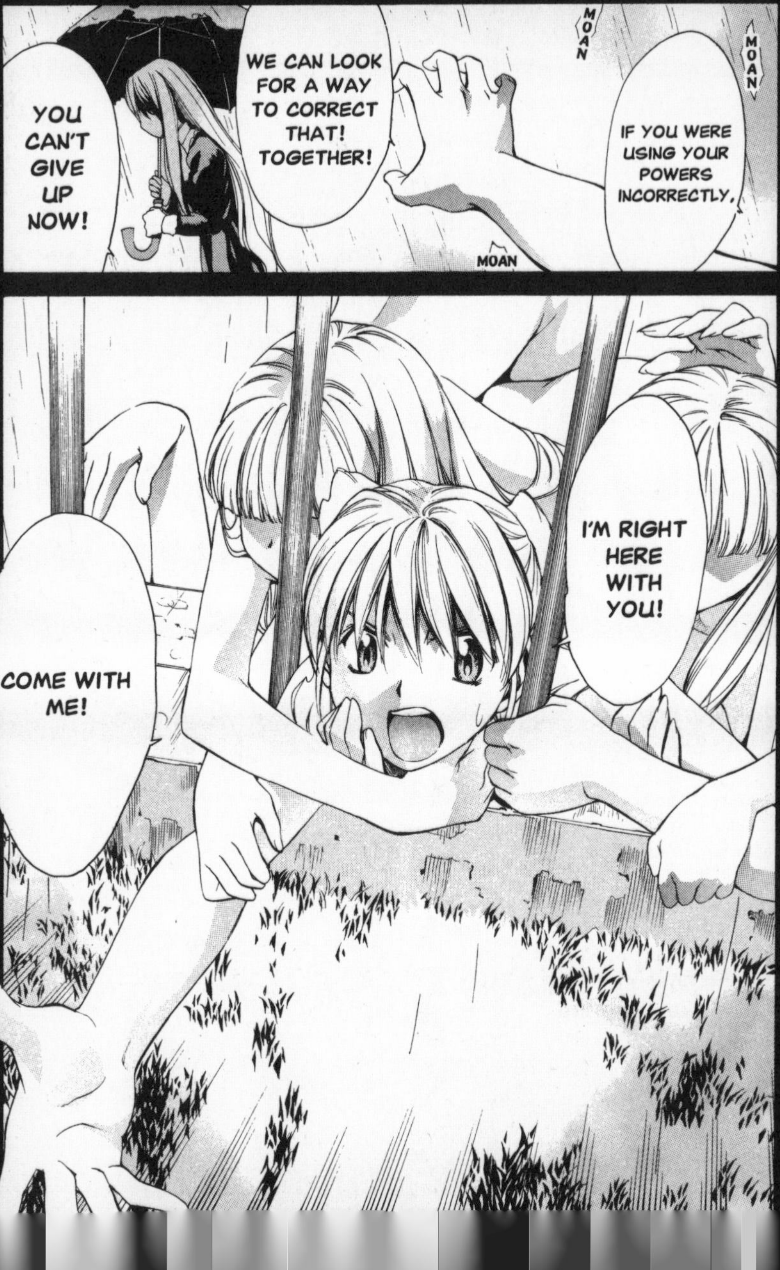
MOAN
MOAN
IF YOU WERE USING YOUR POWERS INCORRECTLY,
WE CAN LOOK FOR A WAY TO CORRECT THAT! TOGETHER!
YOU CAN'T GIVE UP NOW!
MOAN
I'M RIGHT HERE WITH YOU!
COME WITH ME!

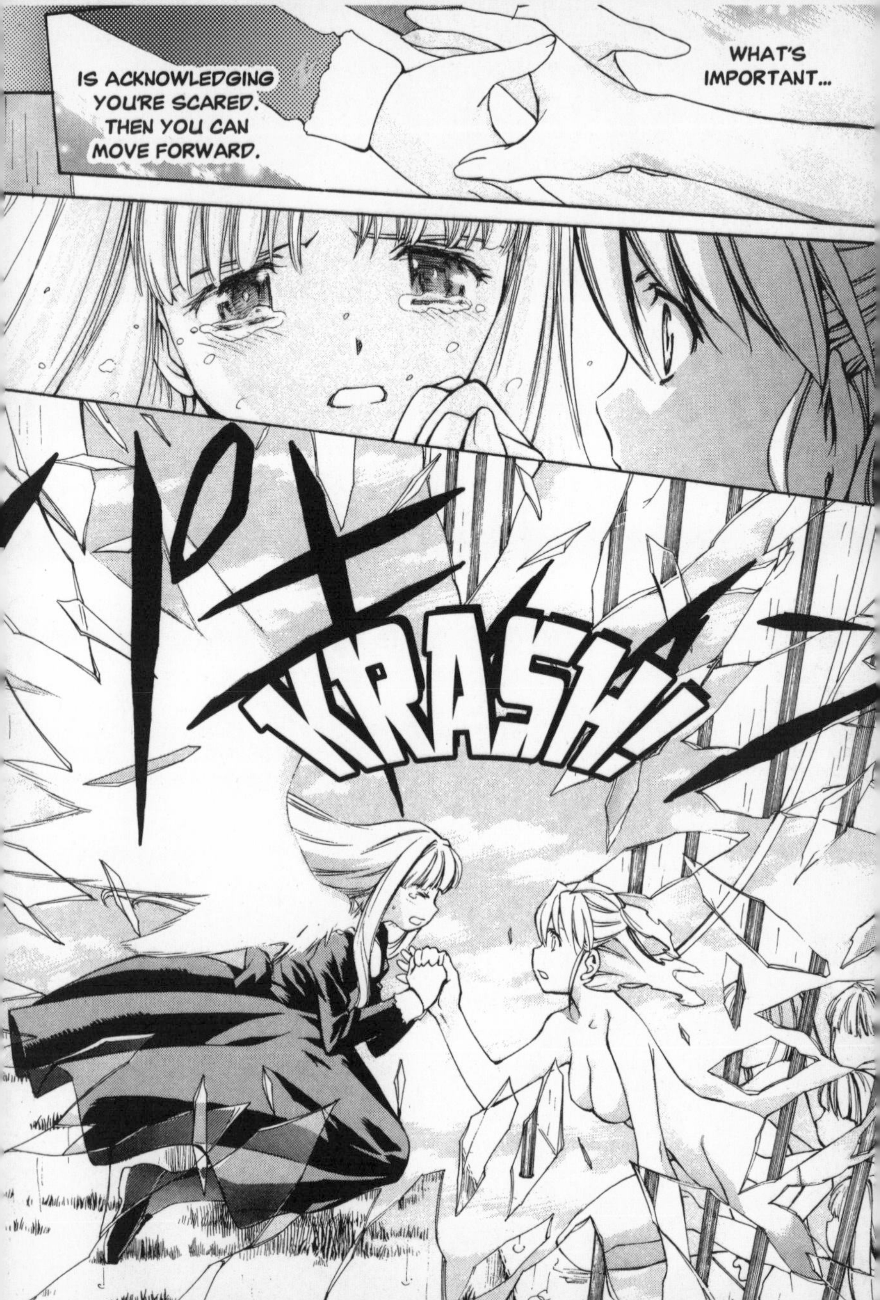
WHAT'S IMPORTANT...
IS ACKNOWLEDGING YOU'RE SCARED. THEN YOU CAN MOVE FORWARD.
KRASH!

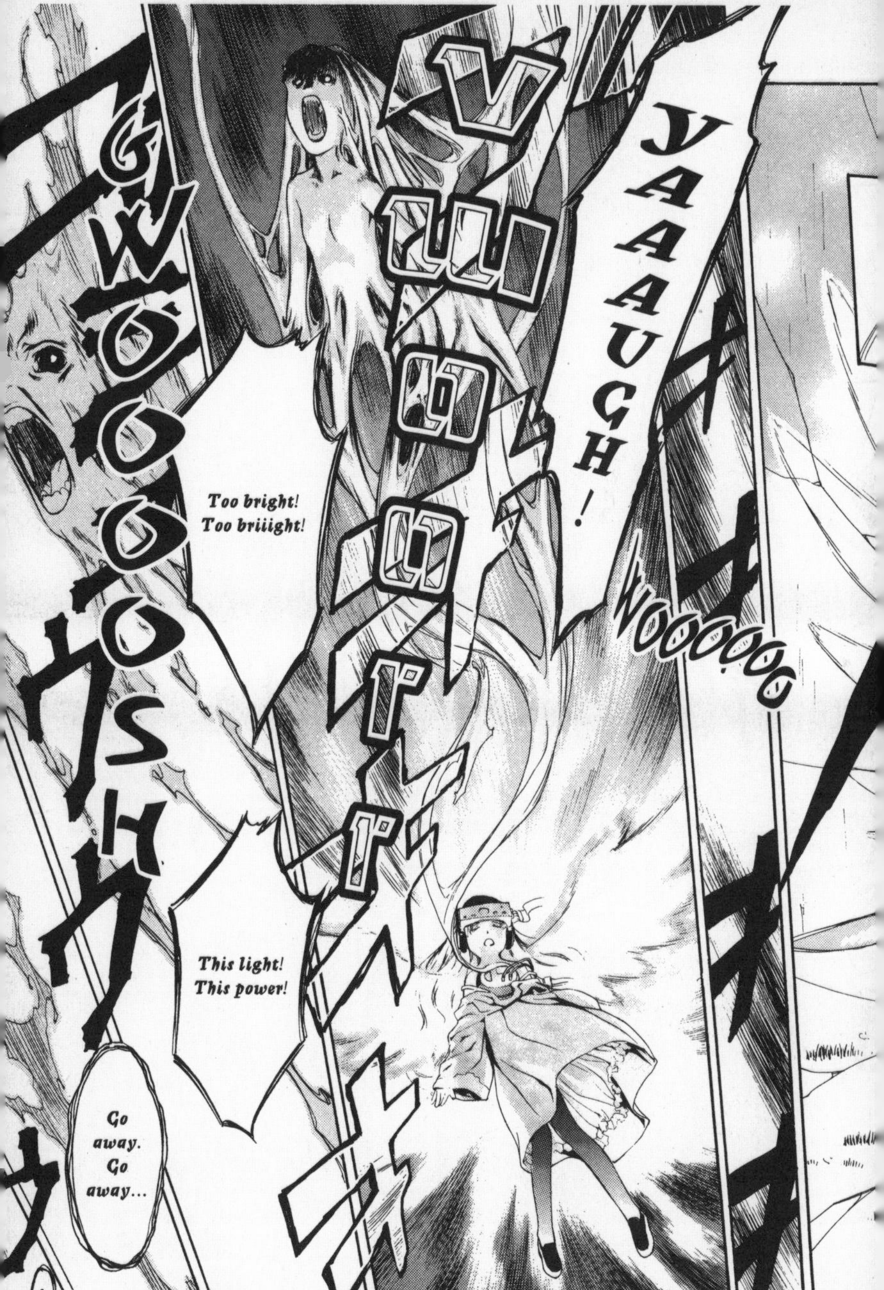
YAAAUCH!
WOOOOOO
Too bright! Too briiight!
This light! This power!
Go away. Go away...
GWOOOOOSH

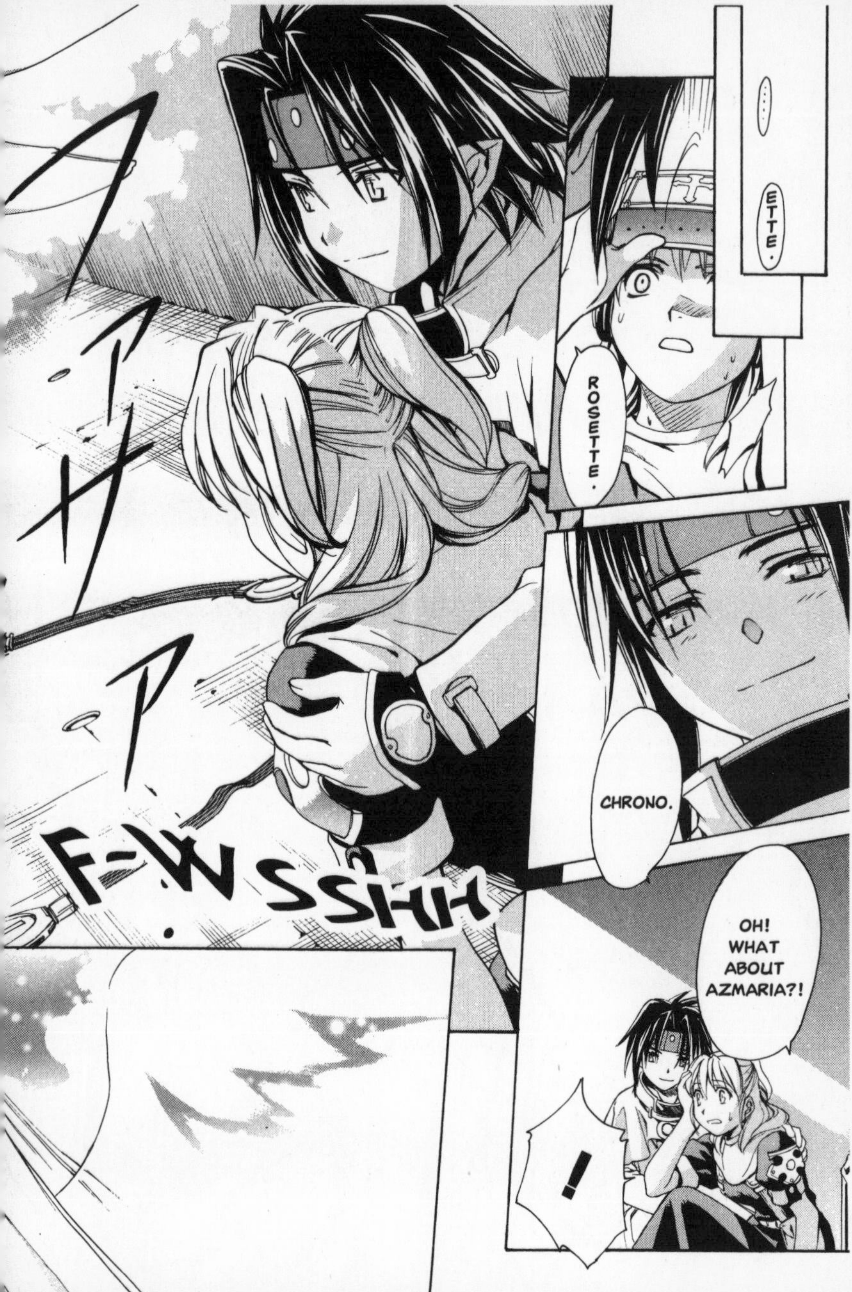

...ETTE.
ROSETTE.
F-WSSHH
CHRONO.
OH! WHAT ABOUT AZMARIA?!
!

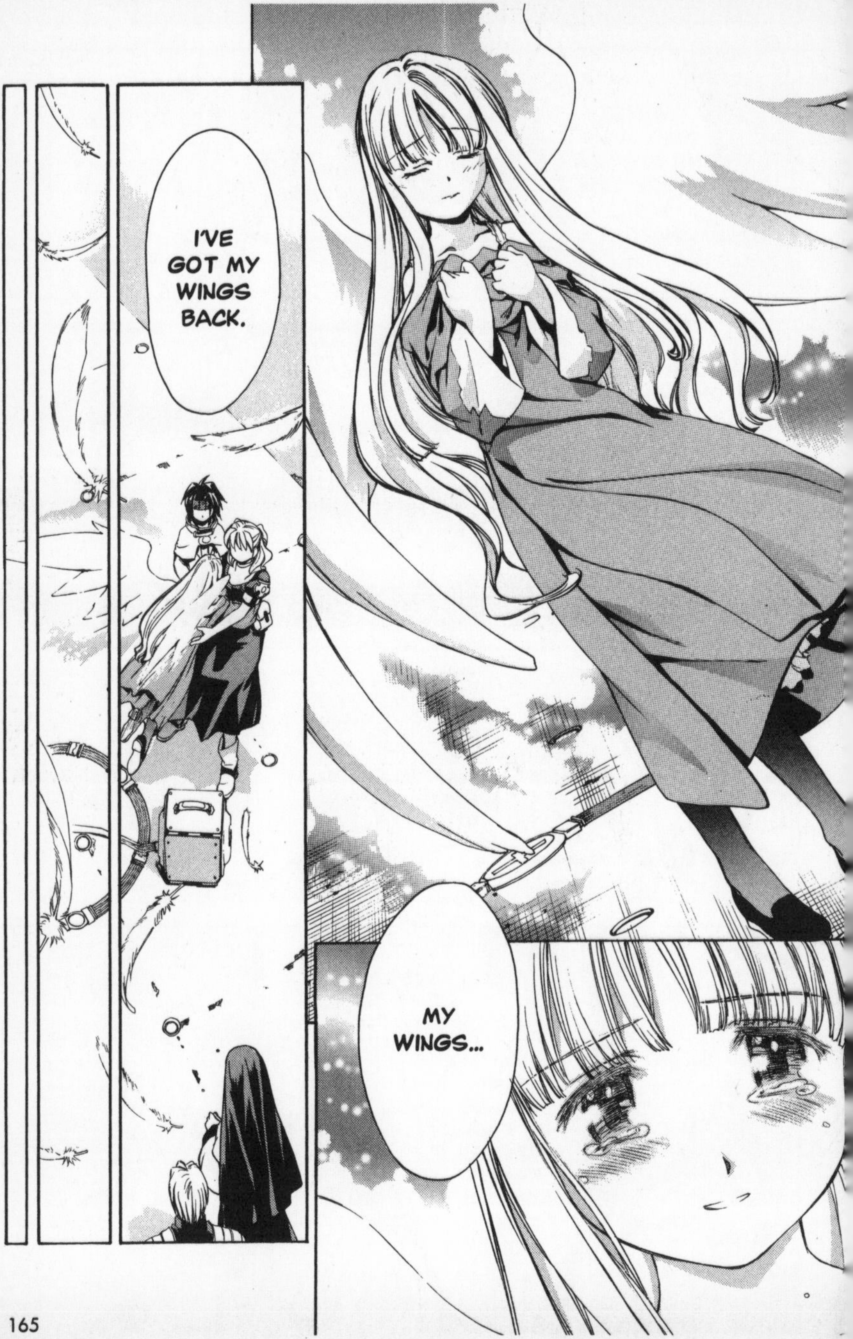
I'VE GOT MY WINGS BACK.
MY WINGS...

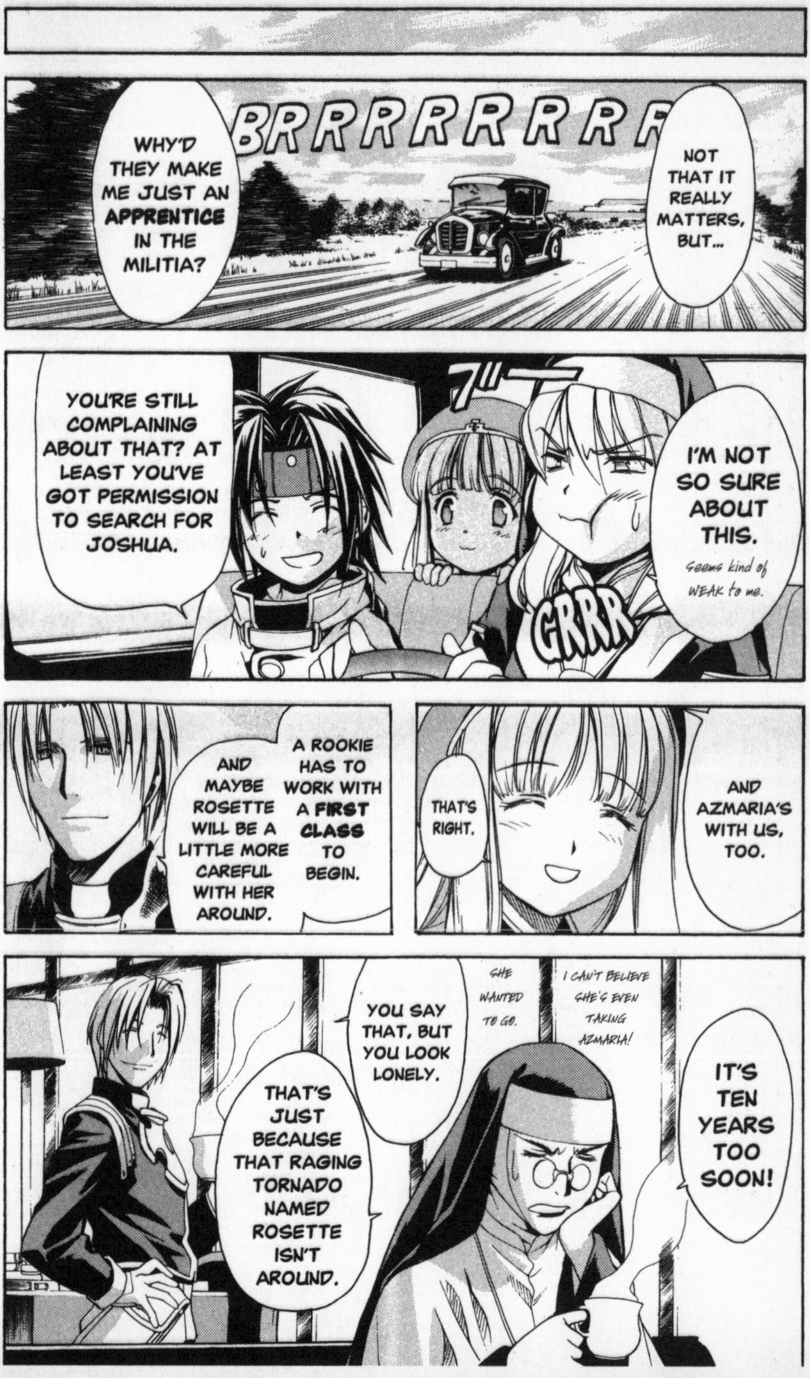
BRRRRRRR
WHY'D THEY MAKE ME JUST AN APPRENTICE IN THE MILITIA?
NOT THAT IT REALLY MATTERS, BUT...
ブー
YOU'RE STILL COMPLAINING ABOUT THAT? AT LEAST YOU'VE GOT PERMISSION TO SEARCH FOR JOSHUA.
I'M NOT SO SURE ABOUT THIS.
Seems kind of WEAK to me.
GRRR
A ROOKIE HAS TO WORK WITH A FIRST CLASS TO BEGIN.
AND MAYBE ROSETTE WILL BE A LITTLE MORE CAREFUL WITH HER AROUND.
AND AZMARIA'S WITH US, TOO.
THAT'S RIGHT.
YOU SAY THAT, BUT YOU LOOK LONELY.
THAT'S JUST BECAUSE THAT RAGING TORNADO NAMED ROSETTE ISN'T AROUND.
SHE WANTED TO GO.
I CAN'T BELIEVE SHE'S EVEN TAKING AZMARIA!
IT'S TEN YEARS TOO SOON!

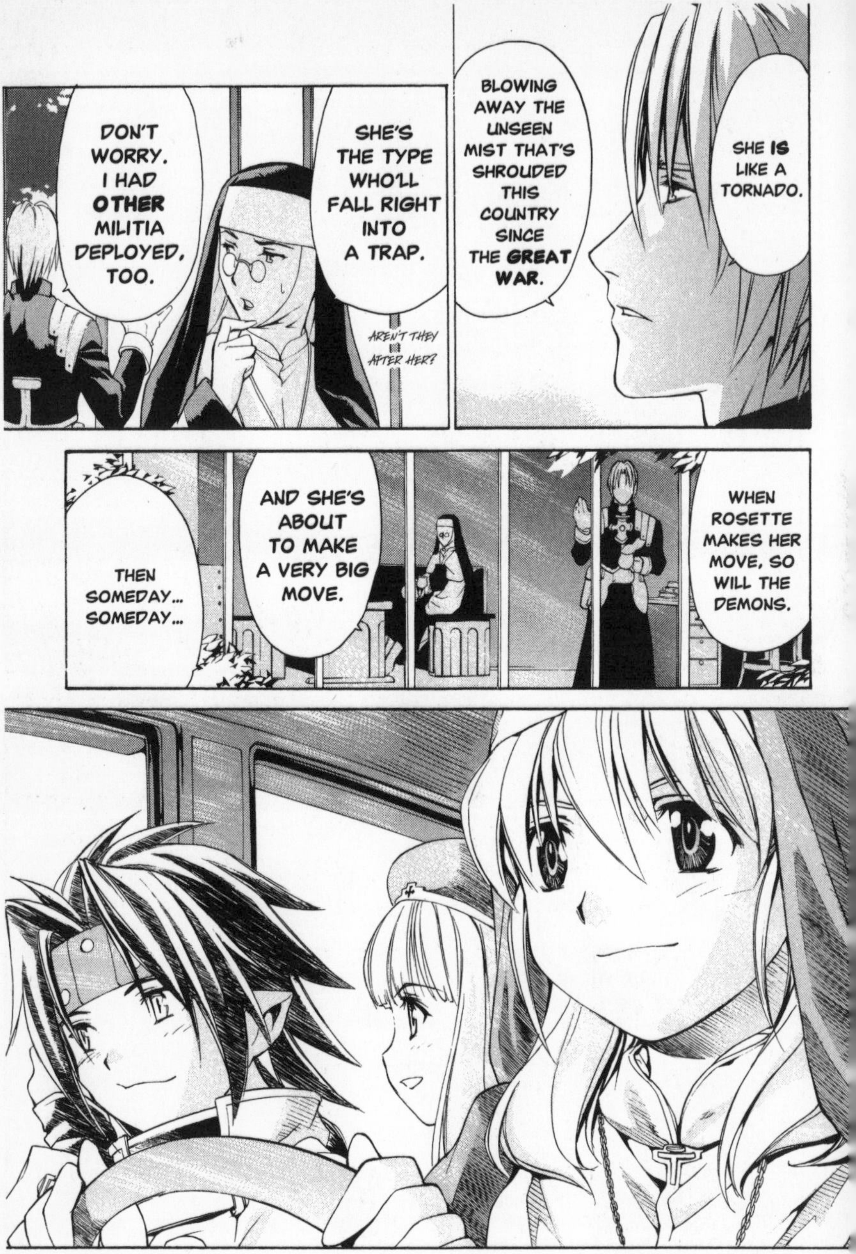
SHE IS LIKE A TORNADO.
BLOWING AWAY THE UNSEEN MIST THAT'S SHROUDED THIS COUNTRY SINCE THE GREAT WAR.
SHE'S THE TYPE WHO'LL FALL RIGHT INTO A TRAP.
AREN'T THEY AFTER HER?
DON'T WORRY. I HAD OTHER MILITIA DEPLOYED, TOO.
WHEN ROSETTE MAKES HER MOVE, SO WILL THE DEMONS.
AND SHE'S ABOUT TO MAKE A VERY BIG MOVE.
THEN SOMEDAY... SOMEDAY...

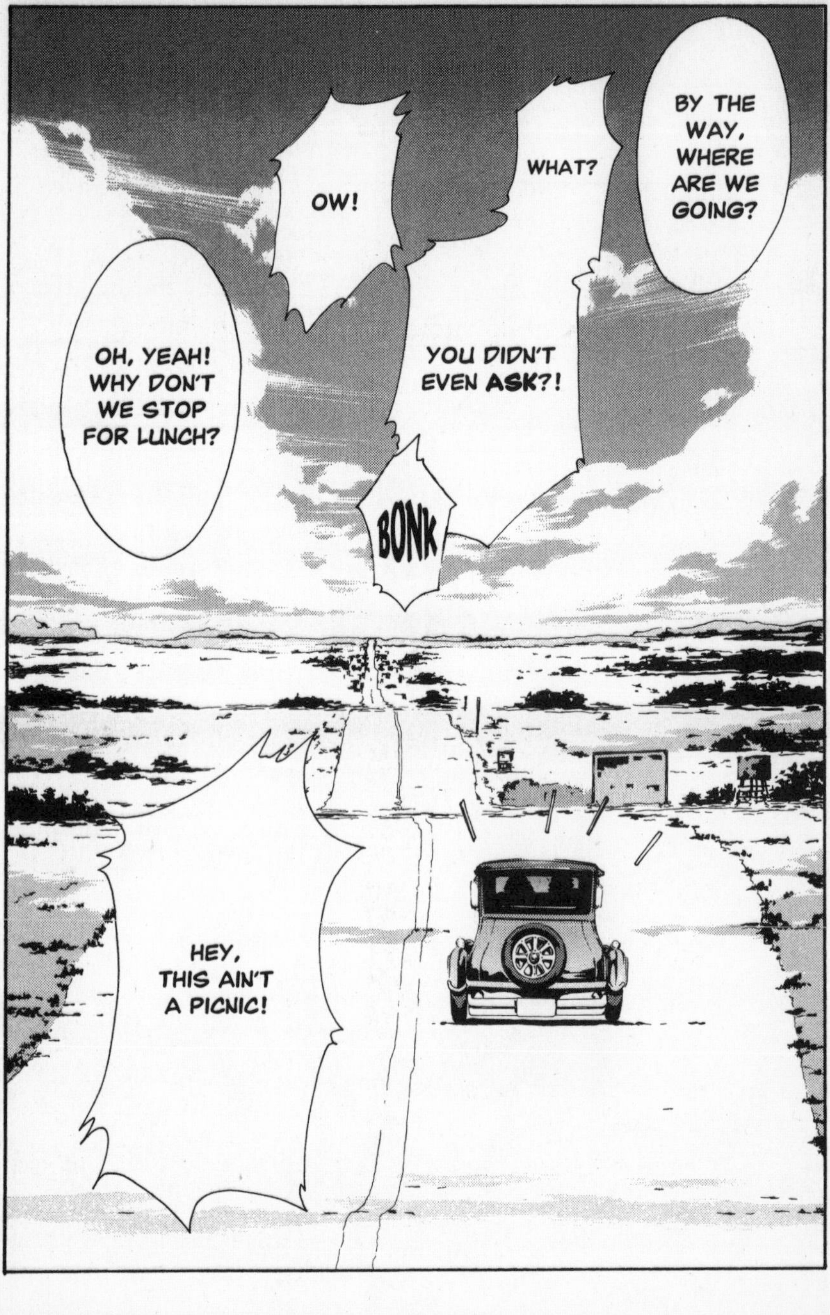
BY THE WAY, WHERE ARE WE GOING?
WHAT?
YOU DIDN'T EVEN ASK?!
BONK
OW!
OH, YEAH! WHY DON'T WE STOP FOR LUNCH?
HEY, THIS AIN'T A PICNIC!

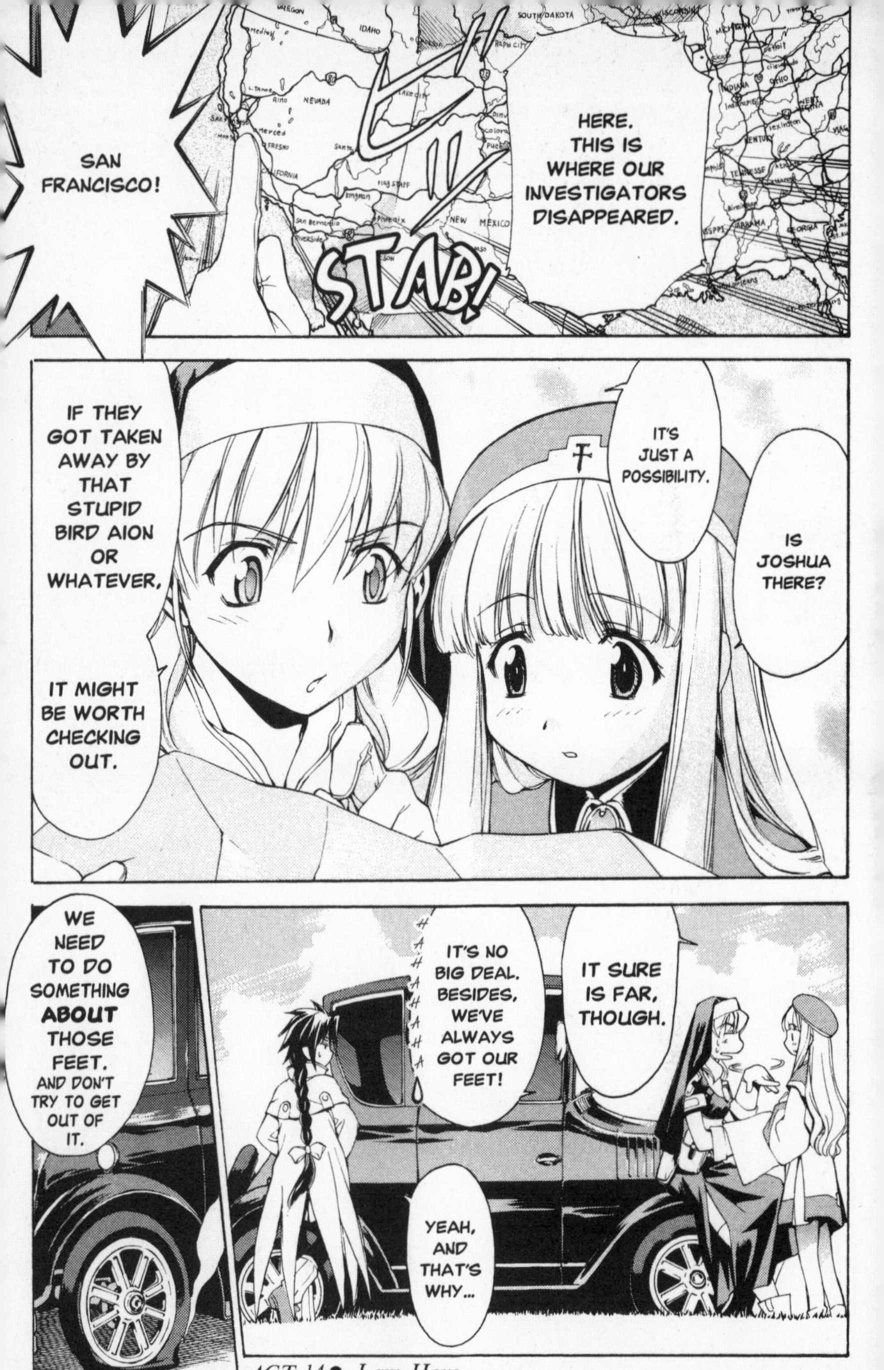
HERE. THIS IS WHERE OUR INVESTIGATORS DISAPPEARED.
STAB!
SAN FRANCISCO!
IS JOSHUA THERE?
IT'S JUST A POSSIBILITY.
IF THEY GOT TAKEN AWAY BY THAT STUPID BIRD AION OR WHATEVER,
IT MIGHT BE WORTH CHECKING OUT.
IT SURE IS FAR, THOUGH.
IT'S NO BIG DEAL. BESIDES, WE'VE ALWAYS GOT OUR FEET!
HAHAHAHA
YEAH, AND THAT'S WHY...
WE NEED TO DO SOMETHING **ABOUT** THOSE FEET.
AND DON'T TRY TO GET OUT OF IT.

ACT 14● *I am Here*

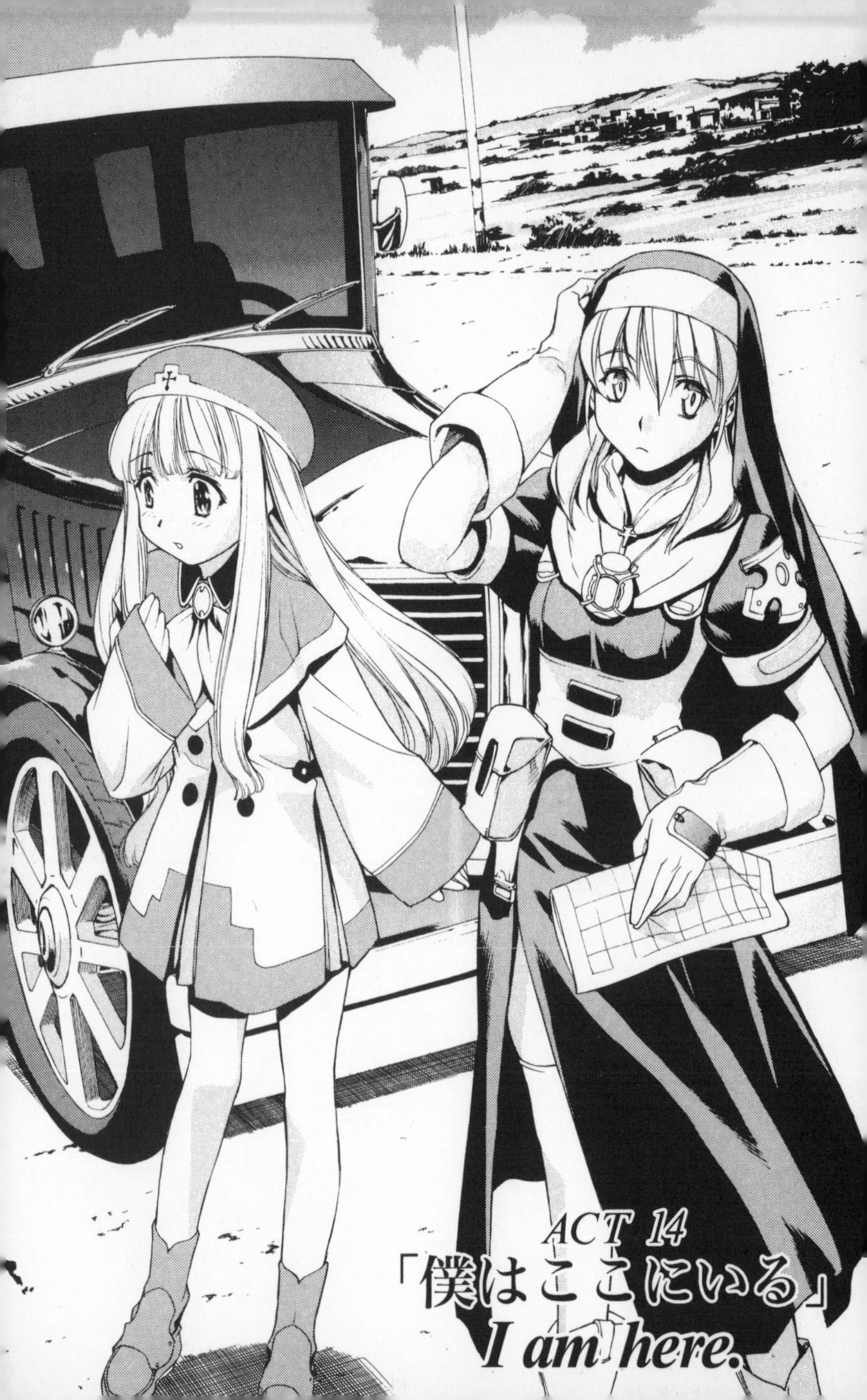
ACT 14
「僕はここにいる」
I am here.

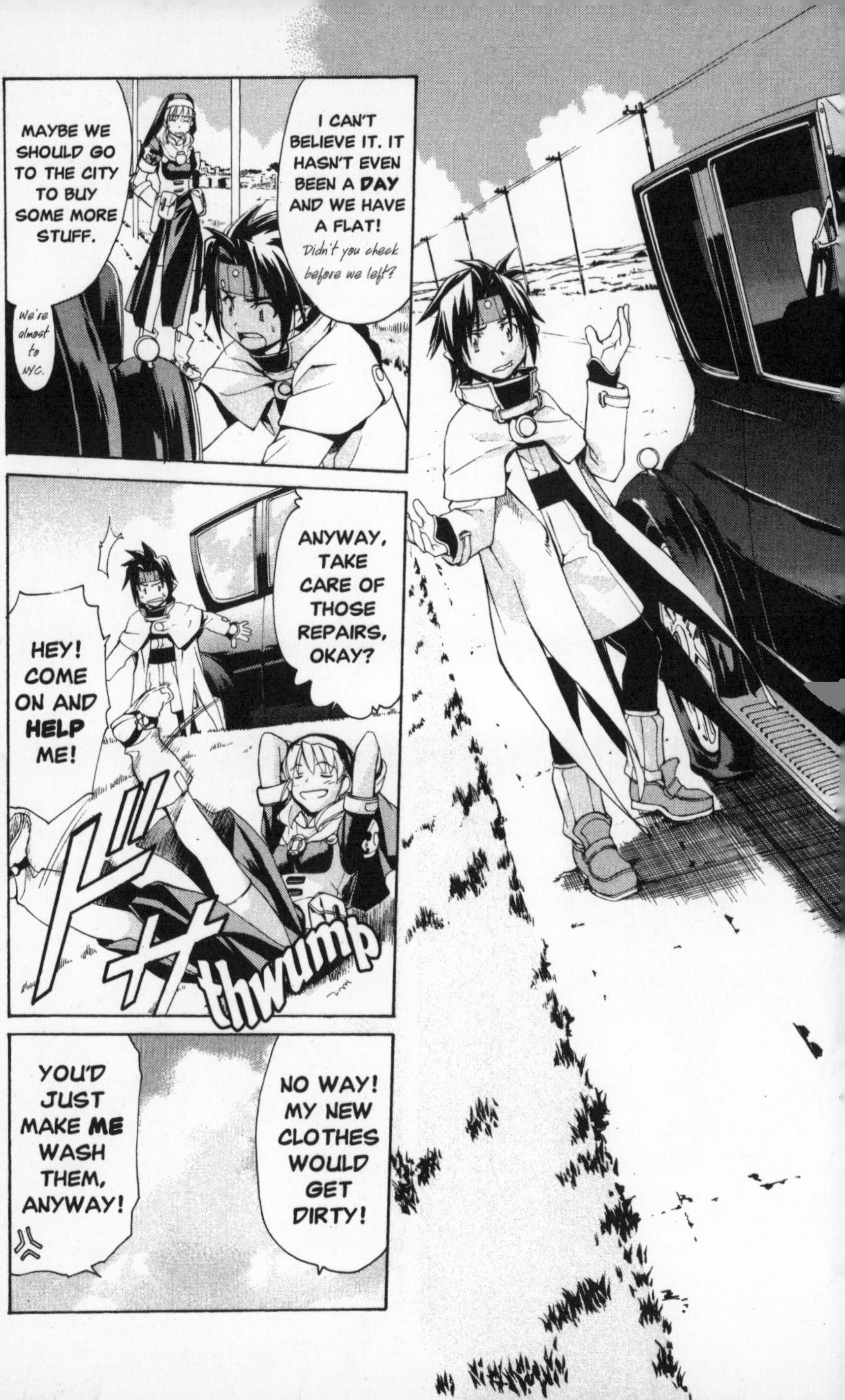
I CAN'T BELIEVE IT. IT HASN'T EVEN BEEN A DAY AND WE HAVE A FLAT!
Didn't you check before we left?
MAYBE WE SHOULD GO TO THE CITY TO BUY SOME MORE STUFF.
We're almost to NYC.
ANYWAY, TAKE CARE OF THOSE REPAIRS, OKAY?
HEY! COME ON AND HELP ME!
thwump
NO WAY! MY NEW CLOTHES WOULD GET DIRTY!
YOU'D JUST MAKE ME WASH THEM, ANYWAY!

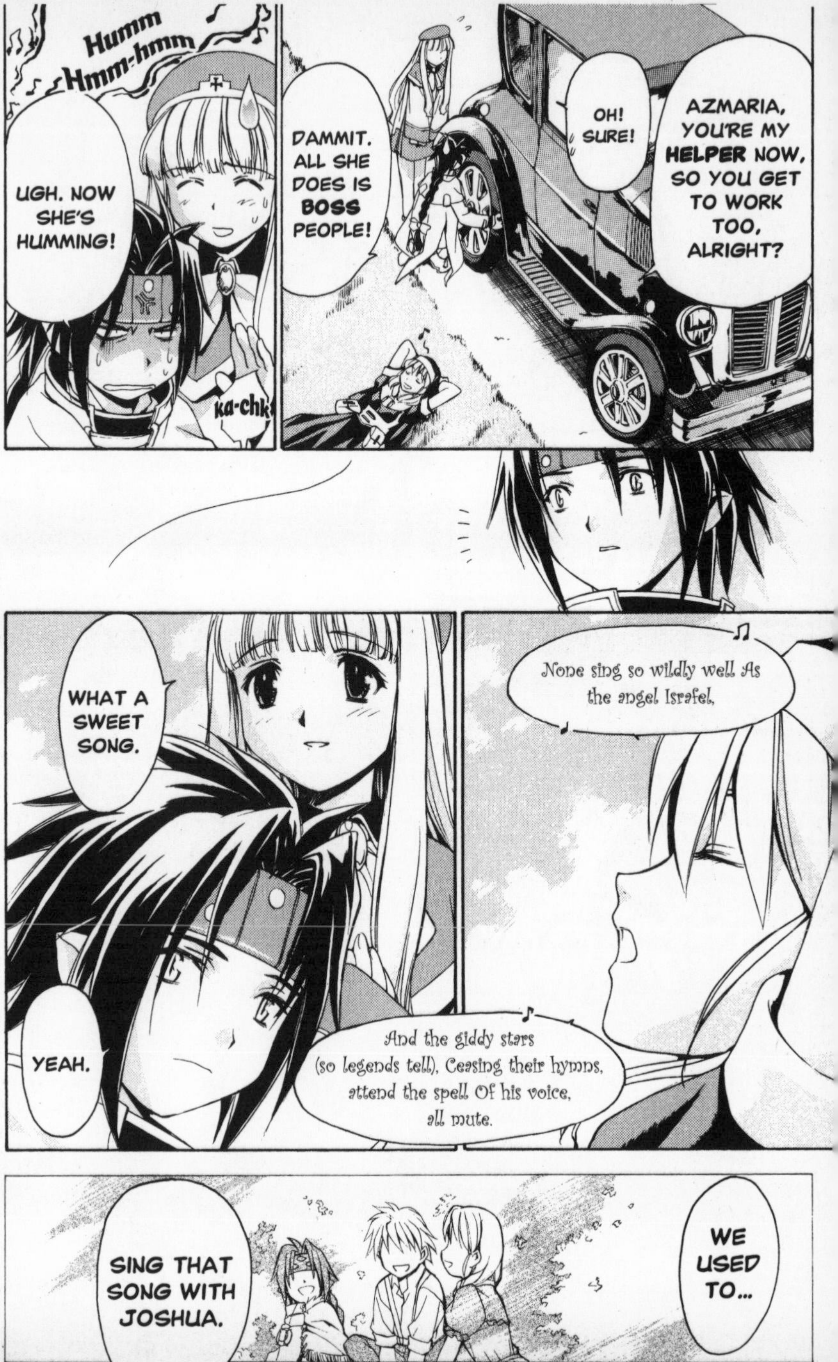

AZMARIA, YOU'RE MY **HELPER** NOW, SO YOU GET TO WORK TOO, ALRIGHT?
OH! SURE!
DAMMIT. ALL SHE DOES IS **BOSS** PEOPLE!
Humm Hmm-hmm
UGH. NOW SHE'S HUMMING!
ka-chk
None sing so wildly well As the angel Israfel,
WHAT A SWEET SONG.
And the giddy stars (so legends tell), Ceasing their hymns, attend the spell Of his voice, all mute.
YEAH.
WE USED TO...
SING THAT SONG WITH JOSHUA.

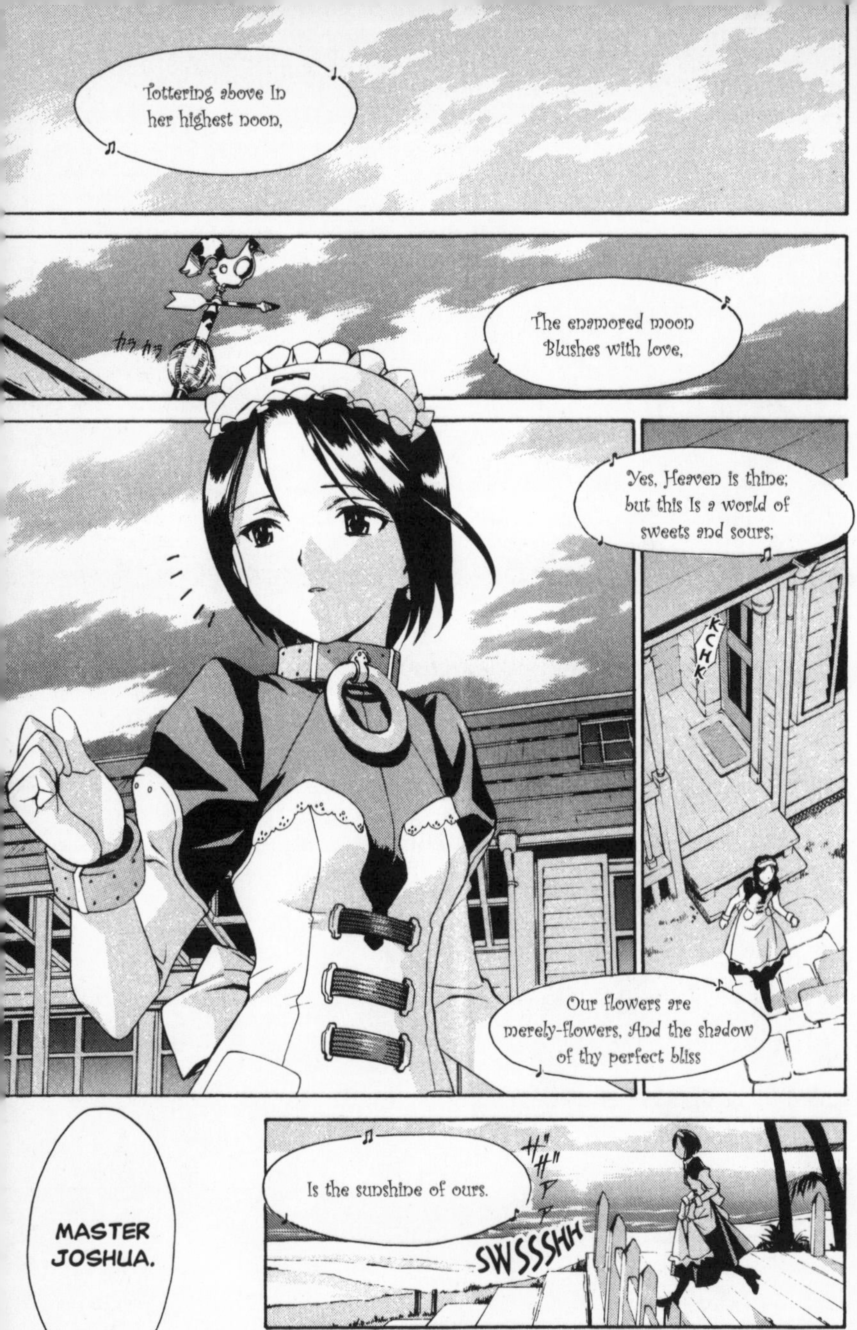
Tottering above In her highest noon,
The enamored moon Blushes with love,
Yes, Heaven is thine; but this Is a world of sweets and sours;
KCHK
Our flowers are merely-flowers, And the shadow of thy perfect bliss
Is the sunshine of ours.
SWSSSHH
MASTER JOSHUA.

Edgar Allen Poe (1809-49) *"Israfel"* (1831)

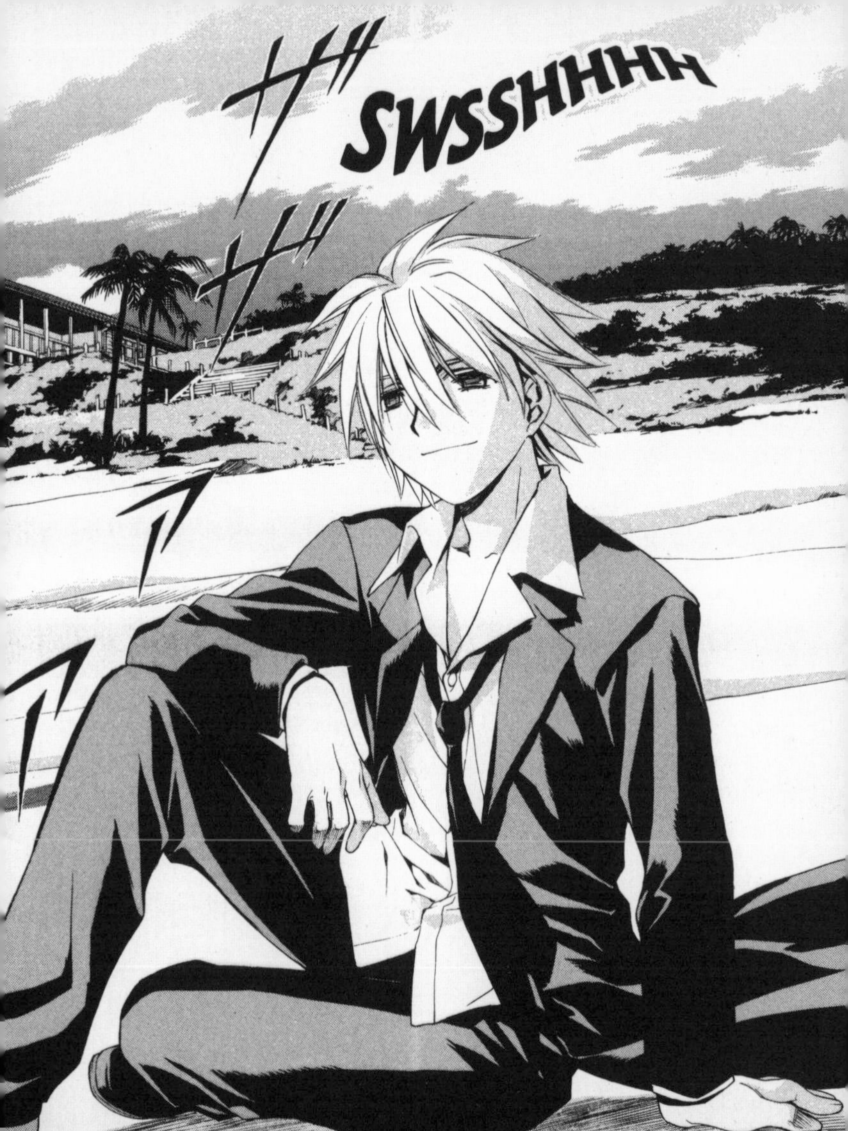
SWSSHHHH

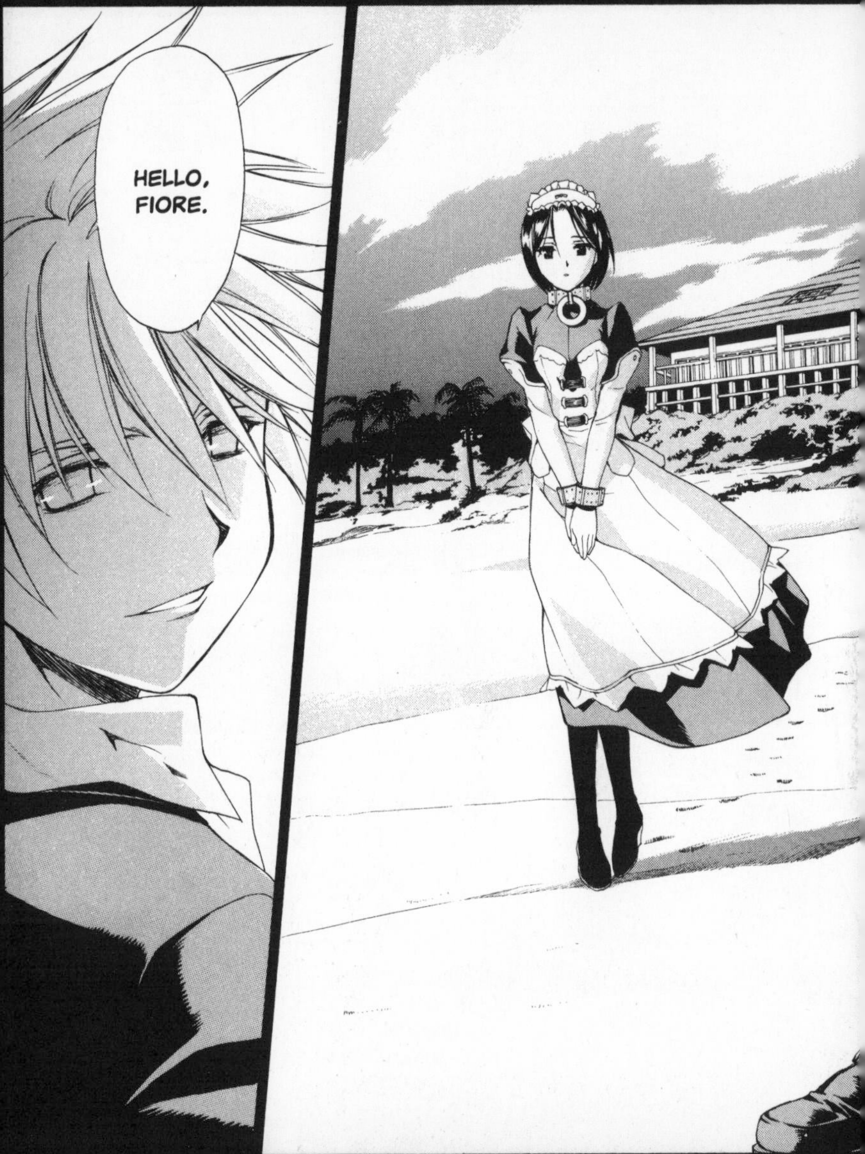
HELLO, FIORE.

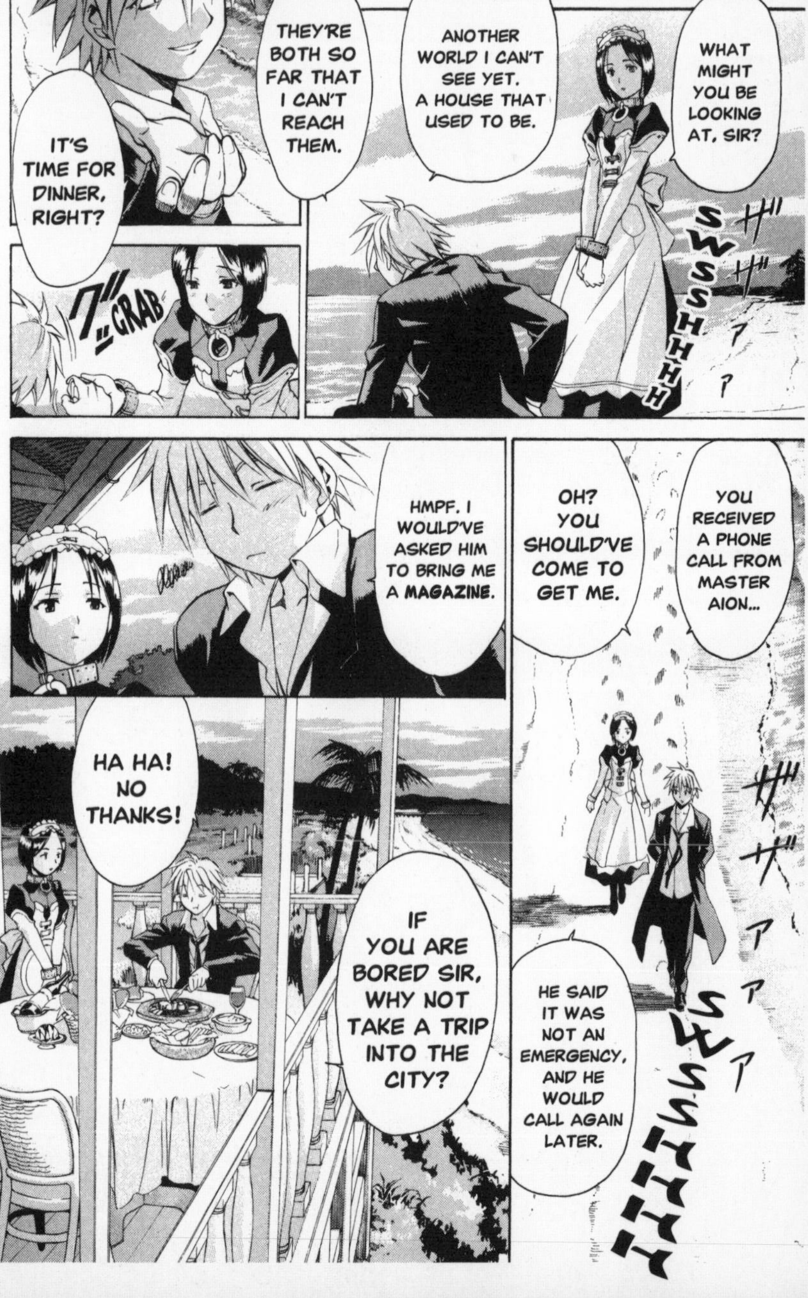
WHAT MIGHT YOU BE LOOKING AT, SIR?
ANOTHER WORLD I CAN'T SEE YET. A HOUSE THAT USED TO BE.
SWSSHHHH
THEY'RE BOTH SO FAR THAT I CAN'T REACH THEM.
IT'S TIME FOR DINNER, RIGHT?
GRAB
YOU RECEIVED A PHONE CALL FROM MASTER AION...
OH? YOU SHOULD'VE COME TO GET ME.
HE SAID IT WAS NOT AN EMERGENCY, AND HE WOULD CALL AGAIN LATER.
SWSSHHHH
HMPF. I WOULD'VE ASKED HIM TO BRING ME A MAGAZINE.
IF YOU ARE BORED SIR, WHY NOT TAKE A TRIP INTO THE CITY?
HA HA! NO THANKS!

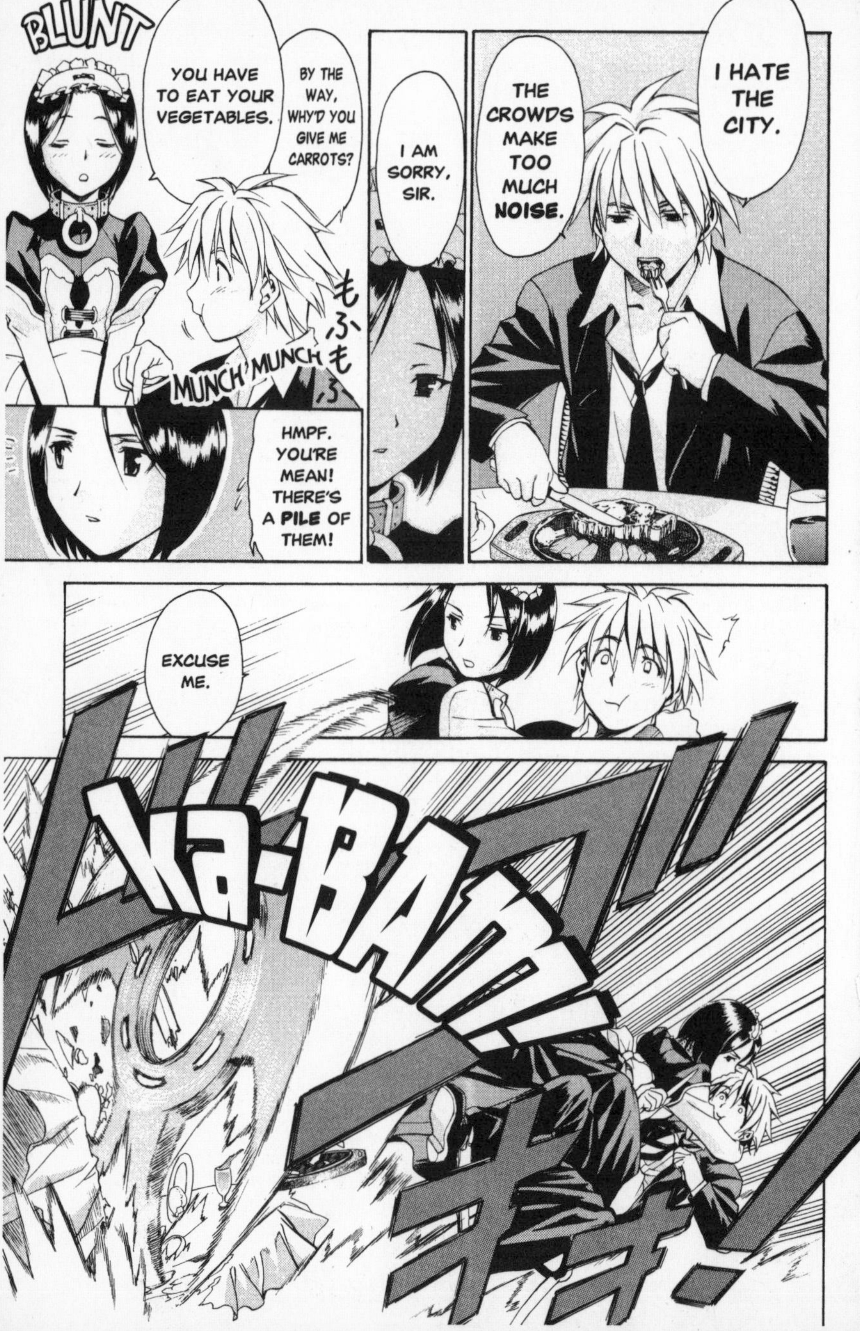
I HATE THE CITY.
THE CROWDS MAKE TOO MUCH NOISE.
I AM SORRY, SIR.
BY THE WAY, WHY'D YOU GIVE ME CARROTS?
YOU HAVE TO EAT YOUR VEGETABLES.
BLUNT
MUNCH MUNCH
もふもふ
HMPF. YOU'RE MEAN! THERE'S A PILE OF THEM!
EXCUSE ME.
Ka-BAM!!

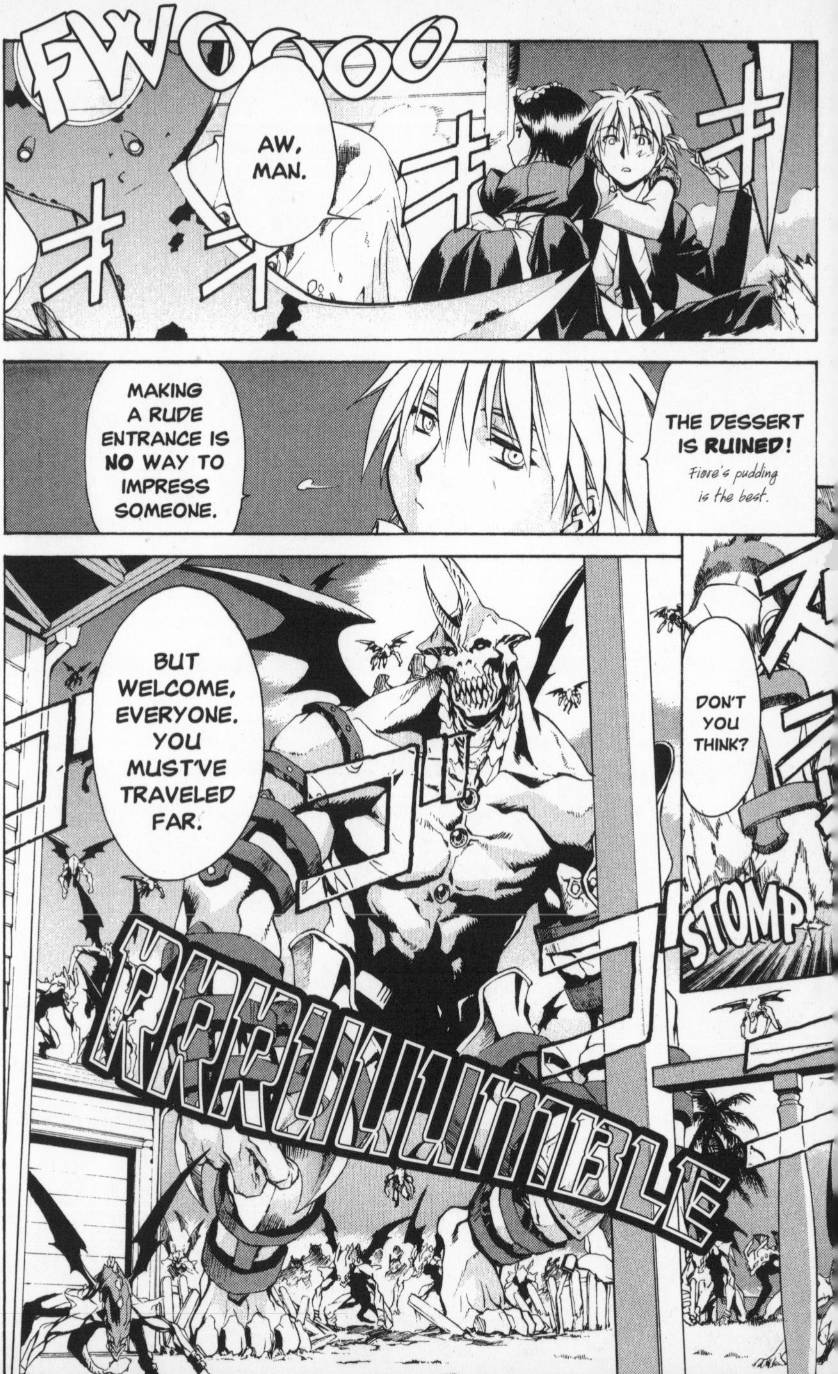
FWOOOOO
AW, MAN.
THE DESSERT IS RUINED!
Fiore's pudding is the best.
MAKING A RUDE ENTRANCE IS NO WAY TO IMPRESS SOMEONE.
DON'T YOU THINK?
BUT WELCOME, EVERYONE. YOU MUST'VE TRAVELED FAR.
STOMP
KRRRUUUMBLE

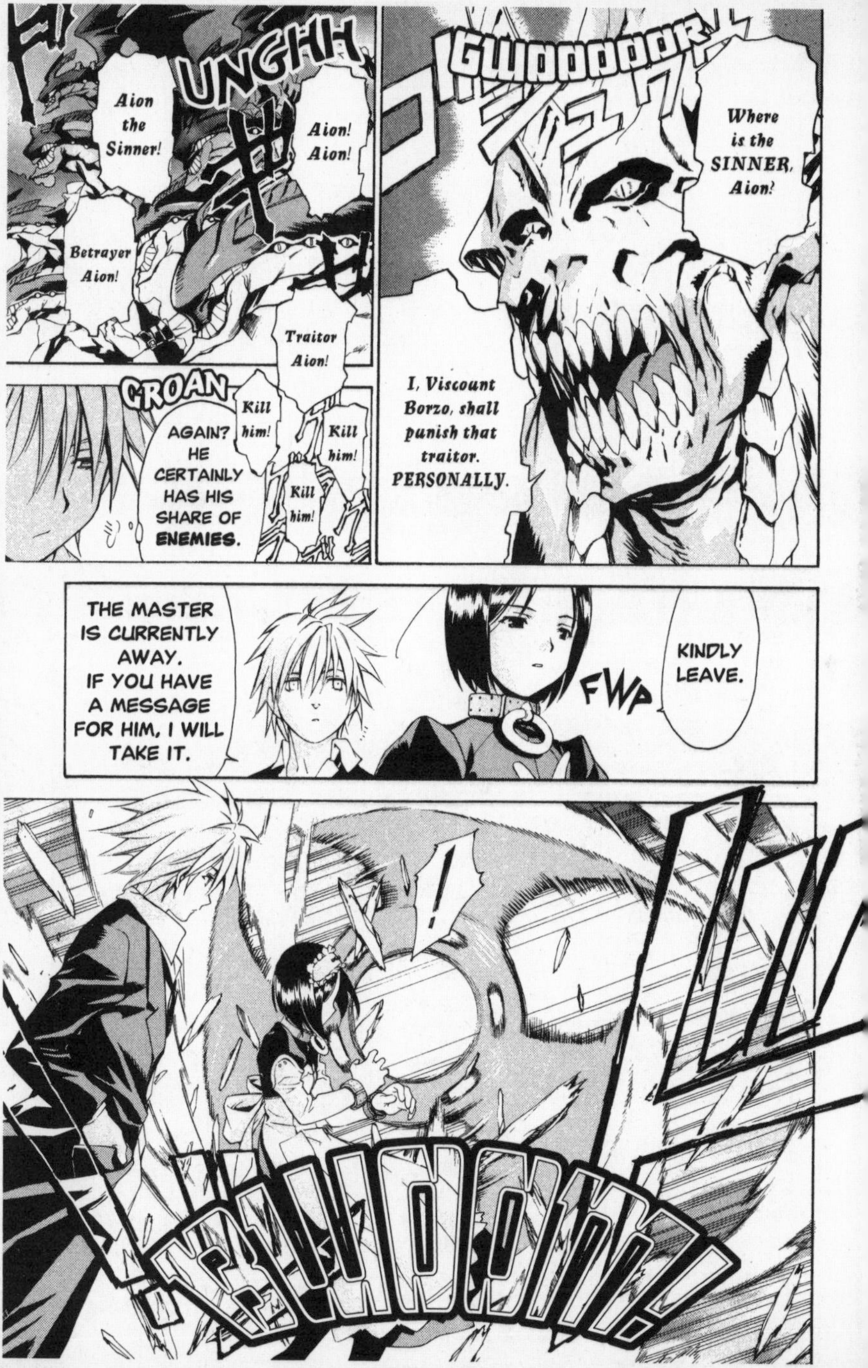
GLUOOOOOOR
Where is the SINNER, Aion?
I, Viscount Borzo, shall punish that traitor. PERSONALLY.
UNGHH
Aion! Aion!
Aion the Sinner!
Betrayer Aion!
Traitor Aion!
GROAN
Kill him!
Kill him!
Kill him!
AGAIN? HE CERTAINLY HAS HIS SHARE OF ENEMIES.
KINDLY LEAVE.
FWP
THE MASTER IS CURRENTLY AWAY. IF YOU HAVE A MESSAGE FOR HIM, I WILL TAKE IT.
!

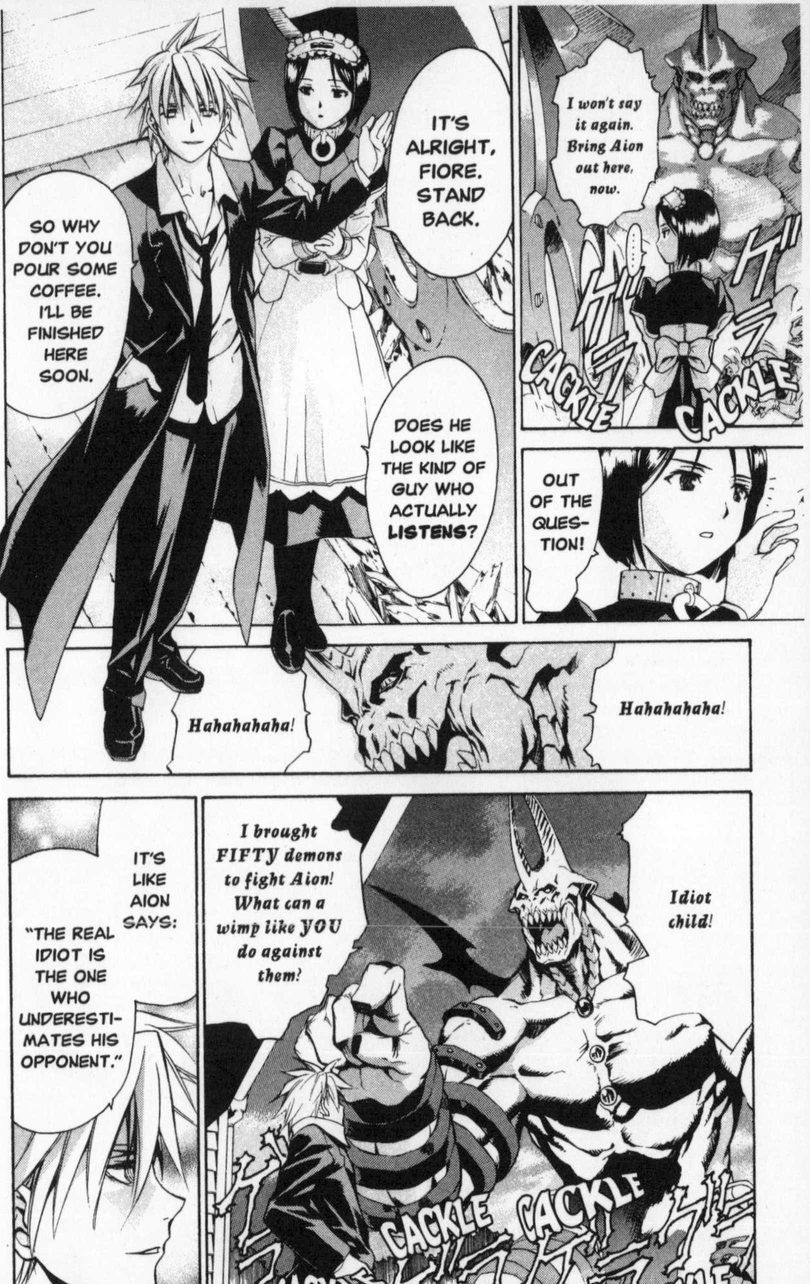
I won't say it again. Bring Aion out here, now.
...
CACKLE
CACKLE
OUT OF THE QUES- TION!
IT'S ALRIGHT, FIORE. STAND BACK.
DOES HE LOOK LIKE THE KIND OF GUY WHO ACTUALLY **LISTENS**?
SO WHY DON'T YOU POUR SOME COFFEE. I'LL BE FINISHED HERE SOON.
Hahahahaha!
Hahahahaha!
Idiot child!
I brought FIFTY demons to fight Aion! What can a wimp like YOU do against them?
CACKLE
CACKLE
CACKLE
CACKLE
IT'S LIKE AION SAYS:
"THE REAL IDIOT IS THE ONE WHO UNDERESTI- MATES HIS OPPONENT."

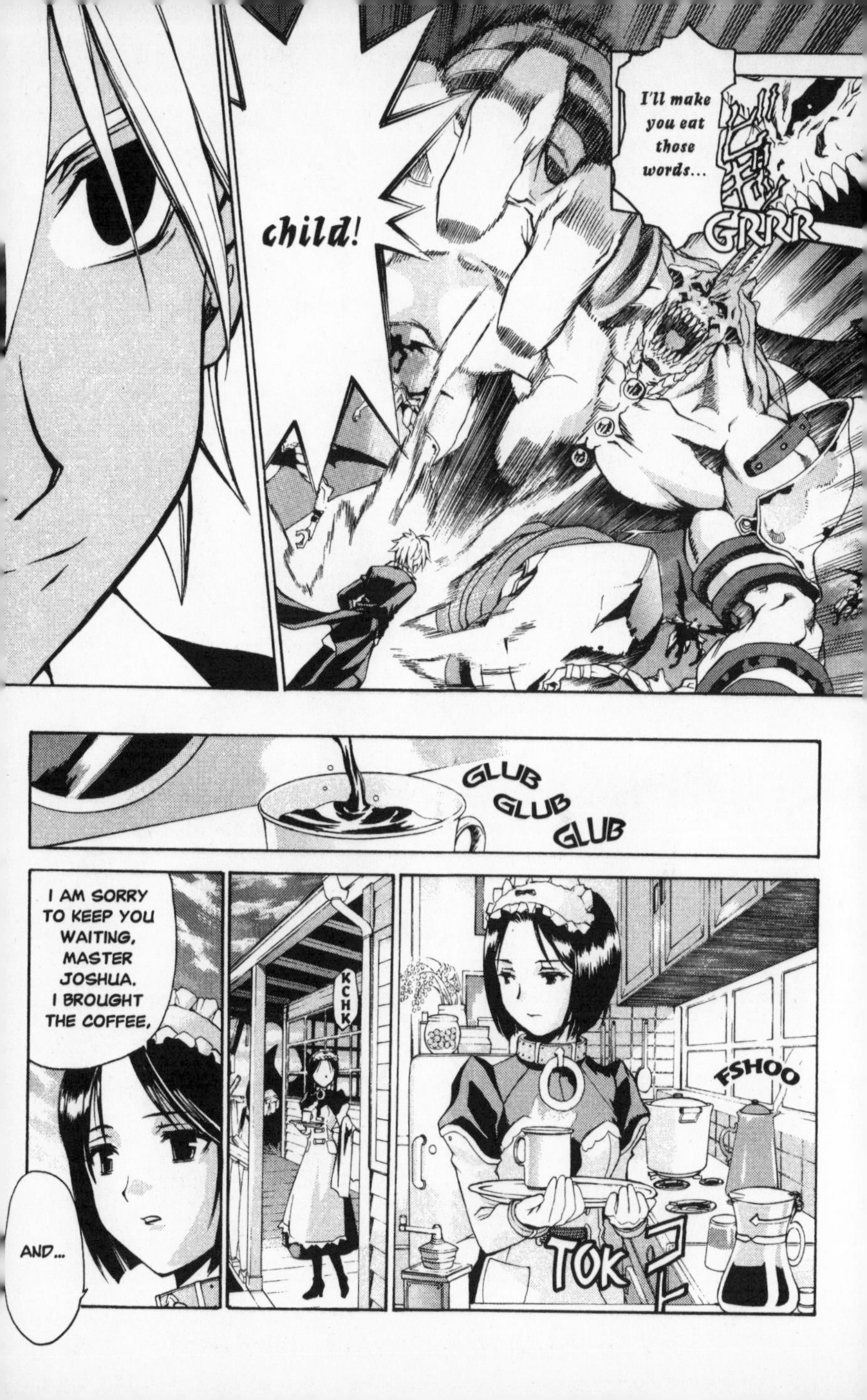
I'll make you eat those words...
GRRR
child!
GLUB GLUB GLUB
I AM SORRY TO KEEP YOU WAITING, MASTER JOSHUA. I BROUGHT THE COFFEE,
AND...
KCHK
FSHOO
TOK

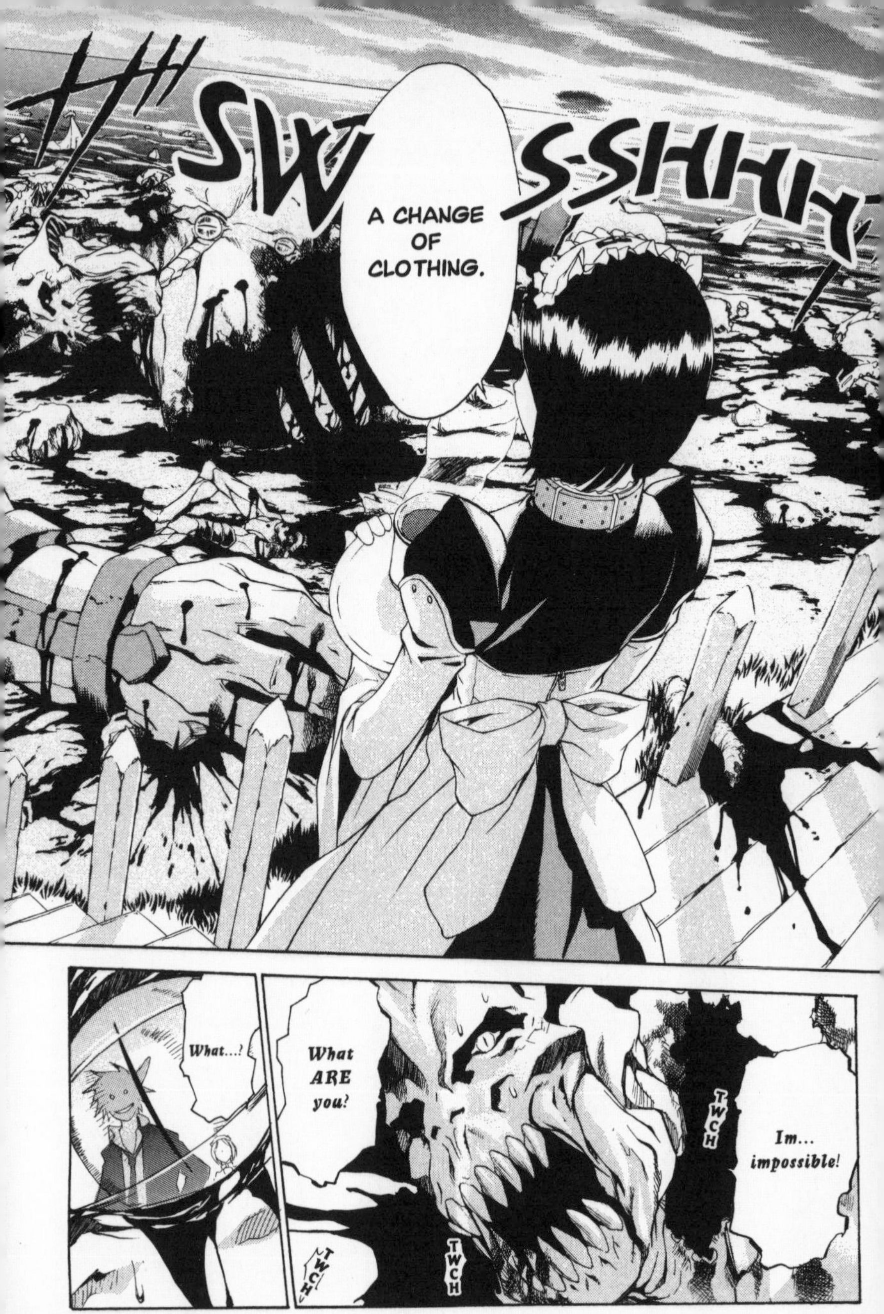
SWISSHHH
A CHANGE OF CLOTHING.
What...?
What ARE you?
TWCH
TWCH
TWCH
Im... impossible!

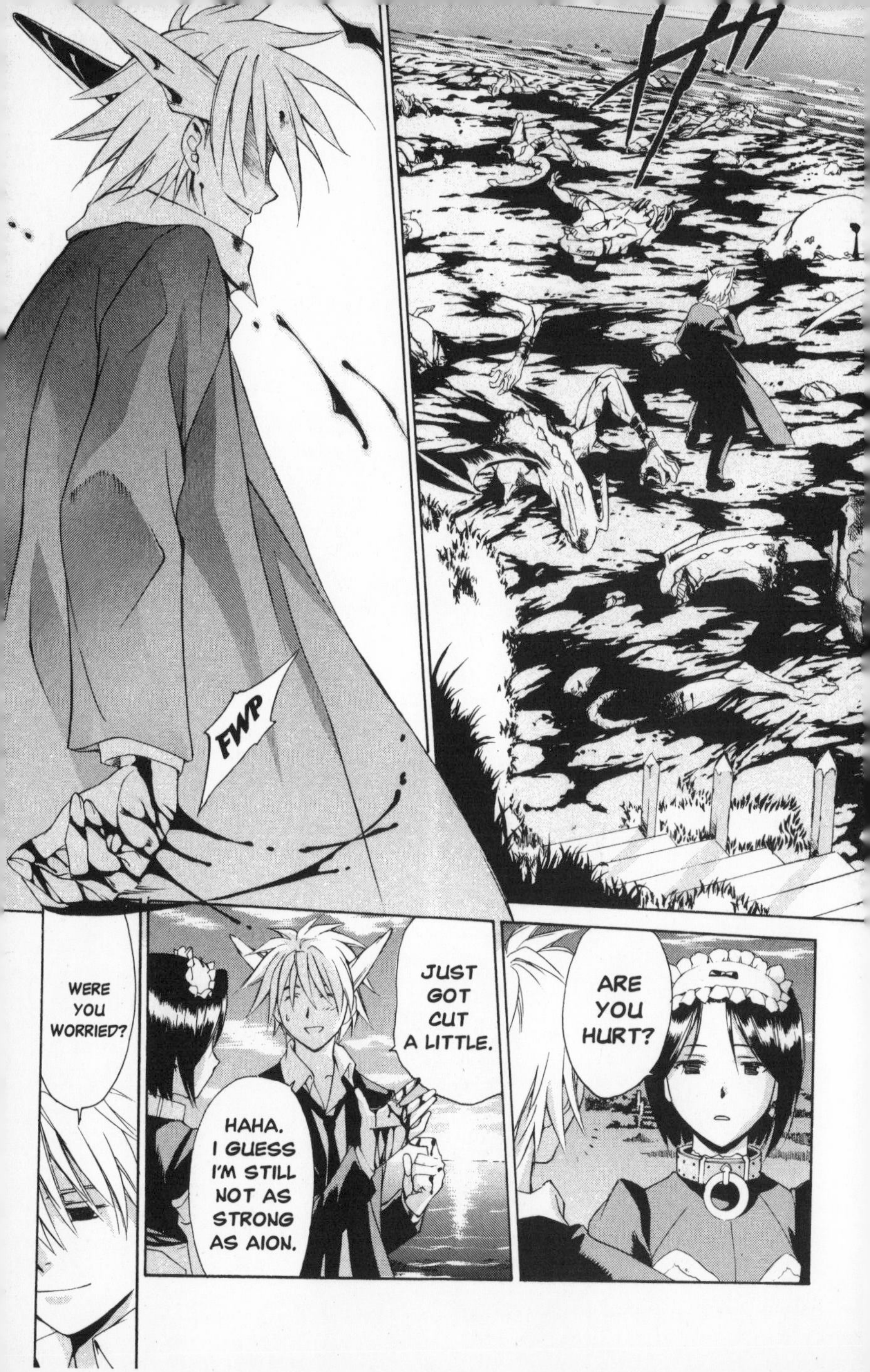
FWP
ARE YOU HURT?
JUST GOT CUT A LITTLE.
HAHA. I GUESS I'M STILL NOT AS STRONG AS AION.
WERE YOU WORRIED?

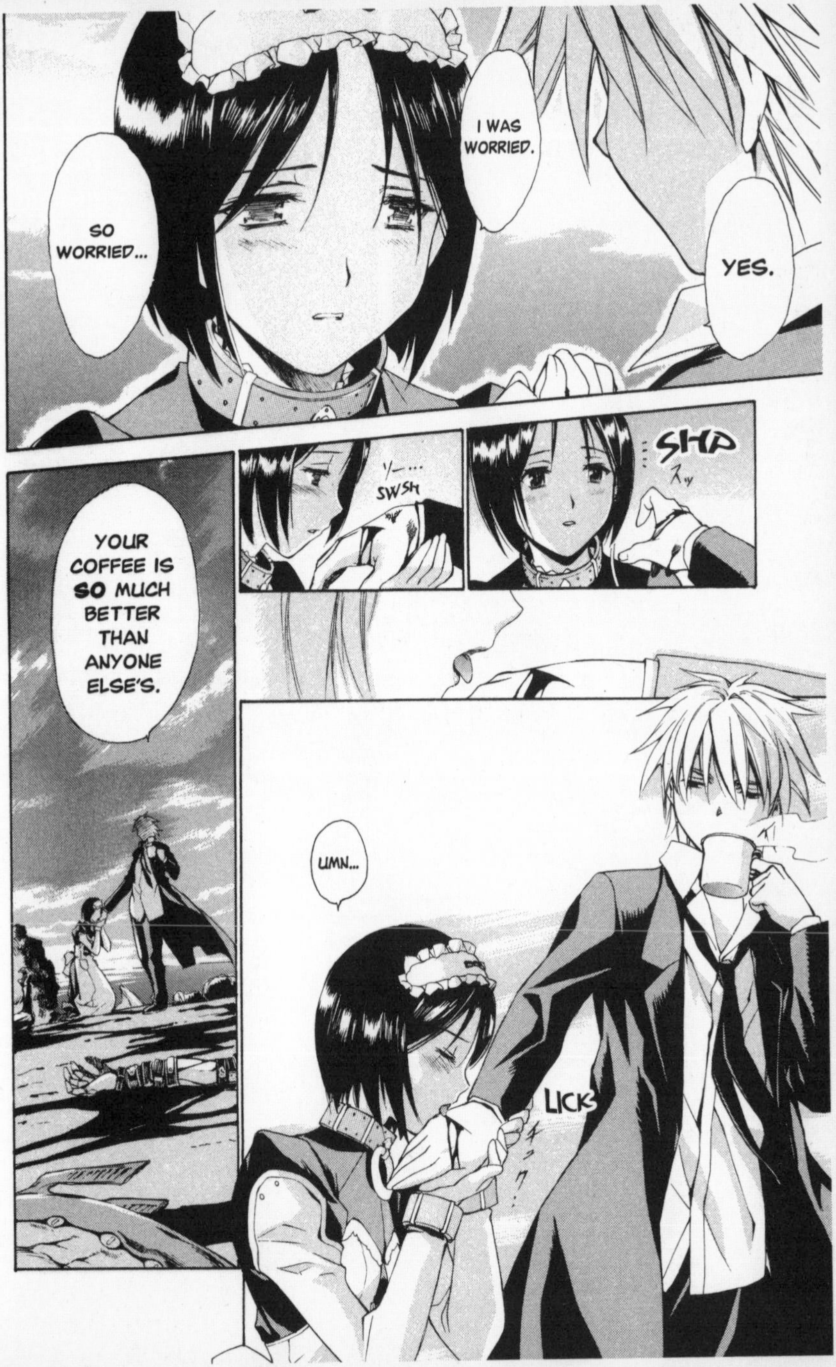
I WAS WORRIED.
YES.
SO WORRIED...
SHP
SWSH
YOUR COFFEE IS SO MUCH BETTER THAN ANYONE ELSE'S.
UMN...
LICK

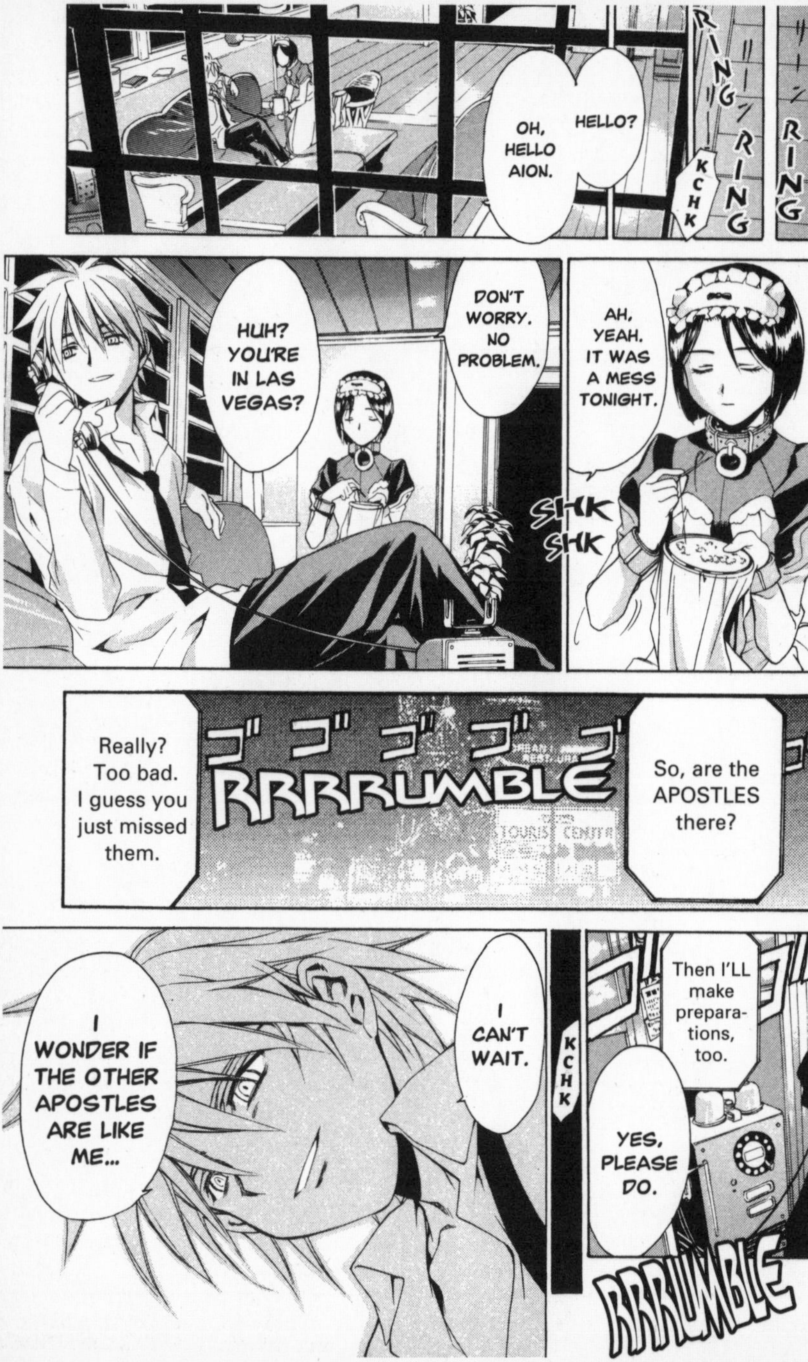
RING RING
RING RING
KCHK
HELLO?
OH, HELLO AION.
AH, YEAH. IT WAS A MESS TONIGHT.
SHK SHK
DON'T WORRY. NO PROBLEM.
HUH? YOU'RE IN LAS VEGAS?
So, are the APOSTLES there?
RRRRUMBLE
Really? Too bad. I guess you just missed them.
Then I'LL make preparations, too.
YES, PLEASE DO.
RRRUMBLE
KCHK
I CAN'T WAIT.
I WONDER IF THE OTHER APOSTLES ARE LIKE ME...

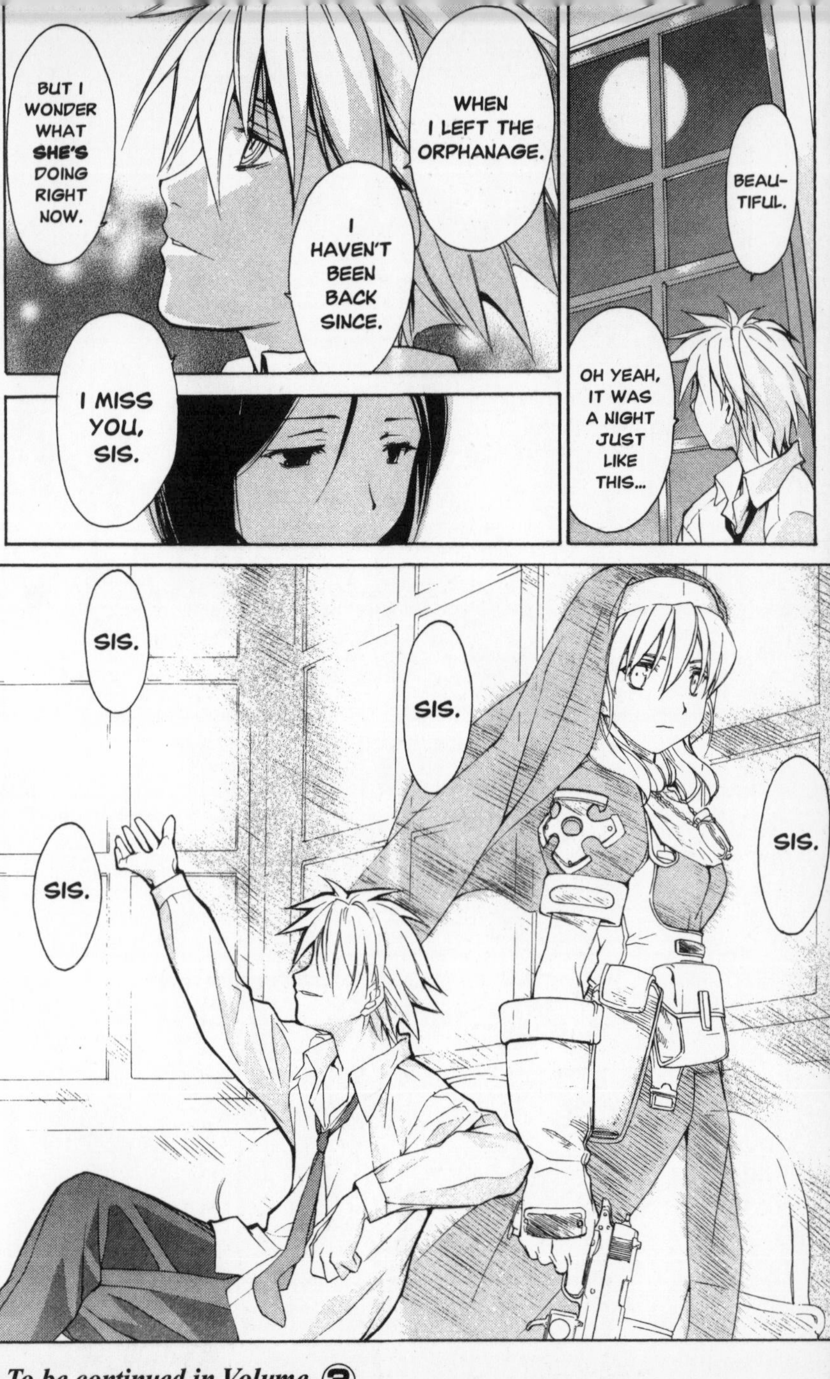
BEAU-TIFUL.
OH YEAH, IT WAS A NIGHT JUST LIKE THIS...
WHEN I LEFT THE ORPHANAGE.
I HAVEN'T BEEN BACK SINCE.
BUT I WONDER WHAT **SHE'S** DOING RIGHT NOW.
I MISS YOU, SIS.
SIS.
SIS.
SIS.
SIS.

To be continued in Volume 3

STAFF
DAISUKE MORIYAMA

TOKUNORI NAKANISHI
TETSUYA NAKATA
MASASHI KASHIWADA
UI SUZUKI
AYA KIGAWA
TSUGUO TAKAMOTO

RYO OGAHARA
ARUMI HIGASHI
JUNYA INOUE

DESIGN
TADAO NAKAMURA (ARTEN)

EDITOR
AKIRA KAWASHIMA (COMIC DRAGON)
TAKESHI KURIHARA (COMIC DRAGON)
MASAYOSHI KEYAKI (DRAGON COMICS)
AKIHIKO NAKADA (DRAGON COMICS)

AFTERWORD

My Dream Life in the Doghouse Part 2

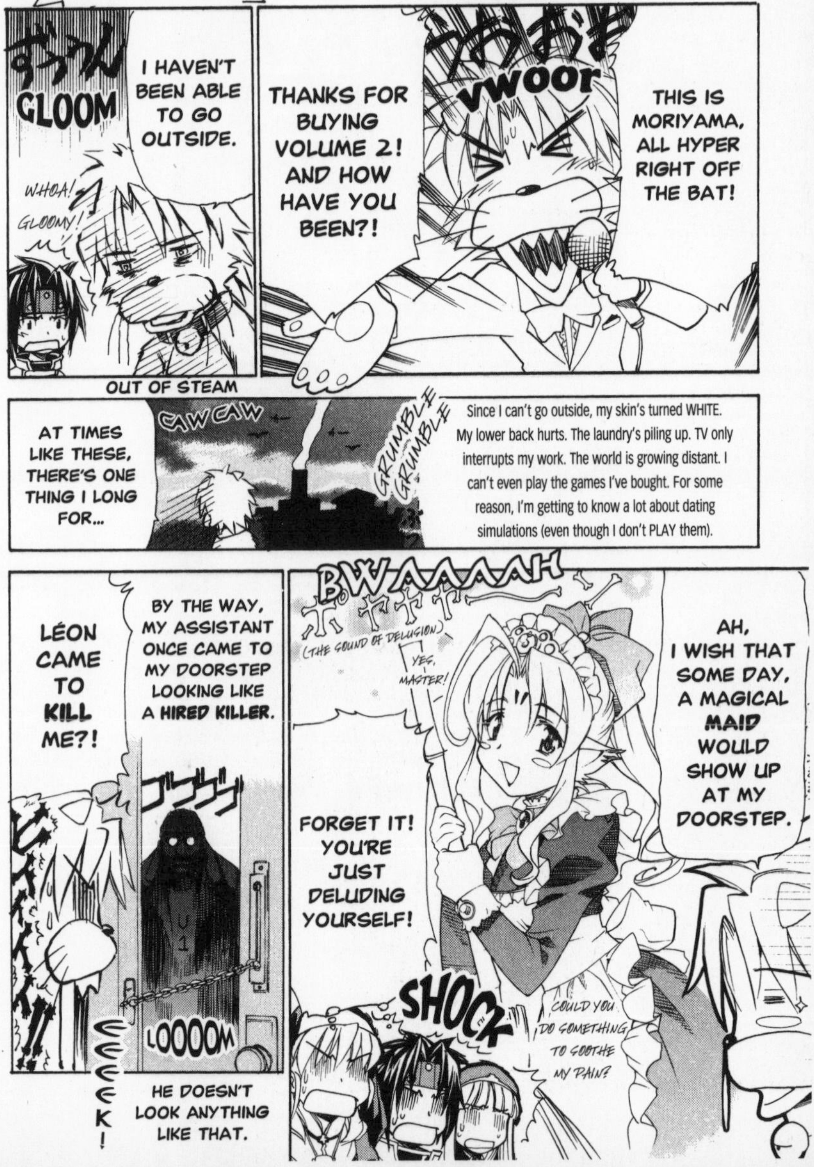
VWOOR
THIS IS MORIYAMA, ALL HYPER RIGHT OFF THE BAT!
THANKS FOR BUYING VOLUME 2! AND HOW HAVE YOU BEEN?!
I HAVEN'T BEEN ABLE TO GO OUTSIDE.
GLOOM
WHOA! GLOOMY!
OUT OF STEAM
Since I can't go outside, my skin's turned WHITE. My lower back hurts. The laundry's piling up. TV only interrupts my work. The world is growing distant. I can't even play the games I've bought. For some reason, I'm getting to know a lot about dating simulations (even though I don't PLAY them).
GRUMBLE GRUMBLE
CAW CAW
AT TIMES LIKE THESE, THERE'S ONE THING I LONG FOR...
AH, I WISH THAT SOME DAY, A MAGICAL MAID WOULD SHOW UP AT MY DOORSTEP.
BWAAAAAH
(THE SOUND OF DELUSION)
YES, MASTER!
FORGET IT! YOU'RE JUST DELUDING YOURSELF!
SHOCK
COULD YOU DO SOMETHING TO SOOTHE MY PAIN?
BY THE WAY, MY ASSISTANT ONCE CAME TO MY DOORSTEP LOOKING LIKE A HIRED KILLER.
LÉON CAME TO KILL ME?!
LOOOOM
EEEEK!
HE DOESN'T LOOK ANYTHING LIKE THAT.

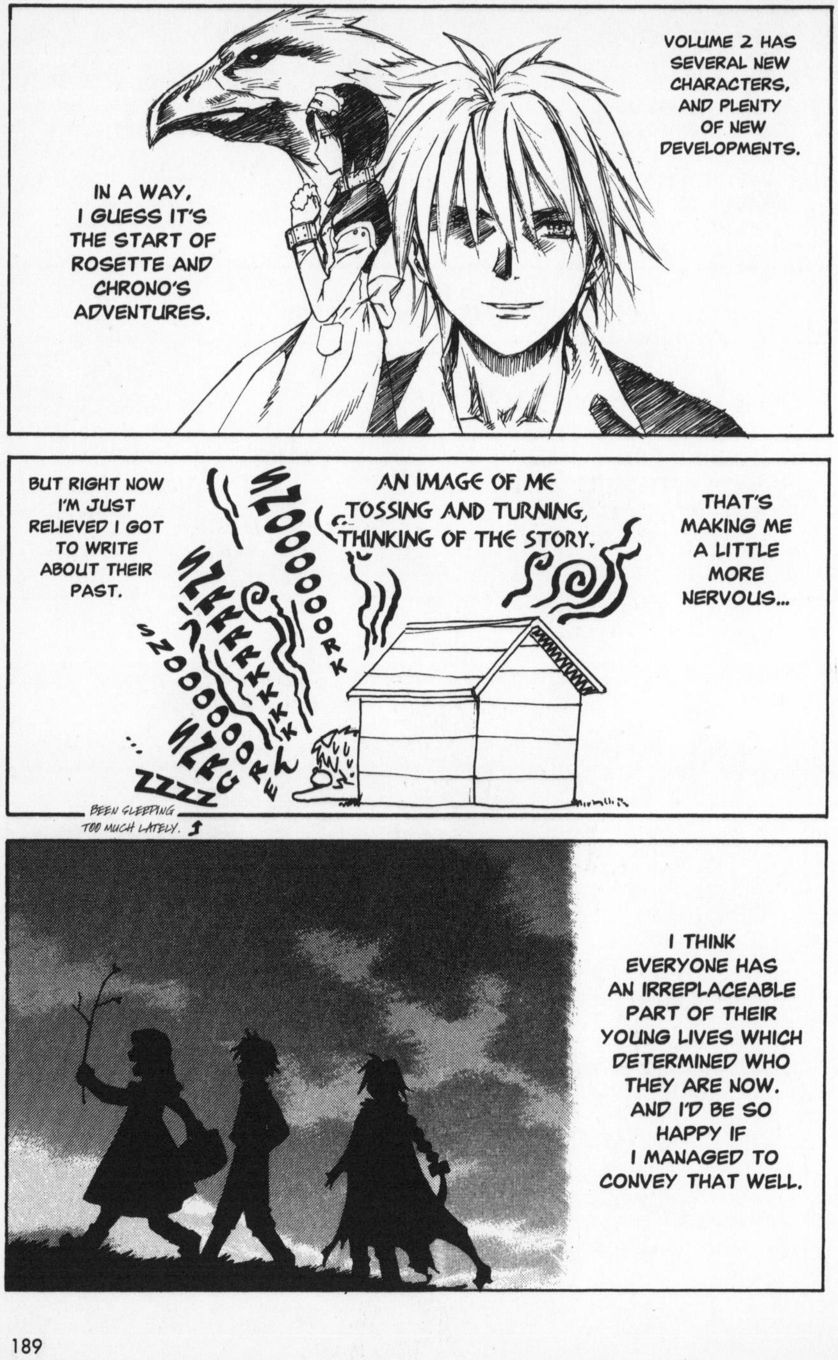
VOLUME 2 HAS SEVERAL NEW CHARACTERS, AND PLENTY OF NEW DEVELOPMENTS.
IN A WAY, I GUESS IT'S THE START OF ROSETTE AND CHRONO'S ADVENTURES.
BUT RIGHT NOW I'M JUST RELIEVED I GOT TO WRITE ABOUT THEIR PAST.
AN IMAGE OF ME TOSSING AND TURNING, THINKING OF THE STORY.
THAT'S MAKING ME A LITTLE MORE NERVOUS...
ZZZZ
BEEN SLEEPING TOO MUCH LATELY.
I THINK EVERYONE HAS AN IRREPLACEABLE PART OF THEIR YOUNG LIVES WHICH DETERMINED WHO THEY ARE NOW. AND I'D BE SO HAPPY IF I MANAGED TO CONVEY THAT WELL.

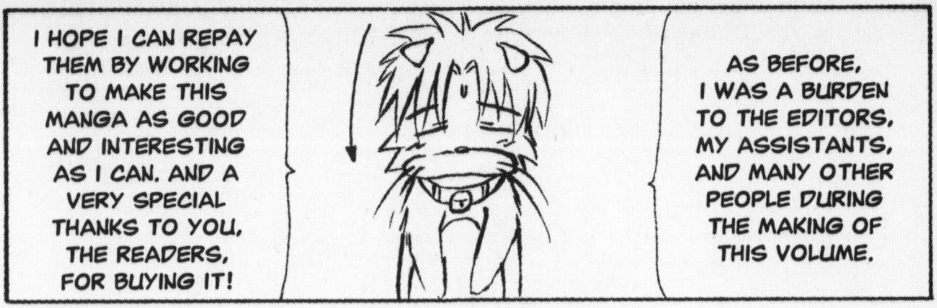
AS BEFORE, I WAS A BURDEN TO THE EDITORS, MY ASSISTANTS, AND MANY OTHER PEOPLE DURING THE MAKING OF THIS VOLUME.
I HOPE I CAN REPAY THEM BY WORKING TO MAKE THIS MANGA AS GOOD AND INTERESTING AS I CAN. AND A VERY SPECIAL THANKS TO YOU, THE READERS, FOR BUYING IT!

Preview of next volume

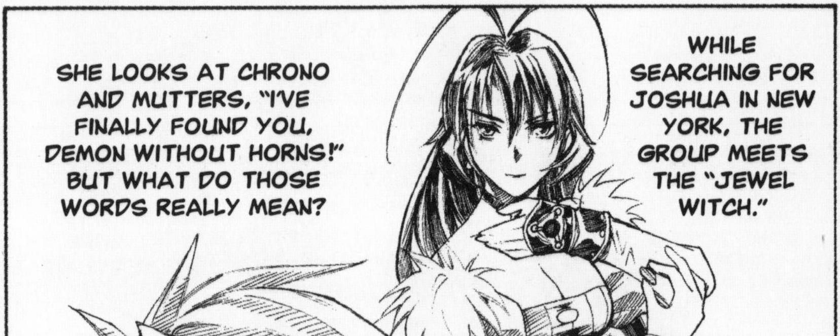
WHILE SEARCHING FOR JOSHUA IN NEW YORK, THE GROUP MEETS THE "JEWEL WITCH."
SHE LOOKS AT CHRONO AND MUTTERS, "I'VE FINALLY FOUND YOU, DEMON WITHOUT HORNS!" BUT WHAT DO THOSE WORDS REALLY MEAN?

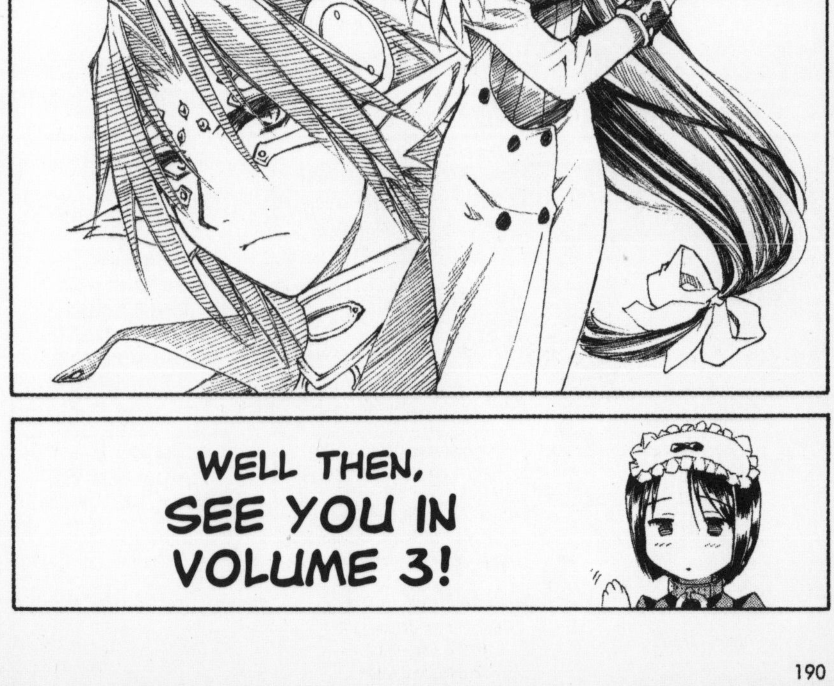
WELL THEN, SEE YOU IN VOLUME 3!

(Originally published as "CHRNO CRUSADE" in Japan.)

© 2000 DAISUKE MORIYAMA
Originally published in Japan in 2000 by KADOKAWA SHOTEN PUBLISHING CO., LTD., Tokyo.
English translation rights arranged with KADOKAWA SHOTEN PUBLISHING CO., LTD., Tokyo.

Translator **AMY FORSYTH**
Lead Translator/Translation Supervisor **JAVIER LOPEZ**
ADV Manga Translation Staff **JOSH COLE, BRENDAN FRAYNE, HARUKA KANEKO-SMITH,
EIKO MCGREGOR, MADOKA MOROE and KAY BERTRAND**

Print Production/ Art Studio Manager **LISA PUCKETT**
Pre-press Manager **KLYS REEDYK**
Art Production Manager **RYAN MASON**
Sr. Designer/Creative Manager **JORGE ALVARADO**
Graphic Designer/Group Leader **SCOTT SAVAGE**
Graphic Designer **NANAKO TSUKIHASHI**
Graphic Artists **CHRIS LAPP, CHY LING, NATALIA MORALES and LISA RAPER**
Graphic Intern **MARK MEZA**

International Coordinator **TORU IWAKAMI**
International Coordinator **ATSUSHI KANBAYASHI**

Publishing Editor **SUSAN ITIN**
Assistant Editor **MARGARET SCHAROLD**
Editorial Assistant **VARSHA BHUCHAR**
Proofreaders **SHERIDAN JACOBS and STEVEN REED**

Research/ Traffic Coordinator **MARSHA ARNOLD**

Executive VP, CFO, COO **KEVIN CORCORAN**

President, CEO & Publisher **JOHN LEDFORD**

Email: editor@adv-manga.com
www.adv-manga.com
www.advfilms.com

For sales and distribution inquiries please call 1.800.282.7202

is a division of A.D. Vision, Inc.
10114 W. Sam Houston Parkway, Suite 200, Houston, Texas 77099

English text © 2004 published by A.D. Vision, Inc. under exclusive license.
ADV MANGA is a trademark of A.D. Vision, Inc.

ISBN: 1-4139-0104-2
First printing, October 2004
10 9 8 7 6 5 4 3 2 1
Printed in Canada

Chrono Crusade Vol 02

PG. 18 — Sacred Spirit
A special bullet developed by the Elder. Its Japanese name translates to "Bullet of the Sacred Fire."

PG. 27 — Grand Central Station
Located in NYC, at 42nd Street and Park Avenue. It is the largest station in the world by number of platforms (44). Three different buildings actually stood on this site. The first, Grand Central Depot, was built in 1871. Around 1900, this building was essentially demolished and replaced with a new building, called Grand Central Station. By the 1920's (when Chrono Crusade takes place), that building had been torn down and replaced with yet another one. This is the building which is still standing in NYC today (and has recently undergone extensive renovation). It is technically named Grand Central Terminal, but is often called Grand Central Station (or just Grand Central) by NYC natives.

PG. 95 — Background text, cell 6
The text swirling in the background of cell 6 reads:
"Sick"
"Worry"
"How many times"
"It's so…"
"I want to scream"
"Fits"
"Are you alright?"
"You're bleeding."
"He's so annoying."

PG. 96 — (1) Background text, cell 6
The text swirling in the background of cell 6 reads:
"His eyes…"
"They're creepy."
"What's WITH him?"

(2) Background text, cell 7
The text swirling in the background of cell 7 reads:
"I'm scared. I'm scared."
"I'm going to run. I'm scared."
"I'm scared."

(3) Background text, cell 8
The text swirling in the background of cell 7 reads:
"Help me!"
"He's going to kill me!"

PG. 188 — Léon
The name of Jean Reno's hitman character in the film of the same name (known in the US as The Professional).

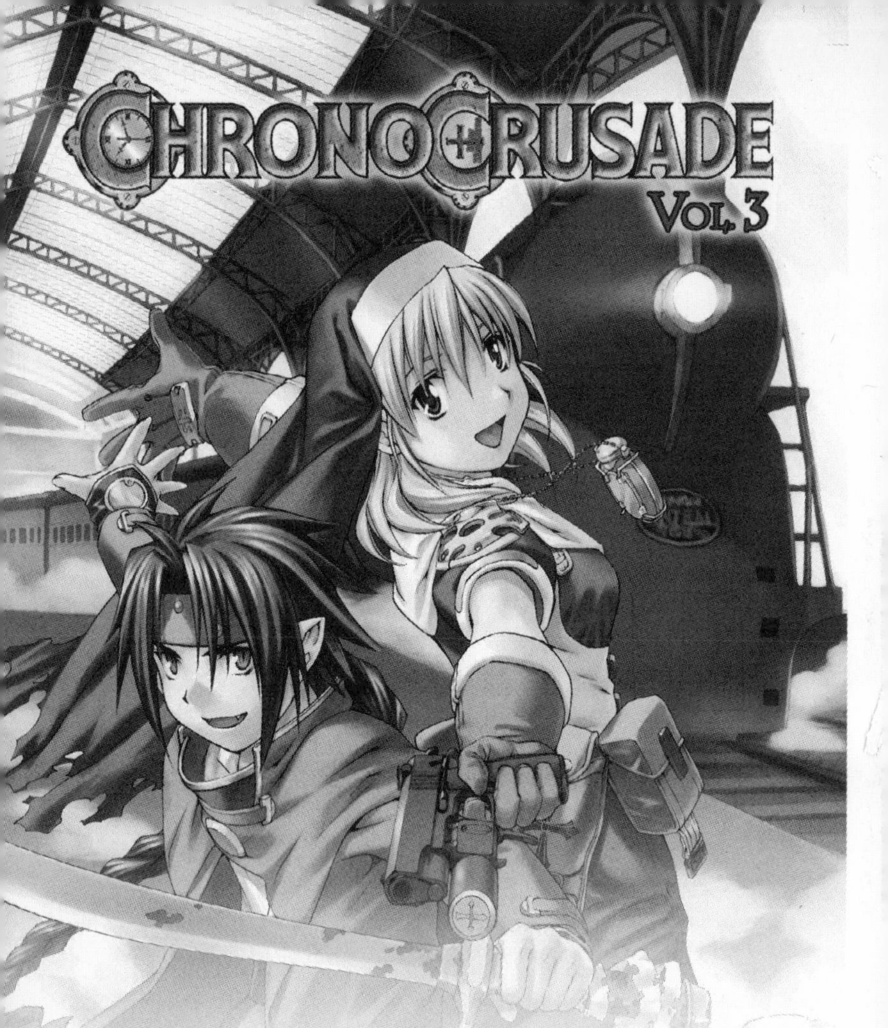
CHRONO CRUSADE
VOL. 3

Sister Rosette and company are about to embark on a mission to find Rosette's long-lost brother, but their journey might end before they leave the bright lights of the city. A powerful witch who threatens even the gun-toting Sister, is on a search of her own, and she is thirsty for revenge. A good ole exorcism won't stop the wicked woman, nor will it rid this evil-crushing team of even worse rivals. The Magdalan Order's finest put their demon-slaying talents aside, only to be confronted head-on with the chilling face of devilry in the holy-rolling action of ***Chrono Crusade Volume 3!***

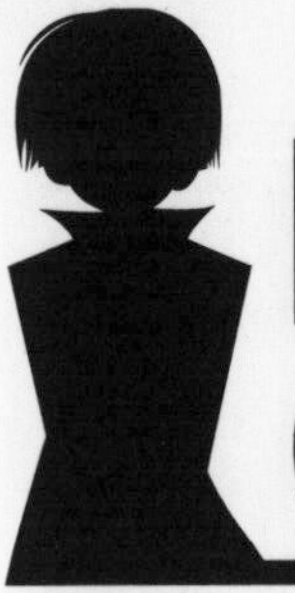

MEET THE CREATOR

Check out ADV's exclusive interview with *Chrono Crusade* creator, Daisuke Moriyama.

1> How long did it take for you to come up with the idea of *Chrono Crusade*?

Work on the project began in 1998, around April or May. I'd already had a kind of half-formed image [of the story], but that was around the time when I began shaping it into an actual work. *Chrono Crusade* began running serially in December of 1998, so it [took] around six months.

2> How did you come up with the name Chrono for Rosette's demon partner?

I'd begun thinking that I'd be dealing with themes of time and lifespan, and I thought it'd be interesting to just be direct and use [that name] for one of the characters appearing in the story. So, I decided on that relatively early into the project.

3> Why did you choose to set the story in the 20s? Did that require that you do a lot of research into America in the 20s?

The main reason was that when I came up with the idea to deal with the theme of time [in the story], I wanted to place it in some bygone era rather than in the present. I wanted to do the kind of story that an elderly grandfather and grandmother could tell, this grand tale of the lives they led when they were younger. I set it in the 1920s because, well, there are people from that time alive even today... I feel like it was a colorful, glamorous time, when the shadow of war had retreated. The actual research, about six months' worth, was done when I first started on the project. I wouldn't exactly call that amount of time *sufficient*, but I investigated various documents to at least capture the feel [of the time].

4> Much of the Catholicism (like Fatima) and the demonology seems like it is based on real religious history. How much research did you do on the religious (and demonic) aspects of *Chrono Crusade*?

That, too, began at the project's start date, April or May of '98. Again, not really what you'd call a sufficient amount of time, but... I made [researching] my first priority. Then, once the story had begun running serially, I began the gradual process of researching in more detail.

5> The bond between Rosette's life span and Chrono's powers seems quite original. How did this idea come to you?

At first glance, making a contract with a demon in order to use him would appear like nothing more than a risk, but I wondered to myself, wouldn't it be possible to change that around, so that [Rosette and Chrono] actually trust and love one another, and that their relationship is *beneficial*? So I made that the setting of the story. As for one of them being male and the other female, I thought that that kind of relationship could be portrayed more appealingly.

6> Who among the characters do you most closely relate to?

I think that all of the characters are, in a sense, a part of me…but if I had to say, I guess it would be Joshua. His childhood dilemma of the gap between the person he wants to be and the person he actually is, it's like that's exactly how I was as a kid, to the point where I can't think of that being someone else.

7> How did the anime come about?

It was in the summer of 2002 that Kadokawa, the company that published [the *Chrono Crusade* manga], said that they wanted to make it into an anime. GONZO, the [animation company] chosen for the project, requested that their version be more serious than the original, and rich with occult elements. The idea was to make the anime a story with strong and dark imagery, which is how the anime shifted [from the manga] to its current form.

8> Did you have much involvement in the anime? Were you pleased with how it turned out?

I didn't participate that much in producing the anime. Not only was the manga gearing up for its climax, and I personally didn't have time for much else, but things were such that pretty much everything [regarding the anime] would be left to GONZO. They were kind enough to address some of the general plot points that will be developing in the manga from here on out, but rather than some run-of-the-mill anime that just follows the course of the manga, I think having it be a reflection of the individuals who are there, where [the anime] is actually being created, will result in a much higher-quality work, which is why I leave the final structure of the show up to them.

9> How is the anime different from the manga?

As I mentioned above, the manga and the anime are approaching the story from two different perspectives. But the *themes* in both are the same—the bond between Rosette and Chrono, and the idea of time running out. But the way that the anime and manga show this is different. With the anime, you have these currents of time and fate, and the challenge to see how far these personal feelings of "trust" can run through all that. At least, that's what I believe. But I think the manga centers more on Rosette's individual ideology, with a focus on things like how the potential strength of will she possesses can actually change her current situation.

To be continued in *Chrono Crusade* volume 3.
Coming December 2004 only from ADV Manga!

EDITOR'S
PICKS

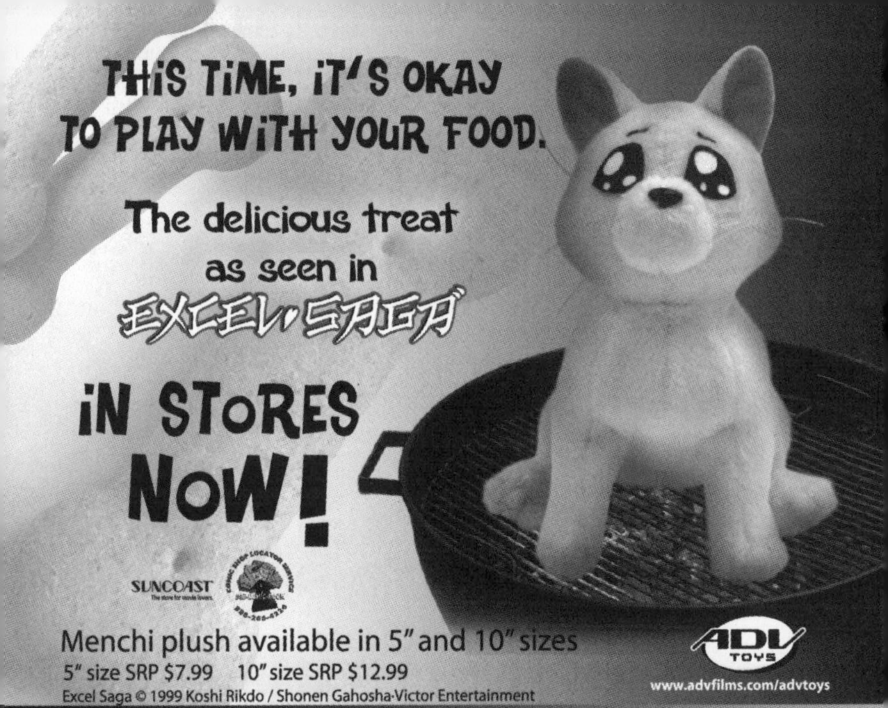

THIS TIME, IT'S OKAY TO PLAY WITH YOUR FOOD.
The delicious treat as seen in
EXCEL SAGA
IN STORES NOW!
SUNCOAST
Menchi plush available in 5" and 10" sizes
5" size SRP $7.99 10" size SRP $12.99
Excel Saga © 1999 Koshi Rikdo / Shonen Gahosha·Victor Entertainment
ADV TOYS
www.advfilms.com/advtoys

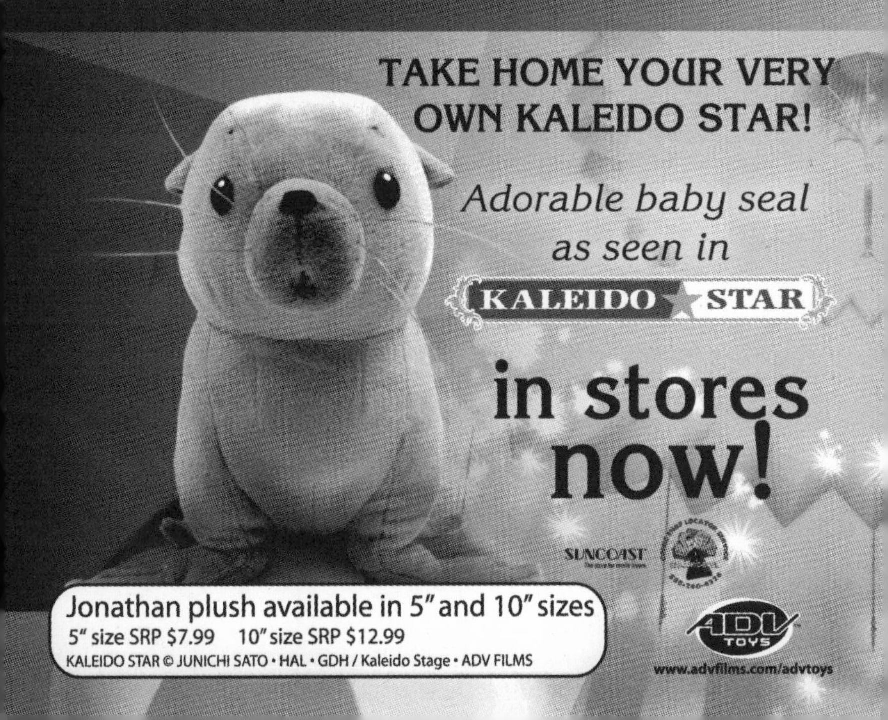

TAKE HOME YOUR VERY OWN KALEIDO STAR!
Adorable baby seal as seen in
KALEIDO STAR
in stores now!
SUNCOAST
Jonathan plush available in 5" and 10" sizes
5" size SRP $7.99 10" size SRP $12.99
KALEIDO STAR © JUNICHI SATO • HAL • GDH / Kaleido Stage • ADV FILMS
ADV TOYS
www.advfilms.com/advtoys

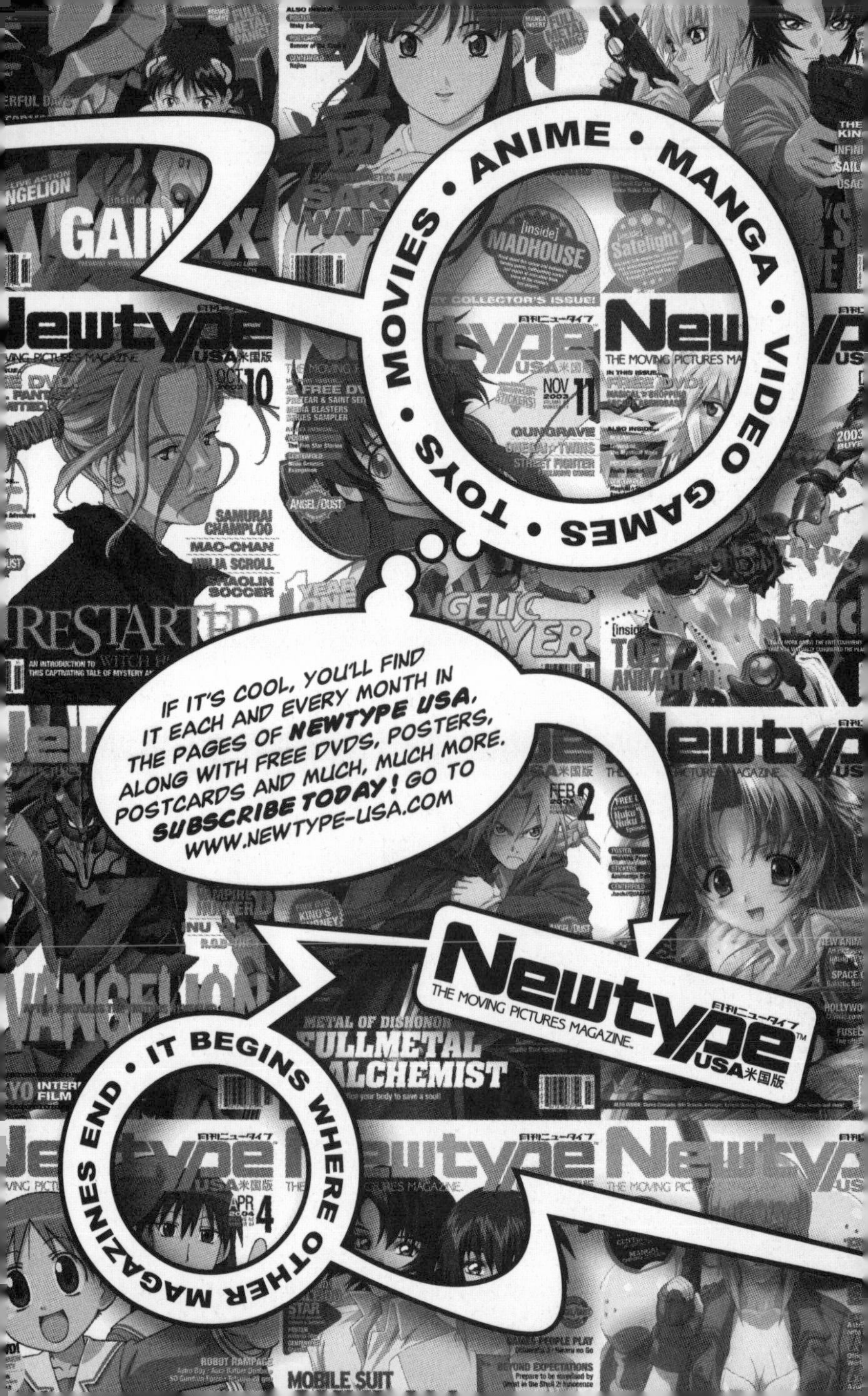
MOVIES • ANIME • MANGA • VIDEO GAMES • TOYS •
IF IT'S COOL, YOU'LL FIND IT EACH AND EVERY MONTH IN THE PAGES OF **NEWTYPE USA**, ALONG WITH FREE DVDS, POSTERS, POSTCARDS AND MUCH, MUCH MORE. **SUBSCRIBE TODAY!** GO TO WWW.NEWTYPE-USA.COM
Newtype USA 米国版
THE MOVING PICTURES MAGAZINE.
IT BEGINS WHERE OTHER MAGAZINES END •

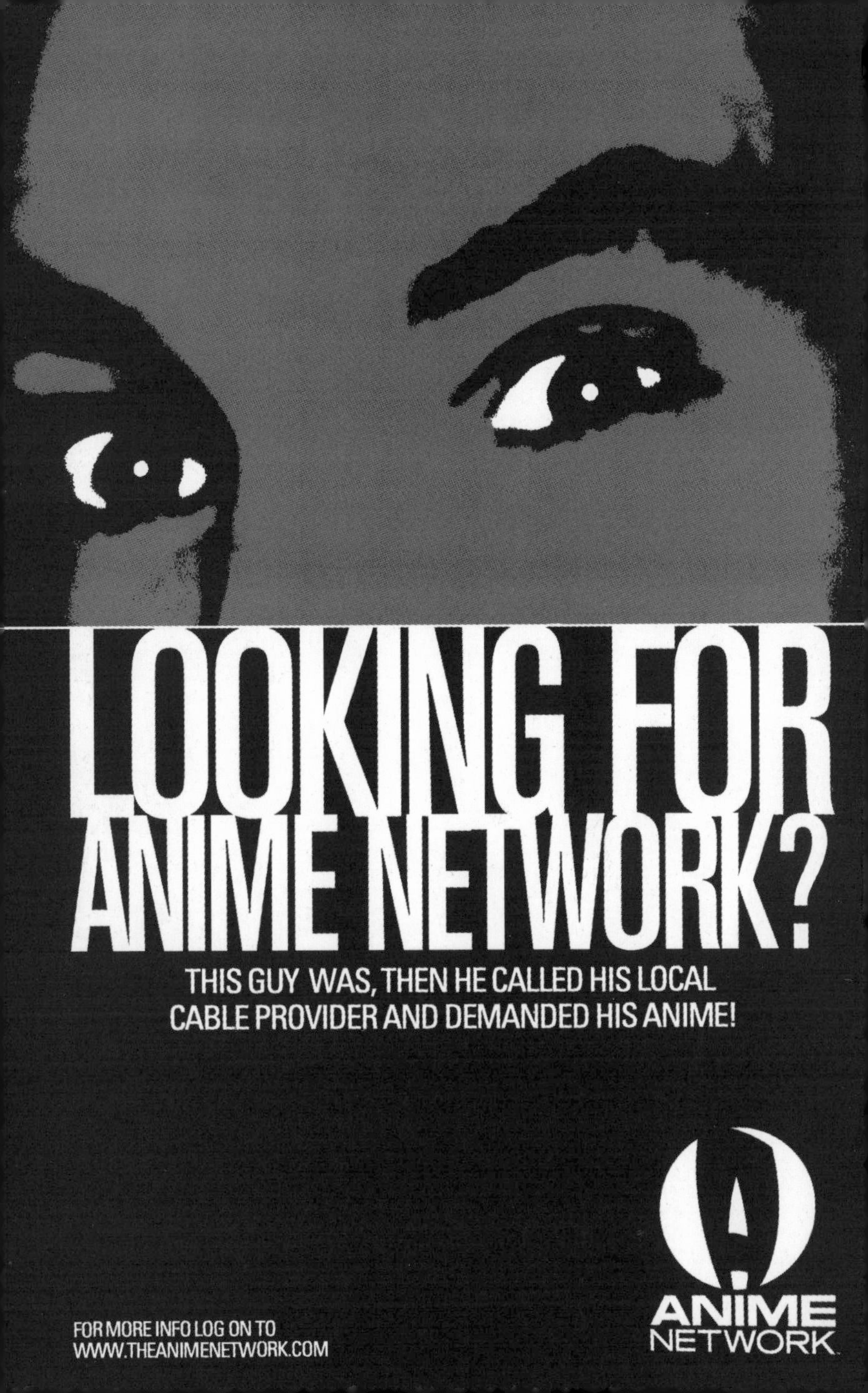
LOOKING FOR ANIME NETWORK?
THIS GUY WAS, THEN HE CALLED HIS LOCAL CABLE PROVIDER AND DEMANDED HIS ANIME!
ANIME NETWORK
FOR MORE INFO LOG ON TO
WWW.THEANIMENETWORK.COM

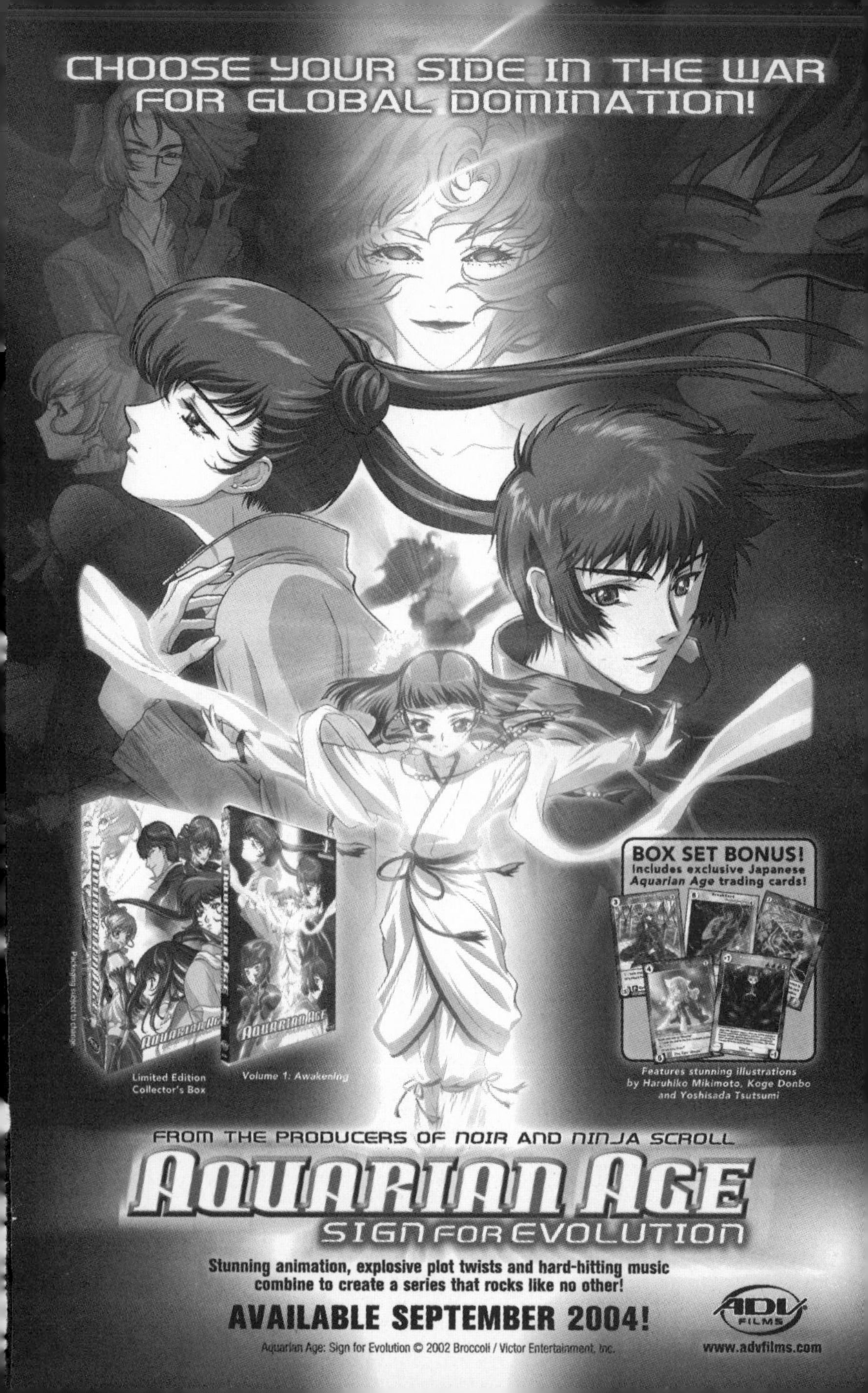
CHOOSE YOUR SIDE IN THE WAR FOR GLOBAL DOMINATION!
BOX SET BONUS!
Includes exclusive Japanese *Aquarian Age* trading cards!
Limited Edition Collector's Box
Volume 1: Awakening
Features stunning illustrations by Haruhiko Mikimoto, Koge Donbo and Yoshisada Tsutsumi
FROM THE PRODUCERS OF NOIR AND NINJA SCROLL
AQUARIAN AGE
SIGN FOR EVOLUTION
Stunning animation, explosive plot twists and hard-hitting music combine to create a series that rocks like no other!
AVAILABLE SEPTEMBER 2004!
ADV FILMS
Aquarian Age: Sign for Evolution © 2002 Broccoli / Victor Entertainment, Inc.
www.advfilms.com